Bridging the Atlantic

THE QUESTION OF AMERICAN EXCEPTIONALISM IN PERSPECTIVE

Bridging the Atlantic compares developments in modern European and American history. The case studies on British, German, and U.S. history since the eighteenth century assembled here seek to establish an integrated vision of Atlantic history. The contributions by European and American historians challenge the concept of American exceptionalism and present a vivid example of the ongoing debate between American and European historians on the structure and nature of European–American relations.

Elisabeth Glaser is a historian of international relations and a student of psychotherapy.

Hermann Wellenreuther is a professor of history at the University of Göttingen.

PUBLICATIONS OF THE GERMAN HISTORICAL INSTITUTE
WASHINGTON, D.C.

The German Historical Institute is a center for advanced study and research whose purpose is to provide a permanent basis for scholarly cooperation among historians from the Federal Republic of Germany and the United States. The Institute conducts, promotes, and supports research into both American and German political, social, economic, and cultural history; into transatlantic migration, especially in the nineteenth and twentieth centuries; and into the history of international relations, with special emphasis on the roles played by the United States and Germany.

Recent books in the series

Norbert Finzsch and Dietmar Schirmer, editors, *Identity and Intolerance: Nationalism, Racism, and Xenophobia in Germany and the United States*

Manfred F. Boemeke, Gerald D. Feldman, and Elisabeth Glaser, editors, *The Treaty of Versailles: A Reassessment After 75 Years*

Susan Strasser, Charles McGovern, and Matthias Judt, editors, *Getting and Spending: European and American Consumer Societies in the Twentieth Century*

Carole Fink, Philipp Gassert, and Detlef Junker, editors, *1968: The World Transformed*

Manfred F. Boemeke, Roger Chickering, and Stig Förster, editors, *Anticipating Total War: The German and American Experiences, 1871–1914*

Roger Chickering and Stig Förster, editors, *Great War, Total War: Combat and Mobilization on the Western Front, 1914–1918*

Bridging the Atlantic

THE QUESTION OF AMERICAN EXCEPTIONALISM IN PERSPECTIVE

Edited by

ELISABETH GLASER

and

HERMANN WELLENREUTHER

GERMAN HISTORICAL INSTITUTE

Washington, D.C.

and

CAMBRIDGE
UNIVERSITY PRESS

PUBLISHED BY THE PRESS SYNDICATE OF THE UNIVERSITY OF CAMBRIDGE
The Pitt Building, Trumpington Street, Cambridge, United Kingdom

CAMBRIDGE UNIVERSITY PRESS
The Edinburgh Building, Cambridge CB2 2RU, UK
40 West 20th Street, New York, NY 10011-4211, USA
477 Williamstown Road, Port Melbourne, VIC 3207, Australia
Ruiz de Alarcón 13, 28014 Madrid, Spain
Dock House, The Waterfront, Cape Town 8001, South Africa

http://www.cambridge.org

GERMAN HISTORICAL INSTITUTE
1607 New Hampshire Ave., N.W., Washington, DC 20009, USA

First published 2002

Printed in the United Kingdom at the University Press, Cambridge

Typeface Bembo 11/13 pt.   *System* QuarkXPress [BTS]

A catalog record for this book is available from the British Library.

Library of Congress Cataloging in Publication Data
Bridging the Atlantic : the question of American exceptionalism in perspective / edited
by Elisabeth Glaser and Hermann Wellenreuther.
p.   cm. – (Publications of the German Historical Institute)
Rev. papers presented at a symposium held at the German Historical Institute in
Washington D.C., June 8–10, 1995.
Includes bibliographical references and index.
ISBN 0-521-78205-8 (Cambridge University Press)
1. United States – Relations – Germany – Congresses.   2. Germany – Relations – United States
– Congresses.   3. United States – Relations – Europe – Congresses.   4. Europe – Relations –
United States – Congresses   5. National characteristics, American – Congresses.   6. United States
– Civilization – Congresses.   7. Germany – Civilization – Congresses.   8. Europe – Civilization
– Congresses.   9. Historiography – Methodology – Congresses.   I. Gläser, Elisabeth.
II. Wellenreuther, Hermann.   III. German Historical Institute (Washington, D.C.)   IV. Series.

E183.8.G3 B75   2000
303.48′273043–dc21   00-034255

0521 78205 8   hardback

Contents

Contributors

Kathleen Neils Conzen is a professor of history at the University of Chicago.

Carl N. Degler is a professor emeritus of history at Stanford University.

Elisabeth Glaser is a historian of international relations and a student of psychotherapy.

Hans R. Guggisberg was a professor of history at the University of Basel.

Ari Hoogenboom is a professor emeritus at Brooklyn College and the Graduate Center of the City University of New York.

Peter Krüger is a professor of history at the Philipps University of Marburg.

Kenneth L. Kusmer is a professor of history at Temple University.

Daniel J. Leab is a professor of history at Seton Hall University.

Hartmut Lehmann is the director of the Max Planck Institute for History, Göttingen.

Gerald Stourzh is a professor emeritus of history at the University of Vienna.

Hans L. Trefousse is a professor emeritus of history at Brooklyn College and the Graduate Center of the City University of New York.

Gerhard L. Weinberg is a retired professor of history at the University of North Carolina at Chapel Hill.

Hermann Wellenreuther is a professor of history at the University of Göttingen.

Introduction

ELISABETH GLASER AND HERMANN WELLENREUTHER

This book presents the revised results of a conference convened to discuss the work of the late Erich Angermann (1927–92). The symposium took place at the German Historical Institute (GHI) in Washington, D.C., from June 8 to 10, 1995. We remember Angermann, the senior historian of America in Germany, as the principal figure behind the foundation of the GHI in 1987. He also served as the first chairman of its academic advisory council. During his tenure as professor for American and European history at the University of Cologne, Angermann more than anyone else worked for a revitalization of what he called "Atlantic history." That conceptual approach, derived from the eighteenth- and nineteenth-century tradition of humanistic historiography, viewed American history as part of an integrated history of North America and Europe. Thus, the concept of *Atlantic history* comprises the common links between European and American history since the beginning of the European settlement of North America as well as comparative social, cultural, and economic developments on both continents.[1]

Angermann's integrated vision of a common Atlantic history of Europe and America remains important for American as well as European historians. During the last decade the historical communities on both sides of the Atlantic have vigorously debated the notion of complementary and comparable historical developments – or of Atlantic history.[2] The meeting

---

1 For similar approaches in American historiography with a different emphasis, see Henry S. Commager, *The Empire of Reason: How Europe Imagined and America Realized the Enlightenment* (Garden City, N.Y., 1977). Angermann described his thoughts on the potentialities and limits of comparative European–American history in *Challenges of Ambiguity: Doing Comparative History*, German Historical Institute, Washington, D.C., Annual Lecture series, no. 4 (New York, 1991). See also Erich Angermann and Marie-Luise Frings, eds., *Oceans Apart: Comparing Germany and the United States* (Stuttgart, 1981).
2 See, e.g., Norbert Finzsch and Robert Jütte, eds., *Institutions of Confinement: Hospitals, Asylums, and*

1

in Washington in 1995 presented an opportunity to reassess pertinent methodological and historiographical questions.

At the conference and in this book, the discussion about American exceptionalism serves as a useful counterpoint to national historiography. Historians of America in both Europe and the United States have opted not to subscribe to an understanding of history that fosters narrow interpretations or promotes the writing of exceptional national histories.[3] The debate over American exceptionalism, as continued in this book, shows how America adopted and transformed European institutions, religions, mores, and political philosophies during the eighteenth and nineteenth centuries. As Hans R. Guggisberg and others have pointed out, a discussion of American exceptionalism implies a comparative context. The chapter on immigration history in this book illustrates that point.[4] Meanwhile, the related issue of whether or not there was a German *Sonderweg* or peculiar path of historical development still provokes sharp criticism and vociferous disagreement, despite overwhelming evidence for the affirmative. Here, however, Kenneth L. Kusmer and Hans L. Trefousse provide qualified support, albeit with caveats.[5]

The discussion of whether historical research can distinguish clearly between comparable or unique national developments, or whether these categories are merely historiographical tools, has increased our knowledge about European–American relations over the last 300 years. Since the early

Prisons in Western Europe and North America, 1500–1950 (New York, 1997); Miles Kahler and Werner Link, *Europe and America: A Return to History* (New York, 1996); Roger Schlesinger, *In the Wake of Columbus: The Impact of the New World on Europe, 1492–1650* (Wheeling, Ill., 1996); James R. Sofka, "Metternich, Jefferson, and the Enlightenment," Ph.D. diss., University of Virginia, 1995; Karen O. Kupperman, ed., *America in European Consciousness, 1493–1750* (Chapel Hill, N.C., 1995); Hermann Wellenreuther and Claudia Schnurmann, eds., *Die amerikanische Verfassung und deutsch-amerikanisches Verfassungsdenken* (New York, 1990); David E. Barclay and Elisabeth Glaser, eds., *Transatlantic Images and Perceptions: Germany and America Since 1776* (New York, 1997).

3 Klaus Schwabe, "Die Vereinigten Staaten und die französische Revolution," in Norbert Finzsch and Hermann Wellenreuther, eds., *Liberalitas: Festschrift für Erich Angermann zum 65. Geburtstag*, Transatlantische Historische Studien, vol. 1 (Stuttgart, 1992), 189–206. See also Byron E. Shafer, ed., *Is America Different? A New Look at American Exceptionalism* (Oxford, 1991); Jack P. Greene, *The Intellectual Construction of America: Exceptionalism and Identity from 1492 to 1800* (Chapel Hill, N.C., 1993); Seymour M. Lipset, *American Exceptionalism: A Double-Edged Sword* (New York, 1996); David K. Adams and Cornelis van der Minnen, eds., *Reflections on American Exceptionalism* (Staffordshire, U.K., 1994); Amy T. Bushnell, ed., *Establishing Exceptionalism: Historiography and the Colonial Americas* (Brookfield, Vt., 1995); David M. Wrobel, *The End of American Exceptionalism: Frontier Anxiety from the Old West to the New Deal* (Lawrence, Kans., 1992); and the chapters by Hans R. Guggisberg and Gerald Stourzh in this book.

4 See Kathleen Neils Conzen's chapter in this book.

5 See Reinhard Kühnl, *Deutschland seit der französischen Revolution: Untersuchungen zum deutschen Sonderweg* (Heilbronn, 1996); Helga Grebing, *Der Deutsche Sonderweg in Europa 1806–1945: Eine Kritik* (Stuttgart, 1986); Karl-Dietrich Bracher, *Deutscher Sonderweg: Mythos oder Realität?* (Munich, 1982).

1980s we have witnessed the stunning growth of complementary comparative historical research and important longitudinal studies.[6] This book pursues that debate and brings together historical essays on comparative themes of modern European and American history. One of the important underlying methodological questions is how the tools of comparative analysis, or, where appropriate, the emphasis on singular national developments can help in drawing the fine line between comparable and distinct national developments.

Angermann insisted on broad historical approaches to studying the history of the Atlantic world – *"multum,* but not *multa"* – inspired by his desire to revive the tradition of humanistic historiography.[7] As a researcher, teacher, and educator he concentrated first on the history of German liberalism in the nineteenth century and then, since the early 1960s, increasingly on American history. He eventually became the leading historian of the United States in the Federal Republic of Germany. His characteristic approach to teaching and writing American history centered on his integrated vision of the history of England and the United States. Thus, Angermann's colleagues in Germany and abroad and his students in Cologne profited from his cosmopolitan yet sound interpretations of British and North American history. He emphasized the fundamental role that British and European settlement of North America played in the development of modern European *and* American or Atlantic history.[8] But he did not stop at that. In practical terms, he worked hard to establish the GHI and his own institute in Cologne as centers for a

---

6 See, e.g., George M. Fredrickson, *The Comparative Imagination: On the History of Racism, Nationalism, and Social Movements* (Berkeley, Calif., 1997); George M. Fredrickson, *Black Liberation: A Comparative History of Black Ideologies in the United States and South Africa* (New York, 1995); David Englander, *Britain and America: Studies in Comparative History, 1760–1970* (New Haven, Conn., 1997); Dirk Hoerder and Jörg Nagler, eds., *People in Transit: German Migrations in Comparative Perspective, 1820–1930* (New York, 1995); Stephen Englehart and John A. Moore Jr., *Three Beginnings: Revolution, Rights, and the Liberal States: Comparative Perspectives on the English, American, and French Revolutions* (New York, 1994); Stephen I. Katz, *The Holocaust and Comparative History* (New York, 1993); Mathias Reiman, ed., *The Reception of Continental Ideas in the Common Law World, 1820–1920* (Berlin, 1992); and the synthetic treatment by Richard Pells, *Not Like Us: How Europeans Have Loved, Hated, and Transformed American Culture Since World War II* (New York, 1997).

7 See Erich Angermann, "Sapientia et Eloquentia: Überlegungen zur Geschichtsdarstellung Franz Schnabels," in Historische Kommission bei der Bayerischen Akademie der Wissenschaften, ed., *Franz Schnabel: Zu Leben und Werk (1887–1966)* (Munich, 1988). In the United States, Peter Gay's work offers an outstanding example of humanistic historiography that seeks to explore broad human themes in eighteenth- and nineteenth-century European history. See, e.g., Peter Gay, *Education of the Senses: The Bourgeois Experience: Victoria to Freud* (New York, 1984), 3–44.

8 For a discussion of Angermann's work, see Hermann Wellenreuther's chapter in this book, as well as Helge Riedel, "Das wissenschaftliche Werk Erich Angermanns," in Finzsch and Wellenreuther, eds., *Liberalitas,* 521–33.

broad scholarly exchange involving different concepts of Atlantic history. The present book highlights some of the results of this work. It seeks to contribute to the ongoing conversation among American and European historians on the structure and nature of European–American relations, the contours of American history, and the important debate on the meaning and possibilities of comparative methodology. The authors here continue what Angermann felt strongly about – an Atlantic dialog.

Part One concentrates on constitutional and political history. Gerald Stourzh (Chapter 1) argues that the American legal framework derived from an exceptional English legal culture of individual rights. From English roots, eighteenth-century Americans evolved a conspicuously different legal culture that was based on the concept of a written constitution and on that of the people as the constituent power. Ari Hoogenboom (Chapter 2) begins where Stourzh leaves off. He deftly sketches what republicanism meant in the late eighteenth century and then describes its various effects on the political, economic, cultural, and religious cultures of the United States. He forcefully insists that the American republican tradition was and still is exceptional. He adds, however, that the term has lost much of its earlier glamour; at the same time he cautions against critical overreaction. True, American foreign policy has lost much of its revolutionary and republican fervor; likewise, he concedes, America's social structure still leaves much to be desired, especially when one considers the starkly unequal distribution of property within American society. Yet, at the same time he points to the vibrant forces within American society that work to improve these social ills, that continue to combat racism and work for a greater integration of ethnic minorities into the American mainstream, and that insist on human rights as a factor in foreign policy – these are values that should be respected everywhere.

Part Two focuses on comparative themes of religion, social philosophy, and nationalism. In his essay on religion in Europe and America in the nineteenth and twentieth centuries, Hartmut Lehmann (Chapter 3) raises questions about the interrelatedness of secularization and Christianity on both sides of the Atlantic. His argument is based on the observation that American society experienced a re-Christianization while de-Christianization progressed within European societies. Because urbanization and industrialization, the latter hitherto considered the prime cause for secularization, shaped societies on both sides of the Atlantic, Lehmann proposes a series of precisely focused comparative studies in order to better understand these processes.

Lehmann also suggests that the concept of exceptionalism could be taken as a starting point for a closer and more searching analysis of European and American social, cultural, political, and religious developments. This concept also intrinsically shapes Carl N. Degler's essay (Chapter 4). In analyzing American and European perceptions of Darwin's concepts Degler demonstrates that each debate is situated in a specific national context, although it simultaneously forms part of an Atlantic dialog. Books were translated, and ideas were exchanged and contested in both Europe and America. In the end, the dividing line did not run between Europe and America but between the Anglo-American and the European continental intellectual worlds.

Hans L. Trefousse (Chapter 5) focuses on yet another important aspect of the Atlantic world of concepts and mentalities: the different ideas and meanings of nationalism. He discusses the nationalism of Abraham Lincoln as an example of idealistic and ethnic nationalism. Trefousse portrays Carl Schurz as an example of ethnic nationalism formed and shaped by his experiences as a Forty-Eighter and a member of the radical republican wing of German liberalism that gradually merged with American idealistic nationalism. Otto von Bismarck, finally, exemplifies the Prussian nationalist. Nationalism not only shaped and structured Bismarck's policies but also may have later prompted the Iron Chancellor to use German unification in 1870–1 as a means for the aggrandizement of Prussia rather than for the formation of a unitary German state.

In Part Three, Kathleen Neils Conzen (Chapter 6), Kenneth L. Kusmer (Chapter 7), and Daniel J. Leab (Chapter 8) address the question of how people in the transatlantic world perceived themselves. Conzen presents a thoughtful analysis of the experience of German Americans in nineteenth-century America. Kusmer addresses the xenophobic responses to immigration in a comparative study of Germany and the United States. In a detailed treatment of American responses to blacks as well as to Chinese, Jewish, and Mexican immigrants in the nineteenth and early twentieth century Kusmer recounts stereotypes and acts of discrimination against these minorities. He also looks at German attitudes toward Poles, Jews, and blacks between 1871 and 1933. His comparisons show important differences between the responses in both societies to mass immigration and modernization, particularly in the reactions of the urban middle class and academics. Leab's discussion of German and American national perceptions in movies before and during World War I also addresses stereotypes and how an increasingly important medium popularized them. Leab shows how a largely negative image of Germans in

American movies preceded World War I and became more propagandistic and pronounced in the years after 1914.[9] German movie depictions of the United States appear mostly positive and admiring, and included popular German-made "Westerns" during the Wilhelmine period. Together, the chapters by Conzen, Kusmer, and Leab demonstrate that national identity is an overdetermined concept in which personal predilections, "imagined" traditions, and religious, social, and political environments all play a role.

Transatlantic politics and economics from 1914 to 1945 are analyzed by Gerhard L. Weinberg (Chapter 9) and Elisabeth Glaser (Chapter 10) in Part Four. Weinberg compares Franklin D. Roosevelt and Adolf Hitler. He pointedly shows how both men had radically different personalities and reacted very differently at times of potential military confrontation. Roosevelt preferred deterrence until the Japanese attack in 1941, whereas Hitler always chose the aggressive option and in fact had propagated a war against America as early as 1928. Glaser deals with America's options for helping the Allies against Germany in 1914–16. She shows how J. P. Morgan & Co. recognized the need to aid the Allies financially, contrary to Washington's official policy, thereby paving the way for more American economic and financial help that turned the war effort in favor of the Allies. Taken together, these chapters underscore the evolving role of the United States as a world power after the turn of the century and how at an early date clear-sighted observers inside and outside the United States perceived that new role, which Washington only gradually accepted.

The historiographical essays in Part Five illuminate the options and limitations of transatlantic history and American exceptionalism as categories for historical interpretation. Peter Krüger (Chapter 11) surveys German historiography since 1945. He emphasizes the slowness with which German historians developed new concepts. Likewise, he demonstrates how transatlantic history in Germany profited from the teachings of Angermann's mentor, Franz Schnabel, one of the few holders of a history chair in postwar Germany who had not been associated with the Nazi Party. In 1936 Schnabel had been forced to leave his job as a professor in Karlsruhe. After 1947, as a professor of modern history in Munich, Schnabel broadened the historical curriculum by including lec-

---

9 Cf. Daniel J. Leab's chapter in this book to Beverly Crawford and James Martel's analysis of post–World War II American movies, "Representations of Germans and What Germans Represent: American Film Images and Public Perceptions in the Postwar Era," in Barclay and Glaser-Schmidt, eds., *Transatlantic Images*, 285–308.

tures about revolutionary wars, including the American War of Independence, and decolonization.[10] German interest in American history, as Krüger points out, was also promoted by the work of Dietrich Gerhard, an émigré historian and the first holder of the American history chair in Cologne. Political scientists, particularly Karl Dietrich Bracher, whose work in turn was influenced by Hannah Arendt, likewise had an impact.[11] In conclusion, Krüger counsels against the inflationary use of concepts such as the German *Sonderweg* or American exceptionalism and pleads instead for using national history and comparative studies of modern nation-states as promising themes of transatlantic history.

The late Hans R. Guggisberg (Chapter 12) reviewed recent American literature on American exceptionalism as a theme in American history. Guggisberg contrasted new interpretations that stress the complementary nature of American exceptionalism in the comparative history of the modern nation-states with the accounts of George Bancroft and Henry Turner, whose romantic images of America's uniqueness still reverberate, even in works of New Left historians. Finally, Hermann Wellenreuther (Chapter 13) depicts the historical world of Erich Angermann. He describes how Angermann's work as a researcher, historian, and teacher depended on his vision of the rootedness of American history in its ties to Europe. As Wellenreuther makes clear, Angermann's views were much influenced by Schnabel but also grew out of Angermann's own active involvement in the teaching of American history as the only holder of a chair in that field in the old Federal Republic. In sum, the reader finds a balanced and careful discussion of German views on American history, American exceptionalism, and transatlantic history as historiographical categories for comparative historical approaches toward American and European history.

With this book the editors hope to encourage further research by German and American historians in the fields explored here. The individual chapters have been inspired by the desire to practice and discuss transatlantic history not as a strict methodological canon but as the focus of multiarchival and comparative research, as Angermann suggested. We therefore dedicate this book to his memory.

The editors sadly report that Hans Guggisberg died a few months after taking part in the conference on which this book is based. Guggisberg

---

10 See Angermann, "Sapientia et Eloquentia," and Eberhard Weis, "Leben und Persönlichkeit Franz Schnabels," in Historische Kommission, ed. *Franz Schnabel*, 25–40.

11 See also Peter Graf Kielmansegg, Horst Mewes, and Elisabeth Glaser-Schmidt, eds., *Hannah Arendt and Leo Strauss: German Emigrés and American Political Thought After World War II* (New York, 1997).

(1930–96) taught American history at the University of Basel and actively supported the European Association for American Studies. He also served as a founding member of the Swiss Association for American Studies. A polyglot historian interested in the early modern history of Europe and the United States, Guggisberg, not unlike Angermann, was a devoted teacher and scholar, although he modestly described himself as simply a "student of history." In 1974 he published a two-volume history of the United States that became a standard textbook. We will remember him fondly.

We thank the GHI and the Volkswagen Foundation for the funding of the original 1995 conference. We also extend our thanks to Erich Angermann's wife, Ursula Angermann, for her kind advice. Hartmut Lehmann, the first director of the GHI, suggested and encouraged plans for the conference. His successor, Detlef Junker, has generously supported the project. Frank Smith at Cambridge University Press recognized the relevance of this subject to the ongoing work of the GHI. Annette M. Marciel copy-edited the manuscript, and Daniel S. Mattern, the senior editor at the GHI, gave patient and expert advice that made publication of this book possible.

PART ONE

Transatlantic Faiths and Beliefs

1

Liberal Democracy as a Culture of Rights

England, the United States, and Continental Europe

GERALD STOURZH

I

"The Commons of *England* for hereditary fundamental Liberties and Properties are blest above and beyond the Subject of any *Monarch* in the World." Thus wrote Edward Chamberlayne in 1669 in his highly successful work *Angliae Notitia*, which was to run through no less than thirty-eight editions until 1755 and was translated into German and other continental languages.[1]

Chamberlayne did not mean the members of the House of Commons; he had in mind free Englishmen who did not belong to clergy or nobility, and he proceeded to enumerate, in what may be considered an early, though unofficial catalog of the rights of Englishmen, these liberties and properties in eight points. I shall mention only a few of them. The first point: "No Freeman of England ought to be imprisoned or otherwise restrained, without cause shewn for which by Law he ought to be so imprisoned." In point two, the Writ of Habeas Corpus was mentioned; in point four, it was stated: "No soldiers can be quartered in the House of any Freeman in time of Peace, without his will." In point five, the Englishmen's property rights were extolled: "Every Freeman hath such a full and absolute property in Goods, that no Taxes, Loans, or Benevolences ordinarily and legally can be imposed on them, without their own consent

I would like to thank James Hutson and Vera Nünning for their thoughtful comments on the occasion of the presentation of this chapter in June, 1995, as well as Ralph Lerner and Jack Pole for their critical reading of the manuscript. This essay has also been published in Thomas Fröschl, Margarete Grandner, and Birgitta Bader-Zaar, eds., *Nordamerikastudien: Forschungen zu den Vereinigten Staaten und Kanada an österreichischen Universitäten*, Wiener Beiträge zur Geschichte der Neuzeit, no. 24 (Vienna, 1999).

1 Edward Chamberlayne, *Angliae Notitia*, 3d ed. (London, 1669), 446–8, reprinted in Gerald Stourzh, "Vom aristotelischen zum liberalen Verfassungsbegriff," in Gerald Stourzh, *Wege zur Grundrechts-demokratie* (Vienna, 1989), 34–5.

by their Representatives in Parliament." Chamberlayne went on to
describe the unrestricted freedom to bequeath one's property, "which
other Nations governed by the Civil Law, cannot do." Those familiar with
the 1628 Petition of Right will recognize in points four and five various
similarities in content and partly even in wording. Point six stated that
no Englishman could be compelled (unless bound by his tenure) to fight
in foreign wars.

Reflecting on this catalog of rights from 1669, two observations are
called for: First, there is an awareness, a proud one at that, that things in
England are different from, and better than, the situation in other countries; a contrast is drawn to the civil law countries, which meant most
continental countries, but partly Scotland as well. The English, or to be
exact their "Commonalty," those belonging to the third estate, are blessed
with fundamental liberties and properties "above and beyond" the subjects of any monarch in the world – thus proclaiming an English "exceptionalism"! The distinction between common law and civil law is certainly
an important element that sets England apart from the rest of Europe –
as has rightly been stressed by Hermann Wellenreuther in his contribution to the festschrift for Erich Angermann.[2]

Second, notwithstanding an awareness of *ständisch* (corporate) differences – the "Commonalty" set apart from clergy and nobility – there is
an almost imperceptible identification of the "Freemen of England" with
"Englishmen." And indeed, what Chamberlayne referred to as the liberties and properties of the Commons of England were, already in the
course of the seventeenth century, often referred to as rights of Englishmen or English subjects, without bothering to refer to any order or estate.
The Petition of Rights of 1628 had enumerated "divers rights and liberties of the subject"; in 1646 the issue was raised in Massachusetts whether
"our due and naturall rights, as freeborne subjects of the English nation"
were respected.[3] In 1675 William Penn summed up "those rights and
privileges which I call English, and which are the proper birthrights of
Englishmen," and in 1687 he initiated the first printing of the Magna
Carta in America – in Philadelphia – in a publication titled *The Excellent
Priviledge of Liberty & Property Being the Birth-Right of the Free-born Subjects
of England*. In the early 1680s there appeared the very popular collection

---

2 Hermann Wellenreuther, "England und Europa: Überlegungen zum Problem des englischen Son-
  derwegs in der europäischen Geschichte," in Norbert Finzsch and Hermann Wellenreuther, eds.,
  Liberalitas: Festschrift für Erich Angermann zum 65. Geburtstag, Transatlantische Historische Studien,
  vol. 1 (Stuttgart, 1992), 97–8.
3 Quoted in Stourzh, "Verfassungsbegriff," 27.

of Henry Care, titled "English Liberties: or, the Free-Born subject's inheritance," which was frequently reprinted, including two American editions in Boston, in 1721, and in Providence, Rhode Island, in 1774.[4] In other words, in the course of the seventeenth century, references to liberties or rights had lost or were about to lose their relation to a specific order or estate; they had become, in an untranslatable German word, *standesunspezifisch*.

Rights – those of the people of England – were the primary concern of the most celebrated attempt to present a system of the laws of England, William Blackstone's *Commentaries on the Laws of England* (1765–9). The rights of the people of England were summarized by Blackstone in three "principal or primary articles" – first, the right to personal security; second, the rights of personal liberty; and third, the right to private property.[5] These three "principal absolute rights" were to be protected by "auxiliary subordinate rights of the subject." The first of these auxiliary and subordinate rights consisted of "the constitution, powers, and privileges of Parliament"; the second of "the limitation of the king's prerogative"; the third was the right to apply to the courts for the redress of injuries; the fourth was the right to present petitions to the king or to Parliament; and the fifth was the right to bear arms for one's defense "such as are allowed by law."[6]

In view of this system of the primary and the auxiliary rights of Englishmen it has been rightly observed – by Sir Ernest Barker – that for Blackstone the constitution was "a body of rights belonging to the subject, and vested in the subject."[7] We may also remind ourselves that Blackstone, according to his own words, was greatly influenced by Matthew Hale's *Analysis of the Law*, written prior to 1676. Hale built his entire system of law, including public law, on a system of legal relations or "rights" (distinguishing between "rights of privilege" and "rights of duties"), and not on top of sovereign power.[8]

One hundred and twenty years after Blackstone, Albert Dicey said that with the English, "the law of the constitution . . . is not the source, but

4 For the preceding, see ibid., 29–30.

5 On the impact of these three absolute rights in revolutionary America, see James H. Hutson, "The Bill of Rights and the American Revolutionary Experience," in Michael J. Lacey and Knud Haakonssen, eds., *A Culture of Rights: The Bill of Rights in Philosophy, Politics, and Law, 1791 and 1991* (Cambridge, 1991), 78–9.

6 William Blackstone, *Commentaries on the Laws of England*, 4 vols. (London, 1765–9), 1:125–39.

7 Sir Ernest Barker, "Blackstone on the British Constitution," in Sir Ernest Barker, *Essays on Government*, 2d ed. (Oxford, 1951), 142.

8 On Hale, see Gerald Stourzh, "Grundrechte zwischen Common Law und Verfassung," in Stourzh, *Wege zur Grundrechtsdemokratie*, 82–4.

the consequence of the rights of individuals, as defined by the Courts."[9]

Now to an observer from the European continent, used to the traditional primacy of the state or its ruler and its highest organs – a primacy respected even in the freest of the civil law countries, the Netherlands, as the writings of the Dutch jurist Ulric Huber show in contrast to Hale or Blackstone – and aware of the Roman legal tradition of the *princeps legibus solutus*, a conception like Blackstone's, explaining the limitations of the king's prerogative as "auxiliary and subordinate" to the rights of the people, is utterly astonishing. Yet, this conception is truly expressive of the English common law tradition that ignored, as Frederick W. Maitland once observed, the term *constitutional law* as a technical phrase.[10] This conception also is expressive, I submit, of the fact that the politico-legal culture of England may justly be called a "culture of rights" – taking this felicitous phrase from the well-known volume published in 1991 by Michael Lacey and Knud Haakonssen on the occasion of the bicentennial of the Federal Bill of Rights.[11]

This phenomenon is something that, I repeat, set England apart from the European continent and that linked it with the emerging political societies of English – I say English rather than British! – origin across the Atlantic Ocean. "Rights were taken seriously in the eighteenth-century British Empire," says John Phillip Reid, obviously alluding to Ronald Dworkin's celebrated book title, at the opening of his *Constitutional History of the American Revolution*, of which the first volume is dedicated to "the authority of rights."[12] I stress this phenomenon now because it is apt, of course, to put a question mark behind the juxtaposition of "Europe" and "America" that plays such a role in the chapters of the current book. I stress it also because in a suggestive discussion of English and American differences with respect to "rights," Alan Ryan has too one-sidedly minimized, I think, the relevance of "rights" in England. He observes that the "common law is based less on rights than on rules, forms of action, and procedures for arriving at right decisions."[13] Yet this means nothing else than the basic principle "no right without remedy," as valid in America as in England. John Adams, at the time of the Stamp Act crisis, noted

9 Albert V. Dicey, *Introduction to the Study of the Law of the Constitution*, 10th ed. (London, 1965), 203.

10 Frederick W. Maitland, *The Constitutional History of England* (Cambridge, 1908), 527.

11 Lacey and Haakonssen, eds., *Culture of Rights*, particularly the introduction by the editors, 1–18.

12 John Phillip Reid, *Constitutional History of the American Revolution*, 2 vols. (Madison, Wis., 1986), 1:3.

13 Alan Ryan, "The British, the Americans, and Rights," in Lacey and Haakonssen, eds., *Culture of Rights*, 378.

from Coke's First Institutes: "Want of right and want of remedy are all one; for where there is no remedy there is no right."[14] Ryan also observes, rightly, that the purpose of the English Declaration of Rights of 1689 "of restricting the freedom of the sovereign was much more evident than any notion of liberating the 'individual,'"[15] and indeed the 1689 document is more concerned with protecting parliamentary privileges than individual persons. Yet, Ryan omits any reference to the Petition of Rights of 1628, which was more "person-centered" than the Bill of Rights of 1689. One also ought not forget the powerful aura surrounding "that second *magna carta*," the Habeas Corpus Act of 1679.[16] Furthermore, I would like to refer to the tremendous significance surrounding the issue of the freedom of the press, at least from the time of Milton's *Areopagitica*, and particularly after the last Licensing Act ran out in 1695 and was not renewed.[17]

I submit that in seventeenth- and eighteenth-century England a process of *fundamentalizing* the rights of persons took place, and that some important phases of this process, apparently neglected by Ryan, had taken place prior to the 1689 Declaration of Rights. This process was not matched by any contemporary parallel development in continental Europe. England was different. Seventeenth-century England, as Alexis de Tocqueville observed in one of his masterpieces of comparative juridico-sociopolitical analysis, was already a truly modern state, *une nation toute moderne*, some feudal remnants notwithstanding.[18] Speaking of the equalization of rights across fading differences of orders or estates, one ought to be mindful of other restrictions of legal capacity like those hitting the indigent or, under the common law doctrine of the *femme covert*, married women.[19]

What did not happen in England, and what was happening across the Atlantic Ocean in North America, was the process of *constitutionalizing* the

---

14 See Gerald Stourzh, "The American Revolution, Modern Constitutionalism, and the Protection of Human Rights," in Kenneth Thompson and Robert Mayers, eds., *A Tribute to Hans Morgenthau* (Washington, D.C., 1977), 169, quoting from John Adams, *The Works of John Adams, Second President of the United States, with a Life of the Author, Notes, and Illustrations by his Grandson, Charles Francis Adams*, 10 vols. (Boston, 1850–6), 2:159.

15 Ryan, "The British," 384.   16 Blackstone, *Commentaries*, 1:135.

17 Gerald Stourzh, "Die Entwicklung der Rede- und Meinungsfreiheit im englischen und amerikanischen Rechtsraum," in Stourzh, *Wege zur Grundrechtsdemokratie*, 175–7, 181.

18 Alexis de Tocqueville, *L'ancien régime et la Révolution*, bk. 1, chap. iv, "folio" ed. (Paris, 1967), 78.

19 On the latter point, see Lee Holcombe, *Wives and Property: Reform of the Married Women's Property Law in Nineteenth-Century England* (Toronto, 1983), 25–31. For early America, see Marylynn Salmon, *Women and the Law of Property in Early America* (Chapel Hill, N.C., 1986). An illuminating discussion with reference to an extremely interesting case is presented by Linda K. Kerber, "The Paradox of Women's Citizenship in the Early Republic: The Case of Martin vs. Massachusetts, 1805," *American Historical Review* 97 (1992): 349–78.

rights of persons. Indeed, as is known to everyone, England – or Great Britain, for that matter – did not develop a set of rules binding the legislative power itself, and it did not develop procedures designed for setting up rules capable of binding the legislator. There were times when the lack of such rules or procedures was felt and bitterly expressed by opposition writers, such as Daniel Defoe in 1701, or opposition politicians critical of the Septennial Act of 1716, when a parliament elected for three years prolonged its own term of office for another four years and opposition speakers argued that this measure violated "the constitution."[20] The case of the Septennial Act was to be noted and commented on decades later in America.

There was, then, no procedural way, no legal way, no easy way out of the dilemma between the primacy of the rights of Englishmen, so forcefully proclaimed by Blackstone and Dicey, and the absolute sovereignty of Parliament (to be precise, the king-in-parliament or the queen-in-parliament), also forcefully expressed in Blackstone's and Dicey's writings. There was, however, a difficult – and risky – way out of that dilemma, once the contradiction became too burdensome, as long as legal and constitutional thinking was pervaded by natural law thinking – which was the case with Blackstone (though not, more than a century later, with Dicey). For cases of extreme emergency Blackstone had this to say: "Indeed, it is found by experience, that whenever the unconstitutional oppressions, even of the sovereign power, advance with gigantic strides and threaten desolation to a state, mankind will not be reasoned out of the feelings of humanity; nor will sacrifice its liberty by a scrupulous adherence to those political maxims, which were originally established to preserve it." To future generations – thus Blackstone concluded a remarkable passage – was left, "whenever necessity and the safety of the whole shall require it, the exertion of those inherent (though latent) powers of society, which no climate, no time, no constitution, no contract, can ever destroy or diminish."[21] The message was heard and understood, in America, at the appropriate time.[22]

In spite of the fundamental place of the rights of persons in the English public mind, then, the legislator was entitled to suspend such rights,

---

20 For details, see Gerald Stourzh, "Vom Widerstandsrecht zur Verfassungsgerichtsbarkeit," in Stourzh, *Wege zur Grundrechtsdemokratie*, 42–9.

21 Blackstone, *Commentaries*, 1:238. See also David Liebermann, *The Province of Legislation Determined: Legal Theory in Eighteenth-Century Britain* (Cambridge, 1989), 52–3.

22 For details, see Gerald Stourzh, "William Blackstone: Teacher of Revolution," in Stourzh, *Wege zur Grundrechtsdemokratie*, 135–53.

including the hallowed one of habeas corpus, and did so on various occasions.[23] Yet, it was precisely the legislative and not the executive power alone that was entitled to suspend habeas corpus, as Blackstone was eager to point out.[24] As almost instinctively critical as one is inclined to be in view of our overwhelmingly constitutionalist perspective – not merely in the United States but in most European continental nations as well – one ought not forget that the sovereign legislator of England, Parliament, by the seventeenth and eighteenth centuries was a remarkable institution, including by far the strongest "Third Estate" of any of the major European states. This parliament, for generations of European observers the very epitome of "representative government," of a "free government," was gradually widening the franchise rights required to elect representatives. The years 1832, 1867, 1884, 1918, and 1928 were landmarks on the road from "representative government" to a "representative democracy," although difficult stretches between these landmarks, be it the Chartist or the Suffragette movements, must not be forgotten. But even the democratically elected parliaments of the twentieth century (I refrain from commenting on the decline plus reforms of the House of Lords during the twentieth century) have remained as sovereign as those described by Blackstone or Dicey in the preceding centuries. The most telling symbol of this legislative sovereignty remains for me the Emergency Powers (Defense) Act of 1940, passed at a time when German invasion seemed imminent. It provided "for requiring persons to place themselves, their services, and their property at the disposal of His Majesty." The bill to this effect passed through all its stages in both houses of Parliament and received the royal assent within one single day! A perspicacious observer commented that this law "put into a legal formula the 'blood and tears and sweat' that Mr. Churchill had promised as the British contribution to the war effort."[25]

II

What were the major transforming elements that contributed to the growth in parts of North America – out of a rich heritage of English legal and political tradition – of a different type of "free government," of

23 For details, see Sir David Lindsay Keir, *The Constitutional History of Modern Britain Since 1485*, 8th ed. (London, 1966), 398.

24 Blackstone, *Commentaries*, 1:132.

25 O. Hood Phillips, *Constitutional and Administrative Law*, 5th ed. (London, 1973), 321, quoting from Sir Ivor Jennings, *Law and the Constitution*, 3d ed. xxv–xxvi.

liberal constitutional democracy, American style, of a liberal democracy expressing itself indeed in a more intensive way than in Britain as a culture of rights? I single out the four following points: (1) republican government; (2) federalism; (3) the rise of a paramount law above the ordinary legislator; and (4) the constitutionalization of individual rights. I shall deal with points one and two rather briefly, with the interrelated points three and four at greater length.

1. Breaking away from the British monarchy produced the sudden and simultaneous rise of the powerful notions of republican government and of the constituent power of the people. So much has been written about the "paradigm of republicanism" within the last twenty-five years that I shall limit myself to a few very brief observations:

As far as the historiographical attention given to the meaning of republican government and "republicanism" is concerned, to which I contributed myself a quarter of a century ago,[26] it seems that the exaggerated juxtaposition of the "republican" and "liberal" paradigm has given way to more balanced interpretations.[27] John Pocock himself, whose great work on the "Machiavellian Moment" had done so much to unleash the "republicanism versus liberalism debate," has admitted that his account of "civic humanism" was a "tunnel history" that "pursued a single theme, that of the *vivere civile* and its virtue, to the partial exclusion of parallel phenomena."[28] Among these parallel phenomena the most important was and is what Pocock rightly calls the "law-centered paradigm."[29] There is no question that in an inquiry about a culture of rights, the "law-centered paradigm" assumes a priority of place, as it does in this chapter. Yet, the question has to be asked whether, and if so in which way, the "republican paradigm" contributes to enlighten us about certain roots of enduringly strong elements of a "culture of rights."

It seems to me that the notion of "citizens," replacing in America the English notion of "subjects" − even freeborn subjects of king or queen − is the most important element that the republican paradigm has con-

26 Gerald Stourzh, *Alexander Hamilton and the Idea of Republican Government* (Stanford, Calif., 1970); see the review article by J. G. A. Pocock, "Virtue and Commerce in the Eighteenth Century," *Journal of Interdisciplinary History* 1 (1972–3): 119–34.

27 Among recent interpretations, the work of Paul A. Rahe, *Republics Ancient and Modern* (Chapel Hill, N.C., 1992), stands out.

28 J. G. A. Pocock, "*The Machiavellian Moment* Revisited: A Study in History and Ideology," *Journal of Modern History* 53 (1981): 53.

29 Idem, *Virtue, Commerce, and History* (Cambridge, 1985), 37. Among the vast amount of scholarly discussion produced by the "republican paradigm" and its critics, I would like to single out, for reference, the collected contributions by Joyce Appleby in *Liberalism and Republicanism in the Historical Imagination* (Cambridge, Mass., 1992).

tributed to the American culture of rights. Citizenship in a republic implies rights, particularly rights of participation, although in the republican tradition, as Rousseau made very clear, citizenship was by no means bound to reach all classes of the population.[30] It certainly was a republican manner of speech that impelled Noah Webster to associate citizenship with suffrage. A citizen for Webster was a person, native or naturalized, "who has the privilege of exercising the elective franchise, or the qualifications which enable him to vote for rulers, and to purchase and hold real estate."[31] It was the republican association of the idea of citizenship with the franchise that inspired the women who drew up the Seneca Falls Declaration of 1848 on women's rights to speak "of the first right of a citizen, the elective franchise," and to denounce man who had deprived woman of this first right, "thereby leaving her without representation in the halls of legislation."[32] Yet, although the "participatory connotations" of citizenship had their origins in classical republicanism,[33] the dynamics of the extension of suffrage to groups hitherto excluded, such as people without property qualifications, colored people, or women, was due to the – modern – tendency to equalize legal capacities, connected with modern natural rights thinking and also, although not exclusively so, with the rise of modern democracy.

The notion of citizenship and the rights pertaining to it, tied to the individual states after independence, nationally defined and entrenched only in the Fourteenth Amendment of 1868, were frequently discussed *without* reference to the franchise question; and women were held to be citizens without having the right of franchise.[34] The central issue of early discussions on citizenship was the status of the free persons of African descent – particularly in connection with the Missouri compromise – and later, with Chief Justice Roger B. Taney's *Dred Scott* decision, the question of whether the status of citizenship was accessible to colored persons at all.[35] The final answer, after years of bloodshed, were the Fourteenth

---

30 See Rousseau's note on the meaning of the word *citoyen* in bk. 1, chap. 7, of the *Social Contract*. See Rogers Brubaker, *Citizenship and Nationhood in France and Germany* (Cambridge, Mass., 1992), 42.

31 Quoted in the magnificent work by Don Fehrenbacher, *The Dred Scott Case* (New York, 1978), 615n55, from Noah Webster, *An American Dictionary of the English Language*, 2 vols. (New York, 1828). The last words echo section 6 of the Virginia Bill of Rights, in which it was stated that "all men, having sufficient evidence of permanent common interest with and attachment to the community, have the right of suffrage" (Henry Steele Commager, *Documents of American History*, 7th ed., 2 vols. [New York, 1963], 1:104).

32 Commager, *Documents*, 1:315.   33 Brubaker, *Citizenship*, 50.

34 Fehrenbacher, *Dred Scott Case*, 65, 615n56. See also the discussion by Kerber, "Women's Citizenship," 376–8.

35 Fehrenbacher, *Dred Scott Case*, 64–8, 340–50.

and Fifteenth Amendments to the Constitution, the latter affirming the right of citizens of the United States to vote, not to be denied or abridged on account of race, color, or previous condition of servitude. I will return to the relevance of status for the theme of this chapter later on.

2. Federalism, as it emerged from the work of the Philadelphia Convention and was embodied in the Federal Constitution, is relevant for the development of a culture of rights on two counts:

First, federalism, as Dicey rightly said, "means legalism." A federal system cannot work with an unspecified sovereign "power" – singular; it needs specified "powers" – plural. In other words, federalism necessitates the attribution of powers in the specific sense of competences. The transformation of "power" into "powers" inevitably produces an additional network of legal norms, unknown and unnecessary in unitary states. The need to settle possible differences of interpretation as to the meaning and extent of respective "powers" enhances the role of the judiciary, and it has been rather well said that particularly during the first century of American constitutionalism (under the Federal Constitution), the theme of *powers* was its central motif: "the extent of the authority of each branch and level of government and their relationship to each other and to the people."[36] Federalism, Dicey also rightly said, means "the prevalence of a spirit of legality among the people."[37]

Second, and more specifically, we must remind ourselves that American federalism injected a new element into "federal" relationships: The powers of the federal – national – government were to extend "to certain enumerated objects only," as James Madison phrased it carefully. Yet within these confines the government of the Union was empowered, again in Madison's words, to operate "on individual citizens, composing the nation, in their individual capacities."[38] This was the truly new departure of the Federal Constitution of 1787, and this was the important wedge with the help of which individuals and their claims would be connected with federal jurisdiction – for instance, concerning interstate commerce – and that jurisdiction's competence to adjudicate conflicting claims of state legislation and the rules of the Federal Constitution – a vast field for developing a culture of rights.

---

36 Morton Keller, "Powers and Rights: Two Centuries of American Constitutionalism," *Journal of American History* 74 (1987–8): 676.
37 Dicey, *Law of the Constitution*, 175.
38 Jacob E. Cooke, ed., *The Federalist* (Cleveland, 1961), nos. 39, 255, 256. See also Gerald Stourzh, "Il 'Federalist': Teoria politica e retorica della persuasione," in Guglielmo Negri, ed., *Il Federalista: 200 anni dopo* (Bologna, 1988), 282.

3. The emergence of the "written constitution" as the "fundamental and paramount law of the nation" – to employ John Marshall's phrase in *Marbury v. Madison* – was a process that began in North America long before independence. The *dissociation* of legislative and sovereign power – a phenomenon central to American constitutionalism – set in during the colonial period. This was indeed an important departure from the English system; it also was a departure from one of the main tenets of early modern political thinking, from Bodin to Hobbes to Rousseau or to Blackstone: The legislator is the sovereign. In colonial America the colonial assemblies did indeed legislate for their respective colonies; they passed laws, they were considered to carry out legislative acts, they imitated – increasingly – the parliament at Westminster in the style of proceedings – and yet they were not by any means sovereign, being subject to various superior norms – frames of government, charters and grants, the disallowance powers of the Privy Council, and finally, if not unequivocally, to the legislative authority of Parliament itself.

An important experience that separated colonials from Englishmen in the mother country was the experience of founding a political community – an experience of contemporary or at any rate recent memory. Conscious founding necessitates conscious organization, and in several cases the foundational documents emphasized the "fundamental" or "paramount" character of the rules laid down in them vis-à-vis the "ordinary" legislature. The "Fundamental Orders" of Connecticut (1639), the "General Fundamentals" introducing the revised code for New Plymouth in 1671, the "Charter or fundamental Laws of West New Jersey agreed upon" in 1676, and Penn's "Frames of Government" for Pennsylvania with a provision of a qualified majority for amending procedures are some cases in point. Thus, Americans, unlike Englishmen in the mother country, had become accustomed to being governed by a hierarchy of legal norms, of which the laws passed by the assemblies held by no means the highest rank.[39]

The Americans' polemics – in the 1760s and 1770s – against what they considered the "unconstitutional" deeds of Parliament in London further encouraged the dissociation of legislative from sovereign power. I have shown in an earlier publication how the use of the word "unconstitutional" suddenly spread in North America, once it had first been used in 1764–5 in Rhode Island.[40] Theoretical awareness that the legislator was inferior to the constitution was greatly helped by the very clear

---

39 Cf. Stourzh, *Wege zur Grundrechtsdemokratie*, 25–34.
40 Ibid., 52–3.

presentation of this subordination in the work of Emmerich de Vattel, *Le droit des gens ou principes de la loi naturelle*, published in 1758.[41] It was immediately translated into English, very soon used and quoted by James Otis in Boston, and unmistakably echoed in the Massachusetts Circular Letter of 1768, in which it was stated that "in all States the Constitution is fixed; & as the supreme Legislative derives its Power & Authority from the Constitution, it cannot overleap the Bounds of it, without destroying its own foundation."[42]

With America's breaking away from Britain in 1776 the need for new fundamental frames of government or (with a more recent name) constitutions produced the first sustained and successful coming into action of the "constituent power of the people" in Western history.[43] Anticipating the Abbé Sieyès in France by twelve years, Thomas Young of Pennsylvania spoke of the "supreme constituent power" of the people, distinguishing it from the delegated powers of the representatives.[44] The process of constitution-making in the United States from 1776 to 1780, with increasing procedural sophistication and culminating in the Massachusetts Constitution of 1780,[45] remains a memorable chapter in the history not merely of constitutional democracy in North America but in the history of liberal democracy *tout court*.[46] In what was one of the earliest uses of a modern expression, Alexander Hamilton in 1777 spoke of the new form of government as a "representative democracy."[47]

The "written constitution" as paramount law: The decisive quality of the "written constitution" did not consist in its quality as a written document but in its rank as paramount law vis-à-vis legislature-made law. The awareness that this was so, and that this was the great innovation of the American system of government was not the invention either of

41 Gerald Stourzh, "Naturrechtslehre, leges fundamentales und die Anfänge des Vorrangs der Verfassung," in Christian Starck, ed., *Rangordnung der Gesetze*, Abhandlungen der Akademie der Wissenschaften in Göttingen, phil.-hist. Klasse, 3d ser., no. 210 (Göttingen, 1995), 24–5.

42 Gerald Stourzh, "*Constitution:* Changing Meanings of the Term from the Early Seventeenth to the Late Eighteenth Century," in Terence Ball and J. G. A. Pocock, eds., *Conceptual Change and the Constitution* (Lawrence, Kans., 1988), 45–6.

43 For the "constituent power of the people" see in particular R. R. Palmer, *The Age of Democratic Revolution: A Political History of Europe and America, 1760–1800*, vol. 1: *The Challenge* (Princeton, N.J., 1959), 213–35. For this and some of the following, see also Gerald Stourzh, *Fundamental Laws and Individual Rights in the 18th-Century Constitution* (Claremont, Calif., 1984), 18–25, reprinted in J. Jackson Barlow, Leonard W. Levy, and Ken Masugi, eds., *The American Founding: Essays on the Formation of the Constitution* (Westport, Conn., 1988), 176–83.

44 Willi Paul Adams, *The First American State Constitutions: Republican Ideology and the Making of the State Constitutions in the Revolutionary Era* (Chapel Hill, N.C., 1980), 65.

45 Oscar Handlin and Mary Handlin, eds., *The Popular Sources of Political Authority: Documents on the Massachusetts Constitution of 1780* (Cambridge, Mass., 1966).

46 See Adams, *First American Constitutions*.   47 Stourzh, *Hamilton*, 49, 223n36.

Alexander Hamilton – in *Federalist* no. 78 – or of John Marshall in *Marbury*. This awareness was widespread and antedated the Federal Constitution, though it certainly was greatly enhanced by the work of the Philadelphia Convention and by the ratification debates accompanying the adoption of the Federal Constitution. As early as May 1776 the town of Pittsfield, Massachusetts, had asked for "the formation of a fundamental Constitution as the basis and groundwork of Legislation."[48] This indeed was done, within a period of less than fifteen years, both on the state level and on the level of the Union.

Among those who grasped and articulated what was new in the American system, the North Carolina jurist James Iredell, subsequently nominated to the Supreme Court of the United States, stands out. As early as 1783 he pointed out that an independent judiciary was "a point of the utmost moment in a Republic where the Law is superior to any or all the Individuals, and *the Constitution superior even to the Legislature*, and of which the Judges are the guardians and protectors."[49] In an article published in the summer of 1786 Iredell extolled the new chance of protecting individual rights, with the help of the courts, against unconstitutional legislation, thus protecting the constitution itself. In North Carolina something was possible that did not exist in England, where the principle of unbounded legislative power prevailed. And Iredell pointed to an event that had taken place in England seventy years before: A parliament elected for three years had prolonged its own duration for another four years; this was not possible in North Carolina. People in England were less free than in North Carolina![50] A year later Iredell considered the judges' obligation "to hold void laws inconsistent with the constitution" unavoidable, "the Constitution not being a mere imaginary thing, about which ten thousand different opinions may be formed, but a written document to which all may have recourse, and to which, therefore, the judges cannot willfully blind themselves."[51]

The contrast to England, even with reference to the same dreadful event seven decades earlier – the Septennial Act of 1716 – was expressed

---

48 Handlin and Handlin, eds., *Popular Sources*, 91.

49 James Iredell, *The Papers of James Iredell*, ed. Don Higginbotham, 2 vols. (Raleigh, N.C., 1976), 2:449 (emphasis added).

50 "To the Public," Aug. 17, 1786, in Griffith J. McRae, ed., *Life and Correspondence of James Iredell*, 2 vols. (New York, 1858), 2:147–8.

51 Iredell to Richard Spaight, Aug. 26, 1787, ibid., 174. I have discussed Iredell extensively in "American Revolution," 170–2, and in *Wege zur Grundrechtsdemokratie*, 60–4. The great significance of Iredell, long neglected by American authors, has now been duly emphasized by Sylvia Snowiss, *Judicial Review and the Law of the Constitution* (New Haven, Conn., 1990), 45–53, although I cannot share all of her interpretations.

by eminent authors. In 1788 Madison, in *Federalist* no. 53, proudly wrote: "The important distinction so well understood in America between a constitution established by the people, and unalterable by the government; and a law established by the government, and alterable by the government, seems to have been little understood and less observed in any other country." He went on to denounce the "dangerous practices" demonstrated by the British Septennial Act, to wit, the possibility of changing "by legislative acts, some of the most fundamental articles of government."[52] For Thomas Paine, writing in *The Rights of Man*, the Septennial Act was proof that "there is no constitution in England."[53]

The most artful of all comparisons between the British and the American systems of government, embellished with all sorts of rhetorical flourishes, came from the pen of James Wilson. His "Lectures on Law" delivered in Philadelphia in 1790–1 – the inaugural lecture was held in the presence of President George Washington and Vice President John Adams – are a monument of American "exceptionalism." Wilson made very clear the dissociation of legislative from sovereign power in America, as opposed to the English doctrine; in America there existed a guard against "legislative despotism": the superior power of the Constitution, the judges called to decide under the Constitution. Above the Constitution, retaining the right of abolishing, altering, or amending the Constitution, stood the sovereign power of the people. Concluding his "parallel between the pride of Europe – the British constitution – and the constitution of the United States," Wilson threw out his challenge: "Let impartiality hold the balance between them: I am not solicitous about the event of the trial."[54]

To return from "exceptionalist" rhetoric to reality: The pattern of the written constitution as paramount law and the practice of judicial review was to become the most characteristic feature of the American culture of rights – both on the relatively neglected level of the state constitutions and on the superior level, in the limelight of public attention and controversy, of the Federal Constitution.[55] Yet this development might not have moved so much into the center of public interest if it had not been

---

52 *The Federalist*, 360–1.

53 As quoted by Charles H. McIlwain, *Constitutionalism Ancient and Modern* (Ithaca, N.Y., 1958), 2.

54 Robert G. McCloskey, ed., *The Works of James Wilson*, 2 vols. (Cambridge, Mass., 1967), 1:185–8, 329–30, 333.

55 The significance of judicial power in the United States was soon recognized in Europe, e.g., as early as 1824 by the young Robert von Mohl, *Das Bundes-Staatsrecht der Vereinigten Staaten von Nord-Amerika* (Tübingen, 1824), 298–302. See also Erich Angermann, *Robert von Mohl 1799–1875: Leben und Werk eines altliberalen Staatsgelehrten* (Neuwied, 1962), 26.

inseparably intertwined with another phenomenon to which I now turn.

4. As part of the constitutionalization of individual rights, I distinguish between two processes – "fundamentalizing" and "constitutionalizing" individual rights. The first, which I used earlier in this chapter in reference to England, is a process that leads to the recognition of certain imperatives or prohibitions – for example, habeas corpus – as fundamental laws of the land *without* thereby creating a special category of legal norms. By constitutionalizing I refer to a process whereby certain imperatives or prohibitions become part of the higher law or paramount law in the technical sense that it cannot be abrogated or changed by normal legislative procedure. This process also could be described as a process of *entrenching* certain rules – protecting individual rights for instance, above and beyond the license of simple legislative majorities – the term entrenching being taken from public law discussions in South Africa and in Canada.

Constitutional developments in North America in the seventeenth and eighteenth centuries added a new dimension to the securing of individual rights. To the dimension of rights secured by the law of the land and considered fundamental, though changeable by the legislator (for example, habeas corpus), the dimension of "entrenched" guarantees was added. A remarkable example of this process in colonial times is a 1676 document titled "Charter or fundamental laws" of West New Jersey.[56] It is part of the "Concessions and Agreements of the Proprietors, Freeholders and Inhabitants of the Province of West New Jersey" of that year. The eleven articles of the "Charter" were alternatively called "the common law or fundamental Rights" of West New Jersey. They chiefly embodied rights with reference to criminal procedure, including habeas corpus. These fundamental rights were agreed on

to be the foundation of the Government which is not to be altered by the Legislative Authority or free Assembly hereafter mentioned and constituted. But that the said Legislative Authority is constituted according to these fundamentals to make such Laws as agree with and maintain the said fundamentals and to make no Laws that in the least contradict, differ, or vary from the said fundamentals under what pretence or allegation so ever.

The clarity of distinguishing between fundamental law (in which various individual rights were "entrenched") and legislative-made law is

---

56 For the following, see Julian P. Boyd, ed., *Fundamental Laws and Constitutions of New Jersey, 1664–1964* (Princeton, N.J., 1964), 71ff. (spelling modernized).

extraordinary; it would not be surpassed by statements made more than a century later like Hamilton's *Federalist* no. 78 or John Marshall's dictum in *Marbury*.

With American independence the tendency of entrenching individual rights in the fundamental – or paramount – law of the Constitution was vastly enhanced. One reason was the appeal to natural rights that pervaded the movement for independence and many of the documents drafted in and around 1776, Jefferson's preamble to the Declaration of Independence and Mason's Virginia Bill of Rights merely being the two outstanding and best known examples.[57] Another reason was the firm determination to protect the rights of persons from legislative arbitrariness, as the activities of Parliament in London had come to be felt. The protection of rights emerged in America as the very raison d'etre of a constitution: This was unsurpassably well said in the Concord town meeting's resolution of October 21, 1776: "We conceive that a Constitution in its proper idea intends a system of principles established to secure the subject in the possession and enjoyment of their rights and privileges, against any encroachments of the governing part."[58] This is, in a nutshell, the liberal idea of a constitution, and it is, if connected with the idea of the constituent power of the people and a democratic franchise, the central idea of liberal democracy. In Europe the central place of rights – of "subjective" rights, as French and German legal terminology has it[59] – in a liberal constitution were aptly expressed thirteen years later in Article 16 of the Universal Declaration of the Rights of Man and Citizen: "Any society in which the guarantee of rights is not assured, nor the separation of powers determined, has no constitution."[60]

Many, although not all, state constitutions included bills of rights. There are examples, such as the well-known North Carolina case of *Bayard v. Singleton* (1786–7), that judicial review, weighing the constitutionality or unconstitutionality of legislation, measured legislation according to the

---

57 See the extensive source material presented in Hutson, "Bill of Rights," 62–80, and, with more emphasis on the moral and public opinion-related aspects of rights, the chapter on "Rights" in Jack N. Rakove, *Original Meanings: Politics and Ideas in the Making of the Constitution* (New York, 1996), 288–338.

58 Handlin and Handlin, eds., *Popular Sources*, 152–3.

59 On the significance of the notion of "subjective" rights and its applicability to English and American notions of rights, see the suggestive study by James H. Hutson, "The Emergence of the Modern Concept of a Right in America: The Contribution of Michel Villey," *American Journal of Jurisprudence* 39 (1994): 185–224.

60 "Toute société, dans laquelle la garantie des droits n'est pas assurée, ni la séparation des pouvoirs determinée, n'a pas de constitution."

criterion of an individual right entrenched in the constitution (in that particular case, the right to trial by jury).[61]

What happened in the United States beginning in 1776 was a process of "constitutionalizing" individual rights that worked, as it were, from two directions. On the one hand, natural rights were reduced, if one may put it this way, to the level of constitutional rights – what German authors have called *die Positivierung des Naturrechts* (the positivizing of natural law).[62] A classic application of this process of transforming natural rights into legal (constitutional) rights is supplied by the well-known "Quok Walker" case in Massachusetts. In 1783 the chief justice of Massachusetts, William Cushing, instructed a jury to the effect that the natural freedom of all men, as asserted in Article 1 of the Massachusetts Bill of Rights (a part of the Constitution of Massachusetts), was incompatible with the idea of slavery. Subsequently, the institution of slavery, which to be sure never had been strong in Massachusetts, vanished in the Commonwealth.[63] On the other hand, the process of "constitutionalizing" individual rights also included the raising of various rights of English common law or parliamentary origin, particularly procedural rights, to the level of constitutional rights.

The early existence of a culture of rights in the United States – awareness of the centrality of rights in a political system, awareness of the various levels on which rights were located – is excellently expressed in an essay published in December 1787:

Of rights, some are natural and unalienable, of which even the people cannot deprive individuals: Some are constitutional or fundamental; these cannot be altered or abolished by the ordinary laws; but the people, by express acts, may alter or abolish them – These individual claims, such as the trial by jury, the benefits of the writ of habeas corpus, and so forth, under the solemn compacts of the people, as constitutions, or at least under laws so strengthened by long usage as not to be repealed by the ordinary legislature – and some are common or mere legal rights, that is, such as individuals claim under laws which the ordinary legislature may alter or abolish at pleasure.[64]

---

61 For details, see Stourzh, *Wege zur Grundrechtsdemokratie*, 60–4.
62 Jürgen Habermas, "Naturrecht und Revolution," in Jürgen Habermas, *Theorie und Praxis* (Neuwied, 1967), 52–88 (often lacking historical precision), quotation on 55; see also on this theme Dieter Grimm, "Europäisches Naturrecht und Amerikanische Revolution: Die Verwandlung politischer Theorie in politische Techne," *Ius Commune* 3 (1970): 120–51.
63 Henry Steele Commager, ed., *Documents of American History*, 5th ed. (New York, 1949), 110. See also Arthur Zilversmit, *The First Emancipation: The Abolition of Slavery in the North* (Chicago, 1970).
64 "Letters from the Federal Farmer" (abbreviated title; anonymous), in Herbert J. Storing, ed., *The Complete Anti-Federalist*, 7 vols. (Chicago, 1981), 2:261, letter VI; the authorship by R. H. Lee, often claimed, has been cast in doubt by several scholars; arguments for the authorship of Melancton Smith, an important moderate anti-Federalist from New York, have been put forward by

The story of the advocacy of a Federal Bill of Rights and of the adoption of the first ten amendments has been told too often to be repeated.[65] Also, the qualitative change of the constitutional protection of individual rights resulting from the passing of the Fourteenth Amendment, making the Supreme Court the ultimate arbiter of the individual states' respect for "the equal protection of the laws," shall not be addressed here. It also cannot be the aim of this chapter to give an account of how the most important provisions of the Federal Bill of Rights became applicable to the states – a process that has been described as the "nationalization of the Bill of Rights."[66]

Constitutional litigation involving the protection of rights has become, in the twentieth century, the major feature of America's culture of rights. As constitutional adjudication during (roughly) the first century of U.S. constitutionalism has (chiefly) been a constitutionalism of "powers," the second century of U.S. constitutionalism has been marked by "a new constitutionalism of rights"; especially since 1945, "the civil rights of racial and other groups have taken center stage in what has become a vigorous constitutionalism of rights."[67] Thus, one encounters the striking phenomenon that in an age of increasing relativism, particularly "cultural relativism,"[68] and in an age in which generally recognized moral obligations seem to be weakening or waning, "rights talk" persists. "The Curious Persistence of Rights Talk in the 'Age of Interpretation'" is the title of a thoughtful article,[69] and it is indeed a phenomenon that calls for comment.

I suggest two answers, one obvious and one perhaps less obvious, both limited to the specifically American culture of rights. I shall return to this

---

Robert A. Webking, "Melancton Smith and the *Letters from the Federal Farmer*," *William and Mary Quarterly*, 3d ser., 44 (1987): 510–28; they are shared by Rakove, *Original Meanings*, 228–9.

65 Most recent interpretation of this process in Hutson, "Bill of Rights," 80–97, and, with a subtle analysis of James Madison's views and motives, see Rakove, *Original Meanings*, 330–8.

66 Cf. Richard C. Cortner, *The Supreme Court and the Second Bill of Rights: The Fourteenth Amendment and the Nationalization of Civil Liberties* (Madison, Wis., 1981); Michael Kent Curtis, *No State Shall Abridge: The Fourteenth Amendment and the Bill of Rights* (Durham, N.C., 1986); very suggestive, and with ample references, Robert J. Kaczorowski, "To Begin the Nation Anew: Congress, Citizenship, and Civil Rights after the Civil War," *American Historical Review* 92 (1987): 45–68. See also the radically egalitarian interpretation by Judith A. Baer, *Equality under the Constitution: Reclaiming the Fourteenth Amendment* (Ithaca, N.Y., 1983).

67 Keller, "Powers and Rights," 686, 688.

68 See the challenging reflections by David A. Hollinger, "How Wide the Circle of the 'We'? American Intellectuals and the Problem of the Ethnos Since World War II," *American Historical Review* 98 (1993): 326.

69 Thomas L. Haskell, "The Curious Persistence of Rights Talk in the 'Age of Interpretation,'" *Journal of American History* 74 (1987–8): 984–1012.

problem in my conclusion, where I attempt to suggest an additional answer applying both to Europe and America.

As far as the United States is concerned, the obvious answer is: The Enlightenment project of the American system of government, as expressed in the Declaration of Independence and the Federal Constitution, rededicated in the Gettysburg Address and the Fourteenth Amendment, and including a considerable potential for conflict resolution through constitutional litigation and adjudication, has generated very strong institutional and emotional (patriotic) support, strong enough to defy intellectual fashions and changing moral currents.

A less obvious answer is this: The culture of rights in the United States draws its peculiar intensity and poignancy from the fact that in no other liberal democracy in the North Atlantic world have the affirmation of human rights and their denial been as closely adjacent to each other. As you see, I am here developing Edmund Morgan's "American Slavery, American Freedom" theme.[70] Joyce Appleby has written that the most radical achievement of the American Revolution was "the abolition movement that brought northern slavery to an end and turned the surveyors' line of Mason and Dixon into the most conspicuous ideological divide in the world."[71] I agree with Hendrik Hartog, who has said that for the past two centuries, "American understandings of constitutional rights have changed as understandings of the interrelated meanings of slavery and of political freedom have changed." Hartog rightly adds, "The long contest over slavery did more than any other cause to stimulate the development of an alternate, rights conscious, interpretation of the Federal Constitution."[72]

In no other liberal democracy has the postulate of equal rights been taken as seriously and at the same time encountered utter denial as directly as in America.[73] One may compare the proposition of the Declaration of Independence that all men are created equal with Chief Justice Taney's denial that citizenship might ever be accessible to the black person,

---

70 Edmund Morgan, "Slavery and Freedom: The American Paradox," *Journal of American History* 59 (1972–3): 5–29, and Edmund Morgan, *American Slavery, American Freedom: The Ordeal of Colonial Virginia* (New York, 1975).

71 Joyce Appleby, "The Radical Recreation of the American Republic," *William and Mary Quarterly*, 3d ser., 51 (1994): 682 (contribution to a forum on Gordon S. Wood's *The Radicalism of the American Revolution*).

72 Hendrik Hartog, "The Constitution of Aspiration and 'The Rights That Belong to Us All,'" *Journal of American History* 74 (1987): 1017.

73 See the very thoughtful work by J. R. Pole, *The Pursuit of Equality in American History*, 2d ed. (Berkeley, Calif., 1993).

whether slave or free. In no other liberal democracy have varieties of legal capacity, ranging from the fullest capacity of the male citizen "having sufficient evidence of permanent common interest with and attachment to the community"[74] to the denial of active legal capacity pertaining to the status of slavery, been as great as in America.[75] Think of status issues arising from the fugitive slave movement and the personal liberty laws in antebellum America,[76] or from transit through or residence in free territory, culminating in the *Dred Scott* case.[77] I believe that the intensity of the pre–Civil War struggle on the status of persons, free/unfree, equal/unequal, continues to provide an ever-present foil for the subsequent debates on inequality of status and its remedies, on discrimination negative and positive – in other words, on rights. After the abolition of slavery, status discrimination concerning people of color, whether de jure in the South ("grandfather laws") or de facto in many places, and more recently status discrimination concerning other groups, notably women, have continued to throw into relief the issue of status inequalities. Hartog has rightly stressed that the history of "rights consciousness" has received an enormous impulse since the end of the Civil War and emancipation. He has emphasized: "All the varying meanings that have been derived from the phrase 'equal protection of the laws' are rooted in contending views of what it was that was overthrown by the end of slavery."[78] All this has supplied an impetus to civil rights or equal rights litigation that is probably not found anywhere else in the North Atlantic world and that indeed characterizes America's culture of rights.

III

The constituent power of the people, which had been exercised in America since 1776, re-emerged on the continent of Europe, in France, in 1789 as the *pouvoir constituant de la nation*. Its most important advocate was Emmanuel-Joseph Sieyès, whose booklet *What Is the Third Estate?* played a powerful role early in 1789, similar to that played by Tom Paine's

---

74 Virginia Bill of Rights of 1776, sec. 6.

75 In 1824, Robert von Mohl divided his chapter on the personal rights of the inhabitants of the United States in three sections: rights of the "free whites," of the "free colored," and of "slaves" – the latter amounting to a list of rights denied, and of the rights of the masters. See Mohl, *Bundes-Staatsrecht*, 385–418.

76 William M. Wiecek, *The Sources of Antislavery Constitutionalism in America, 1760–1848* (Ithaca, N.Y., 1977); Paul Finkelman, *An Imperfect Union: Slavery, Federalism, and Comity* (Chapel Hill, N.C., 1981).

77 On this issue, see the masterly Fehrenbacher, *Dred Scott*.

78 Hartog, "Constitution of Aspiration," 1017.

Common Sense early in 1776.[79] The constituent power of the nation found its institutional expression in the National Assembly, also often referred to as the "constituent" National Assembly or *constituante*. The name "National Assembly" employed in Paris in 1789 was to reverberate through the subsequent history of the constituent power of the people in Europe – in Frankfurt on Main in 1848, in Weimar and Vienna in 1919, in Paris again, and in Rome after World War II. The history of the United States has never known – on the level of the union – such an assembly issued from a nationwide election, uniting the representatives of the whole nation for the task of drawing up the constitution as fundamental law of the nation, but at the same time legislating as well. Such bodies reflected and felt themselves to be in the legitimate possession of the sovereignty of the people.

The French National Assembly of 1789 adopted, as we all know, the Universal Declaration of the Rights of Man and Citizen. Much has been written on the impact, present or absent, of the American states' declarations of rights on the French Declaration. I agree with Georg Jellinek and R. R. Palmer, among others, that such an impact indeed existed.[80] Yet it is also important to see differences between the types of bills of rights prevailing in the United States and the French Declaration of 1789 and its many successors. The French text of 1789 contained in no less than seven of seventeen articles express invitations, or rather authorizations addressed to the legislator, to settle matters *par la loi*, by law. The law (*la loi*) was explicitly declared to be "the expression of the general will" (Article 6); in the constitution of 1791 it was also stated expressly that "there is in France no authority superior to that of the law." Thus, *la loi* assumed a central significance, and consequently so did the lawmaker, the legislator, assumed to be the mouthpiece of the nation's sovereign will.[81] In the American declarations there are more statements

---

79 The best critical edition is Roberto Zapperi, ed., *Emmanuel Sieyès, Qu'est-ce que le Tiers état?* (Geneva 1970).
80 Jellinek's little book, first published in 1895, is conveniently found, together with a number of more recent studies, partly critical, partly revising and developing Jellinek's theses, in Roman Schnur, ed., *Zur Geschichte der Erklärung der Menschenrechte* (Darmstadt, 1964). A parallel printing of the corresponding articles of the Virginia Bill of Rights and the French Declaration of 1789 has been assembled in R. R. Palmer, *The Age of the Democratic Revolution: A Political History of Europe and America, 1760–1800*, 2 vols. (Princeton, N.J., 1959–64), 1:518–21. Among the vast literature published around the bicentennial of 1789, see Stéphane Rials, ed., *La déclaration de 1789*, special issue of *Droits: Revue francaise de théorie juridique*, no. 8 (1988); and Wolfgang Schmale, "Droit," in Rolf Reichardt and Hans-Jürgen Lüsebrink, eds., *Handbuch politisch-sozialer Grundbegriffe in Frankreich 1680–1820*, vol. 12 (Munich, 1992), 78–84.
81 For the following, see Gerald Stourzh, "The Declarations of Rights, Popular Sovereignty and the Supremacy of the Constitution: Divergencies between the American and the French

about what existing law prescribes, in the French *Déclaration* more is said about what the law is supposed to settle. In America the declarations had to do with legislative restraint; the French declarations (of 1793 no less than of 1789), quite apart from their function as a kind of revolutionary "catechism," became guideposts for legislative action rather than legislative restraint. It also has been observed that the French (unlike the English and the Americans) "are more sensitive to grand principles than to the procedures that guarantee them."[82] The consequences of this disposition will be discussed shortly.

Finally, in France no less than in America, a "written constitution" was drawn up and adopted in 1791; the end of the monarchy and the proclamation of the republic in 1792 necessitated a new constitution, more democratic (with strong Rousseauian overtones) in theory; it never was allowed to operate. As we all know, the number of constitutions in France multiplied in later years. In revolutionary France the aura surrounding the notion of "constitution" was even stronger than in America; the relevance of an almost deified "constitution" in the context of dechristianization and revolution in France has been the object of recent thoughtful discussion.[83]

Yet, in spite of the exalted position of the constitution, a logical consequence of the constitution as paramount public law did not develop in France: mechanisms to control the constitutionality of legislation, notably judicial review. In 1791 a project for a special *assemblée de révision* was worked out; this special assembly was to be empowered to investigate whether the "constituted powers" had stayed within the limits prescribed by the constitution. The plan came to nothing. In 1795, under the Directory, someone who grasped the logic of the constitution as higher law and who asked for a kind of special constitutional court was Sieyès; yet his proposal of a *jury constitutionnaire* was not taken up either.[84] An excellent expert on French public law has commented that the reason for the failure of Sieyès's plan can be found "in the concept of the absolute power of the legislative body as representative of the general will."[85]

Certainly, the primacy of legislative sovereignty in France in spite of the existence of written constitutions had various sources. In France, as

Revolutions," in Claude Fohlen and Jacques Godechot, eds., *La Révolution américaine et l'Europe*, Colloques internationaux du Centre National de la Recherche Scientifique, no. 577 (Paris, 1979), 355.

82 Georges Vedel in *Le Monde*, Nov. 10, 1977, 1.

83 Wolfgang Schmale, *Entchristianisierung, Revolution und Verfassung: Zur Mentalitätsgeschichte der Verfassung in Frankreich 1715–1794* (Berlin, 1988).

84 Stourzh, "Declarations of Rights," 361–2.

85 Georges Burdeau, *Traité de Science politique*, vol. 4, 2d ed. (Paris, 1969), 374, also 408–10.

distinct from America, the Revolution was not directed against the "despotism" of a sovereign parliament but against absolutism (and against the *société des ordres*). In France, opposition to the existing judicial organization was strong because it was regarded to be part and parcel of the ancien régime, whereas in America the judiciary, from the time of the Stamp Act, had sided with the "patriots."

Now the concept of the primacy of the legislative assembly as expression of the sovereign will of the nation had far-reaching consequences. It prevented, for a very long time indeed, any kind of judicial review of legislation. Only in 1958 did the constitution of the Fifth Republic create the Conseil Constitutionnel (Constitutional Council), which was empowered to exercise control over the constitutionality of legislation. But it was not and is not a court *stricto sensu* because suits by individual citizens cannot be brought before it; specific complaints as to the unconstitutionality of certain laws or legal provisions may be brought before the council by the government, by the presidents of the two chambers of the National Assembly, and after a reform also by a minority group of deputies, but not by individuals. A proposal by former French president François Mitterrand in connection with the bicentennial of the Revolution to entitle citizens to bring suits before the council was not taken up by the National Assembly. Nevertheless, a constitutional "revolution" took place in 1971, when the council ruled for the first time that the Declaration of the Rights of Man and Citizen of 1789 had constitutionally binding character and that consequently ordinary law was to be measured by the standard of the legally superior Declaration.[86]

Thus, three types of Western democratic government were in the process of emerging and developing: in Great Britain, the primacy of a sovereign parliament without a "written," that is, paramount constitution, and without the constitutional protection of individual rights; in the United States, the primacy of the written constitution including an unequivocal subordination of legislation and the constitutional protection of individual rights; and in France (at least until the onset of the Fifth Republic), a de facto sovereignty of the legislator in spite of the existence of a written constitution and (until 1971) no constitutional protection of

---

86 For the breakthrough in a decision of July 16, 1971, see Louis Favoreu and Loïc Philip, eds., *Les grandes décisions du Conseil Constitutionnel* (Paris, 1975), 267–87. See also Christian Starck, "Der Schutz der Grundrechte durch den Verfassungsrat in Frankreich," *Archiv des öffentlichen Rechts* 113 (1988): 636. For a general discussion of the French development, see Gerald Stourzh, "Verfassungsgerichtsbarkeit und Grundrechtsdemokratie – die historischen Wurzeln," in Verfassungsgerichtshof der Republik Österreich, ed., *70 Jahre Bundesverfassung* (Vienna, 1991), 26–8.

individual rights. The culture of rights in these three nations obviously was influenced by this state of affairs. In a very general way, and with an awareness of and due respect for differences in time and space among various countries, I would say that, in other European nations developing toward liberal democracy, for a long time constitutional systems developed that were rather similar to the French type; only in the second half of the twentieth century did a strong tendency in the direction of the American type develop.

Prior to sketching this fairly new development, I must turn to an aspect of the transformation of the legal landscape of Europe that has wholly altered the culture of rights in Europe. I refer to the process of the "equalization" (*Angleichung*) of individual rights – or technically speaking, of the individuals' legal capacity – that went on from the late eighteenth century well into the twentieth century. This process consisted not merely of the reduction or disappearance of the privileges, immunities, and "liberties" of orders, estates, or other privileged groups in the everyday understanding of the word "privileged." This process also included, in a major way, the lifting of the *privilegia odiosa*, of the special obligations and restrictions burdening most population groups.

One passage from the celebrated book *On the Civil Improvement of the Jews* (1781) by the Prussian author Christian Wilhelm Dohm explains what I wish to convey.[87] Dohm wrote: "The Jew is still more human than Jewish, and how should it be possible that he should not love a state in which he could acquire and freely enjoy property, in which his taxes would not be greater than those of other citizens, and where he, too, could acquire honor and respect? Why should he hate people who would not anymore be separated from him by grievous privileges, with whom he would share equal rights and equal duties?"[88]

Dohm's statement "The Jew is still more human than Jewish" ("Der Jude ist noch mehr Mensch als Jude") is apt to explain – symbolically

---

87 Christian Konrad Wilhelm von Dohm, *Über die bürgerliche Verbesserung der Juden*, 2 vols. (Berlin, 1781; reprint, Hildesheim, 1973), the quotation is on 1:28. The book appeared in a French translation as early as 1782.

88 My translation. In view of the significance of the passage, I quote the original as well: "Der Jude ist noch mehr Mensch als Jude, und wie wäre es möglich, daß er einen Staat nicht lieben sollte, in dem er ein freyes Eigenthum erwerben, und desselben frey geniessen könnte, wo seine Abgaben nicht größer als die anderer Bürger wären, und wo auch von ihm Ehre und Achtung erworben werden könnte? Warum sollte er Menschen hassen, die keine kränkenden Vorrechte mehr von ihm scheiden, mit denen er gleiche Rechte und gleiche Pflichten hätte?" I first drew attention to this passage and the reflections that follow from it in an earlier paper: Gerald Stourzh, "The Modern State: Equal Rights, Equalizing the Individual's Status, and the Breakthrough of the Modern Liberal State," in Janet Coleman, ed., *The Individual in Political Theory and Practice* (Oxford, 1996), 319–21.

and vicariously, as it were – the claim of all groups of people living under a status of limited, or sometimes virtually nonexistent, legal capacity,[89] living, in other words, under the disabilities of a special status. The slave is more human than slave. The serf is more human than serf. A domestic servant or an indentured servant is more human than servant.[90] The comedian – thinking of a category of people to whom during the ancien régime the Church denied the privileges of Christian marriage and burial – is more human than comedian. The member of a religious group denied full access to civil or political rights (for example, Roman Catholics in England prior to 1829) is more human than member of a persecuted or restricted denomination. Woman, finally, – let me evoke Condorcet's *De l'admission des femmes au droit de cité* or the *Déclaration des droits de la femme et citoyenne* of Olympe de Gouges – woman is more human than woman. In terms of the improvement – and equalization – of legal capacity and legal status, all these aspirations tended toward civil equality[91] and citizenship in the fullest sense.[92] The fact that human rights find a protected and respected place most fully within the sphere of civil rights and citizens' rights is demonstrated by the fact that – in an age of the virtually completed equalization of legal capacity – the status of "alien" represents the last great status disability within the world of liberal democracy.

The emancipation of serfs and peasants (*Bauernbefreiung*); the emancipation of slaves, not merely in the United States but in territories under European domination; the emancipation of Catholics in England or Protestants in Catholic nations; the emancipation of the Jews – in France at the time of the French Revolution,[93] in a slower and halting process elsewhere in continental Europe; the legal equalization of the status of domestic servants; the legal improvement and final equalization of the status of women – these and many other stages and chapters in the process of the equalization of legal capacity have had a profound impact on the character of "cultures of rights."

---

89 The German legal term is *Rechtsfähigkeit*.

90 A telling example of the late lifting of legal disabilities even in a democratic society is the fact that domestic servants in France were given the right to sit on juries only in 1932! Georges Ripert, *Le régime démocratique et le droit civil moderne* (Paris, 1948), 100.

91 This development is addressed in the well-known phrase of Sir Henry Sumner Maine that the movement of modern society went from "status to contract." See his book *Ancient Law*, 5th ed. (London, 1874), 170.

92 On this, see T. H. Marshall, *Citizenship and Social Development* (Garden City, N.Y., 1964), including his classic lectures on "Citizenship and Social Class."

93 See, particularly, Robert Badinter, *Libres et égaux. . . . L'émancipation des Juifs 1789–1791* (Paris, 1989).

I stress this transforming process for three reasons: First, there is a vast difference between a society based on unequal legal capacity and a society based on equal legal capacity. A close reading of Tocqueville's writings shows how very great is the role of the transformation of legal capacity in his account of the progress of the *égalité des conditions* – the central term of Tocqueville's work describing the emergence, development, and future tendencies of the vast socio-juridico-political system that he called "democracy."[94]

Second, the traditional story of human rights and civil rights, particularly in Europe, has put too one-sided an emphasis on those rights that were entrenched in the catalogs and declarations of rights drawn up in the tradition of the French declaration of 1789.[95] By the same token, developments in private law concerning property or inheritance legislation, for example, have long been neglected by historians,[96] and there is no question that feminist historical writing has been instrumental in calling attention to the significance of disabilities of legal status and capacity beyond the limited sphere of constitutionally entrenched rights.[97]

Third, attention to the role of legal capacity and legal status sharpens our awareness of threats to individual rights as harbingers of worse things to come. Under National Socialism, as early as 1936, the German Supreme Court (Reichsgericht) denied legal capacity to a Jewish person in a suit for damages, explicitly rejecting "the former liberal notion" of the equal rights of human beings, affirming "older thoughts" on the legitimate distinction between persons of full legal capacity and those of inferior right, a distinction now to be applied according to racial criteria.[98] This statement antedates the November pogrom of 1938 and further degradation and destruction to come. It shows how the reduction or denial of legal capacity is a signal of the destruction of any culture of rights previously extant.

---

94 See Gerald Stourzh, "Alexis de Tocqueville und das Werteproblem in der modernen Demokratie," in Helmut Konrad et al., eds., *Staat = fad: Demokratie heute, Markierungen für eine offene Gesellschaft* (Graz, 1995), 87–106.

95 This is the case, e.g., in the widely used book by Gerhard Oestreich, *Geschichte der Menschenrechte und Grundfreiheiten im Umriss* (Berlin, 1968).

96 Although there are as always exceptions to the rule, such as Elisabeth Fehrenbach, *Traditionale Gesellschaft und revolutionäres Recht* (Göttingen, 1974).

97 See, e.g., the references in note 19 of this chapter.

98 The "Charrell case," brilliantly analyzed by Ernst Fraenkel in his classic study on the "*Dual State*" (New York, 1940), here reference to the German ed.: Ernst Fraenkel, *Der Doppelstaat* (Frankfurt am Main, 1974), 126–7. On this case, and on the process of *Entrechtung* (taking away previously held rights), which led to the genocide of the Jewish population under Nazi rule, see Gerald Stourzh, "Menschenrechte und Genozid," in Heinz Schäffer et al., eds., *Staat – Verfassung – Verwaltung (Festschrift für Friedrich Koja)* (Vienna, 1998), 147–56.

The victory over National Socialism and fascism in 1945 produced a new vigor in the protection of human rights that has led, over the last fifty years, to a new level of the culture of rights in many European nations. The Western world, in the United States no less than in Europe outside the orbit of fascism and communism, was swept by a renewal of the Enlightenment tradition of the natural rights of humankind. The Universal Declaration of Human Rights of 1948 and the many international conventions on the protection of human rights (including the two Covenants on Human Rights of 1966) are important cases in point. On the European level, the European Convention on Human Rights and Fundamental Liberties of 1950 set a landmark for a new culture of rights in those European nations that adhere to the convention. By adopting procedures that enable individuals to apply for remedies against violations of human rights and creating appropriate judicial or semi-judicial institutions (the European Commission of Human Rights and the European Court of Human Rights), the European Convention established the most efficient transnational system for the protection of human rights anywhere in the world.

During 1998 a major revision of the institutional system of the European protection of human rights took place. The European Commission of Human Rights as an intermediate institution between complaining individuals and the European Court ceased to exist, and the European Court of Human Rights was transformed into a court with full-time judges – one judge for every member nation of the Council of Europe. By linking membership in the Council of Europe to adherence to the European Convention of Human Rights, this system was extended to a large number of nations in eastern and southeastern Europe, including Russia and the Ukraine. It will be of great interest to continue to watch the impact of this new European Court of Human Rights on nations with a weak tradition of protecting individual rights.

On the national level of the European democracies, the constitutional protection of human rights has made considerable advances by developing or extending procedures that first were suggested or tried, rather sporadically, in the nineteenth century. The German constitution of 1848, for example, drawn up in Frankfurt's Paulskirche, empowered the Reichsgericht to decide on suits of German citizens concerning the violation of rights guaranteed by the constitution.[99] Yet, the constitution of the

---

99 Cf. Hans Joachim Faller, "Die Verfassungsgerichtsbarkeit in der Frankfurter Reichsverfassung vom 28. März 1849," in Gerhard Leibholz et al., *Menschenwürde und freiheitliche Rechtsordnung: Festschrift*

Paulskirche was never given the chance to be put into practice, and a
provision corresponding to the one just mentioned had to wait until
the Federal Republic of Germany's Basic Law (Grundgesetz) of 1949.
However, the liberal constitutional program of 1848, embodied in the
Austrian "Kremsier" draft constitution as well as in the Frankfurt constitution, was taken up, by virtue of a peculiar political constellation when
the Austrian emperor needed the support of the Austrian liberals, in the
liberal constitution of Imperial Austria of 1867.[100] Redress of violations
of those rights guaranteed under the Austrian fundamental law on citizens' rights could be sought in the Austrian Imperial Court, although
some legal deficiencies impaired the effectiveness of this provision; the
Imperial Court was a forerunner of the Austrian Constitutional Court
created in 1919–20, where, with the significant participation of Hans
Kelsen, a legal theorist turned constitution-maker, the first efficient system
for the constitutional protection of citizens' rights was created. It differed
from the American system by separating the functions, united in the
American Supreme Court, of a Supreme Court (for civil and criminal
matters) and a special Constitutional Court.

Only after 1945 has there been a vast expansion of constitutional jurisdiction, including the creation of special constitutional courts and the
remedy of individual suits (*Verfassungsbeschwerde* and *Individualbeschwerde*).
The Federal Republic of Germany must be mentioned as the nation with
the most highly developed post–World War II tradition of constitutional
jurisdiction (beginning in 1951), yet Italy (1956), Spain (1980), and
Belgium (1984) also deserve special mention; the somewhat exceptional
case of France has already been addressed.[101] More recently, constitutional
courts have been created in Poland, Hungary, the Czech Republic, and
even in Russia (though conclusions as to impartiality and effectiveness in
the latter case are premature). Within the English-speaking world constitutional jurisdiction, although not located in separate courts, has increasingly included jurisdiction concerning "entrenched" provisions or bills of

---

für Willi Geiger zum 65. Geburtstag (Tübingen, 1974), 835, 839–40, 845. On the impact of the
American constitutional principles on the deputies of the Paulskirche, see the excellent study
by Eckhart G. Franz, *Das Amerikabild der deutschen Revolution von 1848/49: Zum Problem der Über-
tragung gewachsener Verfassungsformen* (Heidelberg, 1958), 98–133. On American comments on the
German constititional projects of 1848, see Günter Moltmann, *Atlantische Blockpolitik im 19.
Jahrhundert: Die Vereinigten Staaten und der deutsche Liberalismus während der Revolution von 1848/49*
(Düsseldorf, 1973), 213–35.
100 Gerald Stourzh, "Die österreichische Dezemberverfassung von 1867," in Stourzh, *Wege zur Grundrechtsdemokratie*, 239–58.
101 See note 86 of this chapter.

human rights. A notable example of a transition from the "British" system without an entrenched bill of rights to the "American" system of an entrenched bill of rights has been the creation and operation of the Canadian Charter of Rights.[102] It has been rightly said that the experience of the last decades shows that constitutional jurisdiction (in American parlance, judicial review) has become the institutional protector for the preservation and development of Western democracy. This is particularly true of the function of protecting individual rights.[103]

There remains, of course, Great Britain, without an entrenched bill of rights. The case in favor of a bill of rights removed from Parliament's sovereign legislative will was reopened in 1974 by the eminent British judge Sir Leslie Scarman (later Lord Scarman); it was taken up most prominently by Ronald Dworkin and has also been persuasively argued by Alan Ryan in a study mentioned earlier in this chapter. One most interesting phenomenon must be noted: A kind of subsidiary bill of rights – and a subsidiary court – have been operating for more than three decades: The European Convention of Human Rights and the European Court of Human Rights, and the impact of these institutions and the "Strasbourg" cases on public discussion in Britain has been considerable. The Queen's Speech of May 14, 1997, embodying the legislative program of the new Labour government, announced the "incorporation" of the European Convention of Human Rights into British law. This has enabled British courts to apply directly the provisions of the European Convention, although the exact way in which possible clashes between the European Convention incorporated as British law and other parliamentary enactments might be reconciled still remain to be worked out.

Looking back on the last half century, it can be said that in the liberal democracies of the Western world more than ever before the idea of a liberal constitution expressed in 1776 by the Concord Town Meeting has been fulfilled: "A Constitution in its proper idea intends a system of principles established to secure the subject in the possession and enjoyment of their rights and privileges, against any encroachments of the

---

102 See Anne F. Bayefsky, "Parliamentary Sovereignty and Human Rights in Canada: The Promise of the Canadian Charter of Rights and Freedoms," *Political Studies* 31 (1983): 239–63.

103 For an early survey on judicialism, see Carl J. Friedrich, *The Impact of American Constitutionalism Abroad* (Boston, 1967), 71–96, and the excellent study by Alexander von Brünneck, *Verfassungsgerichtsbarkeit in den westlichen Demokratien: Ein systematischer Verfassungsvergleich* (Baden-Baden, 1992), 151; for a comparative survey of the constitutional protection of individual rights, see 62–125; for the following paragraph, see 150–1; see also Sir Leslie Scarman, *English Law: The New Dimension* (London, 1974), and Ronald Dworkin, *A Bill of Rights for Britain?* (London, 1990); Ryan, "The British," 416–20, 431–9.

governing part."[104] In the United States the background of slavery, emancipation, and racial discrimination has given added intensity to the American culture of rights; in Europe, the horrors of genocide and war wrought by National Socialism have provided, in the years after 1945, a new impetus for the protection of human rights, indeed for a new culture of rights. By the end of the twentieth century, not merely in the United States but in many other countries, particularly in Europe, a new and more intensive level of a culture of rights has been reached or may be in the process of attainment.

IV

My conclusion is very brief and consists of two points only: First, I would like to express – from the vantage point of the theme of liberal democracy as a culture of rights – my skepticism as to simply juxtaposing "America" and "Europe." What about England or Great Britain? What about Canada, so often forgotten in comparative discussions?[105] I have doubts about "exceptionalisms," American or European. In many countries there are certainly assertions of one's own special and providential task or burden.[106] There are certainly various types and even more numerous variants within the family of liberal democracies; there are numerous distinctions to make in that vast development that Tocqueville described and analyzed as the development of those "conditions of equality" that are the core of modern liberal democracy. Yet "exceptionalism" as a category of historical and comparative analysis will not, I fear, open up new insights. Carl N. Degler stated the essential point years ago: "To ask what differentiates one people from another does not mean one has to insist on deviation from a norm, which is clearly implied in the term 'exceptionalism.'"[107] The recent restatement of the United States as exceptional

104 See note 58 of this chapter.
105 For all too rare comparative volumes that consider both the United States and Canada, see Seymour Martin Lipset, *Continental Divide: The Values and Institutions of the United States and Canada* (New York, 1990), and Marian C. McKenna, ed., *The Canadian and American Constitutions in Comparative Perspective* (Calgary, 1993), and the thoughtful review by Willi Paul Adams in *Reviews in American History* 23 (1995): 551, who writes that the latter volume can "serve to jolt students of American as well as Canadian constitutional law and history out of the ruts of the well-trodden paths of homonational historiography."
106 It is in the context of the Americans' consciousness of a special task or mission and its rhetorical implications that Erich Angermann has placed the term "exceptionalism." See Erich Angermann, "Was heißt und zu welchem Ende studiert man anglo-amerikanische Geschichte?" *Historische Zeitschrift* 256 (1993): 648–9.
107 Carl N. Degler, "In Pursuit of American History," *American Historical Review* 92 (1987): 4. See also the thoughtful article by George M. Frederickson, "From Exceptionalism to Variability:

and an "outlier" among nations by a distinguished believer in American exceptionalism has encountered manifold critical comments.[108]

Second, I would like to refer once more to Tocqueville, who said that he knew of only two methods of establishing equality in the political world. "Rights must be given to every citizen, or none at all to anyone." Tocqueville also said that rights – legal rights – are particularly important in a situation in which "religious belief is shaken and the divine notion of right is declining," in which morality is debased and the notion of moral right is therefore fading away. "If, in the midst of this general disruption, you do not succeed in connecting the notion of right with that of private interest, which is the only immutable point in the human heart, what means will you have of governing the world except by fear?"[109] Fear, to a reader of Montesquieu, like Tocqueville, was the principle animating the worst form of government, despotism. The "curious persistence of rights talk in the 'Age of Interpretation,'" or to be more blunt, the care for a culture of rights in an age of increasing relativism, may indeed be the only way to stave off the threats of a new despotism.

Recent Developments in Cross-National Comparative History," *Journal of American History* 82 (1995): 587–604.

108 Seymour Martin Lipset, *American Exceptionalism: A Double-Edged Sword* (New York, 1996), 17. Three critical review essays by experts on Canadian, German, and Japanese history appeared the following year: H. V. Nelles, "American Exceptionalism: A Double-Edged Sword," *American Historical Review* 102 (1997): 749–57 (with an interesting survey of the development of Lipset's exceptionalism in earlier work); J. Victor Koschmann, "The Nationalism of Cultural Uniqueness," *American Historical Review* 102 (1997): 758–68; and Mary Nolan, "Against Exceptionalisms," *American Historical Review* 102 (1997): 769–74, with its devastating conclusion: "The repeated assertion of American exceptionalism masks the complex nature of American society and its similarities with and interconnections to other nations. It dismisses the ways the rest of the world sees the United States. In both Germany and America, exceptionalist arguments produce inadequate history, limited self-understanding, and arrogant politics" (774).

109 Alexis de Tocqueville, *Democracy in America*, 2 vols. (New York, 1953), 1:53, 246 (vol. 1, chaps. iii, xiv, section on "the idea of rights in the United States").

2

American Exceptionalism

Republicanism as Ideology

ARI HOOGENBOOM

I

The relationship of republicanism to exceptionalism poses three problems: the nature of the ideology of republicanism; the extent, if any, of its effect on American development; and finally how, if at all, this relationship caused American society to differ from other societies. The three answers to these problems are that Americans shaped the ideology of republicanism to meet their needs, that in its altered form republicanism had a profound effect on American development, and that republicanism made American society different from other societies.

Throughout the nineteenth and into the twentieth century, Americans were self-consciously republican. They created a republican empire of liberty and equality by admitting new states into the union, and they invented the mass-based political party to facilitate its operation as a democracy. To enable the masses to cast intelligent ballots, Americans advocated universal education at public expense and preached the virtues of adult education. While American literature and fine arts remained indebted to European masters, American poets and painters cast about for inspiration at home, and Walt Whitman appropriately celebrated the virtues of the democratic republic in "free verse." In addition, republican egalitarianism spawned new religions, inspired social reform movements, and, ironically, embroiled both sides in a long civil war. Republican concern over the uneven distribution of wealth and economic power

I have viewed republican ideology – and particularly its relationship to American exceptionalism – through the eyes of nineteenth-century Americans. I am indebted to James H. Hutson of the Library of Congress, Vera Nünning of the University of Cologne, and Edwin G. Burrows, Robert Muccigrosso, and Jerome L. Sternstein, my colleagues in history at Brooklyn College of the City University of New York, for their comments on this chapter.

overcame republican fears of powerful government and gave rise to federal regulatory legislation. Although every country has developed differently and is exceptional in its own way, the history of the United States is quite distinct from other nations, and its republican ideology has differentiated it clearly from the monarchies of Europe.

Because republicanism rejected monarchy and relied on representative government, its classic ideology stressed the need for virtuous political leaders and citizens willing to sacrifice for the commonweal, and for a simple, frugal government too weak to threaten the liberty of its people. Republicanism and its ideology appealed to Americans resisting encroaching British imperial authority. When resistance escalated into revolution, logic and experience compelled Americans to form a republic but also to adapt classic republicanism to their needs. In their Declaration of Independence, Americans embraced the rights of equality and pursuit of happiness, or economic opportunity, as well as liberty.

These added values penetrated the American psyche and spawned democratic and liberal variants that incorporated some, and contradicted other, traditional republican beliefs. For example, the thrust of selfish liberal individualism (already present in the colonies) ran counter to the notion of selfless devotion to the common good. Also, the spread of democracy yearned for by urban radicals appeared to the educated, wealthy elite as a threat to public virtue as well as to their own personal power. And achieving equality for all citizens, indeed for the United States among other nations, required a fairly strong national government. Liberalism and democracy waxed in strength, but traditional republican values, rather than waning, mingled with equality and opportunity. Americans have clung to this expanded and exceptional republican ideology that includes civic virtue, simplicity, frugality, and the least powerful government needed to protect liberty, achieve equality, and promote opportunity.[1]

In conflicts among themselves, Americans have identified their causes

---

1 Some notion of the manifold interpretations by historians of republican ideology, including its relationship to democracy and liberalism, can be grasped by perusing the thirteen articles included in "Forum: *The Creation of the American Republic, 1776–1787*: A Symposium of Views and Reviews," *William and Mary Quarterly*, 3d ser., 44 (1987): 550–640; two valuable articles by Robert Shalhope, "Toward a Republican Synthesis: The Emergence of an Understanding of Republicanism in American Historiography," *William and Mary Quarterly*, 3d ser., 29 (1972): 49–80; and Robert Shalhope, "Republicanism and Early American Historiography," *William and Mary Quarterly*, 3d ser., 39 (1982): 334–56; and Joyce Appleby's essays in *Liberalism and Republicanism in the Historical Imagination* (Cambridge, Mass., 1992). A good introduction to American republicanism is Willi Paul Adams, "Republicanism," in Jack P. Greene, ed., *Encyclopedia of American Political History*, 3 vols. (New York, 1984), 3:1131–46.

with this broad republican ideology by emphasizing elements in it that suit their objectives. While it has reflected their society, this powerful and inspirational ideology has also made it different. (If, however, republican ideology is narrowly defined in the classic terms of civic virtue and a weak state, it has merely inspired ineffectual efforts to "turn the rascals out" and to shrink the federal government.)

The American people have perceived themselves as different and at times as exceptional in the pejorative sense that they are better than any other people. Indeed, the term *exceptionalism*, as commonly used, encompasses obnoxious superiority, irritating paternalism, ugly undertones of racism and imperialism, and has been linked to the excessive nationalism of a chosen people. In attacking and trying to undermine this brand of exceptionalism, some historians deny vigorously that there is anything about America that is unique. Nevertheless, America is different, is exceptional – more often than not in ways in which most Americans can take pride – and the ideology of republicanism, having been adjusted to a unique society, has accentuated this positive uniqueness.[2]

II

Americans abandoned monarchism with astonishing rapidity. In 1760 they rejoiced in the accession of George III, who they anticipated would be "a Patriot King," rooting out corruption and ushering in a new age of selfless virtue. But by July 4, 1776, they had transmogrified a beloved monarch into a foreign tyrant and aspired to replace a corrupt Old World monarchy with a pure New World republic. The reign of public-spirited virtue would begin not with a patriot king but with the sovereign people.[3]

The jump from a monarchy to a republic was not a leap into an unknown abyss. In practice the colonists already had experience with republicanism. With its meeting of eligible voters, each New England town was a miniature republic, and Connecticut and Rhode Island had republican governments. Proprietary and even royal colonies, with their legislatures claiming control of the purse strings, veered toward republicanism, especially in the eyes of royal officials.

2 For conflicting evaluations of American exceptionalism, see Byron E. Shafer, ed., *Is America Different?: A New Look at American Exceptionalism* (Oxford, 1991). I have used "exceptionalism" in its nonpejorative sense.
3 William D. Liddle, "'A Patriot King or None': Lord Bolingbroke and the American Renunciation of George III," *Journal of American History* 65 (1978–9): 951–70.

American colonists identified with prominent defenders of the concept of limited monarchy like John Locke and eighteenth-century British Whigs. In *Two Treatises of Government* (1690) Locke claimed that William and Mary's title to the throne rested on the republican notion of consent of the people, and the Whigs aimed to achieve a virtual republic by enhancing the power of the House of Commons while reducing the king to a cipher. Both Thomas Jefferson and John Dickinson, avid readers of Catherine Macaulay's eight-volume *History of England (1763–1783)*, were steeped in the Whig interpretation of the Glorious Revolution.[4]

Americans followed British politics, and many identified with the out-of-power "country" party of landed Tories. Fearing that big government, with its extensive patronage, would multiply opportunities for corruption and suspecting that the private goals of commercialism would undermine public virtue and raise land taxes, they opposed the "court" party of Whigs. While riding the surging wave of commercialism, that party presided over a financial and administrative revolution.[5] Knowledgeable Americans were aware of Baron Montesquieu's *L'Esprit des lois* (1748), with its separation of powers (derived from the idea of Henry St. John Bolingbroke, a leading Country Tory, that the English neatly balanced king, lords, and commons in their government), and they were cautioned by his observation (derived from Aristotle) that civic virtue and small size were preconditions for a successful republic.

American intellectuals, knowing the history of republics, whether they were ancient Greek and Roman or modern Italian, Swiss, Dutch, or English, were aware of their shortcomings. At times corruption had corroded virtue, patrician families or strongmen had eroded liberty, and states' rights had weakened republican confederacies in foreign affairs. But these Americans also knew adaptations by James Harrington and Algernon Sidney of the republican theories of Niccolo Machiavelli's *Discourses*, designed to correct the abuses of power by Oliver Cromwell's English Commonwealth in the 1650s. To colonists – obsessed with what they believed was a corrupt, rapacious, tyrannical monarchy and with faith in themselves as "a new and uncorrupted people" – a republican confederacy was not frightening. Americans had discarded "the monarchical and taken up the republican government," Jefferson remarked, "with as much

---

4 H. Trevor Colbourn, *The Lamp of Experience: Whig History and the Intellectual Origins of the American Revolution* (Chapel Hill, N.C., 1965).
5 James H. Hutson, "Country, Court, and Constitution: Antifederalism and the Historians," *William and Mary Quarterly*, 3d ser., 38 (1981): 337–68.

ease as would have attended their throwing off an old and putting on a new suit of clothes."

The ideology that accompanied republicanism was admirably suited to American society. It was in many respects a secular version of the Puritan ethic, with its emphasis on regeneration, morality, hard work, thrift, and a common concern for an exceptional community that was likened to a city on a hill. When compared with European society, American society seemed virtuous and simple, free and equal; but revolutionary patriots feared that the connection with monarchical England had sown seeds of idleness and luxury, riches and status. They looked to republicanism to improve and reform the character of the people and to set them apart from other peoples by endowing them with "good manners, and good morals" and making them "sober, industrious, and frugal." A virtuous people would keep in check the tendencies to aggrandize power and wealth and to wallow in idleness and corruption. They would be able to enjoy the rights, proclaimed by the Declaration of Independence, to liberty, equality, and the pursuit of happiness, which by implication included equality of economic opportunity and the right to enjoy the fruits of one's labor.[6]

But as Robert E. Shalhope has observed, each element in revolutionary American society "drew on republican theory selectively." Radicals emphasized egalitarian and communal values and were suspicious of commercialism; liberals stressed equality of economic opportunity; and anti-egalitarian conservatives embraced capitalism and equated social stability with their own political leadership. Viewed regionally, New Englanders emphasized moral communitarian values supported by a strong central government, Southerners feared government as a threat to their libertarianism, mid-Atlantic radicals favored egalitarianism, and mid-Atlantic conservatives wanted an effective government to foster their commercial enterprises.[7]

Americans living from the District of Maine to the state of Georgia, whether radicals or conservatives, merchants or wage earners, farmers or

---

6 On American assimilation of republican thought from abroad, see J. G. A. Pocock, *The Machiavellian Moment: Florentine Political Thought and the Atlantic Republican Tradition* (Princeton, N.J., 1975); Caroline Robbins, *The Eighteenth-Century Commonwealthman: Studies in the Transmission, Development and Circumstance of English Liberal Thought from the Restoration of Charles II until the War with the Thirteen Colonies* (Cambridge, Mass., 1959); Bernard Bailyn, *The Ideological Origins of the American Revolution* (Cambridge, Mass., 1967); Gordon S. Wood, *The Creation of the American Republic* (Chapel Hill, N.C., 1969). The quotations in this paragraph and the preceding one are from Wood, *Creation*, 42, 92, 119–20.

7 Shalhope, "Republicanism and Early American Historiography," 341–2.

planters, tried to legitimize their objectives by appealing to republican ideology. In the turbulent years during and after the Revolution, democratic egalitarianism and liberal individualism and acquisitiveness were embraced by ordinary Americans and incorporated into their republican ideology. America's incredible natural resources — soil, timber, minerals, and waterways — sustained opportunities unknown elsewhere. These opportunities fostered the widely held notion that the ordinary fellow, despite disparities in wealth, was as good as the rich man — the egalitarianism that made the American republic unique.

Nineteenth-century Americans of diverse backgrounds were self-consciously egalitarian republicans — a different breed — in a monarchical world. When in 1838 Gustavus Vasa Fox, a sixteen-year-old midshipman, exclaimed in Italy, "There are Palaces here that a Republican can have no conception of," he identified himself with a republicanism whose salient characteristic was egalitarianism. Sixteen years later Abraham Lincoln, then a lawyer from Illinois, declared "no man is good enough to govern another man, *without that other's consent*. I say this is the leading principle — the sheet anchor of American republicanism." In 1873 Richard T. Greener, the first black graduate of Harvard College, told the *New York Times*, "I am always in favor of mixed schools, believing that under a republican form of government no distinction of color or sex should be made." In 1886 former president Rutherford B. Hayes, a strong advocate of social justice, thought republican institutions and the uneven distribution of wealth were incompatible.[8]

Even as colonists, Americans had believed that they were distinctive. With independence they believed that republicanism, by diffusing political power among a virtuous and vigorous, free and equal people, would produce an exceptional society. Most Americans hoped to prove that equality would bring an orderly society and a flourishing culture, that happiness could be pursued in shops, factories, and farms, that the individual's hard work for private gain would benefit the commonweal as much as self-sacrificing public virtue, and that an effective central government would not threaten liberty. Avoiding a stifling autocracy and a dissipating anarchy, Americans made a religion of republicanism and worked, with a millennial vision, to create a viable government; a dynamic economy; an educated, cultivated people; and a virtuous, reformed society.

8 Fox to Isaac O. Barnes, U.S.S. *Cyane*, Messina, Nov. 22, 1838, Fox papers, New York Historical Society; David Herbert Donald, *Lincoln* (New York, 1995), 176; Greener to the *New York Times*, Aug. 26, 1873, *New York Times*, Aug. 30, 1873; Ari Hoogenboom, *Rutherford B. Hayes: Warrior and President* (Lawrence, Kans., 1995), 493.

They wished to make a republic fully deserving of Johann Wolfgang von Goethe's 1827 observation: "Amerika, du hast es besser / als unser Kontinent, das alte."[9]

III

Balancing their republican ideology with their practical needs, Americans created an exceptional form of government that Jefferson called "the world's best hope." Even prior to adopting the Federal Constitution, they solved the problem of empire and limited the spread of slavery. The Confederation Congress approved the Territorial Ordinance of 1784 (written by Jefferson), which, although not implemented, formed the basis of its Northwest Ordinance of 1787. That law organized the new nation's northwestern lands into territories (not "colonies"), forbade slavery in them, and provided for their admission into the Union "on an equal footing with the original states." Although settlers initially objected to congressional control and denounced the 1787 ordinance as a new form of colonial government, their successors – Salmon P. Chase, for one – revered it as a charter on par with the Declaration of Independence and celebrated its anniversary on July 13.[10]

The establishment in 1789 of a strong federal government in place of a weak confederation demonstrated that republicanism could be flexible and viable. Americans at their 1787 Constitutional Convention had created a republican "empire for liberty" by insisting that all states have a republican form of government. Mitigating traditional republican fears, the Constitution balanced the requirements of an effective national government with the interests of existing state governments.

Enabling federalism and nationalism to coexist, the powers were divided with a brilliant mix of precision and imprecision, providing maneuverability for future generations of politicians. The innovative

9 Bailyn, *Ideological Origins of the American Revolution*, 59; Jack P. Greene, in his *The Intellectual Construction of America: Exceptionalism and Identity from 1492 to 1800* (Chapel Hill, N.C., 1993), 200, found that "a notion of distinctiveness was a significant component in intellectual constructs of America from the beginning." The meaning of Goethe's verse is: "America, you have it better than our old continent."

10 Harold M. Hyman, *American Singularity: The 1787 Northwest Ordinance, the 1862 Homestead and Morrill Acts, and the 1944 G.I. Bill* (Athens, Ga., 1986), 18–34. Hermann Wellenreuther, "'First Principles of Freedom' und die Vereinigten Staaten als Kolonialmacht 1787–1803: Die Northwest Ordinance von 1787 und ihre Verwirklichung im Northwest Territory," in Erich Angermann, ed., *Revolution und Bewahrung: Untersuchungen zum Spannungsgefüge von revolutionärem Selbstverständnis und politischer Praxis in den Vereinigten Staaten von Amerika* (Munich, 1979), 133–85; John Niven, *Salmon P. Chase: A Biography* (New York, 1995), 100; Hoogenboom, *Rutherford B. Hayes*, 442.

concept of dual citizenship – that Americans were simultaneously citizens of the United States and of the state in which they resided – furthered coexistence by enabling the central government to deal directly with citizens, without going through the intermediary of a state. The Constitution made the new government remote by providing for the indirect election of the president and members of the Senate for relatively long terms but simultaneously made it immediate by apportioning the biennially and directly elected members of the House of Representatives according to population.

Ardent republicans, using country party ideas, attacked the Constitution for increasing the power of the central government, while equally ardent republicans supported it, fearing the absence of power as much as its excess. In that "great national debate" Isaac Kramnick discerns that "the languages of republicanism, of Lockean liberalism, of work-ethic Protestantism, and of state-centered theories of power and sovereignty" were used in "profusion and confusion." The ideas represented were neither victorious nor vanquished, and he observes that "American political discourse to this day tends to be articulated in one or another of these distinguishable idioms, however untidy that may seem to professors of history or political philosophy."[11]

To eliminate, or at least to contain, factionalism was the hope of the authors of the Constitution. They neither wanted nor anticipated political parties, which they associated with partisan strife, patronage, and corruption. But biennial elections, widespread voting, and the First Amendment rights of free speech, press, and assembly made parties inevitable. Within a few years James Madison (the father of the Constitution) began, with Jefferson, to organize an opposition; and the first American party system emerged in the 1790s.

Pitting Democratic Republicans against Federalists, the new system marked a sharp break from original republican hostility to parties; and, with political rivals competing for support, it took a big step toward democracy. The American party system, however, with congressional caucuses shaping issues and picking presidential candidates, was similar to the British system, which was dominated by parliamentary leaders. The first American party system was issue-oriented, centralized, and disciplined. Campaigning was informal, voters often deferred to the local gentry, and *viva voce* voting had not disappeared.

---

11 Isaac Kramnick, "The 'Great National Discussion': The Discourse of Politics in 1787," *William and Mary Quarterly*, 3d ser., 45 (1988): 3–32.

During the early nineteenth century, while the United States converted its territories west of the Appalachian Mountains into full partners in the Republic, virtually all its states east and west, north and south were democratized. Because states, not the national government, determined who voted, how presidential electors were chosen, and how seats in Congress and state legislatures were apportioned, the rise of democracy was a state phenomenon. It led to the second American party system, which flourished in the Jacksonian era and was a practical response to meet the requirements of an exceptional democratic republic. To determine the will of the sovereign people in filling myriad local, state, and national offices, mass-based political parties were invented. They organized elections, nominated candidates, and mobilized voters.

In sharp contrast to the previous system, the second party system was decentralized and undisciplined. It developed in the states; relied on local, county, state, and national conventions to nominate candidates; and emphasized winning elections, rather than issues. With frequent elections, numerous offices to fill, and masses of voters to inspire, party organizations were complex and campaigns were spectacular. Although torchlight parades and monster rallies – celebrations of a secular republican religion – appealed to entertainment-starved Americans in the same way that the "pomp, ceremony, and pageantry of the great established churches" appealed to Europeans, there was nothing in the world like an American political party.[12]

The workers required to staff the elaborate party structures were found among civil servants or among those who wished to become civil servants. The emergence of mass-based parties led to the introduction of another unique American phenomenon – the spoils system. European monarchs and their ministers had always dispensed patronage among their favorites, but in America, political patrons appointed party workers to the civil service. While serving the public in local post offices and customhouses, these appointees also staffed their patrons' organizations, contributed money to them (called a political assessment), and worked for their re-election. Whereas the hope of gaining or fear of losing an office provided political machines with ardent campaigners, rotations of government workers in and out of office hurt the public service. It also made reformers out of those who would not or could not break into politics while such "low flung" practices prevailed.

---

12 Richard P. McCormick, *The Second American Party System: Party Formation in the Jacksonian Era* (Chapel Hill, N.C., 1966), 19–31, 329–56.

Civil-service reformers (whose fear of patronage reflected country party ideas) attacked corruption in the public service and advocated the merit system of open-competitive examinations. This system was modeled on the practice of British and European governments. Striking at the source of the spoilsmen's power, the merit system would have encountered strenuous opposition under any circumstances, but its monarchical pedigree made ardent republicans apoplectic. They believed that rotation in office prevented a corrupt aristocracy of lifelong officeholders from bequeathing their offices to their heirs. Representative John A. Logan of Illinois denounced the merit system as unconstitutional, undemocratic, antirepublican, aristocratic, and monarchical. Reformers countered that competitive examinations, open to all, would secure able and virtuous public servants, promote simplicity and frugality in government, and be more in harmony with republican ideology than the spoils system.[13]

Even some patrician, but thoroughly republican, Americans echoed Logan. William M. Evarts, whose grandfather had signed both the Declaration of Independence and the Constitution, could not find a satisfactory answer to his question, "In a Republic what political motive is an adequate substitute for patronage?" Neither could his dinner guest, Representative James A. Garfield, who exclaimed: "This is the central difficulty that underlies the Civil Service."[14]

When it passed the Pendleton Civil Service Reform Act in 1883, Congress tried to make certain that an intellectual aristocracy would not monopolize appointments. In democratic America, merit would be determined by practical examinations (for example, border-patrol candidates had to demonstrate their ability to ride and shoot), rather than by tests of general knowledge. Furthermore, appointments to the Washington bureaucracy would be geographically apportioned to prevent any monopoly by well-educated northeastern candidates.

Despite efforts to shape the merit system for an egalitarian republic, its effect on politics realized some of the fears of Logan, Evarts, and Garfield. As the civil service became depoliticized, political campaigns became less spectacular, corporate contributions replaced political assessments, personal contact between party workers and voters fell off, and voter turnout

---

13 Ari Hoogenboom, *Outlawing the Spoils: A History of the Civil Service Reform Movement, 1865–1883* (Urbana, Ill., 1961), 30–1, 57.
14 Harry James Brown and Frederick D. Williams, *The Diary of James A. Garfield*, 4 vols. (East Lansing, Mich., 1967–81), 3:470 (Apr. 5, 1877).

dropped dramatically. By the twentieth century the civil service had become professionalized and American politics had lost some of its distinction.[15]

IV

Republican ideology permeated not only government and politics but all of society and culture. If the people were to govern, education had to eliminate illiteracy and ignorance. "From the beginning," Alice Felt Tyler observes, "American leaders were interested in the spread of education and the reform of its techniques as a necessity for the success of republican institutions." The Confederation Congress in 1785 adopted the Basic Land Ordinance, which required that in each town of thirty-six lots one lot be set aside to support public schools; and the Northwest Ordinance of 1787 called on the new states to support public education. To prevent tyranny, safeguard freedom, and assure wise and honest government, Jefferson in 1786 sponsored in the Virginia legislature a bill to create the first statewide school system, but it failed to pass. Despite the conviction of leaders like Jefferson and John Adams that universal public education was essential, widespread opposition by parsimonious, conservative, and childless taxpayers postponed the creation of new school systems until the 1830s, 1840s, and later.[16]

Unlike colonial-period schools, which were expected to promote religion and save souls, nineteenth-century schools were expected to preserve the republic and redeem the world: "If we do not prepare children to become good citizens [Horace Mann warned] – if we do not develop their capacities, . . . enrich their minds with knowledge, imbue their hearts with the love of truth and duty, and a reverence for all things sacred and holy, then our republic must go down to destruction, . . . and mankind must sweep through another vast cycle of sin and suffering, before the dawn of a better era can arise upon the world." In the 1880s Senator Henry W. Blair of New Hampshire told his colleagues that if they appropriated federal funds to "educate the rising generation mentally, morally, physically . . . this nation and this world would reach the millennium within one hundred years."[17]

15 Hoogenboom, *Outlawing the Spoils*, 238, 244–5.
16 Alice Felt Tyler, *Freedom's Ferment: Phases of American Social History from the Colonial Period to the Outbreak of the Civil War* (New York, 1962), 232–3; Dumas Malone, *Jefferson the Virginian* (Boston, 1948), 281–4.
17 On January 13, 1836, the *Ohio State Journal* exclaimed, "*these children all about your streets . . . are*

The entwined mission of the republic and its schools was a common theme. While teaching basic practical skills, elementary schools utilized readers – like William Holmes McGuffey's *Eclectic Readers* – that stressed the patriotism, civic virtue, and devotion to freedom and equality of the founding fathers as well as the moral – and material – benefits of obedience, kindness, temperance, generosity, promptness, and work. Francis Grund, a German immigrant, marveled at the "great mass of useful knowledge" that pervaded all classes of Americans, making them unique among other peoples: "Who [he asked] upon entering an American school-room and witnessing the continual exercise in reading and speaking, or listening to the subject of their discourses, and watching the behavior of the pupils toward each other and their teachers, could, for a moment, doubt his being amongst a congregation of young republicans?"[18]

Reflecting both its religious diversity and its new-found concern for secular education, the American republic established an astounding number of colleges in the period between the American Revolution and the Civil War. The handful of colleges that existed in 1776 swelled to 563 by 1870. The revolution encouraged intellectual democracy; and enthusiasts argued that higher education, as well as primary schools, should be within the reach of all citizens to prepare them for life in a democratic society, as well as for the professions. Although Washington, Alexander Hamilton, and Madison were unable to realize their dream of establishing a national university (open to talented young men regardless of their families' incomes), state universities (like that of Michigan, making "it possible for every student to study what he pleases and to any extent he pleases") were opened and were "consistent with the spirit of a free country."[19]

College curricula remained primarily traditional but gradually moved away from the classics toward a more "scientific" curriculum. Increasing choice and the growing vogue for more practical subjects culminated in the passage of the 1862 Morrill Land Grant Act (for the establishment of

your future sovereigns" (original emphasis). Tyler, *Freedom's Ferment*, 233, 239; Rush Welter, *Popular Education and Democratic Thought in America* (New York, 1962), 151. Citation courtesy of Harry Stein.

18 Henry Steele Commager, *The American Mind: An Interpretation of American Thought and Character Since the 1880s* (New Haven, Conn., 1950), 37–40; Tyler, *Freedom's Ferment*, 234.

19 The quotations are from Tyler, *Freedom's Ferment*, 258–9. See also Merle Curti, *The Growth of American Thought*, 3d ed. (New York, 1964), 128–31, 216–18, 352–3; Hyman, *American Singularity*, 36; Linda Kerber, *Women of the Republic: Intellect and Ideology in Revolutionary America* (Chapel Hill, N.C., 1980); Martin Trow, "American Higher Education:'Exceptional' or just Different?" in Shafer, ed., *Is America Different?* 138–86.

agricultural and mechanical colleges) and the adoption of the elective system by Harvard University after the Civil War. With the Morrill Act the American republic supported higher education generously, but in contrast to Europe (where universities were also funded by governments) it supported the training of scientific farmers and technicians for industry. In addition, generous admission standards (eschewing meritocracy) made utilitarian training widely available in America. Although higher education in the United States was predominantly for males, its women were not left in ignorance. Republican mothers had to be educated, it was believed, in order to train their children to be responsible, patriotic citizens. Emma Willard's Troy Female Seminary opened in 1821, and Mary Lyon's seminary (the beginnings of Mount Holyoke College) opened in 1837 in South Hadley, Massachusetts. American higher education differed from higher education in Europe and has remained exceptional to the present day.

Republican America was committed to spreading knowledge as widely as possible. Informal education flourished with the proliferation of newspapers and magazines, the establishment of public libraries, and the participation by scholars in the lyceum lecture circuit. Rejecting the Old World notion "that the mass of the people need no other culture than is necessary to fit them for their various trades," William Ellery Channing, a leading Unitarian minister, in his 1838 address on "Self Culture" called for the education of adults, through books and lectures, to fulfill their intellectual potential and to help them participate effectively in a free republic. The cult of self-improvement took Jacksonian America by storm. The gap in knowledge between ordinary folk, who were bent on improving themselves, and those with the wealth and leisure to pursue learning was still large; but it was narrower than the gap in any other country.[20]

V

Republican Americans were deeply conscious of their real or imagined inferiority to European artists and intellectuals. But they were loathe to admit that the subjects of despots were advancing science and technology, and creating masterpieces of music, art, and literature. Americans were convinced that a free republic would nurture genius as did ancient Greece

---

20 Curti, *Growth of American Thought*, 346–50, 353–7; see the entry on Benjamin Silliman in Malone Dumas, ed., *The Dictionary of American Biography*, 22 vols. in 11 books (New York, 1946), 17:160–3.

and Rome, and no longer make Americans the intellectual colonists of Europe. Philip Freneau exclaimed: "Can we never be thought to have learning or grace / Unless it be brought from that horrible place / Where tyranny reigns with her impudent face?"

A generation later, in 1830, Channing criticized American writers for imitating English models and challenged them to find inspiration at home. He had faith that if the United States were true to itself and if its writers expressed its mind in literature, it would lead in the reformation of the world. Seven years later Ralph Waldo Emerson declared America's intellectual independence, exclaiming: "Let us have done with Europe and all dead cultures, let us explore the possibilities of our own new world." Of course, American writers continued to aspire to produce poetry and prose of intrinsic artistic value, universal in inspiration and appeal. Indeed, Emerson himself, more an advocate of national self-realization than of extreme nationalism, admitted his indebtedness to Thomas Carlyle, Samuel Taylor Coleridge, Goethe, and William Wordsworth.[21]

Although American writers neither reformed the world nor ignored the lessons of European literature, they found ample subjects at home. The novels of James Fenimore Cooper, Nathaniel Hawthorne, Washington Irving, and Herman Melville were thoroughly American but owed much in formula, technique, and inspiration to European writers. The same can be said about the quintessentially American poet William Cullen Bryant, who trumpeted the wonders of American nature.

Influenced by Emerson more than by Europeans, Walt Whitman originated a new form of "free verse" to express the glory of the American democratic republic. Paying little heed to traditional rhyme or meter, Whitman sang of democracy and became, in Mark Van Doren's opinion, the "most original" and perhaps the "most passionate and best" American poet.[22]

Channing's and Emerson's idea that Americans must find their creative inspirations at home rather than abroad is borne out by music. American attempts prior to the Civil War to compose complex music, like opera, were not successful; but American slave songs, folk songs, hymns, and gospel songs have inspired composers like Aaron Copeland, Antonin Dvorak, and Roy Harris. In the twentieth century critically acclaimed

---

21 Curti, *Growth of American Thought*, 142; see the entries on William Ellery Channing and Ralph Waldo Emerson, in Malone, ed., *Dictionary of American Biography*, 4:4–7 and 6:132–41, respectively; Ralph Rusk, *The Life of Ralph Waldo Emerson* (New York, 1949), 197, 236–7, 239, 262–6.
22 See the entry on Walt Whitman, in Malone, ed., *Dictionary of American Biography*, 20:143–52.

American composers have flourished, but American popular music has had a global impact, with musicals, jazz, and rock 'n' roll remaining America's chief contributions to the world of music.[23]

Republican ideology was pointedly expressed in American architecture. With independence, Americans adapted for their modern republic the classic republican architecture of ancient Rome and Greece. More than anyone, Jefferson articulated the new nation's need for an appropriate style, and its most conspicuous expression is the Capitol in Washington. Neoclassicism dominated American architecture from the Revolution to the Civil War and in the twentieth century remained a potent force in the design of public buildings, railroad stations, and banks.[24]

Republican neoclassicism also was influential in the fine arts. In sculpture it came by way of Italy (ironically a collection of degenerate monarchies, where Americans studied) and is most strikingly expressed in Horatio Greenough's statue of Washington, half draped in a toga. Painters interpreted the land, the people, and the history of America. John Trumbull painted *The Declaration of Independence*, the Hudson River School reveled in the American landscape, and genre painters recorded everyday scenes in the lives of ordinary Americans. Thomas Cole, the founder of the Hudson River School, echoed Bryant's love of nature so pointedly in his landscapes that Asher B. Durand, in his picture *Kindred Spirits*, featured them standing together above a wild ravine. In 1829, when Cole embarked on a visit abroad, Bryant in his sonnet, "To Cole the Painter," urged him "to keep that earlier wilder image bright" by remaining true to the American spirit and resisting the temptations of Europe.

During his time abroad Cole yielded to the temptations of European landscapes and painters, but his conservative republican ideology remained unchanged. He was especially inspired by classical ruins in Italy and by J. M. W. Turner, whose *Dido Building Carthage* influenced his *The Course of Empire*. In these five allegorical paintings Cole illustrated what he considered a universal truth: that empires "progress from Barbarism to Civilization – to the state of Luxury – to the vicious state or state of Destruction." Although the empire he depicted was a classical amalgam, he painted it to remind Americans that their modern democratic republican "empire" was not exempt from the cycle of growth and decay. Pro-

---

23 Slave songs with their stress on freedom echoed the republican values in the Declaration of Independence. Unlike virtually every other field, America's biggest contributions in music were made by common people rather than by elitists.
24 There were, of course, other influences on American architecture, which cannot be linked to republicanism. Among these are the Gothic Revival and Egyptian influences.

foundly republican – but of an old school – Cole was averse to commerce and industry, fearing the wealth, luxury, and vice they would produce. Like other conservatives, he was afraid that Jacksonian America – with its spreading democracy, its mass-based political parties, and its rapidly expanding free-market economy – was launched in the cycle of growth and decay.[25]

VI

Unlike Cole, most Americans tailored their republican values to include democracy, the free-market economy, and industry. The adjustment involved some soul searching. Although Hamilton preferred to develop American manufactures, using the familiar strategy of the British Navigation Acts, Americans with their country party ideas initially were reluctant to embrace such favoritism and to enhance the power of the central government. After considerable debate they chartered the Bank of the United States to act as the fiscal agent of the government for twenty years and made it the dominant institution in the fledgling banking industry. In 1811 the Jeffersonian Republicans had allowed the bank's charter to expire; but in 1816 they chartered a second bank and passed a protective tariff in a spasm of nationalistic fervor and Hamiltonian heresy. They remained true, however, to the republican belief that the maldistribution of wealth was a threat to the commonwealth and adhered to that view throughout most of the nineteenth century.[26]

In the course of his administration President Andrew Jackson (aided by his popularity) hammered out a democratic, liberal, and republican policy. That policy gave him enormous support from the West and South as well as significant support from the East. Stressing equality of economic opportunity and maldistribution of wealth, Jackson attacked monopoly – especially a government-supported monopoly – in the form of the Bank of the United States, which made "the rich richer and the potent more powerful." He also reduced the scope of the federal government by opposing federal support of intrastate transportation projects, and, although he vigorously enforced tariff legislation, he favored reducing the protective

25 Alan Wallach, "Thomas Cole: Landscape and the Course of American Empire," in William H. Treuttner and Alan Wallach, *Thomas Cole: Landscape into History* (New Haven, Conn., 1994), 85–95; Malcolm Robinson, *The American Vision: Landscape Paintings of the United States* (New York, 1988), 18–20; Mary Ann Tighe and Elizabeth Ewing Lang, *Art America* (New York, 1977), 65–9.

26 On republicanism and the distribution of wealth, see James L. Huston, "The American Revolutionaries, the Political Economy of Aristocracy, and the American Concept of the Distribution of Wealth, 1765–1900," *American Historical Review* 98 (1993): 1079–105.

tariff. His antimonopoly, laissez-faire attitude promoted individualism and stimulated private enterprise and prosperity. Jackson's mix of Adam Smith's ideas and classic republican notions not only resonated with an expanding economy but also with the integration by Americans of liberalism into the ideology of republicanism.[27]

Most Americans perceived that prosperity for the Republic depended primarily on building roads, canals, and railroads to free inaccessible land for development. Almost invariably, roads and canals were built at public expense by local and state governments, whereas railroads were private enterprises built (especially where settlement was sparse) with local, state, and federal subsidies. These "mixed" enterprises demonstrate that Americans were more interested in results than in adhering to an ideology. Laissez faire and private enterprise were touted when vital needs were met, but when capital was in short supply a degree of public intervention was considered necessary to develop the vast interior of the American republic. By contrast, British railways were built with private capital, whereas in France and Germany (which also were plagued by capital shortages) government played a much larger role in planning and building railroads than in the United States.

As huge corporations developed, the American democratic republic was less tolerant of cartels than European monarchies. German industrialists developed vertical and horizontal combinations with the encouragement of Wilhelmian political leaders who adopted no antimonopoly legislation, but the combinations formed by American industrialists – like John D. Rockefeller's Standard Oil or Cornelius Vanderbilt's New York Central Railroad – provoked such widespread fear and hostility that politicians had to respond. Where railroads intersected railroads or other modes of transportation, they competed for freight and passengers, but along most of their right of way railroads were a monopoly. True to their antimonopoly convictions, Americans regarded railroads as common carriers not allowed to discriminate against freight or passengers. Defying their charters, railroads did discriminate, and by the late nineteenth century flourishing corporations in several industries had also become monopolies.

With laissez faire resulting in unevenly distributed wealth and inequality of economic opportunity, Americans (still influenced by egalitarian republicanism) turned to the federal government for redress. In 1886 former president Hayes, who favored confiscatory taxes, warned: "There

27 Shalhope, "Republicanism and Early American Historiography," 345–6.

can be no republican institutions with vast masses of property . . . in a few hands, and large masses of voters without property."[28] To regulate monopolistic railroads Congress passed the Interstate Commerce Act (1887), and to promote competition in industry it passed the Sherman Antitrust Act (1890). Their results were mixed, and in the twentieth century Americans continued their egalitarian quest in the Progressive and New Deal eras with regulatory and reform legislation.

VII

With the monumental exception of slavery, society in America was more egalitarian than in Europe. Trade unions were organized as early as 1794 (Philadelphia cordwainers); by the 1820s property qualifications for voting were disappearing; in 1842 the right to strike was recognized in Massachusetts; and by 1860 labor had achieved, for the most part, the ten-hour day. Working harder for better pay, American workers have been class-conscious enough to organize labor unions but, in contrast with European laborers, not class-conscious enough "to build either a broad-based labor movement or a powerful socialist party." Amy Bridges has pointed out that antebellum American wage earners were distinguished from their European counterparts in that they had the vote, that they were ethnically diverse thanks to immigration, that their organizations relied on republicanism for "key values" and rhetoric, and that they divided their loyalties between the two major parties.[29] When in the 1870s the ideas of Marxian socialists, Lassallean socialists, and anarchists arrived in the United States, they failed to attract significant numbers.

Socialists did have some influence in organized American labor, but on the whole American labor was conservative and inclined to mitigate rather than accentuate class conflict. Even the Knights of Labor (1869–1893) – an industrial union open to skilled and unskilled, black and white, male and female workers – established producers' cooperatives to restore conditions of the past, when smaller, less impersonal units of production prevailed. The growth of the Knights paralleled labor developments in England and France until, Kim Voss observes, the hostile political environment following the 1886 Haymarket bombing enabled employers to drive a wedge between its skilled and unskilled members. With the demise

28 Hoogenboom, *Rutherford B. Hayes*, 493.
29 Amy Bridges, "Becoming American: The Working Classes in the United States Before the Civil War," in Ira Katznelson and Aristide R. Zolberg, eds., *Working-Class Formation: Nineteenth-Century Patterns in Western Europe and the United States* (Princeton, N.J., 1986), 157–96.

of the Knights, Voss argues, the American labor movement became exceptional in its conservatism. The American Federation of Labor accepted the
reality of big business and quarreled with capitalists (rather than with capitalism) over laboring conditions and labor's share of profits. Strikes aimed
for higher wages, shorter hours, and better working conditions, not for a
new social order.[30]

The failure of American wage earners to organize politically and to
espouse a radical program was rooted in their perception that American
society was upwardly mobile. Children of unskilled laborers often became
skilled workers, while their children often achieved professional careers.
Even among the large number of workers whose jobs were similar to
those of their parents, the children's material possessions usually exceeded
those of their parents. With land relatively inexpensive, a much higher
percentage of American workers have owned their homes than
have laborers elsewhere. For most wage earners, especially those with
European backgrounds, these modest advances fulfilled the dream of
America as the land of opportunity.[31]

Many reformers, however, perceived that the promise of the early
republic was not matched by the reality of American life. Fifty years after
the Declaration of Independence, liberty, equality, and the opportunity to
pursue happiness had not produced the ideal society. Those principles,
however, did encourage experiments in religions and utopias and gave rise
to movements to combat the social evils that remained in the land – evils
that were an affront to American republican ideology.

The republican commitment to freedom of religion and the separation
of church and state (exceptional characteristics in the eighteenth and
nineteenth centuries) enabled an unparalleled multiplicity of sects and
cults to flourish in the United States. Although Jefferson felt that Uni-

30 Kim Voss, *The Making of American Exceptionalism: The Knights of Labor and Class Formation in the
Nineteenth Century* (Ithaca, N.Y., 1993), 2, 4, 231–49. See also Martin Shefter, "Trade Unions and
Political Machines: The Organization and Disintegration of the American Working Class in the
Late Nineteenth Century," in Katznelson and Zolberg, eds., *Working-Class Formation*, 197–276.
For a strong emphasis on class consciousness, see Sean Wilentz, "Against Exceptionalism: Class
Consciousness and the American Labor Movement, 1790–1920," *International Labor and Working
Class History* 26 (1984): 1–24.

31 On the mobility of urban America and the modest gains of the working class, see Stephan Thernstrom, *The Other Bostonians: Poverty and Progress in the American Metropolis, 1880–1970* (Cambridge,
Mass., 1973). Voss, *The Making of American Exceptionalism*, 231–49, argues that American labor is
conservative and exceptional, not because of upward mobility, but because in 1886 and 1887
organized capital defeated organized labor. Among the reasons Aristide R. Zolberg gives for the
more diffuse sense of class in America as compared to Europe is the ease with which American
workers can own their own homes. "How Many Exceptionalisms?" in Katznelson and Zolberg,
eds., *Working-Class Formation*, 441–6.

tarianism, with its emphasis on a loving God and the goodness of people, was most suitable for republican America, its unemotional, rational style limited its appeal. By contrast, frontier revivals in which emotionalism ran amok flourished, Methodist and Baptist denominations grew, and off-beat religions took root in the friendly American soil. Nowhere was it friendlier than in upstate New York, where millenarians, who believed in the imminent Second Coming of Christ (including such diverse groups as Mormons, Millerites, and Shakers), coexisted with spiritualists and perfectionists.

Several utopian experiments – inspired by religious and secular concerns over the crassness and harshness of a competitive, industrial society – were established prior to the Civil War. Humanitarian reformers not only crusaded for universal education but also for temperance, peace, humane asylums and prisons, women's rights, and the abolition of slavery. Daniel J. McInerney has demonstrated how republican ideology "formed the abolitionists' dominant mode of discourse, offering a means of announcing as well as arranging their ideas about slavery" to such an extent that they believed they were "the only true republicans of America."[32]

Abolitionism and slavery put the North and the South on a collision course. While the North condemned and tried to contain slavery and the South sanctified it and attempted to spread it to new territories, each of these sections believed itself to be the keeper of the republican faith. Both sections embraced the ideology of liberty and equal rights, but northerners and southerners interpreted those articles of faith differently. Although racism permeated American society, it was more virulent in the South, which had a huge black minority, than in the relatively homogenous North. This difference made it easier for northerners to view freedom and equality in human terms for all races than it was for white southerners. The southerners insisted that they would not be enslaved or ruled by federal laws, which prevented them from taking their human property into free western territories; and northern members of the Republican Party declared that they would not be enslaved or ruled by a southern "slave power," which was bent on carving out a huge chunk of the West for itself. Northern Democrats occupied a middle position

---

32 Tyler, *Freedom's Ferment*, surveys the cults, utopias, and reform movements between the American Revolution and the Civil War, but for New York, see Whitney R. Cross, *The Burned-over District: The Social and Intellectual History of Enthusiastic Religion in Western New York, 1800–1850* (New York, 1965). On republicanism and abolitionism, see Daniel J. McInerney, *The Fortunate Heirs of Freedom: Abolition & Republican Thought* (Lincoln, Neb., 1994), 3, 150.

(congruent with their republican ideology), emphasizing white supremacy and federal restraint with respect to slavery, coupled with an ardent commitment to the Union.

When the triumph of the Republican Party in 1860 confirmed that slavery would expand no more, the deep South seceded, established the Confederate States of America, and waged war for its survival. Rejecting Jefferson's belief that all men are created equal, the Confederacy was an eighteenth-century-style republic built on the racist cornerstone of white supremacy and black slavery. For whites it would protect life, liberty, and property; promote "perfect equality" by forbidding any protective tariffs; and eliminate corruption and restore republican purity by eschewing the partisanship of party politics.[33]

Abraham Lincoln had a different vision of republicanism and of the mission of the American Republic. It was the wave of the future, he insisted, a model for the world. Embracing Jeffersonian equality and Jacksonian democracy, he hailed the United States as "the last, best hope of earth" and declared: "In *giving* freedom to the *slave*, we *assure* freedom to the *free*." The Civil War tested whether a "nation, conceived in liberty and dedicated to the proposition that all men are created equal" could survive. The hopes of millions of African-American slaves, the aspirations of millions of other Americans (primarily in the North), and the longings of millions of people elsewhere for "an unfettered start and a fair chance in the race for life" required that "that government of the people, by the people, for the people, shall not perish from the earth." With that government's survival, Lincolnian republicanism triumphed over the Confederate model.[34]

VIII

Americans continue to struggle with contradictions between the real and the ideal in their pluralistic society and vigorously dispute how best to

---

33 Lloyd E. Ambrosius, "Introduction," and Joel H. Silbey, "Conclusion," in Lloyd E. Ambrosius, ed., *A Crisis of Republicanism: American Politics in the Civil War Era* (Lincoln, Neb., 1990), 1–10, 129–31; George C. Rable, *The Confederate Republic: A Revolution Against Politics* (Chapel Hill, N.C., 1994), 63; Alexander H. Stephens, "Cornerstone Address, March 21, 1861," in Frank Moore, ed., *The Rebellion Record*, 11 vols. (New York, 1861–9), 1:44–6. Jean H. Baker, *Affairs of Party: The Political Culture of Northern Democrats in the Mid-Nineteenth Century* (Ithaca, N.Y., 1983), 143–76, shows how the views of northern Democrats conformed to the ideology of republicanism, whereas Eric Foner, *Free Soil, Free Labor, Free Men: The Ideology of the Republican Party Before the Civil War* (New York, 1970), does the same for the Republican Party.

34 Roy P. Basler, ed., *The Collected Works of Abraham Lincoln*, 9 vols. (New Brunswick, N.J., 1953–5), 4:438, 5:537, 7:23.

achieve freedom, equality, and economic opportunity. For over two hundred years republican ideology has inspired disputants, has shaped American society, and has made the United States a unique nation. In the late twentieth century, for example, the republican ideology of equality inspired a civil rights movement for blacks, revived the women's rights movement, and gave birth to the gay rights movement. Although prejudice persists, the United States continues to lead the world in the quest for equal rights. The exceptional quality of America has in turn profoundly influenced the rest of the world.[35]

By the 1990s, however, *exceptionalism* had become a pejorative term to describe a belief in national superiority, which in foreign affairs led "either to self-righteous isolationism or equally self-righteous crusading." American foreign policy had been tinged in the past with an idealism that gave it a degree of exceptionalism, but by the late twentieth century it appeared unexceptional because strategic and economic, rather than moral, considerations drove policy. Transnational historians revile American exceptionalism to the point that many of them deny any American distinctiveness. But by ignoring distinctions among peoples and nations and denying the value of comparative history, internationalism can warp history as much as it has been warped by nationalism.[36]

All historians can agree that the peoples of the world are more alike than different and that the United States did not develop in a vacuum. Europe and other continents influenced every aspect of America's growth, and parallel developments may be found elsewhere. In the international relations as well as the broad economic and cultural trends of the United States a convincing argument can be made for its unexceptionalism. Since the late nineteenth century it has become less distinctive as it has interacted more and more with other nations and the world economy; as technology and communications have improved; and as democracy has advanced and other republics have been founded. Indeed, by the 1980s

---

35 Carl N. Degler, "In Pursuit of an American History," *American Historical Review* 92 (1987): 1–12.

36 The "self-righteous" quotation is from my colleague Edwin G. Burrows. See also Akira Iriye, "Exceptionalism Revisited," *Reviews in American History* 16 (1988): 291–7; Ian Tyrrell, "American Exceptionalism in an Age of International History," *American Historical Review* 96 (1991): 1031–55, 1068–72; Michael McGerr, "The Price of the 'New Transnational History,'" ibid., 1056–67; George M. Fredrickson, "From Exceptionalism to Variability: Cross-National Comparative History," *Journal of American History* 82 (1995): 587–604. Fredrickson argues that the nation-state is the most convenient unit for comparative history, that various peoples share basic similarities when dealing with phenomena like nationalism, race, and welfare, but that cultural and structural differences among nations result in peculiarities, variations, singularities that are exceptional in the sense that all peoples are exceptional. For an excellent example of comparative history in this vein, see Katznelson and Zolberg, eds., *Working-Class Formation*.

and 1990s the United States – having forgotten its founders' idealistic republican condemnation of the maldistribution of wealth – had the widest gap between the rich and the poor among industrial nations of the world.[37]

Nevertheless, the republican political institutions and egalitarian society of America – especially from its Revolution through its Civil War – were unique. Furthermore, the present-day United States – a pluralistic, democratic society composed of diverse ethnic, racial, and religious groups with the core values of equality and civic virtue – is different from other nations (but not necessarily better), and most American people continue to believe in American exceptionalism.[38]

37 *New York Times*, Apr. 17, 18, 1995, summarizes the studies of New York University economist Edward N. Wolff and others. In addition the Luxembourg Income Study of eighteen nations announced in 1995 that, except for Israel and Ireland, the poor children in the United States were poorer than children in other Western industrialized nations. *New York Times*, Aug. 14, 1995.

38 On the erosion of American economic exceptionalism in the late twentieth century, see Peter Temin, "Free Land and Federalism: American Economic Exceptionalism," and Richard Rose, "Is American Public Policy Exceptional?" both in Shafer, ed., *Is America Different?* 92–3, 189, 218–21. Andrew M. Greeley, "American Exceptionalism: The Religious Phenomenon," also in ibid., 94–115, argues that from the 1960s to the 1990s the religious beliefs and practices of Americans were unexceptional. The review essays by H. V. Nelles, "American Exceptionalism: A Double-Edged Sword"; J.Victor Koschmann, "The Nationalism of Cultural Uniqueness"; and Mary Nolan, "Against Exceptionalism," which criticized Seymour Martin Lipset's *American Exceptionalism: A Double-Edged Sword* (New York: 1996), all appeared in *American Historical Review* 102 (1997): 749–74, too late to influence this chapter. Lipset and his critics, however, focus on how contemporary America compares with Canada, Japan, and Germany, whereas this chapter concentrates on the impact of republicanism on American society in the nineteenth century and suggests that there was a diminution of republican-inspired American exceptionalism by the 1990s.

PART TWO

Transatlantic Ideologies and the Perception of the Other

3

The Role of Religion in Germany and America in the Nineteenth and Twentieth Centuries

HARTMUT LEHMANN

I

A comprehensive history of modern Christianity on both sides of the Atlantic has yet to be written. There are several difficulties that must be overcome before such a project can be undertaken. First, there is a remarkable unevenness of research. Although there are many studies on religion in America, and although American historians with few exceptions acknowledge the role of religion in nineteenth- and twentieth-century American history, within a largely secularized European historical profession a secularized conception of modern history has led to the result that the impact of religion in the periods after the Reformation has often been neglected, if not ignored.[1] Before a comparative study of religion in the Old World and the New World can be undertaken, what is needed, therefore, is a series of penetrating studies on religion in Europe that can be matched with corresponding American works.

What we know, moreover, is very contradictory. In particular, views on religion in America are quite controversial. On the one hand, there are strong voices that serve to demonstrate the strength of religion in America. Alexis de Tocqueville was among the first foreign observers to

---

1 I should note, though, that in some of the recent research on religion in Europe a new awareness of the importance of religious factors may be observed. This is true for those social historians who attempt to write *histoire totale* on a micro-level; for those intellectual historians who explore the background of ideologies such as socialism and nationalism in the context of a history of mentalities; for those historians of culture who discuss the various aspects of cultural continuity and discontinuity; and for those church historians who want to revise the traditional views of their discipline and include the views and experiences of those who had separated themselves from established churches. At the same time, however, one can still note how little religious matters are often being understood, and when they are being mentioned, it is often in a rather superficial way.

point out that "there is no country in the world where the Christian religion retains a greater influence over the soul of men than in America." In America, he stated in the 1830s, Christianity "reigns without obstacle" and "by universal consent"; in the United States "religious zeal," in his view, was "perpetually warmed" by "the fires of patriotism" as "despotism may govern without faith, but liberty cannot." While in France "the spirit of religion and the spirit of freedom" were "marching in opposite directions," "they were intimately united" in America and "reigned in common over the same country."[2] The strong materialism of Americans, Tocqueville concluded, produced an even stronger interest in things immaterial.[3]

A decade later an American observer confirmed Tocqueville's remarks. In his widely circulated book *Religion in the United States of America: Or, An Account of the Origin, Progress, Relation to the State, and Present Condition of the Evangelical Churches in the United States*, Robert Baird described the "religious character of the early colonists" who in his view had implanted evangelical Christianity on the North American continent. For Baird, therefore, the discovery of the New World by Columbus and the rediscovery of the true word of God through reformers like Luther and Calvin had not been coincidental events but interrelated parts of a divine plan. For Baird, moreover, "the dissolution of the union of Church and State" in America had resulted in a most miraculous, and equally effective, development of "the voluntary principle." Although Baird was aware that not all people living in the United States were true Christians, he hoped that with the help of "the voluntary principle" a complete christianization of the population on the North American continent was possible. For the Presbyterian minister Baird, active in many societies devoted to the work of domestic and foreign missions, Christianity was developing toward a bright future in his country.[4]

However, some recent studies modify, yet in principle support, the assessments made by Tocqueville and Baird. Whereas authors such as Sydney Ahlstrom, Roger Finke, or Rodney Stark are somewhat skeptical with regard to the strength of religion in early nineteenth-century America as portrayed by Tocqueville and Baird, they point out how rapidly religion grew in nineteenth-century America, thus confirming not only Tocqueville's observations but also Baird's optimistic predic-

---

2 Alexis de Tocqueville, *Democracy in America*, ed. Philipps Bradley, 2 vols. (New York, 1954), 1:314–15, 318–19; see also 310–26.

3 Tocqueville, *Democracy*, 2:143.

4 American ed., New York, 1844; the British ed., Glasgow, 1844, cited here: On "the voluntary principle," see book IV, 268–411.

tions.[5] For Ahlstrom the key to understanding this remarkable evolution is the development of religious pluralism; for Finke and Stark, the solution to this problem can be found in the competition of churches in America. The more churches offered their services, they argue, the more the services of churches were accepted. Within what they call the "rise of a free market religious economy," "upstart sects" like Baptists and Methodists with no professional clergy but with preachers who knew how to organize well-planned revival meetings overtook older established churches, such as the Episcopalians. At a later stage Catholics, by forming ethnic parishes, added their own share to the growth of Christianity in America.

The main target of Finke and Stark are those religious sociologists who can be seen as proponents of the secularization thesis. For Harvey Cox, for example, in his *Secular City*, published in 1965, the secularization and the urbanization of America were but two sides of the same coin. Cox's views are supported by Bryan R. Wilson and others who have developed sophisticated models of the process of secularization within the modern world, including the United States.[6] In contrast to the authors who believe in the growth of religion in America, the supporters of the secularization thesis believe in the decline of religion both in the New World and the Old. In his study *A House Divided: Protestantism, Schism, and Secularization* Steve Bruce, for example, argues that despite revivals, the decline of religion in America is inevitable. According to the central thesis of his work, "pluralism has a delegitimating and hence corrosive effect on religion."[7] Of course, Bruce cannot deny the strength of religion especially in the American South. But he explains this phenomenon as a result of retardation; in his view, Christianity is strong in the southern states exactly because religious pluralism as a precondition for secularization

---

5 Sydney Ahlstrom, *A Religious History of the American People* (New Haven, Conn., 1972), 121–509; Roger Finke and Rodney Stark, *The Churching of America, 1776–1990: Winners and Losers in Our Religious Economy* (New Brunswick, N.J., 1992), 54–108.

6 Harvey Cox, *The Secular City: Secularization and Urbanization in Theological Perspective* (New York, 1965); Bryan R. Wilson, *Religion in Secular Society* (London, 1966); Harvey Cox, "Secularization: The Inherited Model," in Philipp E. Hammond, ed., *The Sacred in a Secular Age: Toward Revision in the Scientific Study of Religion* (Los Angeles, 1985), 9–20; see also Steve Bruce, ed., *Religion and Modernization: Sociologists and Historians Debate the Secularization Thesis* (Oxford, 1992); Karel Dobbelaere, "Secularization: A Multi-Dimensional Concept," *Current Sociology* 29 (1981): 3–213; Karel Dobbelaere, "The Secularization of Society? Some Methodological Suggestions," in Jeffrey K. Hadden and Anson Shupe, eds., *Secularization and Fundamentalism Reconsidered* (New York, 1989), 27–44; Lucian Hölscher, "Secularization and Urbanization in the Nineteenth Century: An Interpretative Model," in Hugh McLeod, ed., *European Religion in the Age of Great Cities, 1830–1930* (London, 1995), 263–88.

7 *A House Divided* (London, 1990), 181.

does not as yet exist. According to Bruce it is the persistence of homogeneous subcultures that causes religion not to have declined more rapidly in the United States. Bruce does not doubt, however, that the most appropriate metaphor to describe the future of religion in America is that of a "spiral of decline."[8]

As mentioned previously, there is no research on religion in Europe equivalent to the works on America. As a rule, those religious sociologists who treat Europe discuss the Western world as a whole, and they do so in accordance with the secularization thesis: Industrialization and urbanization on both sides of the Atlantic are interpreted as having caused secularization; in many variations, of course, just as the social, economic, and cultural transformations were not uniform but evolved in many different forms.

This chapter attempts to make a contribution to the debate by advancing two arguments: First, I argue that we should be aware that there may have been contradictory developments on both sides of the Atlantic. Whereas industrialization and urbanization may have caused widespread secularization and dechristianization in Europe, the same factors, under different conditions, may have caused christianization, or after the epoch of enlightenment with a temporary decline of established religion, the rechristianization of America.

Second, I attempt to distinguish specific areas in which this thesis may be tested. Perhaps the most obvious weakness of the debate on secularization is the generalization and subsequent simplification of arguments. In my view, no further insight can be attained if one continues to argue on this general level. Rather, we should address and compare the effects of specific issues, such as the legal framework, the religious context, social and economic preconditions, the role of localism and centralism, or the impact of migration.

It is in these specific areas that a comparison will be made between the United States and Germany. No doubt Germany and the United States offer quite distinct test cases. But this is exactly the reason why they are suited for a comparison that serves not to brush aside but to highlight the differences in the development of religion within the Western world. Comparing religion in a transatlantic framework may help us to differentiate, and qualify, the impact of both secularization and dechristianization as well as of sacralization and rechristianization of certain sectors of culture, the economy, and politics in Europe and

8 Ibid., 209–25.

America. It is hoped that the examples chosen will inspire others to test similarities and differences in other areas, thus furthering our insight into the role of religion in both the Old World and the New World. Gerald Stourzh, for example, has suggested that the question of the establishment of churches, the disestablishment of churches, and nonestablishment be investigated as an additional aspect in helping us to understand variations in the role of religion in the Americas and Europe. One could also compare the development of Jewish religion and culture in the Old World and the New, including the roles of anti-Semitism, philo-Semitism, and the religious pluralism that includes and binds together, as much as it separates, the three major Western religions – Catholicism, Protestantism, and Judaism.

II

The Legal Framework

In 1791, shortly after the ratification of the Constitution of the United States, ten amendments went into effect, the first of which stipulated that Congress shall make no laws regarding the establishment of religion or prohibiting the free exercise thereof.[9] This brief half-sentence, which combined what is called the nonestablishment clause with the so-called free-exercise clause has been much discussed ever since and has certainly had long-lasting consequences. These consequences reach far beyond the numerous opinions on the separation of church and state and on the freedom of religion as formulated by the Supreme Court. Rather, it seems, the first amendment provided a unique legal framework in which religion could blossom and grow. Research on the history of Christianity in the United States from Robert Baird and Philip Schaff to Sydney Ahlstrom and Martin E. Marty unanimously emphasizes the success of the double provision of the nonestablishment and free-expression clauses: In the United States questions of religion should not be decided by the political power of the state; at the same time, the state is legally obliged to guarantee that religious issues can be expressed and discussed freely; this includes the right to form new religious organizations. As a result, from the early nineteenth century onward, the number of active religious groups in the United States grew at an astonishing rate. True, there were

---

9 It is not intended to document the arguments of the five paragraphs that follow with all the necessary bibliographical references.

painful divisions and bitter controversies; there was intolerance, even persecution. But even more important, there also was an almost inexhaustible supply of religious enthusiasm that fueled the religious life of those denominations that had already existed in colonial times and that erupted in unexpected ways and led to the formation of new religious groups, both large and small.

It is hardly necessary to explain how different church-state relations were organized in Germany. Throughout the nineteenth century the famous union of throne and altar, as it was called, remained untouched and unshaken, whereas attempts to introduce something similar to the free-expression clause, for example, at the Paulskirche assembly in 1848–9, failed. Even after the revolution of 1918, and in a modified manner even after 1949, the churches and the state in Germany remained so close that they seemed to be two sides of the same coin. In Germany the status of the average pastor was and still is very similar to that of a civil servant (*Beamter*), the church resembles a state agency (*Behörde*), and church theology appears very much like an aspect of official political doctrine (*Herrschaftsdoktrin*). Of course, over time some changes did occur. Although schools in Germany offer religious instruction up to this day, the Basic Law of 1949 secured complete religious freedom for all West Germans. Into the 1990s most Germans were still nominal members of one of the two major churches (Protestant and Catholic); every year, however, a considerable number decide to leave the church, thus avoiding a church tax (tithe) that is collected by the state. Only a minority of Germans, some Protestant, some Catholic, can be considered active, devout Christians.

The Religious Context

During colonial times some Americans were moved by profound religious revivals. The founding fathers of the new republic were not among them. They believed in the power of pure reason, and their heroes lived in ancient Greece and Rome. Since the early nineteenth century, however, the sheer number, but also the size and extent, of religious revivals grew immensely. Frequently, a religious awakening in one region was followed by another in a different region. Some revivals gained national significance, and no denomination remained unaffected. Rather, even in established denominations revivals were used to activate congregations that had become passive and to lift the spirits of those who had begun to doubt. In all of this, the free exercise of religion was most effectively supported by the principle of voluntarism, and both were furthered by the role of revivals. Furthermore, there existed no aspect of Christian doctrine that gave more meaning to voluntarism and revivals than the belief in the return of Christ and in the approaching millennium. In the area of domestic politics, revivalism and voluntarism were sometimes combined with xenophobia and nativism; in matters of foreign policy, what was considered the manifest destiny of the American republic possessed a sharp anti-Catholic and often an anti-Latin American edge. In describing the religious context of our theme, it is therefore not enough to emphasize the importance of religious tolerance and the role of religious pluralism in the United States. Rather, we must stress that pluralism grew out of religious revivals, which on the one hand had certain common theological features as they were founded on millennial beliefs and expectations but which on the other hand were shaped by local religious leaders who produced many vibrant local communities.

In early nineteenth-century Germany, Protestant circles also were impassioned by a movement similar to the American Great Awakening. Like the Great Awakening, the *Erweckungsbewegung* issued from many centers and was carried forward by many inspired local preachers. In contrast to the situation in the United States, however, millennial expectations never became a dominating force within the *Erweckungsbewegung*; furthermore, church leaders in Germany managed to control and regulate the movement. The same was true in the case of the *Gemeinschaftsbewegung*, a revival among Protestants in late nineteenth-century Germany. In both cases, even the most active elements remained within the traditional churches; voluntarism did not produce new and independent organizations. From the vantage point of church authorities, we can speak of a policy of successful domestication in both cases. Among those striving for Christian perfection we can observe a certain degree of resignation that developed in both countries over time.

In the complex processes described here as christianization and dechristianization, differences in legal frameworks in the United States and in Germany were effectively reinforced by differences in religious context. In the United States factors such as voluntarism, revivalism, and pluralism created a cultural climate that favored the growth of religion and in which religious activism could easily be related to matters of justice and social reform. In Germany, factors such as the close cooperation between state and church, the suppression of nonconformism, and the domestication of active Christian groups produced a cultural climate in which religion was tainted with conservatism and with opposition to "progress."

In a semisecularized version, though, the idea of revivalism gained much influence in nineteenth- and twentieth-century Germany. Since the early nineteenth century, many pious Germans believed that national unification, moral renewal, social reform, and Christian revival should and would occur simultaneously, in one huge act of regeneration of the German people. In 1870–1, after the German victory over France, many Germans considered themselves the people of a new covenant and witnesses of just such an experience of national regeneration. This notion of chosenness was revived in 1914, and it even played a role in 1933, when many Germans were convinced that the rise of National Socialism would not only result in the abolition of the Treaty of Versailles but also in a Christian renewal of the whole German nation. Within a few months of the Nazi seizure of power these hopes were, not surprisingly, shattered. Many of those who were disillusioned filled the ranks of the Confessing Church.

In this scenario of a religious-national German revival, religion served political ends from the beginning.[10] By 1914 power politics had corrupted Christian values, and by 1933 anti-Semitism and racism had as well. Notions of American chosenness, by contrast, have always been characterized by a much more harmonious combination of national and Christian elements, even though African Americans were reluctant to see themselves as partners in what European Americans considered the great Christian experiment in the New World.[11] Interestingly enough, African Americans developed their own version of chosenness.[12]

Social and Economic Preconditions

In nineteenth-century Germany the rapidly growing urban centers soon became strongholds of liberalism and socialism. Whereas the educated and well-to-do middle classes, the *Besitz- und Bildungsbürgertum*, embraced lib-

---

10 See Hartmut Lehmann, " 'God Our Old Ally': The Chosen People Theme in Late Nineteenth- and Early Twentieth-Century German Nationalism," in William R. Hutchison and Hartmut Lehmann, eds., *Many Are Chosen: Divine Election and Western Nationalism* (Minneapolis, 1994), 95–107; with response from Conrad Cherry, in ibid., 109–13.

11 James H. Moorhead, "The American Israel: Protestant Tribalism and Universal Mission," in Hutchison and Lehmann, eds., *Many Are Chosen*, 145–66; see also response from Knud Krakau, in ibid., 167–72. By the early twentieth century, American "chosenness" was being defined in a nonconfessional, that is, rather broad way so that this notion could be shared by American Catholics, while Mormonism developed its own and very particular version of American chosenness.

12 Albert J. Raboteau, "Exodus, Ethiopia, and Racial Messianism: Texts and Contexts of African American Chosenness," in Hutchison and Lehmann, eds., *Many Are Chosen*, 175–95; see also response from Silke Lehmann, in ibid., 197–201.

eralism, some artisans and many members of the well-trained industrial workforce (though hardly anyone who could be called a proletarian) discovered in socialism a convincing explanation of the past, the present, and the future. Those among the workers who based their political activities on tenets of Christian ethics remained rather marginal. As a result, churches lost much of their influence in the new cities; the programs of domestic mission as formulated by Johann Hinrich Wichern and others as a reaction to the revolution of 1848–9 produced the best results in small cities but not in the large urban centers where the supposed dangers of unbelief and immorality loomed largest. Over time, therefore, organized Christian religion in Germany became more provincial, if not rural, and less urban, while at the same time the barriers between Christian theology and the world of modern science, technology, and culture continued to grow. When Adolf Stoecker attempted to reverse this trend with aggressive antisocialist and antiliberal preaching in Berlin in the 1880s, he failed. Whereas Stoecker's city-mission was supported by the Hohenzollern court and some archconservative members of the lower middle class, organized Berlin workers were not even tempted to join. The efforts of German Protestantism most comparable to the "Social Gospel," as for example in the Evangelisch-Sozialer Kongress (Evangelical Social Congress), were timid in perspective and marginal in effect.

Not that nineteenth- and twentieth-century American Christianity was first and foremost an urban phenomenon: Many of the revivals were rural events, many took place on the frontier. However, Jon Butler has shown that for various reasons Christian groups did retain some influence in modern American cities.[13] In addition, in urban America local congregations with an ethnic background successfully attracted new members, whereas socialism never blossomed.

Localism Versus Centralism

More than a generation ago, in his famous study *The Social Sources of Denominationalism*, H. Richard Niebuhr argued that much of the success of Christian churches within American society can be explained by the fact that churches genuinely adapted to different social, regional, ethnic, cultural, and political groupings.[14] Although the clientele of each indi-

13 Jon Butler, "Protestant Success in the New American City, 1870–1920: The Anxious Secrets of Rev. Walter Laidlaw, Ph.D.," in Harry S. Stout and Darryl G. Hart, eds., *New Directions in American Religious History* (New York, 1997).
14 H. Richard Niebuhr, *The Social Sources of Denominationalism* (New York, 1929).

vidual congregation was quite homogeneous, the system as a whole was vastly diverse. In this manner, each American could find a congregation in which he or she was comfortable.

Whereas in America localism in religious matters triumphed, in Germany churches adhered to the principle of centralism. Church policies were being defined at the center, and very often by the state, not at the local level; churchgoers were considered consumers of whatever the central agencies postulated. In late nineteenth-century Germany, for example, nonconforming pastors such as Johann Christoph Blumhardt, who joined the Social Democrats, or Christoph Schrempf, who challenged Lutheran orthodoxy, were censured and disciplined. Even after 1945, in both Catholic and Protestant churches, the centers continue to govern over local parishes, and, with few exceptions, local initiatives are successful only insofar as they are approved of from above. Accordingly, in nineteenth- and twentieth-century Germany there are only few cases in which local congregations have engaged in specific issues of local politics.[15] What Christians should think in political matters generally is neither formulated nor tested at the local level.

By contrast, in America the role of Christian congregations in local politics is a much more active one. Not that members of these congregations would shy away from federal politics and "big issues." It is on the local level, however, that Christian conviction is put to the test, and it is in their home congregations that politicians at the state or federal levels are challenged and where they have to be credible and authentic, both as political experts and as fellow Christians. In many of the ethnically segregated congregations in the second half of the nineteenth century, localism and revivalism even put their imprint on the face of American Catholicism.

The Role of Migration

Experts in migration history agree that most of those millions of Europeans who left their homelands and went to America from the seventeenth century onward desperately sought and hoped for a better life. What "pushed" them was above all economic misery and political oppression, and what "pulled" them was economic opportunity and political

---

15 To be sure, there are exceptions to this statement as there are many examples of "strong" pastors and priests who acted on the local level, both in Protestant as well as in Catholic parishes.

freedom. If we also analyze the motives of German emigrants, religious oppression experienced at home and the hope for more religious freedom beyond the Atlantic may rank but third. At the same time, from the late seventeenth to the late nineteenth century, many religious nonconformists who were persecuted in Germany very consciously searched for a place of refuge in North America. In their view, and in the view of other European emigrants looking for religious freedom, William Penn's colony possessed qualities that were unrivaled. If we look for the very center of the christianization of North America, Pennsylvania may be the place.

During the process of migration there were additional elements that served to reinforce the importance of religion. The long and at times dangerous transatlantic journey caused anxiety, as did the living conditions in the strange new country. In short, those who were "uprooted" were in need of security, and there was no agency, no organization, no part of society that offered more contact and better advice than the many Christian congregations. Christian congregations seemed to understand the needs of immigrants and their wish for more personal security. It is there that anxieties were transformed into hope and that immigrants were made into Americans. In America, it seems, religion provided the kind of social cohesion that the state did not and supported local leadership and responsibility within a diverse society. Even if we lack proof that the average German emigrant was more religious than the average German who stayed at home, there is much to suggest that several years after migration the average immigrant felt more strongly about religion than the cousins he or she had left behind. In the complex processes of assimilation and acculturation, religion is perhaps the most underrated factor, and this appears to be true in rural as well as in urban areas, and even in suburban districts. The role of religion in the context of migration within Europe has yet to be studied.

III

In sum, the areas tested reveal remarkable differences in the development, and the impact, of religion in the United States and in Germany. It is not only new prophets and new religions that distinguish the role of religion in the United States from its role in Germany, but rather a combination of structural factors rooted in various areas of public and private life. As a result, in the course of the nineteenth and twentieth centuries, Chris-

tianity in the United States grew in an impressive manner; moral vigor
was complemented by pluralism, and voluntarism was strengthened by
revivalism. In nineteenth- and twentieth-century Germany, by contrast,
state and church authorities were suspicious of new religious ideas
and the religious activities of ordinary people, whereas bureaucratic super-
vision was matched by anti-church resentments of those who felt
oppressed.

Many new questions arise if we attempt to widen the scope of our
investigation and take a look at Canada, at Latin America, and at other
areas of Europe. Is there a convincing manner in which a typology of
countries, or of societies, can be developed? Are there similar phases of
development, similar causes and consequences of christianization in the
Americas and of dechristianization in Europe? Do obvious differences not
overshadow all those aspects that Christian religion in some countries
seems to have in common with Christian religion in others? To what
degree has nationalism, by insisting on the importance of national differences, blinded our view? No doubt, if we look beyond the two countries that I have attempted to compare, the sheer number of unresolved
problems multiplies. A thorough analysis of these problems is a challenge
for all those who study religion not in a national context, or within
America or Europe alone, but within a transatlantic – or perhaps even a
global – perspective.[16]

IV

The history of Christianity was only a minor theme in Erich Angermann's historical world. In matters of religion he kept, like his early hero
Robert von Mohl, what could be called a loyal distance. The history of
American Christianity was not among the topics he addressed at length
in his history of the United States in the twentieth century. Why, then,
include in a book devoted to the memory of Erich Angermann a chapter
on the role of religion in Europe and America in the nineteenth and
twentieth centuries? In 1970, at the meeting of German historians at
Cologne, Angermann chaired a session in which an attempt was made to
compare Puritanism, Jansenism, and Pietism. On that occasion Eberhard
Weis was one of the speakers, and so was I. But it was Angermann, as I

---

16 Hartmut Lehmann, "A Plea for the Comparative Study of Religion in a Transatlantic Perspective," in Hartmut Lehmann, *Alte und Neue Welt in wechselseitiger Sicht: Studien zu den transatlantis-
chen Beziehungen* (Göttingen, 1995), 261–6.

recall, who best understood the methodological implications of doing comparative history.[17] In one of his last public lectures, the fourth Annual Lecture of the German Historical Institute in Washington, D.C., he again discussed the risks and rewards of a comparative approach to history.[18] This is not the place to recapitulate his words of warning or to repeat his encouraging remarks, but there can be no doubt that his expertise and his insight into all questions concerning comparative history are a substantial and compelling part of his rich legacy as a historian to whom we are deeply indebted.

17 Erich Angermann, "Religion – Politik – Gesellschaft im 17. und 18. Jahrhundert: Ein Versuch in vergleichender Sozialgeschichte: Eine Einführung," *Historische Zeitschrift* 214 (1972): 26–9.
18 Erich Angermann, *Challenges of Ambiguity: Doing Comparative History*, German Historical Institute, Washington, D.C., Annual Lecture series, no. 4 (New York, 1991).

4

The Impact of Darwinism on Religion and Science in America and Europe During the Nineteenth Century

CARL N. DEGLER

Undoubtedly the best-known instance of the conflicted relationship between Darwinism and religion is the encounter in 1860 between Thomas Huxley, Charles Darwin's vaunted "bulldog," and Samuel Wilberforce, the Anglican bishop of Oxford. As we all remember, it was "Soapy Sam's" supercilious inquiry into which of Huxley's ancestors derived from apes that drew from Huxley the famous reprise that apish ancestry was far superior to the ignorance the bishop's remarks had exposed. The encounter, in short, was perceived not only as a triumph of Darwinism over ignorance in the guise of religion but also the first of many such biting encounters over the remainder of the century.

Enduring as that vignette appears, it is a serious mistake to epitomize that incident as a true measure of the century's debate between Darwinism and religion, just as it incorrectly implies the scientific triumph of Darwinism. For one thing, some observers, like local news reporters, did not notice the incident at all, whereas others mentioned Joseph Hooker's response to Wilberforce as more important than Huxley's. As a recent historian of the encounter makes evident, Wilberforce was no ignoramus or general critic of science. Indeed, in an extended review of *The Origin of Species* at that time, Wilberforce told his readers that he was basing his judgment "solely on scientific grounds." For it was his "fixed conviction" that this was the only way by which "the truth or falsehood of such arguments should be tried."[1]

Rather than dismissing Wilberforce, we need instead to recognize that

---

1 J. R. Lucas, "Wilberforce and Huxley: A Legendary Encounter," *Historical Journal* 22 (1979): 313, 317–18.

his remarks foreshadowed important elements in the religious response to Darwinian evolution. Wilberforce's comparison to Isaac Newton, for example, recalls the important role that religion, particularly in the form of Reformation Protestantism, had played in the making of the scientific revolution of the seventeenth and eighteenth centuries. As one historian has noted, Protestants viewed nature "as created, contingent and orderly," and thus fostering empirical research. It was not accidental, as Robert Merton remarked years ago, that English Protestants were active in forming scientific societies before 1800.[2] Many clergymen saw science as displaying the "wonderful perfection of the infinite Creator."[3] Others considered a scientific view of the world to be a measure of God's activities and, because the world was God's, science helped human beings to understand it. As one historian of religion has pointed out, there was a "long-standing Puritan assurance that God had revealed himself both in the book of Scripture and in the book of Nature."[4] William Paley's well-known argument that in nature one could perceive God's design constituted a striking example of how religion viewed science: as support, and as insight into God's relation to men and women. Given such a relatively lengthy history of the value of science to religion, it was to be expected, as Wilberforce pointed out in his review, that the way for religious thinkers to question the validity of Darwinism was to examine critically its scientific support.[5]

It was also evident to many theologians when *The Origin of Species* appeared that many of the biblical descriptions of the earth and its history had been abandoned – often in the face of new scientific knowledge. Given the Copernican conception of the universe, Joshua's halting of the sun's motion no longer was tenable. And no longer was it acceptable to determine the age of the earth simply by counting the generations of human beings since Adam and Eve as listed in the Bible. Science, in short, was not a threat to religion but a bulwark. And one of the most recent

2 John Durant, "Darwinism and Divinity: A Century of Debate," in John Durant, ed., *Darwinism and Divinity: Essays on Evolution and Religious Belief* (Oxford, 1985), 11–12.
3 Quoted in Jon H. Roberts, *Darwinism and the Divine in American Protestant Intellectuals and Organic Evolution, 1859–1900* (Madison, Wis., 1988), 9–10.
4 David N. Livingstone, *Darwin's Forgotten Defenders: The Encounter Between Evangelical Theology and Evolutionary Thought* (Grand Rapids, Mich., 1987), 169.
5 On the close and positive relation between Protestantism and science at the time of Darwin I have drawn from Gertrude Himmelfarb, *Darwin and the Darwinian Revolution* (Garden City, N.Y., 1962), 449; Alfred Kelly, *The Descent of Darwin: Popularization of Darwinism in Germany, 1860–1914* (Chapel Hill, N.C., 1981), 97–8; Livingston, *Darwin's Forgotten Defenders*, 27; James R. Moore, *The Post-Darwinian Controversies: A Study of the Protestant Struggle to Come to Terms with Darwin in Great Britain and America* (Cambridge, 1979), 13; Roberts, *Darwinism and the Divine*, 230.

proofs of that support was Newton's demonstration that the cosmic force that held the planets in their orbits was identical to that which measured the fall of a simple, earthly apple. Yet, implicit in the perception of Newton's achievement was a conception of science that caused Darwinism to be a challenge to, rather than a sustainer of, religion. As many historians of religion have shown, in both America and Europe the most common reaction of theologians and clergymen to the religious impact of Darwinism was that evolution and Darwin's explanation for it – natural selection – constituted poor or defective science. It was not unusual for that objection to Darwinism to be sustained right up to the century's end. The earliest form of that objection stemmed from Darwin's divergence from what, on the basis of Newton's laws, had come to be called scientific proof. Good science was said to contain laws, such as Newton's and Galileo's laws of motion, laws that could be proved experimentally and without exception. These were fundamental laws in physics and chemistry, but Darwin did not announce laws of that nature in biology.

Instead, Darwin was establishing historical principles or hypotheses that could be made acceptable only by a convincing arrangement of evidence. Being merely a naturalist, not a physicist, Darwin could not prove the validity of those principles as Newton had in establishing his laws of motion or as Robert Boyle had in his law of gases. Darwin, however, accumulated an enormous collection of examples to suggest and eventually to persuade observers that all plant and animal forms were connected and that the principle or force that had shaped life forms on the contemporary Earth was natural selection. Natural selection was not a law in the Newtonian sense; rather, it was a principle or conclusion, drawn from history, that became acceptable or convincing only because of the many pieces of evidence that supported it. But as one English philosopher of the time who opposed natural selection remarked, "when we bring these facts [on behalf of natural selection] to the test, we find no strength in them, except that which is gained by a virtual assumption of the hypothesis. No good theory was ever built out of such assumptions – by a series of hypothetical reasonings from the unknown to the known."[6]

To scientists and theologians alike, Darwinism seemed speculative, not scientific. Soon after the appearance of *Origin*, the president of the Linnean Society (before which Darwin and Alfred Wallace had presented

---

6 Quoted in Frederick Burkhardt, "England and Scotland: The Learned Societies," in Thomas F. Glick, ed., *The Comparative Receptions of Darwinism* (Austin, Tex., 1972), 73–4n.

their historic papers on natural selection in 1858) saw no reason for his
group of naturalists in 1860 to "refer to those speculations on the origins
of species, which have excited so much controversy." Such topics, the president continued, were beyond the province of the society: "I certainly
should be sorry to see our time taken up by theoretical arguments not
accompanied by the disclosure of new facts or observations."[7]

As I have been suggesting, simply because religion, especially Protestantism, had long perceived science to be sustaining and providing insight
into God's world, it is almost illusory to seek to separate religion from
science in examining evolution in the Age of Darwin. Some of the most
prominent scientific opponents of evolution and natural selection ultimately came down against Darwinism on religious grounds. The best-
known example was the most celebrated scientist in America, Louis
Agassiz, professor of zoology at Harvard College, who died denying evolution. For him all animal forms were immutable and had always been so.
The order of plants and animals, he contended, "proclaim aloud the One
God, whom man may know, adore, and love."[8] For all his scientific rigor,
in the end it was religion or, to be more precise, metaphysics that determined Agassiz's objection to evolution.

By the same token, even those scientists who supported Darwinian
evolution, such as Agassiz's Harvard colleague, the botanist Asa Gray, often
found that religious values or ideas determined their conception of evolution and natural selection. Gray had been a close supporter of Darwin
during the working out of *Origin* and was the first American naturalist
to defend Darwinian evolution and natural selection. Yet, in the end, like
several other early Darwinians – including Wallace himself – Gray refused
to believe that human beings were a part of the continuum of life forms.
He always saw humanity as a product of God's intervention, not simply
a product of natural selection and evolution.

A third example of the intertwining of science and religion in confronting Darwinism was the work of the English naturalist and fervent
convert to Catholicism, St. George Jackson Mivart, who arguably became
Darwinism's most persistent and vehement opponent throughout the
remainder of the century. Although he started out studying law, Mivart
quickly moved to natural history and by 1870 held the chair of comparative anatomy at St. Mary's Hospital in London. Like Wallace and Gray,
Mivart could accept evolution, that is, the transmutation of animals and

---

7 Quoted in ibid., 47–8.
8 Quoted in Roberts, *Darwinism and the Divine*, 35.

plants through time, but he could not countenance the inclusion of human beings in that pattern. The break between animals and human beings, he insisted, was the work of the Creator. A measure of the religious importance of Mivart and of his critique of Darwinism was the award to him in 1876 by Pope Pius IX of an honorary doctorate of philosophy.

The intermingling of science and religion over Darwinism also is evident among a number of theologians who felt it necessary to learn science in order to confront Darwin's challenge to religion. The German theologian Otto Zöckler, who has been described as the earliest theologian in Europe or America to confront Darwinism, became a student of geology, physiology, and biology so that he could better analyze the myriad facts in *Origin*. His German contemporary, the theologian Rudolf Schmid, also was an ardent student of biology, as his critique of Darwinism makes clear from the types of details he pursued. In fact, one reason Schmid accepted a limited form of natural selection was that only with that principle was he able to explain the existence of mimicry in butterflies. Obviously, Schmid insisted, God would not have played such tricks on his creatures, so mimicry – a form of deception – was better explained by natural selection.[9]

As already implied, Darwinism stood for at least two major ideas that troubled or challenged religious thinkers. One was evolution itself, that is, the transmutation of one species of plant or animal into another through generations; the other was, of course, natural selection, Darwin's theory of how that transmutation had taken place. As is also well known, Darwin himself was extremely apprehensive about the religious implications of *The Origin of Species*. Only on the last page of the book did he mention the place of human beings in writing about evolution and natural selection, and only in a most general way. It was not until 1871 in his *Descent of Man* that Darwin at last admitted that he intended to include humanity in the story of evolution, although the co-founder of natural selection, Wallace, had made that leap five years earlier. Despite Darwin's timidity and dissimulation of his true belief, critics and supporters alike recognized almost immediately that *Origin* carried the clear implication that man was included in Darwin's evolutionary system. As the Anglican bishop of Dublin wrote to one of Darwin's teachers at Cambridge in early 1860, "I felt alarm at the apparent high favor and wide

9 Frederick Gregory, *Nature Lost? Natural Science and the German Theological Tradition of the Nineteenth Century* (Cambridge, Mass., 1992), 177.

celebrity of Darwin's theory . . . because it was likely to establish *our* descent from Molluscs or Insects."

The bishop then went on to say that he doubted that oats could become rye and that he disbelieved that either could become apple trees, "but what I have undertaken to disprove is the conversion of the unaided savage into the civilized man."[10]

Aside from the question of man's inclusion in the pattern of animal life, to which I will return, the earliest problem in Darwinism for many clergymen was evolution itself. For, like many scientists, they noted that there was no way to observe evolution given the great span of time it took, nor could they discover any "missing links" between ancient and modern species as Darwin argued. Throughout the era, both among clergy and scientists, such missing links constituted a persistent problem for Darwinians as it was for Darwin himself. He admitted and feared that the paucity of the fossil record weakened his theory. Evolution, in short, seemed more speculative than scientific or theological. Yet, there were theologians who found it possible to accept Darwinism, at least up to a point.

One of the earliest supporters of Darwinian evolution was the American Protestant theologian James McCosh, who later became president of Princeton University. He easily accepted the idea of transmutation of animals and plants, finding in the details and intricacies of such forms "a design and a unity of design" that took a "predetermined form," which in turn is "made to conspire, to secure a progress through indeterminate ages." This was, of course, the traditional argument from design in accounting for the being and power of God. Like many Protestant leaders, McCosh saw science – as he understood Darwinism – as a support for religion. He thought religious people, instead of doubting evolution, "might be more profitably employed in showing them the religious aspects of the doctrine of development; and some would be grateful to any who would help them to keep their new faith in science."[11] Like some other theologians and scientists, McCosh could accept natural selection as but one of several ways by which God had shaped life forms. The continuing Protestant interest in science as a part of God's world is demonstrated by the creation in 1865, six years after the publication of *Origin*, of a Princeton professorship to harmonize science and religion.

For some Christian supporters, Darwin's conception of scientific evo-

10 Quoted in Himmelfarb, *Darwin and the Darwinian Revolution*, 270.
11 Quoted in Livingston, *Darwin's Forgotten Defenders*, 108–9.

lution held the promise of enhancing the Christian message. As English theologian Aubrey Moore wrote in 1889, "The scientific evidence in favour of evolution as a theory is infinitely more Christian than the theory of 'special creation.' For it implies the imminence of God in nature, and the omnipresence of His Creative powers."

Opponents of evolution who seem to believe that evolution involves a continual intervention by God in nature, Moore pointed out, "seem to have failed to notice that *a theory of occasional intervention implies as its correlative a theory of ordinary absence*," whereas natural selection reflects God's continuous or uninterrupted intervention. In 1891 Moore complained that the Deists may have pushed out God almost entirely just when "Darwinism appeared, and, under the disguise of a foe, did the work of a friend."[12]

Although theologians like Moore and McCosh rather easily accepted evolution and even natural selection, that conception of Darwinism could not bridge the spiritual gap that separated human beings from all other living forms. Take away the "revealed truths" of religion, McCosh insisted, "and civilized man could see in himself only a developed animal; his highest and purest culture would be accepted as but the gradual outcome of savage bestiality; and the image of God be lost in the image of an ape."[13]

For many theologians, the sticking point in Darwinism was the essentially materialistic or naturalistic conception of evolution that Darwinian natural selection required. For theologians and many preachers, natural selection was anathema. For such opponents, when they talked about nature and its history, they separated mind, that is, God, from matter. Even Herbert Spencer, an important pre-Darwinian evolutionist, accepted purpose or what theologians referred to as teleology. For Spencer was in principle, if not in belief, a Lamarckian who saw in evolution a direction and a goal, namely, the perfection of mankind. As Spencer's biographer remarked, "Spencer invented the Unknowable because it implanted into the theory of evolution the necessary element of purpose."[14]

Spencer and many theologians, particularly those in Britain and America, were content to accept competition, for that process was perceived as being directed by some kind of supreme being or force, such as Spencer's "unknowable." Darwin, however, saw no purpose in evolu-

12 Quoted in Arthur Peacock, "Biological Evolution and Christian Theology Yesterday and Today," in Durant, ed., *Darwinism and Divinity*, 110–11.
13 Livingston, *Darwin's Forgotten Defenders*, 112.
14 David Wiltshire, *The Social and Political Thought of Herbert Spencer* (Oxford, 1978), 208.

tion. Organisms were simply the product of competition for survival in a changing environment. Of American theologians, none was more scathingly hostile to Darwinism than Princeton's Charles Hodge, the great leader of Old School Calvinists. He was modern enough to have long accepted the new time scale of humanity that recent geology had brought forth. Biblical fundamentalism was not at the center of his rejection of Darwinism. Hodge's book *What Is Darwinism?* (1874) achieved European recognition especially from his concluding response: "We have thus arrived at the answer to our question, What is Darwinism? It is atheism."[15] Like so many theological opponents of Darwinism, Hodge objected primarily to Darwin's rejection of purpose. Hodge listed three distinctive elements in Darwinism: evolution, natural selection, and "by far the most important and only distinctive element of [Darwin's] theory, that this natural selection is without design, being conducted by unintelligent physical causes."[16] Or as he wrote in another place: "It is that Darwin rejects all teleology, or the doctrine of final causes. He denies design in any of the organisms in the vegetal or animal world."[17]

In England, W. B. Carpenter held a similar negative conception of Darwinism: "That the 'accidents' of natural selection should have produced that orderly succession, is to my mind inconceivable. I cannot but believe that its evolution was part of the original creative Design."[18]

It was just that materialist conception of Darwinism that the German theologian Rudolf Otto rejected in 1904 in his widely read book, *Naturalistische und religiöse Weltansicht* (first published in English as *Naturalism and Religion* in 1907). After reviewing all the theories of evolution to the end of the century, Otto concluded that natural selection lacked both vital force and teleology.[19]

Perhaps the most striking instance of religious objection to Darwinism by the end of the century was that of Abraham Kuyper, the founder of the Free University of Amsterdam, even though he strongly encouraged the advancement of science. Although he came to oppose Darwinism because he believed it contradicted the Bible, he nonetheless accepted it as a hypothesis, one that he thought would eventually be found to be incorrect. Yet, it is worth noting that he was no traditionalist, for he delib-

---

15 Charles Hodge, *What Is Darwinism?* (New York, 1874), 176–7.
16 Ibid., 50–1.
17 Quoted in Livingston, *The Forgotten Defenders*, 104.
18 Quoted in M. J. S. Hodge, "England," in Glick, ed., *Comparative Reception of Darwinism*, 21–2.
19 Rudolf Otto, *Naturalistische und Religiöse Weltansicht* (Tübingen, 1904), English ed.: *Naturalism and Religion* (London, 1907), 154–9.

erately sought change in the form of seeking a broader suffrage in the Netherlands, urging government support for working people, and firmly opposing the individualism of the growing middle class in his country. By the end of the century, in a lecture at Princeton University in 1898, Kuyper expressed fear that one of the results of the impact of Darwinism was the development of an alternative religion to Christianity, a change that he dreaded would presage another fall of the Roman Empire. He urged his Princeton audience to cease "to whore with Evolutionism."[20]

Although the theological objections and defenses of Darwinism varied in both America and Europe, the significant varieties were relatively few and generally overlapped across oceans and national borders. But there were also differences between religious groups, especially among Protestants. In Britain, for example, Unitarians and so-called Broad Church of England members tended to be more favorable to Darwin's ideas than evangelicals like Methodists and members of the Low Church. In America, the Unitarians were the most receptive to Darwinism, whereas Congregationalists and Presbyterians were the most articulate and influential. Congregationalists Washington Gladden, Lyman Abbott, and Henry Ward Beecher accommodated early to Darwinian ideas. Beecher, for example, already sought scientific support in the early 1870s. As in England, Methodists, Baptists, and Lutherans in America were either hostile to Darwinism or uninvolved.

Catholicism's reaction to Darwinism was generally single-mindedly hostile. As one Catholic theologian remarked, a Catholic cannot accept "the hypotheses of the purely animal origin of man" and so "body and soul are still formed by the immediate intervention of God."[21] Although the general Catholic reaction to Darwinism was negative, differences of reaction did appear among Catholics in the nations of Europe. Given the English origins of Darwinism, it is worth remarking that an English Catholic, St. George Mivart, pronounced what was perhaps the most vehement and persistent Catholic rejection of Darwinism. His scathing review of *The Origin of Species* wounded Darwin to the quick: "You never read such strong letters as Mivart wrote to me about respect toward me," Darwin wrote to his friend Joseph Hooker, "begging that I should call on him; yet in the *Quarterly Review* he shows the greatest scorn and ani-

---

20 Ilse N. Bulhof, "The Netherlands," in Glick, ed., *Comparative Reception of Darwinism*, 303–4.
21 Quoted in Harry W. Paul, "Religion and Darwinism: Varieties of Catholic Reactions," in Glick, ed., *Comparative Reception of Darwinism*, 435.

mosity towards me, and with uncommon cleverness says all that is most disagreeable. He makes me the most arrogant, obvious beast that ever lived. I cannot understand him; I suppose that accursed religious bigotry is at the root of it."[22]

Mivart's major attack on Darwinism came in his 1871 book, the title of which made a clever play on the title of Darwin's own book: *On the Genesis of Species*. The religious significance of Mivart's denunciation of Darwinism was quickly acknowledged by Cardinal Newman soon after the publication of *Genesis*. Newman conceded that he was neither for nor against "any great dislike or dread" of Darwinism, but he thought it good to "find that the first real exposition of the logical insufficiency of Mr Darwin's theory comes from a Catholic." Newman thought that "many good people are much troubled" by Darwin's ideas "and at all events, without disrespect to him, it is well to show that Catholics may be better reasoners than philosophers."[23]

In the Catholic countries of Europe reactions to Darwinism varied considerably, principally because of variations in the reactions of scientists of those countries to *Origin*. French Catholics, for instance, found no great need to respond to a biological theory that among French scientists had gained neither prominence nor controversy. On the one hand, the great French paleontologist, Georges Cuvier, had repudiated the whole idea of changing forms, or evolution, as early as the 1830s, a repudiation that shaped the general outlook of most French zoologists and botanists. On the other hand, if anyone wanted to follow the evolutionary views of Jean Baptiste Lamarck, despite Cuvier's denunciation, Lamarck's conception of evolution carried none of the challenges to religion that Darwin's materialistic and nonteleological conception of evolution immediately aroused. Indeed, as will be seen, Lamarckianism proved to be a major support for those Christians who wanted to accept evolution but could not live with Darwinism's rejection of mind, teleology, and progress.

Quite the opposite picture from France occurred in Italy, where there was neither a Cuvier nor a Lamarck to obliterate the so-called Darwinian Revolution. Things had been so negative in France, for example, that Darwin had had difficulty finding a translator for *Origin*. One historian reported that out of some thirty-four articles published in eleven French periodicals on evolution between 1859 and 1862, only ten directly mentioned Darwin, some mentioned him in passing, and thirteen made no

22 Quoted in Jacob W. Gruber, *A Conscience in Conflict: The Life of St. George Jackson Mivart* (New York, 1960), 87.
23 Quoted from ibid., 73.

mention of him at all! However, a fine Italian translation of *Origin* appeared as early as 1864. Darwin himself was elected to various Italian academies and in 1875 was presented with the prestigious Bressa Prize.

Without a strong scientific challenge to Darwinism in Italy, Catholic reaction against evolution and natural selection lacked a serious presence. It certainly lacked the potency of the Catholic challenge in Spain, where even a major novelist took it on herself in 1877 to write a critique of *Origin* in an influential Catholic journal. Emilia Pardo Bazan's goal was to calm the fears of Spanish Catholics that Darwinian evolution was apparently triumphing even though she believed fundamentally that God was the true creator and not natural selection. The religious challenge to Darwinism in Germany was most prominent among Protestants, but Ludwig Windthorst, the leader of the Catholic party in Germany, had no doubt that his party's Catholicism repudiated any idea that human beings were in any way related to apes or lesser animals.

The impact of Darwinism on religion in general in Germany, however, differed strikingly from that of much of Europe and of America; the difference derives in part from the works of David Friedrich Strauss, a theologian, and Ernst Haeckel, a scientist. Both espoused to the fullest extent the ideas of Darwin and natural selection; both included human beings in their conception of evolution – a crucial barrier for most Christian scientists. Among scientists and theologians, neither Darwinians nor anti-Darwinians anywhere were comparable in influence and authority to Strauss and Haeckel.[24] Their intellectual relation was not personal or direct, so far as I know, although they were close contemporaries. Indeed, so convinced was Haeckel of the future and importance of Darwinism in the lives of modern people, for example, that he attempted to create an alternative religion to Christianity in the shape of what he called "monism."[25]

Strauss, born in 1808, just one year before Darwin, not only became a Darwinian, but his revolutionary *Life of Jesus* (1835) prepared German and then European and American theologians for the challenges that *Origin* would soon bring. As a political liberal and theologian, Strauss, with his *Life of Jesus*, opened the subject that came to be known as "the higher

---

24 "No other country of Europe, or for that matter even in the United States, did the ideas of Darwinism develop as seriously as a total explanation of the world as in Germany" (Daniel Gasman, *The Scientific Origins of National Socialism: Social Darwinism in Ernst Haeckel and the German Monist League* [London, 1971], xiii). "Darwinism became a kind of popular philosophy in Germany more than in any other country, even England" (Kelly, *Descent of Darwin*, 5).

25 For a full, if rather highly critical, examination of Haeckel's monism, see Gasman, *Scientific Origins*.

criticism" of the Bible. The gist of that work was that the Bible should be interpreted as a work of history, its sources examined and criticized as one would study any other man-made document. One of the reasons Darwinism won quick and wide-ranging acceptance in Germany, compared with that of any other country, was the innovative, even shattering religious work of Strauss. The great German theologian Adolf Harnack remarked in 1907 that historical criticism did more to weaken religion than the attacks from science.[26]

The political and theological reaction to Strauss's *Life of Jesus* was devastating to him personally, for he lost all his university and church connections and for a while fled to Switzerland. Despite the opposition and obloquy, Strauss quickly integrated the ideas of Darwin into his theology. In the highly popular second edition of his *Life of Jesus* (1864) he challenged his opponents: "Do they know that their only choice is between the miracle – the divine hand of the Creator – and Darwin?"[27] He explained to a friend that "I have become interested in Darwin since his theory has become known. I read his major work when it came out and have since seized everything referring to this theme." And by 1869, when writing to an acquaintance, he contended that Darwin first freed human beings from the idea of creation.[28]

In his later work, *The Old Faith and the New* (1874), Strauss made his acceptance of Darwinism in theology complete. Connecting those ideas with a great name in German thought, he asserted that "no greater joy could have been experienced by Goethe than to have lived to see the development of the Darwinian theory." Unlike Lamarck, Darwin could explain "miraculous agency," Strauss explained, for Darwin "has demonstrated this force, this process of Nature; he has opened the door by which a happier coming race will cast out miracles, never to return. Everyone who knows what miracles imply will praise him, in consequence, as one of the greatest benefactors of the human race."[29]

Unlike Strauss, Haeckel was no precursor to Darwin, but Haeckel's prolific writings, public agitation, and immense popularity in support of Darwinism far exceeded the impact of Strauss's 1835 *Life of Jesus*. Born in 1834, Haeckel began as a physician only to shift quickly to zoology, where he settled for the remainder of his life into a professor-

---

26 Kelly, *Descent of Darwin*, 76.
27 Quoted in Gregory, *Nature Lost?* 101.   28 Quoted in ibid., 100.
29 David Friedrich Strauss, *The Old Faith and the New: A Confession*, 3d English ed., 2 vols. (London, 1874), 2:205–6.

ship at the small University of Jena. From that platform he released a flood of scientific and popular works, the latter almost exclusively based on his total commitment to the ideas of Darwin. It was a commitment he elaborated on, repeated endlessly, and ultimately developed into the quasi-religion of monism. Haeckel's book, *The Riddle of the Universe* (1900), was the single best-selling book of German nonfiction as late as 1914.

In a sense, the impact of Darwinism on religion in Germany was largely the result of Haeckel's own determined Darwinism. Again and again, it was Haeckel who appeared as the enemy of religion, whether by intention, as in his open opposition to Catholicism, or by his commitment to Darwinian ideas. Haeckel, for example, heartily supported Bismarck's *Kulturkampf* against the Catholic Church in the 1870s and always regretted Bismarck's ultimate surrender in 1880. Anti-Darwinians in both Spain and the Netherlands saw in Haeckel's books and agitation the true source of their fear of Darwinian ideas. It is true that Haeckel's conception of Darwinism deliberately challenged established religion because he rejected teleology, which he fully recognized was absent from Darwin's conception of evolution even though teleology stood at the heart of Christian theology. Haeckel's best-selling books, *The Natural History of Creation* (1868) and the aforementioned *Riddle of the Universe*, spread his ideas across Europe. Their content, though, stemmed originally from his scientific elaboration of Darwinism, *General Morphology of Organisms* (1866), which he ruefully remembered thirty years later as "a large and laborious work, which had had but a limited circulation."[30] And it was in that earliest book that Haeckel's philosophy was most stringently defined. "According to our view," he wrote in *General Morphology*, "chance collapses together with teleology into nothing. For 'chance' no more exists than does purpose in nature or a so-called 'free-will.'"[31] Or as he put his conception of a world without purpose and direction in the *Riddle of the Universe*, "As our mother earth is a mere speck in a sunbeam in the illimitable universe, so man himself is but a tiny grain of protoplasm in the perishable framework of organic nature."[32] Haeckel followed Darwin closely, denying the uniqueness of man and finding in animal life the

---

30 Ernst Haeckel, *The Riddle of the Universe at the Close of the Nineteenth Century* (New York, 1900), vii.
31 Quoted in Timothy Lenoir, *The Strategy of Life: Teleology and Mechanics in Nineteenth Century German Biology* (Boston, 1982), 271.
32 Haeckel, *Riddle of the Universe*, 14.

beginnings of human abilities and moral conceptions. For Haeckel, as for Darwin, man's physical and mental abilities were only quantitatively different from those of animals. Haeckel also understood, as too many scientists of that time did not, that biological evolution was an historical, not a mathematical science. This is why he was able to link the humanities with natural science.[33]

Yet it would be a misreading of the influence of Haeckel's popular writings and activities to see Darwinism as triumphant. For example, Haeckel's effort to introduce Darwinism into the German school system in the 1870s was hardly a success. In his effort to spread both science and Darwinism in Germany, Haeckel urged the school system to introduce Darwinian ideas into the curriculum. Rudolf Virchow, though a liberal politically and, like Haeckel, a vehement opponent of the Catholic Church as well as a reputable scientist, denounced Haeckel's effort largely on the ground that Darwin's ideas were not scientifically acceptable. One consequence of the confrontation between Haeckel and Virchow was that biology was not introduced into the Prussian school curriculum for many years, whereas the doctrines of the church were expected to be given "special weight" in the schools.[34]

Meanwhile, prominent German clerics and theologians castigated Haeckel and Darwin. For example, Adolf Stoecker, the Prussian court chaplain, denounced a professor at Berlin University for daring to praise Darwin, asserting that to put animals on a level with human beings was impious. Important theologians such as Rudolf Schmid and Otto Zöckler proclaimed that they could not be both Christian and Darwinist. "I cannot, to appease myself, be a Christian with my heart and an atheist with my intellect," Schmid wrote.[35]

By the end of the century the long debate over religion and Darwinism had come to a close. It was not so much that they had become reconciled but that each had gone in its own direction. Insofar as religion was concerned, the scientific weaknesses of Darwin's ideas were still being pursued and dissected, and the ideas were found to be flawed. In *Naturalism and Religion*, Rudolf Otto eagerly reported on the zoologist Albert Fleischmann's most recent attack on Darwinism in his book *Die Descendenztheorie* (The theory of descent, 1901) as well as the objections to Haeckel's famous "biogenetic law": Ontogeny recapitulates phylogeny.

The true denouement of the conflict between religion and Darwin-

---

33 William M. Montgomery, "Germany," in Glick, ed., *Comparative Reception of Darwinism*, 108.
34 Quoted in Kelly, *Descent of Darwin*, 60.   35 Quoted in Gregory, *Nature Lost?* 186.

ism was the complete separation of religion from Darwin's material world. Otto at some length explained where the separation must be made: "Surely we have now left far behind us the primitive expressions of the religious outlook that were concerned with the creation of the world in six days, the making of Eve out of Adam's rib, the story of Paradise and the angelic-demoniac forces, and the accessory miracles and accompanying signs by means of which the Divine control the world" was supposed to be displayed. By now, Otto continued, we can distinguish between the simple myths and legendary histories "and their spiritual values and ethical content. We give to natural science and to religious feeling what is due to each, and thus have done forever with tedious apologetic discussions."[36]

Schmid came to his resolution between religion and Darwinism by continuing to doubt that Darwinism was scientifically based because it accepted chance and by so doing lacked the determination that he thought science required in order to be legitimate.[37] A modern theologian and chemist has summarized the modus vivendi that was arrived at between Darwinism and religion by the end of the century: "Contemporary evolutionary biology," Arthur Peacock wrote in 1985, "continues to raise new questions and so continues to provide a stimulus" for a living theology. "Christian theology," Peacock pointed out, "continues to be vastly indebted to that view of the transformations of the living world into which Darwin initiated us."[38]

Religion may have been compelled to recognize the impact of Darwinism, but before the century was out Darwinism had also been reshaped by religion. Today, of course, Darwinism is acknowledged as a central theory of modern biology; evolution as Darwin explained it through natural selection is no longer dubious among students of the life sciences. And for many people in the late twentieth century, that scientific acceptance of Darwinism is generally envisioned as a primary explanation for the alterations in late-nineteenth-century religious thought. That, however, was not the way it happened; at the end of the century Darwinism was far from triumphant over religion. Indeed, even before the century's end the persistent criticisms and challenges from theologians and scientists alike left much of the Darwinian argument in tatters. The idea of evolution, which had begun even before Darwin's *The Origin of Species* appeared, had been widely accepted, although certainly not unanimously,

36 Otto, *Naturalism and Religion*, 1–2.   37 Gregory, *Nature Lost?* 180–1.
38 Peacock, "Biological Evolution and Christian Theology," 127.

as Fleischmann's 1901 work reminds us. Yet, the big questions or doubts about Darwinism persisted: Was natural selection the primary catalyst of change in species? Whence came the small differences between individual animals within a species, which were, after all, the bases for natural selection? And finally, what were the principles of heredity on which Darwin's theory depended?

Darwin himself right up to his death in 1882 sought to answer these questions and the myriad objections his opponents brought forward. But as we know today, he never found convincing answers.[39] Scientists as well as theologians found the conception of evolution by Lamarck much more persuasive than Darwin's. For, unlike natural selection, Lamarckianism did not draw on chance or deny mind in order to explain evolution. Lamarck's conception of evolution began with purpose and ended with the idea that evolution was progressive, leading to a future goal. Theologians and scientists such as the American paleontologist Edward Drinker Cope could comfortably fit that explanation of evolution into a divine or nonmaterial process. Lamarck's theory could also bypass a formidable obstacle for Darwinian evolution, namely, that humankind was included in the sequence of life. Under Lamarckian principles evolution easily included humankind because the Lamarckian force that linked animals and human beings was beyond material explanation. As one authority has written, "By the end of the century there were probably more Neo-Lamarckians than Darwinians in American science."[40]

By the turn of the century, Darwinism was not only still under attack but was also thought to be out of date. In 1904 Eberhart Dennert, a German biologist, published his *At the Deathbed of Darwinism* in which he reviewed all the dissatisfactions German scientists felt about Darwin and the work of Haeckel. "My object in these pages," Dennert wrote, "is to show that Darwinism will soon be a thing of the past, a matter of history," for to imagine that the wonderfully regulated world of organisms is "at the mercy of chance is utterly monstrous, and for this very reason Darwinism, which is throughout a doctrine of chance, must be rejected; it is indeed a myth."[41]

---

39 See, e.g., the often poignant pages on Darwin's last years in Peter J. Vorzimmer, *Charles Darwin: the Years of Controversy; The Origins of Species and Its Critics, 1859–1882* (Philadelphia, 1970), chap. 11.

40 Edward J. Pfeifer, "United States," in Glick, ed., *Comparative Reception of Darwinism*, 199. For the work of Edward Cope, see Peter J. Bowler, *The Eclipse of Darwinism: Anti-Darwinian Evolution Theories in the Decades Around 1900* (Baltimore, 1983), 121–7.

41 Eberhart Dennert, *At the Deathbed of Darwinism* (Burlington, Iowa, 1904), 28, 122.

It is not accidental, of course, that the scientific objections to Darwinism by the end of the century reflected in their arguments and evidence the same kind of philosophical issues that had troubled theologians: the inclusion of human beings in the process of evolution, the role of chance in natural selection, and the absence of supernatural forces. In sum, the connection between scientists and theologians with which our story began continued right up to the end of the century.

One reason why a benign adjustment between religion and Darwinism came about was that Darwinian evolution no longer was a live subject among scientists, who once had been pressing theologians and preachers for change and adjustment. Ironically enough, a solution to one of Darwin's ancient and persistent deficiencies in accounting for natural selection further undermined his theory. As we know, Darwin had tried unsuccessfully to explain the origin and function of the small differences between individuals within species that were the bases for natural selection. Around the turn of the century that explanation was finally provided. Put in present-day terms, Darwin, along with almost every other biologist of the time, lacked any understanding of modern Mendelian genetics. That deficiency was remedied with the discovery, or more accurately the rediscovery of Gregor Mendel's principles of genetics. The idea that mutations might offer a better way of accounting for evolutionary change than natural selection thus deepened still further the shadow that had fallen for some time on Darwin's theory. The mutation theory had the additional advantage of permitting its adherents to escape the unattractive competitive aura surrounding Darwin's popular cliche, "the survival of the fittest." As the leading American geneticist Thomas Hunt Morgan wrote in rejecting natural selection, the mutation conception of evolution allowed one to escape that "dreadful calamity of nature, pictured as the battle for existence."[42]

For the next thirty years Darwinian evolution was increasingly pushed aside. As the American biologist Vernon L. Kellogg wrote in his important survey *Darwinism Today*, "The fair truth is that the Darwinian selection theories . . . stand to-day seriously discredited in the biological world." Even more dismissive of Darwin's ideas were the words of a major historian of biology, the Swedish scientist Erik Nordenskiöld in 1928. Contrasting Darwin with Newton, Nordenskiöld wrote that "to raise the theory of selection, as it has often been, to the rank of a 'natural law'

---

42 Quoted in Carl N. Degler, *In Search of Human Nature: The Decline and Revival of Darwinism in American Social Thought* (New York, 1991), 23.

comparable in value with the law of gravity established by Newton is, of course, quite irrational, as time has already shown; Darwin's theory of the origin of species," Nordenskiöld remarked, "was long ago abandoned."[43]

This turn-of-the-century dismissal of Darwin evokes a couple of rather sad or ironic thoughts, especially in the context of the impact of Darwinism on religion. One is the way in which Thomas Huxley's long and untiring defense of Darwinism and his almost implacable opposition to religion seemed to reverse themselves. The reversal can be observed in his *Romanes* lecture delivered at Oxford in 1893, thirty-three years after his famous encounter with Bishop Wilberforce. His lecture was titled "Evolution and Ethics." The burden of his *Romanes* lecture was that ethics and nature were at odds. Many ancient writers, like the Stoics, Huxley reminded his audience, believed that the natural way was the good way, and so had more recent thinkers such as Adam Smith and Jeremy Bentham. But evolution now shows us, Huxley pointed out, that nature is not the source of our ethics, but of their destruction: "The practice of that which is ethically best – what we call goodness or virtue," Huxley insisted, "in all respects, is opposed to that which leads to success in the cosmic struggle for existence. In place of ruthless self-assertion it demands self-restraint; in place of thrusting aside, or treading down, all competitors, it requires that the individual shall not merely respect, but shall help his fellows; its influence is directed not so much to the survival of the fittest, as to the fitting of as many as possible to survive. It repudiates the gladiatorial theory of existence," he reminded his audience.[44] "Let us understand, once and for all," he warned, "that the ethical progress of society depends, not on imitating the cosmic process, still less in running away from it, but in combating it."[45]

He was hoping, in effect, to use the Christian ethical system as a way of overcoming the amoral consequences of Darwinian evolution. Once he had been an opponent of traditional religion, and in his mind he remained so. But his *Romanes* lecture also showed that at least religiously based ethics were at odds with Darwinism. It was a striking example of how a major protagonist in the course of the conflict between Darwinism and religion had been reshaped by his experience.

In point of fact, though, Huxley's personal conflict between Darwin-

---

43 Erik Nordenskiöld, *The History of Biology: A Survey* (New York, 1928), 476.
44 James Paradis and George C. Williams, *Evolution and Ethics* (Princeton, N.J., 1989), 139–40.
45 Ibid., 141.

ism and ethics was a misreading of Darwin's conception of the origins of human morality. It also was an English reading, for both Haeckel and Strauss gave, in effect, a German and more Darwinian reading. In contradistinction to a philosophical assertion of the separation of science and ethics, Haeckel defended his view of the uniting of ethics and Darwinism "on the solid ground of social instinct, as we find in the case of all social animals."[46] Strauss, too, saw the beginning of morals in animals' "social instincts . . . which bear on the rearing of young, the care, the pains, the self-sacrifice there lavished," and which constitute "a deposit of the higher moral faculties in the animal kingdom."[47]

The contrast between Huxley's conception of Darwinian ethics and that of Haeckel and Strauss is useful in elucidating the differences between German and English (and American) conceptions of Darwinism. From the beginning, English and American thinkers about Darwin emphasized the individualistic and competitive side of Darwinism. Hence Huxley's worry that good ethics would not emerge from evolutionary thought. German defenders of Darwinian ideas came out of a much more organic conception of science and social life. It is revealing, in this context, that the term *social Darwinism* bore different meanings for Anglo-Americans and Germans. Among the former the term emphasized competitive behavior that produced the so-called fittest and unfit in society, whereas among Germans the term frequently meant simply a connection with, or relation between, evolution and society, often with an organic conception of the social order. It is not surprising, therefore, that Haeckel and Strauss were so impressed by Darwin's social or cooperative side of evolutionary theory.

Scientific theory was only part of the difference between German and Anglo-American conceptions of Darwinism. It just so happened that at the time that Darwinian ideas were being advanced, Germans, scientists and lay persons alike, saw the new ascendancy of German science as a part of the rising political movement looking toward the consummation of the unification of the German states. Many German scientists considered the German nation to be a *Kulturstaat*. It was not accidental, for example, that Haeckel was a strong admirer of Bismarck; he even bestowed an honorary degree on the Iron Chancellor at his university at Jena! It followed, therefore, that despite some continuing objections to Darwinism in Germany, Darwinian evolution carried a deeper and more pervasive appeal to Germans than it did to the English and American

---

46 Haeckel, *Riddle of the Universe*, 350.   47 Strauss, *Old Faith and the New*, 2:15.

publics.[48] In any event, the rise of eugenics in the early twentieth century brought Americans to an equally positive rethinking of the relation between biology and society, but that is a story of the twentieth century.

The fate of St. George Mivart reveals yet another way by which time and circumstances altered the relation between Darwinism and religion. Like Huxley, Mivart was a practicing biologist, but unlike Huxley he was, as we have seen, an unrelenting opponent of Darwinism. And that opposition endeared him to the Roman Church, of which he was a devoted supporter. In 1884, for example, the conservative Catholic publication *The Tablet* praised him for his devotion to Catholic Christianity. But sixteen years later, after the Church began to have doubts about Mivart's conception of animal evolution and his conception of such ecclesiastical beliefs as the nature of Hell, *The Tablet* denounced him as un-Christian. Mivart had made clear that he was neither an agnostic nor an atheist, but he was convinced that science was a search for truth and not something to be determined by ecclesiastical dogma. As he wrote in 1900, "the inscrutable, incomprehensible energy pervading the universe and (as it seems to me) disclosed by science, differs profoundly as I read nature from the God worshipped by Christians."[49] When he died in April 1900, Mivart was buried in unhallowed ground, for he had been excommunicated by the Church for his conscientious effort to reconcile the science he admired – though not Darwinism, of course – and the Church he had loved.

At century's end, then, Darwinism was neither a dominant force in science nor a seriously negative force in religion. Religion could still see itself as beyond the grasp of materialist science.

---

48 For the contrast between German and American and British conceptions of Darwinism in the nineteenth century, see Paul J. Weindling's complex book *Darwinism and Social Darwinism in Imperial Germany: The Contribution of the Cell Biologist Oscar Hertwig (1842–1922)* (Stuttgart, 1991), chap. 1.
49 Quoted in Gruber, *Conscience in Conflict*, 141.

5

Nationalism as a Civil Religion in the Thought of Abraham Lincoln, Carl Schurz, and Otto von Bismarck

HANS L. TREFOUSSE

I

Any discussion of nationalism in the thought of nineteenth-century states-men must begin with a definition of the term. According to Hans Kohn, *nationalism* is "a state of mind in which the supreme loyalty of the individual is felt to be due to the nation-state." Carlton J. Hayes called it a "modern emotional fusion and exaggeration of two very old phenomena – nationality and patriotism," and Boyd C. Shafer explained that it existed "when a people are devoted to the entity they call their country . . . and consider themselves to be separate and one and so different from other peoples that they should have an independent state." Adrian Hastings thought that it derived from a "belief that one's own ethnic or national tradition is especially valuable and needs to be defended at almost any cost through creation or extension of its own national state," and Drew Gilpin Faust stressed the necessity of an idea in the creation of Confederate nationalism. According to Peter Loewenberg, all these emotions can be traced back to early childhood, the home, and considerations of "us" and "them." The idea that every nation, often defined by language, should have its own state became so powerful a movement during the nineteenth century that hardly any major or minor country remained untouched by the concept. It truly developed into a civil religion, a faith so strong that it virtually competed with the older theistic variety.[1]

1 Hans Kohn, *Nationalism: Its Meaning and History* (New York, 1965), 9; Carlton J. Hayes, *Essays on Nationalism* (New York, 1926), 6; Boyd C. Shafer, "Nationalism, Internationalism, and Peace," in Michael Palumbo and William H. Shanahan, eds., *Nationalism: Essays in Honor of Louis L. Snyder* (Westport, Conn., 1981), 3–32; Peter Loewenberg, "The Psychodynamics of Nationalism," *History*

There were, however, varying forms of nationalism. In most European countries the sentiment was based on ethnicity, with the stress on the uniqueness of one people. In the United States, however, national fervor was slightly different. The American variety was not based on ethnic unity alone – after all, the United States was a country of immigrants from many backgrounds – but also on shared ideas of democracy, republicanism, and representative government. These concepts presupposed majority rule by the people, male suffrage (often restricted to whites), minority rights, and the various freedoms guaranteed in the Bill of Rights – freedom of speech, religion, assembly, and petition. American nationalism rested on an endorsement of all of these as the nation's special gift to mankind. As Eric Foner has pointed out, American nationalism rests on principles that are universal, not parochial, whereas Anthony Smith emphasized that Americans, when mentioning "the Nation," might often talk of their political values or their founding. Although this national feeling was by no means exceptional in the way that it, like that of other peoples, tried to differentiate itself from outsiders, often various minorities, it is evident that this was not the same as exultation of one's nation for its own sake, and nobody articulated this type of nationalism more poignantly than Abraham Lincoln.[2]

Widely hailed as the Great Emancipator, Abraham Lincoln remains America's most popular historical figure. More than five thousand volumes have been written about him, and the last few years alone have witnessed the appearance of at least four more works dealing with the sixteenth president.

This popularity is easy to understand. Who else so exemplified the American dream, the ability to rise from rags to riches? And who else was so successful in accomplishing his objectives, those of preserving the Union and liberating the slaves? If this were not enough, the president's martyrdom on Good Friday of 1865 made his career especially remarkable, and an aura of sanctity has clung to him ever since.

of European Ideas 15, nos. 1–3 (1992): 93–103; Adrian Hastings, *The Construction of Nationhood: Ethnicity, Religion, and Nationalism* (Cambridge, 1997), 4; Drew Gilpin Faust, *The Creation of Confederate Nationalism: Ideology and Identity in the Civil War South* (Baton Rouge, La., 1998), 27–9.

2 Eric Foner, "Race and Citizenship in American History," in Anna Maria Martellone, *Towards a New American Nation: Redefinitions and Reconstruction* (Staffordshire, U.K., 1995), 76; Anthony Smith, *The Ethnic Origins of Nations* (Oxford, 1986), 3; Merrill D. Peterson, *Lincoln in American Memory* (New York, 1994); William Hanchett, *Out of the Wilderness: The Life of Abraham Lincoln* (Urbana, Ill., 1994); Philip S. Paludan, *The Presidency of Abraham Lincoln* (Lawrence, Kans., 1994); David Herbert Donald, *Lincoln* (New York, 1995). Jay Monaghan listed some 4,000 books in his *Lincoln Bibliography, 1839–1939*, 2 vols. (Springfield, Ill., 1943–5); the figure 5,000 seems to be justified for the present.

Lincoln's thoughts on nationalism were formed early in his career. He believed that the United States, with its democratic government anchored in the Declaration of Independence, was the world's last best hope, to be preserved at all costs not merely for its own sake but for the salvation of the rest of mankind as well.

He expressed these ideas many times in some detail, usually equating his nationalism with the concept of republican freedom. As early as 1838, in his famous Lyceum Address, he said that the perpetuation of American political institutions was a "task of gratitude to our fathers' justice to ourselves, duty to posterity, and love for our species in general." Knowing that Americans were much attached to their government, he warned that if the rights of freedom were constantly disregarded, an alienation of this affection would be the result.[3] In the equally well-known Peoria Address of 1854, delivered after Senator Stephen A. Douglas (D-Illinois) had brought about the repeal of the Missouri Compromise of 1820 prohibiting slavery in the territories north of 36° 30', he denounced the senator for his blindness to the evils of human bondage by stating:

This declared indifference, but as I must think, overt real zeal for the spread of slavery, I cannot but hate. I hate it because of the monstrous injustice of slavery itself. I hate it because it deprives our republican example of its just influence in the world – enables the enemies of free institutions, with plausibility, to taunt us as hypocrites – causes the real friends of freedom to doubt our sincerity, and especially because it forces so many good men amongst ourselves into an open war with the very fundamental principles of civil liberty – criticizing the Declaration of Independence, and insisting that there is no right principle of action but self-interest.[4]

To emphasize this point, he added, "It deprives our republican example of its just influence in the world," thus stressing the connection of American nationalism with the notion of freedom for all nations, a sentiment very different from the ethnic nationalism of other peoples.

Lincoln, convinced of the lasting validity of the Declaration of Independence, often returned to this theme. Strongly believing that the liberal party throughout the world was apprehensive that the only retrograde institution in America was undermining the principles of progress, fatally violating "the noblest political system the world ever saw," on June 26, 1857, in Springfield, Illinois, he said that he thought the Declaration of Independence contemplated "the progressive improvement of all men

3 Roy P. Basler, ed., *The Collected Works of Abraham Lincoln*, 9 vols. (New Brunswick, N.J., 1953), 1:108 (hereafter *LW*).
4 *LW*, 2:255.

everywhere." Then, during the campaign against Douglas in 1858 in Edwardsville, he again stated: "What constitutes the bulwark of our own liberty and independence? . . . Our reliance is on the love of liberty which God has planted in our bosoms. Our defense is the preservation of the spirit which prizes liberty as the heritage of all men, in all lands, every-where."[5] His insistence on the idealistic nature of American nationalism was unmistakable.

His theories were put to the test when, after his election as president, he was confronted with the necessity of maintaining the Union by force. Determined to do so, he justified his action by citing America's unique position in the world and the importance of his frequently expressed beliefs in the protection of popular government not only in the United States but throughout the world, and asked his fellow countrymen to support the Union as well as the principles it represented. "This issue embraces more than the fate of these United States," he declared in his message to Congress on July 4, 1861. Lincoln continued, "It presents to the whole family of man, the question, whether a constitutional repub-lic, or a democracy, a government of the people, by the same people – can or cannot maintain its territorial integrity against its own domestic foes." Calling the war "essentially a People's contest," he characterized it as "a struggle for the maintaining in the world that form of, and the sub-stance of government, whose leading object is, to elevate the condition of men; to lift artificial weights from all shoulders; to clear the path of laudable pursuit for all; to afford all, an unfettered start and a fair chance in the race for life."

It was an experiment, a trial of popular government, and it was nec-essary to show "that the ballots are the rightful, and peaceful successors of bullets; and that when ballots have been fairly, and constitutionally decided, there can be no successful appeal back to bullets."[6]

Lincoln continued to stress his belief in this central issue of the U.S. Civil War as long as he lived. In his first annual message in December 1861 he called the insurrection "largely, but not exclusively, a war upon the first principle of popular government – the rights of the people."[7] When a delegation of Lutherans expressed their support in May 1862 he told them he accepted their assurance of sympathy "in an important crisis which involves, not only the civil and religious liberties of our own dear

5 *LW*, 2:407; 3:95.
6 James D. Richardson, ed., *A Compilation of the Messages and Papers of the Presidents, 1789–1907*, 9 vols. (Washington, D.C., 1908), 6:23.
7 Ibid., 56.

land, but in a large degree the civil liberties of mankind in many countries and through many ages." And he gave the best expression of his conviction in the Gettysburg Address where he not only stated that "four score and seven years ago, our forefathers brought forth on this continent, a new nation, conceived in Liberty, and dedicated to the proposition that all men are created equal" but also that "Now we are engaged in a great civil war, testing whether that nation, or any nation so conceived and so dedicated, can long endure."[8] It was this emphasis on the universality of the American appeal that made this nationalism, expressed in notions of freedom, different, and nobody phrased it more clearly than the Great Emancipator.

II

Carl Schurz's thoughts about nationalism were not exactly the same as Lincoln's. Born in Germany and involved in the nationalistic uprising of 1848, he first adhered to the ethnic variety so common in Europe, only to attempt to fuse it with the American type when he came to the United States.

This astonishing nineteenth-century liberal had an arresting career. Unlike Lincoln, who was brought up on farms in still largely undeveloped parts of Kentucky and Indiana, Schurz, the son of a local schoolmaster and storekeeper, was born in Liblar near Cologne in 1829. Attending the University of Bonn, he came under the influence of Gottfried Kinkel, a professor of German literature and art history, and a flaming advocate of German nationalism and democracy. During the revolution of 1848, Schurz, a lieutenant in the parliamentary army, barely avoided capture by the Prussians by escaping through a sewer from the besieged fortress of Rastatt and reaching safety in France on the other side of the Rhine. He returned to Germany in disguise to free Kinkel, who had been condemned to life imprisonment and was serving his sentence in prison at Spandau, and accomplished this feat by bribing a guard to lower the professor from the roof so that he could spirit him away to the coast of Mecklenburg, from where he managed to escape to Scotland. This exploit made him famous when he was only twenty-one, and an advantageous marriage to the daughter of a Hamburg merchant rendered him financially independent for a time. After a brief stay in France and Great Britain, he emigrated to America in 1851, eventually

8 *LW*, 5:212; 7:23.

settling in Wisconsin, where there were many German-Americans. Thus, he acquired an ethnic base for his political career, which he soon resumed by acting as a spokesman for his countrymen in the Republican Party. After campaigning for Lincoln in 1860 he became U.S. minister to Spain. But he was anxious to enter the army and in 1862 was commissioned brigadier general. Although his military career was not brilliant, he attained the rank of major-general and the respect of his German-American compatriots.

After the Civil War, Schurz undertook a tour of the South at the behest of President Andrew Johnson. But because of his radical bias, he broke with the president and wrote a scathing report about conditions in the former Confederacy, which was used as a radical campaign document. Then he turned to journalism, finally becoming the co-owner and editor of the *Westliche Post*, a German-language newspaper in St. Louis. As temporary chairman of the Chicago convention that nominated Ulysses S. Grant in 1868 and as active campaigner for the general, he again rallied the German-Americans to the party and in 1869 was elected United States senator from Missouri.

In the Senate, Schurz's excellent speeches captured the ear of the public, but he soon fell out with the president, whose foreign and Reconstruction policies, lack of interest in civil service reform, and corrupt associates he steadily denounced. One of the founders of the short-lived Liberal Republican Party, he was disappointed in the nomination of Horace Greeley for the presidency but loyally supported him, only to return to the Republicans to back Rutherford B. Hayes in 1876. Appointed secretary of the interior by Hayes, he made a name for himself by introducing civil service rules in this previously notoriously corrupt department, attempting to reform the Indian Bureau and furthering conservation policies. He retired to New York at the expiration of his term, again became active in journalism, and devoted himself to civil service reform. In 1884 he was a leading Mugwump supporter of Grover Cleveland, and in the 1890s and early 1900s furthered municipal reforms and opposed America's imperialist policies until his death in 1906.[9]

As a good German, Schurz initially believed strongly in the ethnic type of nationalism. "The patriotic heart loved to dwell on the memories of the 'Holy Roman Empire of the German Nation,' which once, at the zenith of its power had held leadership in the civilized world," he wrote in his *Reminiscences* when recalling his youthful thoughts.

9 Hans L. Trefousse, *Carl Schurz: A Biography* (Knoxville, Tenn., 1982), passim.

From these memories sprang the Kyffhäuser romanticism, with its dreams of the rebirth of German power and magnificence, which had such poetic charm to German youth: the legend telling how the old Kaiser Friedrich Barbarossa sitting in a cave of the Kyffhäuser mountain in Thuringia, in a sleep centuries long . . . and how one day the old Kaiser would awaken and issue from his mountain, sword in hand, to restore the German Empire to its ancient glory.[10]

Combined with his indictment of German princes devoid of all national feeling, willing to serve the interests of foreign powers, and his enthusiasm for the uprising against Napoleon in the German Wars of Liberation, this account could have been written by any nationalist proud of his country and devoted to the idea of national unification. In addition, he proved his ethnic nationalism by his participation in the revolution of 1848, an uprising designed to bring about the unification of Germany, first as a collaborator with the most radical faction in Bonn and then by his service in the revolutionary army in the Palatinate and in Baden. But he came to America and his German nationalism gradually gave way to, or rather merged with, his new American loyalties. Considering the usual definitions of nationalism this sounds like a contradiction, however Schurz not only accomplished this melding but built an entire career on his belief in it.

Ethnic politics became the hallmark of Schurz's political rise. Consciously seeking out areas with large numbers of German-Americans, he settled in Wisconsin and later in Missouri. "I expect to go to Wisconsin," he wrote to Kinkel in 1855:

The German element is powerful in that State, the immigrants being so numerous, and they are striving for political recognition. They only lack leaders that are not bound by the restraints of money-getting. There is the place where I can find a sure, gradually expanding field for my work without truckling to the nativistic elements, and there I hope in time, to gain influence that may also become useful to our cause.[11]

The last phrase demonstrates that he still was not certain about his primary loyalties, "our cause" being the procurement of American help for German unification, but he carried out his design without much delay and became less and less interested in returning to Europe. Moving to Watertown, Wisconsin, after 1855, he soon took an active part in the affairs of the German immigrant community in the vicinity. Unfortunately, however, most of these newcomers were Democrats, and that

10 Carl Schurz, *The Reminiscences of Carl Schurz*, 3 vols. (New York, 1907), 1:103.
11 Frederick Bancroft, ed., *Speeches, Correspondence, and Political Papers of Carl Schurz*, 6 vols. (New York, 1913), 1:19.

party's southern connections repelled him. Thus, when after a brief return to Europe he came back to Wisconsin in 1856, in spite of protestations of shyness, he was not at all hesitant to follow the invitation of Louis P. Harvey, an astute state party leader, to lecture to the German-Americans on the evils of slavery on behalf of the Republican Party. His support might lure the immigrants away from the Democrats in spite of the nativists among the opposition.

Schurz's political career was effectively launched during the presidential campaign of 1856. At a German meeting in nearby Jefferson, the young immigrant was introduced to the crowd. He delivered a speech in German and then continued to campaign among his compatriots.[12]

In his appeals to his countrymen, Schurz, like Lincoln invoking a universal role, ably recalled German ideas of freedom in 1848 to justify the American struggle against slavery. As the Milwaukee *Sentinel*, reporting one of his speeches, commented, "The German heart beats for freedom here as in the fatherland." The newspaper identified him as the liberator of Kinkel, and the fusion of the two nationalisms began to take shape.[13]

After a few years Schurz described his melding most succinctly to his American sponsors. After mentioning various heroes of German ethnic nationalism – Berthold Schwarz, the inventor of gunpowder in Europe, Johann Gutenberg, and Martin Luther – in the "True Americanism" speech in 1859 in Boston's Faneuil Hall he turned to the idealistic type of American nationalism so often cited by Lincoln. Declaring that in the "colony of free humanity," the mother country of which was the world, Americans had established "the Republic of equal rights, where the title of manhood" was the title of citizenship; he expressed the wish that the words of the Declaration of Independence asserting the equality of all men were inscribed on every gatepost within the limits of the republic. "From this principle the Revolutionary Fathers derived their claim to independence; upon this they founded the institutions of this country, and the whole structure was to be the living incarnation of this idea," he continued. Schurz went on to say, "Equality of right, embodied in general self government; there is our mission, there is our greatness, there is our safety; there, and nowhere else! This is a true Americanism, and to this I pay the tribute of my devotion."[14]

Schurz's appeal to American idealistic nationalism did not interfere with

---

12 Trefousse, *Schurz*, 58, 61.
13 Milwaukee *Sentinel*, Sept. 12, Oct. 3, 1856.   14 Schurz, *Speeches, Correspondence*, 1:52, 57–9.

his reliance on his German origins in the furtherance of his career. His Republican sponsors were so impressed with his efforts among his fellow Germans that in 1857 they nominated him for lieutenant governor. In spite of his failure to be elected, he took a prominent part in the 1860 presidential campaign, attempting to create a strong coalition devoted to the support of Lincoln's effort to maintain the Union with its world-wide message of idealism; he was generally credited with bringing many Germans over to the Republican ticket. In fact, it was widely believed that the German vote for Lincoln and Hamlin was large enough to make all the difference in several northwestern states. And although we know today that this analysis was far from true, Schurz shared this opinion.[15] Writing to his friend Congressman John F. Potter that he thought he deserved an appointment from the new administration, he pointed out that, as he was generally looked on as the representative of the German element, it was his duty to those he represented not to take an inferior place. His insistence on his ethnic connections paid off, and after much back and forth Lincoln sent him to Madrid as American envoy.[16]

When, within less than half a year, Schurz returned to join the army, he again used his ethnic connections to full advantage. Anxious to be promoted to major general, he wrote to Charles Sumner:

To stand behind such men as Dan Sickles and T. Steele . . . is a rather severe thing for me. . . . Were it not for the influence I want to possess in the army, and for the relations with my large constituency, with whom a certain kind of success gives prestige and power, I would perhaps care little for promotion. . . . But as matters stand I do care. This time the jeers of the German pro-slavery papers . . . will be disagreeable to my ears.

He became a major general.[17]

After the war he continued to build on his ethnic appeal. Entering the contest for senator from Missouri, as the representative of the Germans he was able to overcome all opposition, and in the U.S. Senate he was considered not merely the spokesman for his state but for all German-Americans.[18] In his speeches on the floor he emphasized his belief in the fusion of the two nationalisms, the German and the American, the idealistic nature of which he had earlier pointed out. Thus, when Senator

15 Frederick C. Luebke, ed., *Ethnic Voters and the Election of Lincoln* (Lincoln, Neb., 1973), passim.
16 Schurz, *Speeches, Correspondence*, 1:165–8.
17 Schurz to Charles Sumner, Mar. 8, 1863, Sumner papers, Harvard University.
18 Max Weber to Schurz, Jan. 18, 1870; Frederick Meyer to Schurz, March 21, 1870, Schurz papers, Library of Congress (hereafter LC); St. Louis *Missouri Democrat*, Apr. 22, 1870.

Frederick T. Frelinghuysen of New Jersey accused him of trying to help the German Empire rather than his own country, he gave a ringing reply:

Although I am certainly not ashamed of having sprung from that great nation whose monuments stand upon all the battlefields of thought; that great nation which . . . seems at this moment to hold in her hands the destinies of the Old World . . . while I am by no means ashamed of being a son of that great nation, yet I may say I am proud to be an American citizen. This is my country. Here my children were born. Here I have spent the best years of my youth and manhood. All the honors I have gained, all the aims of my endeavors and whatever of hope and promise the future has for me it is all encompassed in this my new fatherland. My devotion to this great Republic will not yield . . . to that of any man born in this country.

He also emphasized that he believed "those who would meanly and coldly forget their old mother could not be expected to be faithful to their young bride."[19]

The war of 1870 brought forth outbursts of German nationalism among most German-Americans, and Schurz did not remain immune to their enthusiasm. The news of the capitulation of Napoleon III so excited him that he wrote to his wife: "The Germans are now the greatest and mightiest nation of the Old World, and no one can deny them this rank any longer. This fact contrasts so tremendously with the past, that the German himself can hardly assimilate it. And yet . . . it is so. May it remain so. Hallelujah!"[20]

But soon Schurz returned to his dual allegiance and made every effort to fuse his two national identities and loyalties. Believing strongly in the assimilation of German-Americans, he nevertheless thought this could be accomplished without jettisoning German heritage; he served his countrymen as a role model by showing them that they could hold some of the highest offices in the land and be encouraged not only in the acquisition of English but also in the retention of the German language. He spoke German in his home, conversed and corresponded with Germans in German, and wrote the first volume of his *Reminiscences*, the part dealing with his experiences in Europe, in German, and the other two, describing his American career, in English.[21] As he explained in his speech to the New York Deutsche Liederkranz Society on January 9, 1897, "I

19 *Congressional Globe*, 42d Congress, 2d Session, Ap. 111.
20 Schurz to Mrs. Schurz, Sept. 3, 1870, Hogue Collection, Schurz papers, LC.
21 Hans L. Trefousse, "Carl Schurz Reconsidered," *Lincoln Herald* 83 (spring 1981): 570–1; Schurz, *Speeches, Correspondence*, 5:337.

have always been in favor of sensible Americanization, but this need not mean an abandonment of all that is German. It means that we should accept the best traits of American character and join them to the best traits of German character."[22]

He knew that American character included a nationalism with a worldwide message he had made clear years earlier in his "True Americanism" speech. He was to make it clear again at the turn of the century in his fight against imperialism. Still adhering, like Lincoln, to the truths of the Declaration of Independence, he said, "Here was . . . the natural birthplace of that great charter of human rights and human liberty, the Declaration of Independence, pointing out the goal to be reached, and destined to serve as a guiding star to all mankind." If the American experiment in imperialism were to be continued, he maintained, then the great American republic would soon cease to be an encouragement to the progress of political liberty and become a warning example to all the world.[23] It was a succinct formulation of American nationalism, and Carl Schurz can be cited as one of the best examples of an American nationalist who truly not only fully embraced the nonethnic, ideologically democratic nationalism of a great part of the United States but, by fusing it with his continuing regard for his German roots, showed how well it could be adapted to a country of immigrants.

III

Otto von Bismarck's attitude was entirely different. An East Elbian Junker, brought up in the traditions of his class, his primary loyalty was to his king and to Prussia. As Otto Pflanze has pointed out, a number of authorities have maintained that the chancellor began as a Prussian patriot and made the transition to German nationalism rather late.[24] At first, at least, if he was interested in German nationalism at all, and he maintained that he was, it was merely as a means for the aggrandizement of Prussia.[25] According to Lothar Gall, "in terms of his image of Germany, this meant that Germany must embrace and preserve both the territorial and political identity of Prussia; every Prussian had to be a German without any distinction, and Prussia's political weight in Europe and its freedom of

---

22 Ibid.   23 Schurz, *Speeches, Correspondence*, 6:152.
24 Otto Pflanze, *Bismarck and the Development of Germany*, 3 vols. (Princeton, N.J., 1990), 1:67.
25 Otto Pflanze, *Bismarck and the Development of Germany* (Princeton, N.J., 1963), 124, 198; Erich Eyck, *Bismarck and the German Empire* (New York, 1968), 81, 83–4, passim; Pflanze, *Bismarck* (1990), 1:67.

decision in foreign policy must be in no way diminished by its German ties and obligations."[26]

Bismarck naturally tended to obfuscate these particularistic beginnings. In his *Memoirs*, written when he had become a national hero, he merely admitted that his "task was the establishment or initiation of German unity under the leadership of the king of Prussia."[27] But it was this last phrase that guided him, so that his use of nationalism as a civil religion, a new concept for many Germans, was, at least in the early stages, merely a means to an end. As he said to a French journalist in 1866, he had been brought up in admiration of Austrian policy. But when he came to the Frankfurt Parliament it was not long before he lost the illusions of his youth and became Austria's determined enemy: "The humiliation of my country, Germany sacrificed to foreign interests, a crafty and perfidious policy – all this was not of a nature to please me." Bismarck continued, "From that moment I conceived the idea, which I am now seeking to realize; namely, the rescue of Germany from Austrian oppression, at all events that part of Germany that is united by its genius, religion, manners, and interests to the destinies of Prussia – the Germany of the North." It was this idea to which he devoted himself, the "establishment of North Germany under the aegis of Prussia."[28] Eventually, he would go further. But at the time he was thus not a modern nationalist but a Prussian patriot whose loyalty was not to the nation but to the dynastic state.

Bismarck gave many proofs of this attitude. As early as June 9, 1848, he said to the journalist Hermann Wagener, "We are Prussians and Prussians we shall remain. . . . We do not wish to see the Kingdom of Prussia obliterated in the putrid brew of cozy South-German sentimentality."[29] In 1849 he admitted that everybody wanted German unity, but with the Frankfurt constitution, he did not desire it and preferred that Prussia remain Prussia. In 1852 Sir Alexander Mallet, the British minister to the German Confederation, reported that Bismarck was "in the first place Prussian, in the second out and out Prussian, and in the third place German by Prussia."[30] In the conflict concerning Schleswig-Holstein,

---

26 Lothar Gall, *Bismarck the White Revolutionary*, 2 vols. (London, 1986), 1:60.
27 Otto von Bismarck, *The Memoirs*, ed. Horst Kohl, 2 vols. (New York, 1966), 2:51.
28 Louis L. Snyder, *The Blood and Iron Chancellor: A Documentary Biography of Otto von Bismarck* (Princeton, N.J., 1967), 146–7.
29 Otto von Bismarck, *Die Gesammelten Werke*, 2d ed., 15 vols. (Berlin, 1924), 7:13.
30 Eyck, *Bismarck*, 27, quotation on 52.

pitting Germany against Denmark, he did not see the problem from a German but from a purely Prussian point of view and even encouraged Great Britain to interfere on the side of Denmark.[31] All these acts and statements were hardly those of a nationalist.

In time, of course, he became a great German nationalist, at least in the eyes of the people. That this shift was a matter of convenience, a change of strategy rather than of conviction, has long been recognized. Again citing Pflanze, "He was not a convert to German nationalism, but had come to appreciate its potential utility for the expansion of Prussian power." In 1866 he used German nationalism as a prop to Prussian monarchism and then to pacify the annexed states.[32] He posed as a nationalist, was considered to be Germany's great national hero, and tried to make the utmost use of the sentiment that had become a veritable civic religion bridging the country's divisive religious differences. Telling General Grant that he was sorry that Americans had to fight their own people in the Civil War and hearing that it had to be done, he answered: "Yes, you had to save the Union just as we had to save Germany."[33] In the Reichstag in 1881 he stated that he had always acted according to the question of what was useful for his fatherland, for his dynasty, as long as this was only Prussia, and now for Germany. The nation came first, he asserted, "its position in the world and its independence."[34] In his *Memoirs* he wrote that in the German national sentiment he saw the preponderant force always elicited by the struggle with particularism, and to a delegation from Posen he explained, "We confined our demands to what was necessary for our existence and what enabled the big European nation we are to draw a free breath." Love between the various German "races," as he called the different clans, had been growing during the past eighty years and would continue to do so, and neither Posen nor Alsace-Lorraine would ever be surrendered. "Forty years ago we were far behind other nations in national feeling and love for one another," he boasted. "Today, we are no longer behind them."[35]

Thus, Bismarck easily accomplished his transformation from a Prussian patriot to a German nationalist. Having used German national sentiment for his own purposes – the enlargement of Prussia – he now professed to believe in it. It had served him well, and, for all we know, he may have convinced himself of its validity.

31 Ibid., 81.
32 Pflanze, *Bismarck* (1963), 136, 324.
33 John Russell Young, *Around the World with General Grant*, 2 vols. (New York, 1879), 1:412–18.
34 Snyder, *Blood and Iron Chancellor*, 274.
35 Bismarck, *Memoirs*, 1:325.

IV

The three statesmen under consideration obviously constitute three different types of belief in nationalism as a civil religion. It is for this reason that they were selected. Lincoln represented the American notion of nationalism based on an ideal as well as on ethnicity, the ideal of democracy. Schurz illustrated the effort to meld the two nationalisms, the German ethnic variety with the American idealistic type, and Bismarck used the movement for his own goals and then appropriated it. Comparing the three – Carl N. Degler has done so for Lincoln and Bismarck, maintaining that both built nationalism forged in blood and iron, violated their respective constitutions, and allegedly played a part in starting wars – it is apparent that there are great differences.[36] Whereas Lincoln and Schurz were idealistically convinced of their interpretation of national feeling, Bismarck, more pragmatically interested in power, used the movement for his own ends. Even after embracing German nationalism, the Iron Chancellor tended to stress the ethnic variety, thus differing from Lincoln's idealistic interpretation. And because Bismarck's early Prussian "patriotism" was not nationalistic but dynastic, it differed substantially from Schurz's initial devotion to German ethnic pride. Whatever the differences among them, however, all three certainly were affected by nationalism as a civil religion and demonstrated its triumph in their time.

36 Carl N. Degler, *One Among Many: The Civil War in Comparative Perspective* (Gettysburg, Pa., 1991), 17–20.

PART THREE

People in the Transatlantic World: The Perception of Self

6

German Catholic Communalism and the American Civil War

Exploring the Dilemmas of Transatlantic Political Integration

KATHLEEN NEILS CONZEN

I

Consider the dilemma of returning U.S. Civil War veteran George Hansen – German, Catholic, and American. Hansen had had what a later generation would term a "good war." He had enlisted in Company G of Minnesota's Fourth Volunteer Infantry Regiment in the late autumn of 1861. He was a 23-year-old carpenter at the time, an active member of the younger crowd that, with its drinking, dancing, politicking, and institution-building, set the tone for German life in St. Cloud, the county seat of Minnesota's German and Catholic-settled Stearns County. He had been born in Obersgegen, Kreis Bitburg, under the shadow of the great, dismantled Luxemburg fortress at Vianden, as the youngest of six sons of a Napoleonic veteran, and was named Gregor after his godfather. His family may have regarded themselves as among the peasant elite in Germany and certainly quickly acquired security and status in America. His older siblings emigrated in 1852 to the stone quarry area near Joliet, Illinois, and three years later trekked north in covered wagons to the new Stearns County frontier, driving twenty head of cattle before them. Here they were joined by their youngest brother and aging parents in 1857. The family military tradition may have played a role in young Gregor's decision to join the St. Cloud City Guards, the Democratic Party-linked militia company formed by the town's Germans in June 1860. But the decision also may have grown out of the same commitment to his new country evident in the anglicizing of his name to George.

At the outbreak of the Civil War, the Guards resisted enrollment in the Union's volunteer army, claiming that they had organized purely for frontier defense. But when some of the Guards were finally shamed into forming what became the nucleus of the Fourth Minnesota's Company G, George was among their number, beginning his service as the company's lowest-ranking sergeant. His steady series of promotions culminated in the first-sergeant's position after he was wounded at Vicksburg in May 1863, and shortly thereafter a second lieutenancy. This he declined, probably because as an officer he would have been ineligible for the $400 reenlistment bounty credited to him when he veteranized in early 1864. The Fourth Minnesota was now a battle-hardened unit, proud of its status among Sherman's hard-bitten troops, and when news of draft resistance back home reached the front, Sergeant Hansen began sending a series of letters home to St. Cloud's English-language Republican newspaper, describing the doings of the troops and in no uncertain terms urging his German compatriots to demonstrate their support for their adopted country. "I was very much pleased to hear that the draft had taken effect in Stearns County," he wrote. "I hope that our father Abraham Lincoln will bring them to terms and teach them how to save their country."

Hansen survived the siege of Atlanta and the bummers' march to the sea and beyond to stride in glory beside his company when the Fourth Minnesota was chosen to lead Sherman's victory parade through the streets of Washington at the war's end. Not even subsequent charges of mutiny were able to tarnish his glory. When the crack regiment was retained in Kentucky for possible service against the Emperor Maximilian in Mexico, and forced to suffer the indignities of poor rations and politically motivated promotions, he and several other veteran sergeants led a vigorous and ultimately successful protest. Instead of a court-martial, the mutineers were promoted and the regiment was demobilized. Hansen thus came home in July 1865 "sunbrowned . . . hearty and rugged," a second lieutenant after all "by merit alone" and as close to a wartime hero as Stearns County's German community managed to produce.

Soon, on the strength of his war record and patriotic newspaper correspondence, he was invited to join as candidate for county treasurer a Republican-inspired Union ticket of veterans running in the fall elections on a platform that aspired to unite Republicans and Democrats, Yankees and immigrants alike, in creating a new and harmonious postwar order in Stearns County. But the Union Party went down to ignominious defeat, and Hansen, one of two Germans on the ticket, not only failed to attract German votes for the ticket but even ran behind it in some of the German towns. It was not the Yankees who failed to support him; it was his German compatriots. He no longer was one of them. His war was not their war, his vision of their place in the America created by the war not their vision. One of his stay-at-home brothers would subsequently serve eighteen years as a Democratic county commissioner in a series of German-dominated, inward-looking county governments. George, with his war-gained integrative nationalist perspective, never held local office. He spent his life as a farmer and hotel keeper, haunting the fringes of local politics.[1]

II

In his farewell academic address (*akademische Abschiedsrede*) Erich Angermann issued a resonant call for embedding the interpretation of American history firmly within an "Atlantic" perspective sensitive to the constant interplay between the new nation's ever more autonomous development trajectory and the ceaseless flow of influences among the nations and cultures of the Atlantic basin.[2] The exchange of peoples represents one of the most visible manifestations of such cultural cross-fertilization. A significant part of the case for an American exceptionalism, as Angermann notes, has long rested on America's pre-eminent role as an immigrant nation.[3] Although the burgeoning recent scholarship produced by migration historians on both sides of the Atlantic has undermined America's claim to uniqueness as an immigrant-receiving state, it also has highlighted the significance from a comparative perspective of assessing

---

1 For Hansen family background, see William Bell Mitchell, *History of Stearns County Minnesota* (Chicago, 1915), 1048–9; Stearns County Heritage Center (St. Cloud, Minnesota), Hansen Family Biographical file; and George Hansen's military and pension files (National Archives, Washington, D.C.) which also provide information on his wartime and postwar careers, as does Alonzo L. Brown, *History of the Fourth Regiment of Minnesota Infantry Volunteers during the Great Rebellion 1861–1865* (St. Paul, 1892). For Hansen's letters, see St. Cloud *Democrat* (hereafter SCD), which despite its title was a staunchly Republican organ, May 5, June 2, June 23 (quotation), July 24, Aug. 11, Nov. 17, 1864, Apr. 6, 1865. For the description of Hansen at his homecoming, see SCD July 27, 1865. The election is reported in SCD, Oct. 19, Nov. 9, 1865. Glimpses of Hansen before the war emerge in various court cases generated by the kinds of lives that young Germans were shaping for themselves in the colony; e.g., *State of Minnesota v. Edelbrock*, Stearns County District Court, criminal case files, Minnesota Historical Society (hereafter MHS), St. Paul. His older brother served three years as an engineer in the Prussian army, and that fact, along with his father's Napoleonic service, was prominently mentioned in the family's biographical listing in the county history. Their identification of their home in Germany as "Villa Massingen," suggesting an old estate independent of communal village lands, further hints at the family's sense of social position.
2 Erich Angermann, "Was heisst und zu welchem Ende studiert man anglo-amerikanische Geschichte?" *Historische Zeitschrift* 25 (1993): 638–9, 658–9; see also Hermann Wellenreuther's chapter in this book.
3 Angermann, "Was heisst," 649.

immigrant influences within American society.[4] Yet the immigrant role within even that most central of American institutions, politics, remains particularly underconceptualized.[5]

How, for example, should we interpret the dilemma that George Hansen faced? He was a German immigrant who was purposefully constructing an American identity for himself. But he also was a Catholic peasant who abandoned communal loyalties for national allegiance. It was seemingly his nationalization as much as his Americanization that alienated him from the Minnesota German Catholics among whom he lived. He was a hero to his adopted country. To his local community he was a traitor. Understanding the dilemma created by Hansen's mixed loyalties necessarily takes us deep into the microhistory of his Minnesota community. But scattered across the rural Midwest were numerous other German Catholic communities like Hansen's, whose residents faced similar dilemmas. And it is only the intense localism of the focus itself, I would argue, that permits us to recognize the challenge that immigrant-derived communalism could present to the American state, as well as the critical role of the American Civil War in its precipitation.[6] Why this was so, and the implications for understanding broader connections between transatlantic migration and state-making in the American context, form the subject of this chapter.

We are not accustomed to thinking of American immigration historically in those terms. The unproblematic integration of its agrarian population into the American nation remains an unchallenged bastion of American exceptionalism. Nation-building in Europe may have faced the

---

4 For recent surveys of this transatlantic scholarship, see, e.g., Dirk Hoerder, ed., *Labor Migration in the Atlantic Economies: The European and North American Working Classes During the Period of Industrialization* (Westport, Conn., 1985); Virginia Yans-McLaughlin, ed., *Immigration Reconsidered: History, Sociology, and Politics* (New York, 1990); Rudolph J. Vecoli and Suzanne M. Sinke, eds., *A Century of European Migrations, 1830–1930* (Urbana, Ill., 1991); Nicholas Canny, ed., *Europeans on the Move: Studies in European Migration, 1500–1800* (Oxford, 1994); and, from a specifically German perspective, Dirk Hoerder and Jörg Nagler, eds., *People in Transit: German Migrations in Comparative Perspective, 1820–1930* (New York, 1995).

5 John Higham, "The Future of American History," *Journal of American History* 80 (1994): 1289–309, notes the stateless focus of much immigration historiography. In the community studies so central to the genre, political behavior is often treated as peripheral to the ethnic identity that is the main focus of inquiry, and the implications for the nation at large of the identities that immigrants adopted often remain unexplored. Important exceptions to these strictures include David Gerber, *The Making of an American Pluralism: Buffalo, New York, 1825–1860* (Urbana, Ill., 1989); Gary Gerstle, *Working-Class Americanism: The Politics of Labor in a Textile City, 1914–1960* (Cambridge, 1989); Lizbeth Cohen, *Making a New Deal: Industrial Workers in Chicago, 1919–1939* (Cambridge, 1990).

6 Cf. Higham's critique of the decentered localism of social history microstudies in a world in which we "need to rethink the vehicles of tradition and the agencies of authority"; Higham, "Future of American History," 1304.

problem of converting provincial peasant communalism into national identity and allegiance, of making *Bauern* into *Bürger*, peasants into Frenchmen.[7] But it has seemed absurd even to posit as problematic the making of farmers into "Americans," given the centrality of a largely rural populace in the very creation of the American state. Americans certainly faced the task of gradually converting local allegiances into a sense of national identity – building national walls to belatedly support the roof of state that they had initially constructed, in John Murrin's telling phrase – but this was a task that equally involved all sectors of any given local population.[8] The main American problems were those of crafting a national identity from state and sectional allegiances, and a national citizenry from racial differences, rather than that of converting peasant communalism to a bourgeois conception of nationhood.

Nor, it has seemed, did transatlantic migrants pose any more fundamental a challenge to national integration. "The immigrant," asserted President Ulysses S. Grant in 1872, "is not a citizen of any State or Territory on his arrival, but comes here to become a citizen of a great Republic, free to change his residence at will, to enjoy the blessings of a protecting Government, where all are equal before the law, and to add to the national wealth by his industry. On his arrival he does not know States or corporations, but confides implicitly in the protecting arms of the great, free country of which he has heard so much."[9] Native-born Americans – Grant included – have periodically worried about immigrant threats to the nation's basic institutions and have sought to bar newcomers from public affairs, force their acculturation, or exclude them

7 Eugen Weber, *Peasants into Frenchmen: The Modernization of Rural France, 1870–1914* (Stanford, Calif., 1976); Liah Greenfeld, *Nationalism: Five Roads to Modernity* (Cambridge, Mass., 1992).

8 John Murrin, "A Roof without Walls: The Dilemma of American National Identity," in Richard Beeman, Stephen Botein, and Edward C. Carter II, eds., *Beyond Confederation: Origins of the Constitution and American National Identity* (Chapel Hill, N.C., 1987), 333–48; see also Paul C. Nagel, *This Sacred Trust: American Nationality, 1798–1898* (New York, 1971); Fred Somkin, *"Unquiet Eagle": Memory and Desire in the Idea of American Freedom, 1815–1860* (Ithaca, N.Y., 1967); Philip Gleason, "American Identity and Americanization," in Stephan Thernstrom, ed., *Harvard Encyclopedia of American Ethnic Groups* (Cambridge, Mass., 1980), 150–60.

9 Cited in Hans Kohn, *American Nationalism: An Interpretive Essay* (New York, 1957); re-cited in Greenfeld, *Nationalism*, 560, who notes (434–5), "Even less than Western settlers did immigrants share in the divisive loyalties of the original states . . . their loyalty was to the nation as a whole, which they tended to regard in much more cohesive terms than did the experienced native population. . . . The love of country, allegedly a primary sentiment, was based on the national commitment, rather than generating it." For an interpretation of nineteenth-century German-American discourse on the subject, see Kathleen Neils Conzen, "German-Americans and the Invention of Ethnicity," in Frank Trommler and Joseph McVeigh, eds., *America and the Germans: An Assessment of a Three-Hundred-Year History*, 2 vols. (Philadelphia, 1985), 1:131–47. Ulysses S. Grant in other settings revealed a deep-seated anti-Catholicism and suspicion of immigrants, as Tyler Anbinder has demonstrated in "Ulysses S. Grant, Nativist," *Civil War History* 43 (1997): 119–41.

altogether. Such policies, historians have argued, owed more to broader American fears and delusions than to any actual challenges posed by immigrants themselves.[10] Thus, it is the contours of immigrant political participation that historians have delineated – ethnic electoral preferences, immigrant involvement in machine politics, the relationship between ethnicity and class in labor politics.[11] But what of the immigrant's more fundamental conceptions of the place of the individual within society, and the proper structure and role of the state itself? As Hansen's dilemma makes clear, transatlantic currents could carry new agendas, new conceptions of nationhood, into nineteenth-century American public life, with immediate consequences during the Civil War, and longer-term implications for debating the structure and role of the American state.

The dualisms that confused Hansen's rural German-American identity were cross-cutting rather than congruent. It is conventional to equate the Germany that immigrants like Hansen left with peasant localism and to equate Americanization with nationalization. Hansen's own family may have been moving out of the traditional communal world even before their emigration, as their pride in their military service and social status suggests, a movement that may have contributed to his problematic relationship with his Minnesota community. For the majority of his Stearns County neighbors, however, their departure from Germany was in good part a flight from nationalization – not only from the consequences of a nationalizing economy, but from the impositions of nationalizing states, from state efforts to constrain communal self-governance, collect taxes, oversee the use of fields and forests, control their marriages, conscript their sons, and reshape their religious practices.[12] The appeal of America for

---

10 For the classic statement, and for its author's bemusement that it has remained unchallenged, see John Higham, *Strangers in the Land: Patterns of American Nativism, 1860–1925*, 2d ed. (New Brunswick, N.J., 1988); a recent argument for the coercive role of the state in Americanization can be found in Gary Gerstle, "Liberty, Coercion, and the Making of Americans," *Journal of American History* 84 (1997): 58.

11 For summary discussions of some of this literature, see Ronald P. Formisano, "The Invention of the Ethnocultural Interpretation," *American Historical Review* 99 (1994): 453–77; Steven Erie, *Rainbow's End: Irish Americans and the Dilemmas of Urban Machine Politics, 1840–1985* (Berkeley, Calif., 1988); Richard Oestreicher, "Urban Working-Class Political Behavior and Theories of American Electoral Politics, 1870–1940," *Journal of American History* 74 (1988): 1257–86. For a challenging recent summary of literature on immigration, labor, and race relations, with an eye to its implications for the shaping of the broader American social order, see Russell A. Kazal, "Revisiting Assimilation: The Rise, Fall, and Reappraisal of a Concept in American Ethnic History," *American Historical Review* 100 (1995): 437–71; in *The American Political Nation, 1838–1893* (Stanford, Calif., 1991), Joel H. Silbey effectively integrates ethnocultural factors into his synthesis of nineteenth-century public life.

12 Cf. the peasant grievances discussed in Jonathan Sperber, *Rhineland Radicals: The Democratic Movement and the Revolution of 1848–49* (Princeton, N.J., 1991).

such people was economic, certainly, but it was also political. Germans told the story of an exasperated government official who sarcastically queried a prospective emigrant whether he really believed that in America roasted pigeons would simply fly into his mouth; not really, replied the peasant, "but we know that if it did happen there, we'd be permitted to keep the pigeon."[13] The liberty they celebrated in their letters home was the freedom from government officials telling them what to do.[14] Those most concerned for whatever reasons to reconstruct communal autonomy would have been those most apt to respond to the opportunity to form the isolated and clustered colonies that Minnesota's frontier offered. The Indian missionary whose letters encouraged Stearns County's initial German settlement made the attraction explicit to peasants attempting to make lives for themselves in the nativist America of 1854: "good, pious" German Catholics who desired fertile land, a healthy climate, religious services, like-thinking neighbors, and a refuge from nativism were invited; "work-shy city vagabonds, proud freethinkers, and godless naturalists" were warned away.[15]

Their peasant version of an ideal state, one combining market-driven prosperity with limited external direction or exaction, coincided to a great extent with the loose-knit state they encountered in America, and they found its realization in the abundant land and local self-government of the American frontier. But by the mid-1850s many Americans themselves were questioning the viability of the state held together only by the parties and courts that Jacksonian Democracy had constructed.[16] The old Federalist–Whig countercurrent, with its emphasis on the need for greater centralized governmental promotion of economic development, ran strong within the new Republican Party, bringing with it a parallel logic of cultural integration that resonated with the postmillennial reformism of evangelical Protestantism. Could a democratic society without a shared set of restraining and directing values be trusted to formulate effective centralized policy? And could national regeneration be achieved without

13 Quoted in *Allgemeine Auswanderungs-Zeitung* (Rudolstadt), 48 (Apr. 24, 1851), 191.
14 Wolfgang Helbich, Walter D. Kamphoefner, and Ulrike Sommer, *Briefe aus Amerika: Deutsche Auswanderer schreiben aus der Neuen Welt 1830–1930* (Munich, 1988).
15 Letter of Francis Pierz, Missionary, Crow Wing, Minnesota, to the editor of the *Wahrheitsfreund* (Cincinnati), June 8, 1854, typescript in Pierz papers, MHS. For an introduction to the conscious colonizing that scattered German Catholic colonies throughout the middle west, see Sister Mary Gilbert Kelly, O.P., *Catholic Immigrant Colonization Projects in the United States, 1815–1860* (New York, 1939); scholarship has failed to adequately address the issue of the selectivity of migrants attracted to various kinds of settlements.
16 The description is that of Stephen Skowronek, *Building a New American State: The Expansion of National Administrative Capacities, 1877–1920* (Cambridge, 1992).

central direction?[17] The Jacksonian Democrats, by contrast, envisaged the state not as an organic, integrated whole but as a loosely articulated web of communities whose local values and shared white race were the only possible and necessary guarantors for the virtue and common interests of the restless profit-seekers who moved through them. They thus were also the most appropriate sites for policy making, and in such a context, national integration could mean only special privileges for some rather than opportunity for all. These assumptions found renewed expression in Stephen Douglas's squatter sovereignty and his "Freeport Doctrine" affirmation that national policy was meaningless without local support, as Jean Baker has noted.[18]

Historians, enmeshed in part in a "Civil War synthesis" that sees sectional and slavery-related issues as dominating antebellum politics and implicitly regards Republican-led abolitionism as the only rational and moral choice for antebellum northerners, have been hard-pressed to account for the patent preference of so many immigrants, including most German Catholics, for the Democratic Party.[19] Immigrants were misled by the populism of the party's rhetoric and name, they have suggested, or entrapped by habit and patronage, or diverted by racism; or they sought refuge among the Democrats from the nativism with which the Republicans were tinged, or from Republican temperance and Sabbatarian proclivities. The immigrants who opted for the Democratic vision of America, seemingly, were variously deluded, venal, frightened, or merely pleasure-seeking – judgments that curiously echo nineteenth-century dismissals of immigrants as "voting cattle." Any ideological basis for their stance lay in the fact that as priest-led "liturgicals" they remained pro-

17 Daniel Walker Howe, *The Political Culture of the American Whigs* (Chicago, 1979); Daniel Walker Howe, "The Evangelical Movement and Political Culture in the North During the Second Party System," *Journal of American History* 77 (1991): 1216–39; Tyler Anbinder, *Nativism and Slavery: The Northern Know-Nothings and the Politics of the 1850s* (New York, 1992); William E. Gienapp, *The Origins of the Republican Party, 1852–1856* (New York, 1987); Richard J. Cawardine, *Evangelicals and Politics in Antebellum America* (New Haven, Conn., 1993).

18 Jean H. Baker, *Affairs of Party: The Political Culture of Northern Democrats in the Mid-Nineteenth Century* (Ithaca, N.Y., 1983); see also Joel H. Silbey, *A Respectable Minority: The Democratic Party in the Civil War Era, 1860–1868* (New York, 1977).

19 Joel H. Silbey in "The Civil War Synthesis and American Political History," *Civil War History* 10 (1964): 130–40, reprinted in Joel H. Silbey, *The Partisan Imperative: The Dynamics of American Politics Before the Civil War* (New York, 1985), 3–12, noted the extent to which the focus on sectional issues was blinding historians of the period to the salience of other kinds of issues, including those related to religion and ethnicity. Subsequent efforts of the so-called "ethnocultural school" of historians to address such issues collided with revivified concerns to underscore the centrality of the slavery issue to national politics, and were inhibited by the paucity of studies directly addressing the political cultures and mentalities of immigrant voters themselves.

foundly skeptical of any kind of earthly reform.[20] All these factors may well have played a role. But as far as rural German Catholic communities like Stearns County were concerned, a Milwaukee German Democratic newspaper came closer to the mark in an 1860 editorial. Stephen Douglas, it argued, represented "the principle of the right of communities – be they states or territories [or by extension, more local units, his readers would have inferred] – to regulate their internal affairs according to their own standards."[21]

Douglas lost the 1860 presidential election, of course, and a Republican-led war for the Union followed. That war, German-American spokesmen soon argued, was a formative event in the ethnic group's development, its contributions to Union victory exhibiting its strength and unity and confirming its positive place in American society.[22] Although subsequent scholarship has deflated filiopietistic claims of exceptional wartime service – Germans were overrepresented only among the draftees and bounty enlistments of the later years of the war and underrepresented among the volunteers – it has tended to retain the insistence that the Civil War represented a critical stage in the integration of German immigrants and their acceptance by American society.[23] For the liberal Forty-Eighters who dominated German-American leadership circles and public discourse, the war completed a decisive shift of focus from German to American concerns; an American state without slavery was one to which they could finally give wholehearted allegiance. The heightened group consciousness and unity provoked by wartime defense of the treatment and reputation of German-born soldiers and generals encouraged the ethnicization that proved an important intermediate phase in the evolution from immigrant to American. And the group's demonstrable share in the great national project certainly eased immediate

20 E.g., Paul Kleppner, *The Cross of Culture: A Social Analysis of Midwestern Politics, 1850–1900* (New York, 1970); Richard J. Jensen, *The Winning of the Midwest: Social and Political Conflict, 1888–1896* (Chicago, 1971); see also the summary discussion in Robert P. Swierenga, "Ethnoreligious Political Behavior in the Mid-Nineteenth Century: Voting, Values, Cultures," in Mark A. Noll, ed., *Religion and American Politics: From the Colonial Period to the 1980s* (New York, 1990), 146–71.

21 *Tägliches Banner und Volksfreund* (Milwaukee), June 27, 1860.

22 E.g., Daniel Hertle, *Die Deutschen in Nordamerika und der Freiheitskampf in Missouri* (Chicago, 1865); Benno Haberland, *Das deutsche Element in den Vereinigten Staaten von Nord-Amerika* (Leipzig, 1866); J. G. Rosengarten, *The German Soldier in the Wars of the United States* (Philadelphia, 1886); Wilhelm Hense-Jensen, *Wisconsin's Deutsch-Amerikaner bis zum Schluss des neunzehnten Jahrhunderts* (Milwaukee, 1900); Wilhelm Kaufmann, *Die Deutschen im amerikanischen Bürgerkriege* (Munich, 1911).

23 For the wartime service record, see Ella Lonn, *Foreigners in the Union Army and Navy* (Baton Rouge, La., 1951), 493, 606–7; William L. Burton, *Melting Pot Soldiers: The Union's Ethnic Regiments* (Ames, Iowa, 1988); James M. McPherson, *Battle Cry of Freedom: The Civil War Era* (New York, 1988), 493, 606–7.

nativism and moderated negative group stereotypes.[24] Whereas scholars have noted the incidence of draft resistance among rural German Catholics in particular, they have failed to query either its roots or its consequences.[25]

Those consequences, the Stearns County case suggests, were lasting and significant. Before the war the local communalism German Catholics sought was appropriate for citizens of the American world they found. The war brought home to them the realities of life in the New World that the Republicans were struggling to make – realities that took an all too familiar form of higher taxes, conscription, diminished local autonomy, even midnight government raids on their homes. Although the new nationalism would remain, the new state would again recede until the end of the century.[26] But in Stearns County it left in its wake the implacable resentment that George Hansen encountered, an abiding determination to construct walls of communal autonomy strong enough to withstand the pressures of an alien state, and an oppositional stance toward the state itself. The war, in effect, turned gradually nationalizing peasants into stubborn localists by shifting the defining locus of the nation itself.

III

The depth of the wartime trauma can be understood only in comparison with the optimistic local integration of the prewar period. German

24 Ella Lonn, "The Forty-Eighters in the Civil War," in A. E. Zucker, ed., *The Forty-Eighters: Political Refugees of the German Revolution of 1848* (New York, 1950), 182–220; Carl Wittke, *Refugees of Revolution* (Philadelphia, 1952); Jörg Nagler, *Fremont contra Lincoln: Die deutsch-amerikanische Opposition in der Republikanischen Partei während des amerikanisches Bürgerkrieges* (Frankfurt am Main, 1984); Bruce Levine, *The Spirit of 1848: German Immigrants, Labor Conflict, and the Coming of the Civil War* (Urbana, Ill., 1992); Marino Mania, *Deutsches Herz und amerikanischer Verstand: Die nationale und kulturelle Identität der Achtundvierziger in den U.S.A.* (Frankfurt am Main, 1993); Stephen D. Engle, *Yankee Dutchman: The Life of Franz Sigel* (Fayetteville, Ark., 1993). Interestingly, most published monographic studies with detailed focus on nineteenth-century German-American communities either end before or begin after the U.S. Civil War; e.g., see Kathleen Neils Conzen, *Immigrant Milwaukee, 1836–1860: Accommodation and Community in a Frontier City* (Cambridge, Mass., 1976); Gerber, *Making of an American Pluralism*; Walter D. Kamphoefner, *The Westfalians: From Germany to Missouri* (Princeton, N.J., 1987); S. J. Kleinberg, *The Shadow of the Mills: Working-Class Families in Pittsburgh, 1870–1907* (Pittsburgh, 1989); Stanley Nadel, *Little Germany: Ethnicity, Religion, and Class in New York City, 1845–80* (Urbana, Ill., 1990) spans the period, but mentions the Civil War only in passing, and fails to probe its implications for the ethnic community.

25 E.g., Frank L. Klement, "Catholics as Copperheads During the Civil War," *Catholic Historical Review* 80 (1994): 36–57, finds in traditional accounts for why Catholics became Democrats an explanation for their wartime behavior, stressing racism in particular.

26 Richard F. Bensel, *Yankee Leviathan: The Origins of Central State Authority in America, 1859–1877* (Cambridge, 1990); Morton Keller, *Affairs of State: Public Life in Late Nineteenth-Century America* (Cambridge, Mass., 1977).

Catholic migration to the unsettled wilderness of Minnesota – initially from other Catholic colonies in America, soon directly from Germany itself – began in the autumn of 1854. Almost from the outset the new county had a German Catholic majority that by 1860, when the county's total population stood at 4,505, included close to 58 percent of the males of voting age.[27] Four fundamental factors shaped the emergent political culture of the German Catholics of Stearns County and its wartime reorientation: their Catholicism, the structure of rural government, their imported assumptions about governance, and the local context of party politics.

Catholicism may have played one of its most important roles by defining the fundamental logic of settlement itself. Prolonged resistance to the rationalizing forces within eighteenth-century German Catholicism, to Napoleonic-era secularization, and to the revolutionary upsets that followed lent a certain chiliastic fervor to Germany's peasant Catholicism that was only strengthened by the Church's nineteenth-century devotional revival.[28] Family, farming, and faith were bound by tradition and practice into a seemingly inseparable trinity in which each became necessary to reinforce the other. The first major Catholic emigrations of the 1830s and 1840s sought not only plentiful land but insulation from non-Catholic contamination, and the numerous colonies they established throughout the Midwest and Texas were more than just accidental by-products of chain migrations from Catholic areas. Catholic channels of communication – newspapers, visiting missionaries, letters among priests – stimulated their initial formation, while European Catholic mission societies financed the provision of religious services and structures, and American bishops

---

27 Tabulation of German-born males 21 and over, 1860 federal manuscript census, Stearns County, Minnesota. All evidence suggests that few of these Germans were anything but Catholic; there were some German Protestants to be found in the St. Cloud business community, and two small Protestant settlements on the fringes of the county that by 1860 may have accounted for at most a couple dozen voters. Native-born Americans constituted 32 percent of the voters (this number also includes a few men who were born in the U.S. of German parentage and whose religion and residence placed them culturally among the Germans); predominantly Protestant Maritimers and British constituted another 4 percent, as did generally Catholic Irish and French Canadians. Other immigrants, mainly Scandinavian (1.4 percent) and "unknown," accounted for the remainder of the electorate. Minnesota permitted foreign-born white males to vote provided they had filed their declaration of intent to become citizens; since most Stearns County Germans filed such papers at the same time that they filed their federal land claims, this provision probably excluded very few from the suffrage.

28 Wolfgang Schieder, "Kirche und Revolution: Sozialgeschichtliche Aspekte der Trierer Wallfahrt von 1844," *Archiv für Sozialgeschichte* 14 (1974): 169–95; Jonathan Sperber, *Popular Catholicism in Nineteenth-Century Germany* (Princeton, N.J., 1984); Margaret Lavinia Anderson, "Piety and Politics: Recent Work on German Catholicism," *Journal of Modern History* 63 (1991): 681–716, provides a guide to the voluminous recent literature.

and priests guided inquiring immigrants to the nearest rural colony, creating large and heterogeneous communities united less by kinship and close common origin than by language and peasant religiosity.[29]

The Stearns County settlement eventually grew to encompass thirty separate Catholic parishes whose members dominated a 650-square mile rural core that by 1880 remained more than 80 percent German by birth and parentage.[30] At its heart as early as 1857 were a Benedictine abbey and convent. Early on precious resources were poured into churches, bells, and mission crosses, and the rhythms of prayer and religious procession joined with those of frontier farm-making and weekly conviviality to structure local life.[31] Stearns County settlers subscribed to German-language Catholic journals like Cincinnati's *Wahrheitsfreund* and Milwaukee's *Seebote* (as well as St. Paul's *Der Wanderer* after 1867), and relied on priests for secular as well as religious leadership. Benedictines sat on local school boards, served as town clerks, even captained local militias during the Indian uprising of 1862. Priestly numbers were always too few, and lay people were often left to organize the first parishes and conduct the initial services on their own. But there can be little question that Catholicism, in the form of institutional church as well as pious belief and practice, permeated virtually every aspect of Sauk Valley life.[32]

Dominating entire townships as their settlement imperative insured, these German Catholics could enjoy the benefit of democratic self-government. The federal survey township was the basic unit of local government, and at annual town and school district meetings these immigrants had to elect officers, decide on roads and bridges, regulate stray animals, license peddlers, provide for their poor, and set their local tax rates. They elected their own justices of the peace, set school terms, taxes, and curricula, built the schools and hired the teachers. Nor were the duties of county governance any less inescapable. Jury duty quickly

---

29 Kelly, *Catholic Immigrant Colonization Projects*; Benjamin J. Blied, *Austrian Aid to American Catholics, 1830–1860* (Milwaukee, 1944); Kathleen Neils Conzen, "German Catholics in America," in Michael Glazier and Thomas J. Shelley, eds., *Encyclopedia of American Catholic History* (Collegeville, Minn., 1997), 571–83.

30 Tabulation of the 1880 manuscript population census. For an overview interpretation of the development of this settlement, see Kathleen Neils Conzen, "Making Their Own America: Assimilation Theory and the German Peasant Pioneer," German Historical Institute, Washington, D.C., Annual Lecture series, no. 3 (New York, 1990), 1–33.

31 Colman J. Barry, *Worship and Work: Saint John's Abbey and University, 1856–1956* (Collegeville, Minn., 1956); Sister M. Grace McDonald, *With Lamps Burning* (St. Joseph, Minn., 1957).

32 Father Bruno Reiss, "Memoirs," holograph, St. John's Abbey Archives (hereafter SJAA), Collegeville, Minn., provides a rich narrative of the activities of an early Benedictine who worked among the German immigrants of Stearns County during this period.

acquainted the newcomer with another facet of democratic self-governance, while the uncertainties of frontier land titles, credit arrangements, and personal relationships made the ordering role of the court only too immediate. County government in its other guises had an equally direct impact as it surveyed land, valued property, collected taxes, supervised the transmission of estates, regulated morality, and maintained the peace.[33] Nor was access to state or federal government irrelevant even to isolation-seeking peasants. The federal government regulated land claims, distributed postmasterships, and provided much needed markets through Indian reservation and army supply contracts, while the state hoarded the promise of railroad routes. To achieve the goals for which they came to Minnesota, German Catholics had to pay attention to politics and become actively involved in self-government.

They were not without previous political experience to guide them. In these early years of settlement most had spent time elsewhere in the United States, where a similar logic of governance had already socialized them to the American system. But their German experiences too stood them in good stead. Although few may have ever voted in a national election, most were familiar with some level of parish and village self-governance, and with the village's jealousy of its own rights and its collective habits of resistance, litigation, and negotiation with higher and often hostile levels of government. They may have been unused to self-governance and politics in the American mode, but they had well-formed conceptions of property and order, of the proper purposes and principles of government, and of the ideal relationship of the individual to the community and to the state that would inevitably influence their actions in America.[34]

Nor were Stearns County's German Catholics left to work out their political accommodation in a vacuum. Although the first German pioneers arrived before there were barely a dozen permanent settlers in the county, a power structure was already in place, inherited in part from the fur trade era, in part generated by the promise of settlement itself. A

---

33 Kathleen Neils Conzen, "German-Americans and Ethnic Political Culture: Stearns County, Minnesota, 1855–1915," Working Paper series, no. 16, John F. Kennedy Institute for North American Studies, Free University of Berlin, 1989. The St. Cloud and St. Augusta Township Minute Books, Stearns County Heritage Center (hereafter SCHC), St. Cloud, Minn., are a rich source for the functioning of local governments in the German settlements; *Cram v. Burghardt*, Stearns County District Court, civil case files, MHS, documents the significance Germans attached to county-level governance.

34 Conzen, "German-Americans and Ethnic Political Culture"; A. G. Roeber, *Palatines, Liberty, and Property: German Lutherans in Colonial British America* (Baltimore, 1993) is an important explication of this issue in an earlier context.

cluster of Indian traders had located in the area in 1848, and when Indian title was cleared in 1854, these founding members of what came to be called the local Moccasin Democracy moved quickly to consolidate land claims, plan townsites, and monopolize government offices and contracts.[35] The territorial spoils system insured that many of the area's subsequent Yankee migrants were Democrats drawn by their ties to this Moccasin ascendancy, although the new county's promise soon attracted others of a different political persuasion as well: particularly abolitionist Yankees from Ohio's Western Reserve seeking farms for their growing families, Downeasters who made county farms a base for logging operations in the pineries to the north, and Pittsburgh-area Pennsylvania Dutch entrepreneurs with ties to an earlier Whig territorial governor.[36]

Most of the Germans probably already regarded themselves as Democrats on arrival, for reasons already discussed. The Pennsylvanians, many of whom shared the language and drinking habits if not the religion of the immigrants, might have had some success in altering that allegiance in Minnesota's more tolerant political climate, but the Moccasin ascendancy never gave them a chance.[37] First, the Moccasins drew the Germans quickly into the distribution of local offices. When the first Democratic county convention met in August of 1855, a German was called to the chair, another was among the three candidates for county commissioner, yet another was nominated for sheriff, and another claimed the treasurer's slot. Two years later, the latter was one of the seven Democrats and one Republican representing the upper country in Minnesota's constitutional convention.[38] When some within the party attempted to block a German candidate running for registrar of deeds later that year on grounds that "the Germans are trying to control, and they must be put down," the editor of the local Democratic paper observed that, "A majority of the voters in Stearns County are German, but they have asked to have none of their number nominated either for Senator or Representative, as they justly might have done, but have put forward Americans and have supported them heartily for those offices." Some expressly noted that the

---

35 This story can best be followed through correspondence in the Henry Sibley papers, MHS, and in Letters Received, Winnebago Agency and Minnesota Superintendency, Bureau of Indian Affairs, NARS microfilm. See Kathleen Neils Conzen, "The Winnebago Urban System: Indian Policy and Townsite Promotion on the Upper Mississippi," in Rondo Cameron and Leo F. Schnore, eds., *Cities and Markets: Studies in the Organization of Human Space* (Lanham, Md., 1997), 269–310.

36 These statements are based on biographical tracing of all county residents present in 1857 when a territorial census was taken.

37 E.g., SCD Sept. 2, 1861.

38 Sauk Rapids (Minnesota) *Frontiersman* (hereafter SRF), Sept. 6, 20, 1855; Mitchell, *Stearns County*, 48.

Moccasin alliance was all that kept Germans from totally commandeering the county.[39]

Local Republicans might jeer that no free people on earth were so "trained to habits of veneration and obedience" as these German Catholics, but in return for single-minded loyalty at the polls, Germans received from the Moccasin Democracy more than mere status affirmation. The county offices that they tended to claim as their due in the antebellum years – registrar of deeds, treasurer, and sheriff – were those that most immediately affected their ability to direct the farm and family affairs that lay closest to the heart of their culture, although by 1859 only the auditor, the district attorney, and the probate judge among countywide officials were still Yankee.[40] Postmasterships who insured that addresses could be read and that trade would flow to German villages, ferry franchises and courthouse construction contracts, a colonelcy in the new state's paper militia, a share in federal supply contracts, low saloon license fees – these were all benefits that flowed from the alliance with the Moccasin Democracy. When Indians bothered German farmers, they went to the Moccasins to get them to move away. Land claim contests were fended off and influence was exerted in Washington to postpone payments for preempted land.[41]

The system rested less on shared ideology than on mutual interest in the region's economic development. But Germans were not passive partners when their vision for the community they were constructing collided with Moccasin boosterism. Thus, in late 1857 Germans angered their local allies when they sent representatives down river to seek donations of food and seed grain following a disastrous grasshopper infestation; this was airing dirty linen in public. "The famine here appears to be Democratic thunder," the local Republican editor insisted. "The German Catholics hold the balance of power in this county. They insist on their right to contributions from abroad, for which the Republicans and a portion of the Democrats deny the necessity."[42] Similar concerns were expressed when the struggling German farmers failed to support a railroad loan bill.[43] Germans also were caught up in the Lecomptonite split within the Democracy, when Anti-Lecomptonites presented themselves locally as "conservative" reformers fighting Moccasin corruption.[44] Nevertheless, any German Catholic who broke completely with the Democ-

39 SRF Oct 8, 1857; SCD Oct. 7, 1858.   40 SRF Sept. 29, Oct. 20, 1859.
41 SCD Mar. 24, 1859, SRF Mar. 4, 1858, SCD Aug. 11, 1859, SCD Sept. 8, 1859.
42 St. Cloud *Visiter* (hereafter SCV), Dec. 10, 1857.
43 SRF Mar. 18, 1858.   44 SCD Oct. 7, 14, 31, 1858.

racy could expect to receive scurrilous personal criticism from his compatriots, and there is no better indicator of the strength of the alliance
between Germans and Moccasins than the manner in which, in 1861 and
1862, the county's Germans marched to war: under the aegis of the
Democracy, in two locally recruited companies that united German
Catholics with fur trade-connected Yankees, French Canadians, and mixed
and full-blood Ojibwas – Democrats all – with an officers' roster as ethnically balanced as any ticket the party ever fielded.[45]

Although county Republicans explicitly rejected nativism, they
demanded a level of cultural conformity fundamentally at odds with the
entire ethnoreligious logic of the German settlement process. "I care not
where a man is born," rhymed a local Republican lawyer and banker,
"since birth is accidental/ The question is, doth he adorn/ Both physical
and mental/ For if he does, I'll chance the rest/ And from some point
above him/ I'll try my very *very* best/ to make a Yankee of him."[46] By
contrast, Moccasin Democracy offered German Catholics a free-
wheeling, tolerant, sometimes cynical, and frequently profitable initiation
into the frontier version of the patronage politics of the machine. In
return for their reliable support at the polls it assured them a willing
partner in local government and a powerful patron to promote and
protect their interests at higher levels of government.[47] In a process of
pluralistic integration, their cultural distinctiveness was acknowledged and
used to draw them as a group into the core elements of the loose-knit
state while they used the powers of the state, such as it was, to help build
their own community.

But the system's efficient functioning depended on access to power and

45 SCD Nov. 15, 1860; collective biographies of the officers and men of Company G, 4th Minnesota, and Company G, 9th Minnesota, based on military and pension records at the National
Archives, county histories, and manuscript census entries. The Minnesota state constitution gave
the franchise not only to unnaturalized immigrants but also to mixed-blood and "civilized" full-
blood Indians.

46 Henry C. Waite, holograph, Waite papers, MHS; this undated poem encapsulates the general stance
taken toward the area's Germans by Republican editor Jane Grey Swisshelm in SCV throughout
the prewar period. Waite himself after the Civil War became a convert to Catholicism and an
important power broker between the local German Catholic community and the state Republican ascendancy.

47 I have not attempted here to statistically correlate party preference with ethnicity in county elections for two reasons: neither the 1857 nor the 1860 ms. censuses reported the population according to the township boundaries that formed the basis for election reporting precincts, and by all
accounts the population fluctuated widely from year to year, owing in particular to the effects of
the 1857 depression and the 1862 Indian uprising. However, an effort to chart the 1857 and 1860
census-taker's route using initial land claims and plat maps from 1876 for guidance, suggests that
there is little reason to doubt contemporary commentators' assumptions that the extremely lop-
sided township-level election returns that characterized every election in this period, mirrored
fairly accurately the ethnic distribution of the various towns' populations.

favor that was already waning by the beginning of the Civil War. The election of 1859 had confirmed the young state's decisive shift into the Republican column, thanks in part to increased Yankee migrations and to the influence of national political trends, but thanks also to the end of territorial status with its dependence on the party in power in Washington. The war only hastened this transfer of power, and not until 1898 would anyone other than a Republican again sit in the governor's chair; not until 1912 would a Republican presidential candidate fail to carry the state. Minnesota became to all intents and purposes a one-party state.[48] Stearns County's German Catholics were losing their protective umbrella and soon felt the rain. Land disputes that had simmered for years, for example, were now settled in 1862 and 1863 in favor of Yankee claimants; a good portion of the German lot titles in St. Cloud were invalidated, and owners had to pay again to retain their homes, while the Benedictines were forced to vacate their city site altogether and move their monastery to the country. Feelings ran so high that one of the successful claimants asserted that it was impossible for him to receive a fair trial in the county because he was a "native American" and his opponent a "German" – descriptive terms that in the original brief had read "native American Protestant" and "German Catholic" but were then crossed out when better judgment prevailed.[49]

But it was not only the shift in political party dominance that affected the Germans. It was the war itself and the enhanced state powers with which it was fought. There is virtually no direct evidence for local German Catholic attitudes to the war. There was no German Catholic newspaper in the state until 1867, the county's Germans would not support their own press until the middle 1870s, and even the St. Cloud parish book of mass announcements for the period is silent on the subject of prayers for victory or peace.[50] That silence is itself suggestive, however. Thanks to the Lecomptonite controversy we know that there were German Catholics in Stearns County who held firm anti-slavery convictions, but for most, slavery was a distant issue, one about which their church had few strong negative feelings, and one that seemed irrelevant to their own community-forming project.[51] Union as the fundamental

48 William Watts Folwell, *A History of Minnesota*, 4 vols. (St. Paul, 1924), vol. 2; see also Bruce M. White et al., compilers, *Minnesota Votes: Election Returns by County for Presidents, Senators, Congressmen, and Governors, 1857–1977* (St. Paul, 1977).
49 *Cram v. Burghardt*; see also Barry, *Worship and Work,* 47–83, passim.
50 St. Mary's Parish, St. Cloud, Mass Announcement Book, SJAA.
51 Cf. Benjamin J. Blied, *Catholics and the Civil War* (Milwaukee, 1945).

basis for the right of self-government – the prime value worth fighting for in the war, according to the local Democratic editor – was a concept they could understand and support, but not, they argued when their militia company refused to respond to the governor's call for mobilization in the spring of 1861, at the expense of families eking out a living on marginal farms at the edge of Indian country.[52]

One result was a dramatic difference in both the incidence and the character of Yankee and German military service. Only 24 percent of the 365 soldiers credited to Stearns County during the war were German. Those who served in the two main Yankee Republican companies recruited in the county acted as representatives of their communities; those in the two German Democratic companies were effectively hostages for theirs. One Yankee company was recruited mainly among the farmers' sons of the Maine Prairie area, the other among the farmer-loggers of the Downeast settlement to the north. Their officers in both cases were community leaders – the local minister captained the Maine Prairie boys, the biggest sawmill owner led the men of the north. Community organizations oversaw their welfare and that of their families while they were away, and community provision of enlistment bounties and substitutes insulated those who remained behind from the consequences of the draft. By contrast, it took a concerted campaign of public shame to recruit the first German company in the autumn of 1861, and the threat of the draft to stimulate the second the following summer. Their commanders, while German, were not members of the rural communities from which the ranks were largely recruited, but St. Cloud businessmen who were also Prussian army veterans. Both, significantly, were Protestant. The two oldest rural German settlements and the city of St. Cloud were able to raise money for bounties and substitutes, although they had to do it through bonds issued against future taxation revenue rather than through voluntary subscription like their Yankee neighbors, but most of the other German townships lacked the resources to do anything other than let the draft run its course. Seventy-one percent of the draftees and substitutes credited to the county were German; draftees, substitutes, and late bounty recruits constituted 47 percent of the county's German contingent. The two groups differed even in the form of their service during the Indian uprising of 1862: The Yankees organized two cavalry companies that were formally mustered into state service, while the Germans remained behind, uncredited and later unpensioned, to man the Home Guard. If there was

52 St. Cloud *Union* (hereafter SCU), July 1861; SCD, Apr. 25 and May 2, 1861.

a positive reason why Germans enlisted after the initial months of the war, it lay in the bounty system: They were gambling their lives for a farm.[53]

The consequence of such attitudes became evident as Stearns County began to face the prospect of a military draft in the winter of 1863–4. The state provost marshal's office was securely in Republican hands, insuring that both the local deputy provost marshal and the enrolling officers in each town were Republicans and, with only two exceptions, Yankees. Some fifty Germans, the deputy provost marshal reported at Christmas, had formed a secret organization to resist the draft. "I shall endevour [sic] to get all of their secrets without exciting their suspicion," he assured his superiors.[54] The level of popular feeling against the draft ran so high that it spilled over into barroom brawls and a farcical duel between a returned German soldier and a Yankee officer stationed in the area, and led another officer to assert that "there is not one spark of loyalty or genuine unionism in the place."[55] The joint Yankee-German Fourth of July celebrations that had characterized the prewar years were a thing of the past. Fraud, flight, and other forms of evasion accompanied the October 1864 draft; a "wanted" poster offering a $30 dollar reward for information leading to the arrest of county draft evaders contained the names of fifty-one Germans, three Irish, and only two American-born. "In no single instance," complained the deputy provost marshal, "can I prevail on an Enrolling Officer to serve a single notice, or render any assistance. They are intimidated by threats from the German population. And these Germans are so completely banded together, men, women, and children, that they will give no information of any kind whatever. They even deny their own names, and in many instances assume another."[56] There were never full-fledged draft riots in the county, thanks to the soldiers stationed at three forts within the county to deter Indian attack. Instead, Germans

---

53 These patterns are derived from the analysis of company rosters described above, from wartime reporting in the local press (SCD, SCU, SCT), and from Minute Books for the towns of St. Cloud and St. Augusta (SCHC). Full documentation would be too extensive to cite. Extreme fluctuations in the county's population after the 1860 census – first from the influx of new settlers, then from the exodus following the Indian uprising, then from resettlement that picked up speed in the summer of 1864 – make it almost impossible to establish a base from which to calculate formal rates of recruitment from the different sectors of the eligible population; what is clear is the definite underrepresentation of the Germans, as the experience with the draft to be discussed below confirms.

54 Z. Morse to Minnesota State Provost Marshal, Dec. 25, 1863, Provost Marshal Records (hereafter PMR), Minnesota, record group 111, NARS.

55 SCU, Mar. 17, 1864.

56 Morse to Provost Marshal, Nov. 20, 1864, PMR.

fled to Canada or hid out in the bush near their homes, sleeping in one another's cabins at night, leaving their wives to fend off inquiring officers with pitchforks, and staging intimidating raids on countrymen suspected of informing on them. Midnight raids by troops from the forts became a fact of life in the county.[57] The official credence given to a bizarre rumor that county Germans knew of Lincoln's assassination the day before it occurred, and were obviously in league with the Catholics in Booth's conspiracy, grew perhaps inevitably out of these two years of turmoil.[58]

In the midst of that turmoil, Stearns County's Germans inevitably supported George McClellan rather than "Wittwenmacher" Lincoln – the creator of war widows – in the 1864 presidential election. The campaign, the local English-language Democratic newspaper thundered, was a crusade "to prevent our threatened institutions from being submerged in the whirlpool of war, extravagance and fanaticism." St. Paul's German-language Democratic paper, to which influential county Germans subscribed, similarly defined the issues in terms not only of arbitrary federal power but of high taxes, corruption, and families left alone to starve when their men were dragged from their arms. It also played the race card ever more strongly, emphasizing in particular the willingness of the Lincoln administration to let northern soldiers rot in southern prisons – there were significant numbers of Minnesota German boys, including close to a dozen from Stearns County, dying in Andersonville, Georgia – because the South would not agree to treat captured black Union soldiers as prisoners of war.[59] Needless to say, McCllellan carried Minnesota Democracy's banner county.

The wartime experience was a powerful lesson in the vulnerability of the local community to outside control. It produced an equally potent demonstration of the kinds of defensive weapons the community had at its disposal. The sheriff could refuse to serve warrants, justices of the peace could refuse to remand, grand juries could refuse to indict, juries if forced by law and evidence to convict could set ridiculously low damages – all tactics that were used in the resistance effort against the draft, and all possible owing to local political control.[60] Germans also, and not coinciden-

---

57 The story can be followed in the Provost Marshal files, local newspapers, and court cases, particularly _Linneman v. Kulzer et al._, Stearns County District Court, civil case files, box 1, MHS.
58 PMR.
59 SCU, Feb. 25, 1864; St. Paul _Volks Blatt_, July 12, Sept. 24, Oct. 18, Nov. 5, 1864.
60 _State of Minnesota v. Kulzer, Cram v. Burkhardt, R. I. Cromwell v. Kramer et al._; District Court case files, MHS.

tally, used their wartime dominance of local government to reduce the liquor license fee from $50 to $10.[61]

There may be no better symbol of the new political order that the war produced than Stearns County's refusal to support that old Moccasin half-breed war horse, Peter Roy, in his 1865 race for state representative, despite their support for the rest of the ticket; the old Moccasin alliance was finished.[62] But it was, ironically, returning German soldiers like George Hansen who were some of the first to experience the lasting political consequences of the county's wartime purgatory. Historians, I have noted, have often argued that the Civil War had the effect of Americanizing many of the immigrants who fought in it and drawing their communities more closely into the broader local society. But for most of the German "boys" from Stearns, the dual alienation that marked their mustering in – alienation from the patriotism of their fellow soldiers and from the pacifism of their own community – seems to have followed them through the war. Few chose to veteranize, and when they returned, most seem to have done their best simply to blend back in; disproportionately few joined the Grand Army of the Republic (GAR), attended regimental reunions, or even kept regimental organizations informed of their addresses.[63] There has never been a Civil War soldier's statue adorning the county's courthouse square. Republicans after the war could count on German votes in the few Protestant pockets in the county. They never fully abandoned their hope of using veterans – if they had "suffered the miseries of a Southern prison," all the better – to reach other German Catholics, their attempts to recruit disgruntled Catholic office seekers, or their promotion of local Union, Citizens, and Peoples tickets. Such efforts, however, usually proved fruitless.[64] The despair and suicide of one German Catholic former officer in a colored regiment following the county's rejection of his attempt to publish a German Republican newspaper was a tragic marker of the passionate resentment that survived the war.[65]

---

61 Mitchell, *Stearns County,* 103.
62 SCT Oct. 1865.
63 Mitchell, *Stearns County,* 1465–7; Bishop, *Fourth Minnesota: Ninth Minnesota Regimental Reunion Souvenir Address Books,* MHS. The comments concerning alienation within their regiments derive from efforts to trace the wartime experiences of members of the two German companies through official records, military and pension files, and memoirs and letters of others in these regiments; the complete lack of surviving personal accounts of the war from any of these county German veterans is itself indicative. Catholic suspicion about the GAR as a secret organization also deterred German membership.
64 E.g., numerous letters from 1866 through 1868 in Christopher Columbus Andrews, Letter Press Book, vol. 77, Andrews papers, MHS; St. Cloud *Journal,* Oct. 24, 1867, Sept. 17, 1868.
65 Frederick E. Schilplin pension file, NARS.

Der Wanderer, the new German Catholic paper in the state capital founded by one of Stearns County's Benedictines and read by dozens of households in every Stearns County parish, defined the issues in the 1868 presidential elections in terms that were unmistakably resonant to anyone who had lived through the war in the county. The issues, the *Wanderer* insisted, were "too much governance, arbitrary exercise of power, political corruption" (*Zuvielregieren, Willkürherrschaft, politische Fäulnis*). The purpose of the U.S. Constitution was to secure completely the "local interests" of each state, thereby also insuring the flourishing and prosperity of the whole nation and the enjoyment of freedom, creating a nation where the immigrant, "instead of taxes and oppression," would find "a simple, cheap, almost unnoticeable, yet powerfully protecting and beneficial government. The true functions of a government are few and simple." Instead, German readers learned, the Republicans were offering not only high taxes, shoddyism, and bribery, but the same militarism that had led to the downfall of the Roman republic. Paraphrasing a familiar German nationalist poem, a correspondent asked, "What defines the Union as a free nation?" ("Was ist der Union freies Land?"). His answer: A country where everyone does his duty and does not waste time shouting about Negro suffrage, where the law has a free hand, where rich and poor have the same rights, where subjugation is banished and factory owners and bondholders have to pay cash when the tax collector comes – in short, the old Union but without slavery.[66]

The postwar German Catholic political order, it quickly became clear, would rest on two fundamental principles: absolute refusal to support at the polls anyone or anything that looked Republican, and tenacious control of those areas of county government that Germans required to shape and defend their distinctive way of life. This meant continued control of tax assessment and collection procedures – "the Germans of the county should never underestimate the advantage of having a fellow countryman as county assessor," their new German-language Democratic newspaper editorialized in 1876.[67] It meant control of justice of the peace courts, juries, and the probate court where family property was settled; it meant control of welfare measures at both the town and county level; it meant control of the sheriff's office; and fundamentally, it meant control of the schools, through local school boards that could effectively convert

---

66 *Der Wanderer* (St. Paul), Sept. 12, Oct. 31, Oct. 3, 1868. Readership can be determined by the subscription receipt lists published regularly in the paper.
67 St Cloud *Nordstern*, Oct. 12, 1876.

public into parochial schools, and through the county supervisor of schools less than two years after that position was established in 1867. Germans never demanded a total monopoly of local offices; village values imported from Germany demanded a certain level of dignity, of ability to participate in the higher affairs of state, from those who held higher office. Thus, despite German numerical dominance, until the 1880s the chairman of the county board was generally a Yankee; not until the 1890s did Germans consistently chair St. Cloud's city council, and until 1911 only four Germans, at widely spaced intervals, ever served as the city's mayor. Not until the early twentieth century, despite the availability of German attorneys, were Germans elected as clerks of court or circuit court judges, but the vital Probate Court passed into German hands as early as 1876. Germans after the Civil War aggressively utilized certain powers of local government – road building, taxation, education, justice, and public welfare in particular – to shape the kind of world they wanted, but remained willing to follow the Yankee lead in what might be called the "external affairs" of economic development, provided that some of the benefits flowed their way. Not until after the bust following the economic boom of the late 1880s brought about a farm crisis and rising levels of government indebtedness, and an American-born second generation came of age, would Germans finally begin to take full control.[68]

In effect, these German-speaking Catholics in America experienced the Civil War and its aftermath as the functional equivalent of their homeland's *Kulturkampf,* and their response was an analogous retreat into a self-sufficient Catholic milieu.[69] Within Stearns County they reproduced the political strategy of the German village. The war had stripped them of powerful patrons and converted state and federal governments into distant, hostile overlords whom they had little ability to influence; the best they could do was signal their continued contempt for those overlords with their solid Democratic votes, and then focus their attention inward, using local politics to help construct and defend a bounding set of institutions and conditions to reinforce the enduring trinity of family, farm, and faith.[70] Their self-denying refusal to participate more than symbolically in

---

68 The contours and logic of this system are documented in Conzen, "German-Americans and Ethnic Political Culture."

69 Michael Klöcker, "Das katholische Milieu," *Zeitschrift für Religions- und Geistesgeschichte* 44 (1992): 241–62, evaluates recent literature on the concept of Germany's Catholic milieu; for Reconstruction-era American "culture wars," see Ward M. McAfee, "Reconstruction Revisited: The Republican Public Education Crusade of the 1870s," *Civil War History* 42 (1996): 133–53; Anbinder, "Ulysses S. Grant."

70 Kathleen Neils Conzen, "Peasant Pioneers: Generational Succession among German Farmers in

the wider political sphere, however, was not without consequences. It forced them to rely as clients on a series of Republican brokers – first the Pennsylvania Germans, then a Yankee Catholic convert, later Swedes and Norwegians – for the favors they still needed from higher levels of government, making them sometimes susceptible to "courthouse ring" corruption in return.[71] It also made them susceptible to third-party movements when issues arose that their one-party system proved incapable of articulating; progressivism and farmer-laborism later became their main escape routes back into the political mainstream. And it meant that they continued to find real ideological and practical resonance in Democratic rhetoric defending limited central government and the right of a region to embed its own distinctive social arrangements in the structure of local institutions.

IV

Transatlantic currents created disturbing eddies in the reconstructed national identity that was, as Angermann emphasized, a central consequence of the Civil War crisis.[72] Stearns County's German Catholics seemingly negotiated the initial transition from their German to their American world with relative ease. It was the parallel transition from the communal world of the peasant to the national world of the modernizing state that gave them pause. The statist demands that they fled from in Germany caught up with them in America in the maelstrom of civil war. But America also provided them with the instruments of local self-government, and during and after the war they used those instruments to erect effective though never impermeable barriers around their culture.

In so doing, it might be argued, they also inadvertently helped construct postwar Republican America's temporary solution to the dilemma posed by ethnic difference. Democrats could tolerate ethnic difference because they assumed a state composed largely of autonomous, internally homogeneous communities needing little integration other than that provided by the market. The *St. Paul German Democratic* editor's response to a proposed 1865 state constitutional amendment to permit blacks to vote

Frontier America," in Steven Hahn and Jonathan Prude, eds., *The Countryside in the Age of Capitalist Transformation: Essays in the Social History of Rural America* (Chapel Hill, N.C., 1985), 259–92.

71 E.g., SCT Aug. 30, 1882.

72 Erich Angermann, "Abraham Lincoln und die Erneuerung der nationalen Identität der Vereinigten Staaten von Amerika," *Historische Zeitschrift* 239 (1984): 77–109.

in Minnesota – they have their own part of the country, why do they have to come to ours – provides an important key to the logic of "separate but equal" that they found so compelling: The consequences of difference could be contained by physical separation and limited central governmental power. By contrast, the Republican logic of national economic integration demanded cultural integration as well, which the Evangelical mindset that pervaded the party almost seems to have assumed could be achieved through a self-willed process analogous to religious conversion. When, as in the case of the freed slaves of the South, that sort of immediate cultural conversion proved illusory, they tacitly acceded to the South's segregation. The Indian reservation effectively became the Republican model for dealing with difference: isolate it, contain it geographically, and separate it from any broader participation that might enable it to influence or corrupt the centralizing polity. Stearns County's self-constructed encapsulation fit within this framework as efficiently as did the contemporaneous Democratic machine ghettos of the cities. By the end of the century Stearns County's new generation, finding the encapsulation confining, would join the fight to redeem Minnesota from its Republican trammels.[73] But the years of inward-looking localism left their mark, most importantly in an almost reflexive mistrust of the state and its agents, and in an enduring political alliance with that other long-lasting bastion of Democratic localism, the South.[74]

The provincial world into which Minnesota's German Catholics retreated after the Civil War never imperiled the stability of the nationalizing state they rejected, of course, not even during World War I when their localism probably played as strong a role as old-country loyalties in their opposition to American entry.[75] It will require further research to estimate the prevalence, and hence the broader significance, of the Stearns County pattern, although there are clear intimations that broad swathes of the German-Catholic Midwest experienced the Civil War in similar terms and subsequently maintained similar cultural and political orienta-

---

73 For an overview of Minnesota politics in this period, see Carl H. Chrislock, *The Progressive Era in Minnesota, 1899–1918* (St. Paul, 1971).

74 For a characterization of Stearns County's political culture in the 1950s as moralistic and isolationist, see Samuel Lubell, *The Future of American Politics* (New York, 1951); Barry M. Casper and Paul David Wellstone, *Powerline: The First Battle of America's Energy War* (Amherst, Mass., 1981), explore facets of its continuing mistrust of outside agencies a generation later; see also Kevin P. Phillips, *The Emerging Republican Majority* (New Rochelle, N.Y., 1959).

75 On the World War I crisis, see Sister John Christine Wolkerstorfer, "Nativism in Minnesota in World War I: A Comparative Study of Brown, Ramsey, and Stearns Counties, 1914–1918," Ph.D. diss., University of Minnesota, 1973.

tions.[76] But whatever its prevalence, the Stearns County story is a useful reminder of the limits of exceptionalist interpretations of American national integration. Immigrant political incorporation was not necessarily as straightforward, nor rural nationalization as unproblematic, as some of our myths would have us believe. America's great war of national integration may have hastened the Americanization of the educated elite within the German immigration, as historians have long argued.[77] But peasant communalists were also part of that immigration, and for them the war took on a very different meaning, as George Hansen discovered to his detriment.

76 Klement, "Catholics as Copperheads"; Blied, *Catholics and the Civil War*; Kathleen Neils Conzen, "Immigrants in Nineteenth-Century Agricultural History," in Lou Ferleger, ed., *Agriculture and National Development: Views on the Nineteenth Century* (Ames, Iowa, 1990), 303–42; Phillips, *Emerging Republican Majority*.
77 Cf. Bruce Levine, "The Migration of Ideology and the Contested Meaning of Freedom: German Americans in the Mid-Nineteenth Century," German Historical Institute, Occasional Paper series, no. 7 (Washington, D.C., 1992); Levine, *Spirit of 1848*; Nagler, *Fremont contra Lincoln*; Conzen, "German–Americans and the Invention of Ethnicity."

7

Toward a Comparative History of Racism and Xenophobia in the United States and Germany, 1865–1933

KENNETH L. KUSMER

The past decade has witnessed the revival of ethnic and religious conflict in eastern Europe, a disastrous civil war in the former Yugoslavia, and the rise of right-wing movements and extremist violence against minority groups in Austria, France, Germany, and Italy.[1] In the United States there has been a growing hostility toward immigrants from Haiti, Mexico, and Southeast Asia and increasing evidence of racism and violence against African Americans and Jews.[2] Studies purporting to prove blacks mentally inferior no longer are dismissed out of hand, as was once the case, and to some degree it has become intellectually and politically respectable in America to support immigration restriction based on openly racial criteria.[3]

In light of these events, it is imperative that we revisit the history of xenophobia and racial intolerance to gain a better understanding of the causes and consequences of the hostile and sometimes violent conflict between natives and newcomers, majority and minority. The purpose of this chapter is to provide a historical perspective on this phenomenon by comparing and contrasting the response of two societies – the United States

---

1 For a country-by-country survey of this phenomenon, see Bernd Baumgartl and Adrian Favell, eds., *The New Xenophobia in Europe* (London, 1995). On the historical development of neo-fascism in Italy, Germany, France, and Great Britain, see Robert Eatwell, *Fascism: A History* (New York, 1996), 245–362.

2 See, e.g., Deborah Sontag, "Across the U.S., Immigrants Find the Land of Resentment," *New York Times*, Dec. 11, 1992; for examples of violence, see Ronald Takaki, *Strangers from a Different Shore: A History of Asian Americans* (Boston, 1989), 481–4.

3 See, e.g., Richard Herrnstein and Charles Murray, *The Bell Curve: The Reshaping of American Life by Difference in Intelligence* (New York, 1994) and Peter Brimelow, *Alien Nation* (New York, 1995). For a brilliant critique of *The Bell Curve*, see Stephen Jay Gould, "Introduction to the Revised and Expanded Edition," *The Mismeasure of Man* (New York, 1996), 31–6.

and Germany – to the ethnic and racial minorities in their midst in the late nineteenth and early twentieth century, a period of economic change and intensified racism that has much in common with our own time.

I

The race issue in the United States after the Civil War is traditionally defined in black/white terms, with the primary focus on the struggle of African Americans to achieve equality during Reconstruction and the subsequent return of white supremacy after 1890, an era marked by the emergence of legal segregation and the disenfranchisement of African Americans and increasing violence in the form of lynchings. Whereas black/white conflict in the American South was undoubtedly paramount in the eyes of most Americans, it was not the only racial issue agitating American society at the time. In a broader sense, in the half-century following the Civil War native-born white Americans were increasingly concerned about an emerging *multiracial* society that now included Chinese, Japanese, and Mexican immigrants, newly freed slaves, and, at the turn of the century, a growing population of newcomers from southern and eastern Europe.

The "new" European immigrants, as John Higham demonstrated in his classic study *Strangers in the Land*, were increasingly defined in racial terms by nativist writers such as Madison Grant, who expressed the fear that whites of Nordic stock (Anglo-Saxons and other northern Europeans) might be overrun by "inferior" groups from southern and eastern Europe.[4] What is often neglected in discussions of Grant and other nativist authors, however, is the breadth of their racial concerns. In *The Passing of the Great Race* (1916) and its sequel, *The Conquest of a Continent* (1933), Grant spent considerable time discussing the nonwhite races as well as categorizing the various European nationalities. He praised the white South for maintaining its racial pride and deplored the "racially suicidal" weakness of Nordics who "are encouraging the Negro within, and the black, brown and yellow races without, to dispute the dominance over the world at large of Christian Europeans and Americans."[5] Concern about nonwhites was even stronger with Lothrop Stoddard, a Harvard-

---

4 Madison Grant, *The Passing of the Great Race* (1916; reprint, New York, 1944). On the background of racial nativism, see John Higham, *Strangers in the Land: Patterns of American Nativism, 1865–1925* (New York, 1955), chap. 6; Thomas F. Gossett, *Race: The History of an Idea in America* (1963; New York, 1965), chap. 14.

5 Grant, *Passing of the Great Race*, 86–92; Madison Grant, *The Conquest of a Continent, or the Expansion of Races in America* (New York, 1933), 344–5.

trained Ph.D. in history whose book *The Rising Tide of Color Against White World Supremacy* (1920) was popular enough to be satirized in F. Scott Fitzgerald's *The Great Gatsby*. Stoddard continued to disseminate his racist theories into the 1930s in such volumes as *Clashing Tides of Colour* (1935). In 1939 he served as a correspondent in Germany, interviewed Adolf Hitler, and produced a study sympathetic to the German dictator's ideas, if not to all of his methods.[6]

With the exception of Native Americans and, in some regards, African Americans, Asian immigrants received the harshest treatment of all minority groups in the United States during the decades between the Civil War and the Great Depression.[7] Only Asian newcomers (including Koreans and Filipinos) were denied the right of becoming citizens through naturalization.[8] This not only created legal difficulties for them not faced by European immigrants but also declared them to be an outcast group that, in effect, was *incapable* of assimilation. Popular stereotypes of African Americans and Chinese had much in common. Both were perceived as lazy, lascivious, unintelligent, and superstitious.[9] The Chinese, like blacks and Indians, were defined as nonwhite and prohibited from testifying in court against whites or intermarrying with whites.[10]

Throughout the Civil War and Reconstruction period, as Najia Aarim has demonstrated, legislative debates over the extension of civil rights to African Americans were inextricably connected to the contemporaneous

6 Lothrop Stoddard, *The Rising Tide of Color Against White World Supremacy* (New York, 1920); Lothrop Stoddard, *Clashing Tides of Color* (New York, 1935); *DAB: Supplement, 1946–1950* (New York, 1974), 791–3; F. Scott Fitzgerald, *The Great Gatsby* (New York, 1925), 13–14. See also Mathew Frye Jacobson, *Whiteness of a Different Color: European Immigrants and the Alchemy of Race* (Cambridge, Mass., 1998), 96–8.

7 I have purposefully excluded discussion of the American Indian from this essay. By the end of the 1870s, most Native American groups had been exterminated or forced onto reservations. The subjugation of Native Americans is obviously at least partially a product of racism, but this topic lies outside the main purview of this chapter.

8 After 1898 Filipinos came from an American territory, so they could not be denied entrance to the United States. Like other Asian groups, however, they were prohibited from becoming naturalized citizens because the Naturalization Act of 1790 limited this right to "white persons." See Takaki, *Strangers from a Different Shore*, 325, 331.

9 See Stuart Creighton Miller, *Unwelcome Immigrant: The American Image of the Chinese, 1785–1885* (Berkeley, Calif., 1960); Dan Caldwell, "The Negroization of the Chinese Stereotype in California," *Southern California Quarterly* 53 (1971): 123–7; Alexander Saxton, *The Indispensable Enemy: Labor and the Anti-Chinese Movement in California* (Berkeley, Calif., 1971), 20–2; Takaki, *Strangers from a Different Shore*, 100–2. The origins and development of black stereotypes is thoroughly discussed in Winthrop Jordan, *White over Black: American Attitudes toward the Negro, 1550–1812* (New York, 1968) and George Fredrickson, *The Black Image in the White Mind: The Debate over Afro-American Character and Destiny* (New York, 1971).

10 Tomas Almaguer, *Racial Fault Lines: The Historical Origins of White Supremacy in California* (Berkeley, Calif., 1994), 162–4; Takaki, *Strangers from a Different Shore*, 101–2; Sucheng Chan, *Asian Americans: An Interpretive History* (Boston, 1994), 48.

argument over the status of Chinese immigrants. In the post-Reconstruction era the movement to restrict Chinese immigration struck a responsive chord across the nation, but it was especially appealing to white Southerners at a time when they were still grappling with their own "race" problem, and a solid bloc of southern votes helped push through the Chinese Exclusion Act of 1882.[11] Over the next twenty years Chinese immigrants were able to limit the law's impact through judicial appeals, but after 1905 exclusion became much tighter when control over appeals was shifted to the Commissioner of Immigration.[12] Considering their relative population size, Chinese immigrants in the American West were probably lynched as frequently as were blacks in the South. As in the case of the African Americans, we will never know how much violence took place against the Chinese because "many crimes against them went unpunished."[13] This violence gradually subsided, and by 1915 the Chinese were beginning to build up legitimate businesses and restaurants in Chinatowns to attract middle-class white patrons. Nevertheless, prior to 1945 the Chinese remained highly segregated, largely excluded from the body politic and often forced to labor in low-paying jobs in laundries, restaurants, or sweatshop factories.[14] Japanese immigrants also suffered discrimination and ostracism. The "gentlemen's agreement" of 1907 limited immigration from Japan, and the National Origins (Johnson-Reid) Act of 1924 ended it altogether. Discrimination and the Alien Land Laws of 1913 and 1920, promoted by such nativist organizations as the Native Sons of the Golden West, inhibited the upward mobility of the Japanese in California, and many second-generation Japanese were forced into less lucrative small businesses and service occupations.[15] Despite a complete

11 For a thorough discussion of the relationship between the response to African Americans and the Chinese, see Najia Aarim, "Chinese Immigrants, African Americans, and the Problem of Race, 1848–1882," Ph.D. diss., Temple University, 1996.

12 See Lucy Salyer, *Laws as Harsh as Tigers: Chinese Immigrants and the Shaping of Modern Immigration Law* (Chapel Hill, N.C., 1995); Charles McLain, *The Struggle against Discrimination: The Chinese Experience in the Nineteenth Century* (Berkeley, Calif., 1995); K. Scott Wong, "Cultural Defenders and Brokers: Chinese Responses to the Anti-Chinese Movement," in K. Scott Wong and Sucheng Chan, eds., *Claiming America: Constructing Chinese American Identities During the Exclusion Era* (Philadelphia, 1998), 3–40; and Sucheng Chan, ed., *Entry Denied: Exclusion and the Chinese Community in America, 1882–1943* (Philadelphia, 1991).

13 W. Eugen Hollen, *Frontier Violence: Another Look* (New York, 1974), 85; Chan, *Asian Americans* 48–51.

14 Shihshan Henry Tsai, *The Chinese Experience in America* (Bloomington, Ind., 1986), 95–110; Takaki, *Strangers from a Different Shore*, chap. 6.

15 See the superb overview of Roger Daniels, *The Politics of Prejudice: The Anti-Japanese Movement in California and the Struggle for Japanese Exclusion* (New York, 1974); John Modell, *The Economics and Politics of Racial Accommodationism: The Japanese of Los Angeles, 1900–1942* (Urbana, Ill., 1977), chaps. 5–6; Takaki, *Strangers from a Different Shore*, chap. 5. On the legal basis of anti-Asian racism, see Ian Haney-Lopez, *White by Law: The Legal Construction of Race* (New York, 1996), chap. 4; and

lack of evidence of treasonous activity, Japanese immigrants (*Issei*) and their children (*Nisei*) would suffer a massive violation of their civil rights when they were incarcerated in concentration camps during World War II.[16]

Like African Americans and Chinese, Mexicans were burdened with a largely negative image that preceded their political incorporation into the United States.[17] However, the position of Mexicans during the thirty years after 1848 was more favorable than that of Asians or the indigenous Indian population, primarily because they acquired citizenship rights under the Treaty of Guadalupe Hidalgo (1848). They suffered far less violence than the Chinese and were able to retain significant political and economic power until the 1870s.[18] By 1900, however, conditions had greatly changed. The *Californio* group was overwhelmed by the influx of Anglo settlers, leading to their rapid decline and to the barrioization and proletarianization of the Mexican population as a whole. The Mexican immigrants who began to come north in the 1890s would play a distinctly subordinate role in the economy and society of southern California in the following decades.[19]

The tide of predominantly Catholic and Jewish immigrants pouring into eastern and midwestern cities beginning in the 1880s posed a different kind of threat to old-stock Americans. Almost nine million newcomers arrived in the first decade of the twentieth century alone.[20] The nativist movement that arose in response to this massive influx was less

Mae M. Ngai, "The Architecture of Race in American Immigration Law: A Reexamination of the Immigration Act of 1924," *Journal of American History* 86 (June 1999): 80–8.

16 The paranoid climate of opinion leading up to the internment of the Japanese is discussed in Roger Daniels, *The Decision to Relocate the Japanese Americans* (Philadelphia, 1975), and Takaki, *Strangers from a Different Shore*, 379–94. On the legal justification for the internment, see Peter Irons, *Justice at War: The Story of the Japanese American Internment Cases* (New York, 1983); and Peter Irons, ed., *Justice Delayed: The Record of the Japanese American Internment Cases* (Middletown, Conn., 1989).

17 Albert Camarillo, *Not Black but Not White: Mexicans and Ethnic/Racial Borderlands in American Cities* (forthcoming), chap. 1, is the best source on the evolving image of Mexicans in the nineteenth century; see also David J. Weber, " 'Scarce More than Apes': Historical Roots of Anglo-American Stereotypes of Mexicans in the Border Region," in David J. Weber, ed., *New Spain's Far Northern Frontier* (Albuquerque, N.M., 1979); and Arnoldo De Leon, *They Called Them Greasers: Anglo Attitudes Toward Mexicans in Texas, 1821–1900* (Austin, Tex., 1983).

18 Almaguer, *Racial Fault Lines*, 4, 45–65.

19 Albert Camarillo, *Chicanos in a Changing Society: From Mexican Pueblos to American Barrios in Santa Barbara and Southern California, 1848–1930* (Cambridge, Mass., 1979); Richard Griswold del Castillo, *The Los Angeles Barrio, 1850–1890: A Social History* (Berkeley, Calif., 1979); Almaguer, *Racial Fault Lines*, 65–104; George J. Sanchez, *Becoming Mexican American: Ethnicity, Culture and Identity in Chicano Los Angeles, 1900–1945* (New York, 1993), 194–5. For a parallel case in Texas, see Mario T. Garcia, *Desert Immigrants: The Mexicans of El Paso, 1880–1920* (New Haven, Conn., 1981).

20 Leonard Dinnerstein and David M. Reimers, *Ethnic Americans: A History of Immigration and Assimilation* (New York, 1975), 11, 36–7.

broadly based than the anti-Asian agitation. Significantly, however, it now included some non-Anglo-Saxon elements drawn from the older immigrant groups, spearheaded by members of the conservative craft unions. Most American Federation of Labor (AFL) unions, made up primarily of workers of English, Irish, and German ancestry, rejected both Asians and African Americans for membership. After 1906 the organization moved toward acceptance of restrictions on European immigration as well. Later, AFL leaders endorsed the discriminatory National Origins Act, largely accepting the racist arguments of its leading proponents.[21]

During the period between the Haymarket Riot of 1886 and American entry into World War I, a new stage in the process of ethno-racial formation was taking place in the United States, with old-stock, non-Anglo-Saxon groups now being accepted, to a substantial degree, into the fold as parts of the self-defined designation as "Nordics."[22] Madison Grant was even willing to place the long-hated Irish Catholics in this category, and the philosopher John Fiske favorably compared the Irish to the Italians.[23] Occupational convergence with the native-born group of British ancestry in major urban areas, especially the movement of younger Irish, German, and Scandinavian Americans into an opportunity structure increasingly defined by large corporations dominated by Anglo-Saxons or by public service employment, probably smoothed the way for this shift in ethno-racial identity.[24] Certainly this trend did not please all Anglo-

---

21 Sterling D. Spero and Abram L. Harris, *The Black Worker: The Negro and the Labor Movement* (New York, 1931), chaps. 4–5; Higham, *Strangers in the Land*, 163, 321–2; Bernard Mandel, "Samuel Gompers and the Negro Workers, 1886–1914," *Journal of Negro History* 40 (1955): 34–60; Alexander Saxton, *The Rise and Fall of the White Republic: Class, Politics, and Culture in Nineteenth-Century America* (London, 1990), 310–14; Yuji Ichioka, *The Issei: The World of the First Generation Japanese Immigrants* (New York, 1990), 96–102; Robert Asher, "Union Nativism and Immigrant Response," *Labor History* 23 (1982): 325–48; Gwendolyn Mink, *Old Labor and New Immigrants in American Political Development: Union, Party, and State, 1875–1920* (Ithaca, N.Y., 1986), 76–7, 96–7, 118–29.

22 This term is a variation on that used by Michael Omi and Howard Winant, *Racial Formation in the United States: From the 1960s to the 1980s* (London, 1987).

23 On Grant, see Gossett, *Race: The History of an Idea*, 361; on Fiske, see Higham, *Strangers in the Land*, 65.

24 On the Irish, see John R. McKivigan and Thomas J. Robertson, "The Irish American Worker in Transition, 1877–1914: New York as a Test Case," in Ronald Bayor and Timothy Meagher, eds., *The New York Irish* (Baltimore, 1996), 312–13, 315–18; Lawrence J. McCaffrey, "Overview: Looking Forward and Looking Back," ibid., 219; Hasia Diner, *Erin's Daughters in America: Irish Immigrant Women in the Nineteenth Century* (Baltimore, 1983), 70–105. On the Germans, see Russell A. Kazal, "Becoming 'Old Stock': The Waning of German-American Identity in Philadelphia, 1900–1930," Ph.D. diss., University of Pennsylvania, 1998. Historical studies of the new white collar group that grew rapidly in the early twentieth century focus on gender rather than race and ethnicity, but the latter was clearly important, especially for second- and third-generation Irish and Germans. On the changing opportunity structure of the industrializing city generally, see Olivier Zunz, *The Changing Face of Inequality: Urbanization, Industrial Development, and Immigrants in Detroit, 1880–1920* (Chicago, 1982), 220–4.

Saxon Americans. Nevertheless, there was a significant movement toward the acceptance of commonalities among northern Europeans at this time. Even the Ku Klux Klan, although it could hardly appeal to the Irish, accepted sizeable numbers of (presumably Protestant) German-Americans and Scandinavians into its ranks, suggesting that these groups had become assimilated enough to be welcomed into an organization openly hostile to new immigrants and blacks.[25] Perhaps the best symbolic acknowledgement of this trend was the emerging ethnic and racial patterns in major-league baseball, which was quite integrated along northern European lines as early as the 1890s but had few Italian or Jewish players prior to the 1930s, and no Asian, Latin American, or African-American players at all until after World War II.[26]

The "new immigrants" occupied a highly ambiguous place in the ethno-racial hierarchy of early twentieth-century America – somewhat above blacks, Asians, and Mexicans but certainly not fully equal to northern Europeans either. Southern and eastern Europeans were sometimes characterized as nonwhite, or at least as sharing traits with nonwhites. "Make New York University a white man's college," proclaimed an anti-Semitic flyer distributed in 1923 in response to the increase in Jewish students there.[27] In industrializing America, anti-Semitic stereotypes often overlapped with widespread negative images of the Chinese (clannish, materialistic) and blacks (sensual, immoral). Some nativists even believed Jews and Italians to be part African in ancestry, and Slavic immigrants were also compared with African Americans in a pejorative manner.[28]

---

25 See the data on membership in Shawn Lay, *Hooded Knights of the Niagara: The Ku Klux Klan in Buffalo, New York* (New York, 1995), 86–101.

26 McCaffrey, "Overview," 231; Stephen Reiss, *Touching Base: Professional Baseball and American Culture in the Progressive Era* (Westport, Conn., 1980). Blacks did have their own, separate "Negro leagues," but except in exhibition games, they did not play against the white major league teams. See Robert Peterson, *Only the Ball Was White* (New York, 1970).

27 Higham, *Strangers in the Land*, 169; James R. Barrett and David Roediger, "Inbetween Peoples: Race, Nationality, and the 'New Immigrant' Working Class," *Journal of American Ethnic History* 16 (1997): 3–44; Michael N. Dobkowski, *The Tarnished Dream: The Basis of American Anti-Semitism* (Westport, Conn., 1979), 167–8n (quotation); see also the perceptive discussion of Jews in Jacobson, *Whiteness of a Different Color*, 171–87.

28 Robert Singerman, "The Jew as Racial Alien: The Genetic Component of American Anti-Semitism," in David Gerber, ed., *Anti-Semitism in American History* (Urbana, Ill., 1986), 117; Barbara Miller Solomon, *Ancestors and Immigrants: A Changing New England Tradition* (Cambridge, Mass., 1956), 167; Leonard Dinnerstein, *Antisemitism in America* (New York, 1994), 66; Iver Bernstein, *The New York City Draft Riots: The Significance for American Society and Politics in the Age of the Civil War* (New York, 1990), 120. For the case of Slavic immigrants, see David Roediger, "Whiteness and Ethnicity in the History of 'White Ethnics' in the United States," in David Roediger, *Towards the Abolition of Whiteness: Essays on Race, Politics, and Working-Class History* (London, 1994), 190–1. The

Violence directed against minority groups was a significant aspect of racism and xenophobia in the late nineteenth and early twentieth century. Relatively little systematic work has been done on the history of violence against Asian immigrants, and even less on Mexicans and European immigrants. There does exist an extensive literature on racial violence directed against African Americans, however, and an analysis of race riots and lynchings can provide one important window on the history of intolerance during the industrial era.

Traditionally, students of urban racial violence have stressed competition between groups for jobs or housing as a fundamental cause of race riots.[29] This explanation is most persuasive when applied to the massive riots in East St. Louis, Chicago, and elsewhere in the North during World War I, when overcrowding and labor conflict created enormous racial tensions. Such conditions, however, were not necessary for a race riot to take place. In her careful analysis of the 1908 race riot in Springfield, Illinois, Roberta Senechal found no evidence of "social strain" or job competition behind the riot. Whites did view blacks as "a danger to their dignity and status," but not because they feared them as economic competitors. In fact, working-class white rioters singled out successful, affluent black men or their businesses for attack.[30] Throughout the nineteenth and early twentieth century, such hostile reaction to black progress was a recurrent theme of large-scale racial violence. Pogrom-style riots in antebellum Philadelphia and New York often focused on black churches, schools, and the homes of the black middle class, as well as interracial recreational establishments.[31] Although unskilled workers participated in these riots, skilled workers were disproportionately represented, and leadership often came from "gentlemen of property and standing."[32] During Recon-

main focus of this stimulating essay is the process by which successive European groups may have in turn become acceptable as "whites" rather than as ethnic minorities, by differentiating themselves from blacks. What is not addressed by Roediger is the attitude of these groups toward each other, specifically how older groups viewed more recent arrivals, or their attitude toward other racial groups, such as the Chinese or Mexicans.

29 Elliot Rudwick, *Race Riot at East St. Louis, July 2, 1917* (Carbondale, Ill., 1964); William Tuttle Jr., *Race Riot: Chicago in the Red Summer of 1919* (New York, 1970). For a discussion and critique of this approach to the history of race riots, see Roberta Senechal, *The Socio-Genesis of a Race Riot: Springfield, Illinois in 1908* (Urbana, Ill., 1990), 1–14.

30 Senechal, *Socio-Genesis of a Race Riot*, 151. For another example, see Jonathan B. Streff, "Reading Race: The Roots of the Chester, Pennsylvania, Race Riot of 1917," M.A. thesis, Temple University, 1999.

31 John Runcie, " 'Hunting the Nigs' in Philadelphia: The Race Riot of August 1834," *Pennsylvania History* 39 (1972): 209; Linda K. Kerber, "Abolitionists and Amalgamators: The New York City Race Riots of 1834," *New York History* 48 (1967): 32–3.

32 Leonard Richards, *"Gentlemen of Property and Standing": Anti-Abolitionist Mobs in Jacksonian America* (New York, 1970); Paul Gilje, *The Road to Mobocracy: Popular Disorder in New York City, 1763–1834*

struction, notes Eric Foner, to racist whites "the most 'offensive' blacks seemed to be those who achieved a modicum of economic success, for, as a white Mississippi farmer commented, the Klan 'do not like to see the Negro go ahead.' "[33] Such attitudes help explain the attacks on elite blacks in the 1906 Atlanta race riot, as well as the violent response of upper-middle-class whites to black professionals in northern cities in the 1920s. Because black professionals had a mostly black clientele, they were not in competition with whites. The real motivation for these attacks, as one white Cleveland homeowner explained, was that "colored people had no right to purchase such a nice home."[34] Fears of blacks gaining respectability, either through economic achievement or political power, were a prime motivation of much urban racial violence.

It is probable that job competition played a larger role in anti-Chinese xenophobia and violence than it did in assaults on African Americans. The Chinese laboring in the mines and railroad construction in the West were used by some businessmen as a wedge against white labor, which on several occasions led to mob attacks on Chinese workers.[35] Still, many Chinese worked in menial jobs that did not compete with whites, and attacks on the Chinese did not come primarily from those elements of the white working class most likely to compete with unskilled labor. It was largely skilled workers, with little to fear from coolie labor directly, who led the drive for Chinese exclusion.[36]

(Chapel Hill, N.C., 1987), 157, 164–6. Gilje's reassessment of the composition of the 1834 New York mob leads him to a different conclusion than Richards, and he argues it suggests "white apprehension over competition with black labor." I find the argument unpersuasive, because it is hard to see why shoemakers or other skilled workers should feel threatened by unskilled black laborers. In Philadelphia, unlike New York, John Runcie reports that most of the rioters were unskilled Irish immigrants. Still, a quarter of them were skilled artisans and several others apprentices, which probably means the skilled workers were overrepresented in the mob compared to the Irish population as a whole. As in New York, "the instigators of the riot were powerful people" (Runcie, " 'Hunting the Nigs,' " 194–5, 296).

33 Eric Foner, *Reconstruction: America's Unfinished Revolution, 1863–1877* (New York, 1987), 479.

34 Nell Irvin Painter, *Standing at Armageddon: The United States, 1877–1919* (New York, 1987), 219; Kenneth L. Kusmer, *A Ghetto Takes Shape: Black Cleveland, 1870–1930* (Urbana, Ill., 1976), 167, 168–9; Richard W. Thomas, *Life for Us Is What We Make It: Building Black Community in Detroit, 1915–1945* (Bloomington, Ind., 1992), 135–43. On the role of the white middle and upper class in the 1898 Wilmington, North Carolina, race riot, see Michael Honey, "Class, Race, and Power in the New South: Racial Violence and the Delusions of White Supremacy," in David S. Cecelski and Timothy B. Tyson, eds., *Democracy Betrayed: The Wilmington Race Riot of 1898 and Its Legacy* (Chapel Hill, N.C., 1998).

35 See, e.g., Craig Storti, *Incident at Bitter Creek: The Story of the Rock Springs Chinese Massacre* (Ames, Iowa, 1991).

36 See the data in the neglected study of Ping Chiu, *Chinese Labor in California, 1850–1880: An Economic Study* (Madison, Wis., 1963), 53, and, generally, Saxton, *The Indispensable Enemy*, which focuses on the ideological and political uses of anti-Chinese agitation by white labor leaders and politicians. I am indebted to Professor Najia Aarim for bringing Chiu's study to my attention.

The fact that direct economic competition was seldom a motivation for racial violence does not mean that economic factors played no role in attacks on racial minorities. Recent studies of lynching in the South by W. Fitzhugh Brundage and by Stewart Tolnay and E. M. Beck demonstrate that economic conditions did indeed affect the level of violence directed against black southerners during the period from 1880 to 1930.[37] The late nineteenth-century South experienced dynamic change in agriculture, with growing dependency on cotton and a steady increase of farm tenancy among whites, as well as some industrial development and urban growth.[38] Tolnoy and Beck found that almost two-thirds of all lynchings took place in counties dominated by cotton farming, and that especially before 1900 there was a strong inverse relationship between the number of lynchings and the price of cotton. Counties with a high level of tenancy (over 40 percent) exhibited consistently high rates of lynching.[39] Brundage's study confirms the importance of cotton farming as a factor, although rural industrialization and nascent urbanization also promoted mob violence.[40] Conflicts between black tenant farmers and white planters sometimes led to violence, but the wider context for lynchings involved the uncertainties created by the unpredictable market for cotton and growing class differences among whites. It is probable that many white tenants or marginal farmers "resorted to mob violence in order to shore up the caste line" based on skin color.[41] Interestingly, however, the relationship between lynching and white tenancy only took hold when the tenancy rate exceeded 40 percent. Apparently, class differences among whites had to reach a fairly high level before triggering racial violence.

Despite the strong underlying economic connection to lynching, the immediate incidents that precipitated violence often had little to do with economic conditions per se. Prior to 1910, the alleged "cause" of a majority of lynchings in Georgia was sexual assault against white females, a sensationalistic charge that for decades would be used to deflect criticism away from the lynchers.[42] As Ida B. Wells argued in denouncing lynching, the charge of rape was for the most part a figment of white men's

---

37 W. Fitzhugh Brundage, *Lynching in the New South: Georgia and Virginia* (Urbana, Ill., 1993); Stewart E. Tolnay and E. M. Beck, *A Festival of Violence: An Analysis of Southern Lynchings, 1882–1930* (Urbana, Ill., 1996).
38 See Gavin Wright, *Old South, New South: Revolutions in the Southern Economy Since the Civil War* (New York, 1986), chaps. 3–6.
39 Tolnoy and Beck, *Festival of Violence*, chap. 5.
40 Brundage, *Lynching in the New South*, 106–39.
41 Tolnay and Beck, *Festival of Violence*, 253.
42 Brundage, *Lynching in the New South*, 78–9, 112.

imagination.[43] It nevertheless provides one key to understanding the roots of racial violence. Clearly, some of those roots lay in the realm of gender relations. The "rape myth" was largely a product of the period from 1880 to 1920.[44] Economic and social changes forced more white women into the work force while opening up new opportunities for middle-class white women to take part in organizational and recreational activities. As Jacquelyn Dowd Hall has noted, the image of the black "beast rapist" in popular culture reflected fears that both black men and white women might move outside their expected subordinate spheres.[45] It also submerged class divisions among whites by arguing that *all* white women were at risk from the black rapist.[46]

Racial conflict outside the South could also result from the need of some white ethnic groups to guard against perceived threats to the traditional family. Fears of racial "amalgamation" and the defense of tight-knit ethnic communities were one cause of the New York draft riots of 1863. Anti-Chinese organizations, one historian notes, also "used gender to strengthen their cause by drawing on domestic values and women's traditional role in Victorian America," claiming that "white workingmen were family men with starving wives and children, unlike Chinese bachelors who sent money home to China."[47] The threat to white women was viewed in sexual as well as economic terms. The Chinese sexual stereotype stressed seduction, not assault, but such behavior was no less threatening to white families and could lead to violence as deadly as that of any southern lynch mob.[48]

In contrast to Chinese Americans and blacks, the new European

43 Ida B. Wells, *Crusade for Justice: The Autobiography of Ida B. Wells*, ed. Alfreda M. Duster (Chicago, 1970), 69–71; Patricia A. Schechter, "Unsettled Business: Ida B. Wells Against Lynching, or, How Anti-Lynching Got Its Gender," in W. Fitzhugh Brundage, ed., *Under Sentence of Death: Lynching in the South* (Chapel Hill, N.C., 1997), 292–317.

44 On the lack of such a myth, and the lynchings it inspired, during the antebellum era, see Diane Miller Sommerville, "The Rape Myth of the Old South Reconsidered," *Journal of Southern History* 61 (1995): 481–518.

45 For a brilliant exploration of these themes, see the introduction to Jacquelyn Dowd Hall, *Revolt Against Chivalry: Jesse Daniel Ames and the Women's Campaign Against Lynching*, rev. and expanded ed. (New York, 1993), xv–xxxviii; Grace Elizabeth Hale, *Making Whiteness: The Culture of Segregation in the South, 1890–1940* (New York, 1998), 131–5. On the emergence of vicious racial stereotypes in the post-1880 period, see Fredrickson, *Black Image in the White Mind*, chap. 9.

46 On this point, see the statement of one wealthy Virginian in 1889, quoted in Joel Williamson, *The Crucible of Race: Black-White Relations in the South since Emancipation* (New York, 1984), 121; and Hale, *Making Whiteness*, 236–8.

47 Bernstein, *The New York City Draft Riots*, 104–24; Margaret K. Holden, "Gender and Protest Ideology: Sue Ross Keenan and the Oregon Anti-Chinese Movement," *Western Legal History* 7 (1994): 230–44.

48 Similar sexual anxieties led to violence against Filipino immigrants in the 1920s. See Takaki, *Strangers from a Different Shore*, 327–30.

immigrants were much less subject to violent attack; Italians in the South prior to World War I were the main exception to this rule.[49] Instead of physical violence, xenophobic reaction to European newcomers manifested itself in discrimination in social organizations, campaigns for Americanization, and especially in the drive for immigration restrictions. As with the response to nonwhite groups, changing economic circumstances played an important part in promoting xenophobia directed against southern and eastern Europeans. John Higham has shown how the immigration restriction movement had its origins in the depressions of the 1880s and 1890s, but as Higham acknowledges, the economic argument cannot explain the rapid upsurge of nativism in the South and West after 1905.[50] The intensification of nativism must be sought not in economic causes alone, but in the intertwining of economic change with social and cultural factors related to broader questions of racial formation in the industrial era. It surely cannot be a coincidence that xenophobia intensified against the new European immigrants at the time (1905–7) when the Japanese immigration issue was re-emerging on the West Coast, and more important, when the white South was struggling to resolve its own race "problem" through the imposition of a system of racial apartheid and political disenfranchisement of African Americans. As the writings of Grant, Stoddard, and others made clear, these issues were not separate in the mind of racists. They were part of the larger problem of racial categorization and definition that would not reach political resolution until passage of the National Origins Act (which virtually excluded immigrants from southern and eastern Europe) and would not attain social/economic resolution for decades afterward.

The organization that best represented this trend was the second Ku Klux Klan, which grew enormously after 1919, only to go into rapid decline after 1925. The Klan combined the various strands of nativism, anti-Semitism, and anti-black racism into a powerful message that appealed to millions of white Protestants. The Klan was particularly disturbed about threats to conventional moral codes and, as Kathleen Blee and Nancy MacLean have emphasized, it also represented a strong patriarchal impulse to control the behavior of white Protestant women at a time when traditional gender roles were being questioned. Klansmen suffered from economic insecurity, to be sure, but more generally from the

---

49 See George E. Cunningham, "The Italian: A Hinderance to White Solidarity in Louisiana, 1890–1898," *Journal of Negro History* 50 (1965): 22–36; Richard Gambino, *Vendetta: A True Story of the Worst Lynching in America* (New York, 1977); Higham, *Strangers in the Land*, 264–5.
50 Higham, *Strangers in the Land*, chaps. 3–4, esp. 165–73.

social and cultural consequences of a modernizing society. Mostly skilled workers, lower white-collar employees, or small businessmen, Klansmen felt hedged in by "conflicts of class and gender" that arose in the context of the 1920s, and "imagined racial Others," perceived as genetically inferior to Anglo-Saxons (or Nordics) like themselves, became the convenient scapegoat for their anxieties.[51]

II

The specific circumstances of Germany after its defeat in World War I, circumstances that ultimately would help provide a breeding ground for Nazism, make any point-for-point comparison of xenophobia and racism in the United States and Germany in the early twentieth century difficult.[52] If one takes a broader perspective, however, viewing those two nations as premier examples of societies undergoing rapid social change, it is possible to at least assay this historical territory in a preliminary way. Both Germany and the United States underwent massive industrialization and urbanization during the pre–World War I era; both struggled with the far-ranging consequences in society, economy, and culture wrought by the processes of modernization. Both, in their way, were obsessed with the problem of race and with questions of national identity arising, ultimately, from the issue of race.

The differences between the two social systems, however, were almost as great as the similarities. Germany had only been unified as a nation since 1871, and in the 1920s its democratic political institutions were still in their relative infancy. The United States, despite its failure to incorporate nonwhites fully into the system, was one of the oldest functioning political democracies in the world. The unification of Germany forced a number of small and medium-size states to come together, but the regional differences within the created nation were counteracted by the strength of the centralized bureaucracy inherited from the Prussian state. In the United States – except in a purely linguistic sense – regional

---

51 Emerson Hunsberger Loucks, *The Ku Klux Klan in Pennsylvania: A Study in Nativism* (Harrisburg, Pa., 1936), 40; Charles C. Alexander, *The Ku Klux Klan in the Southwest* (New York, 1966), 55–82, 245–6; Nancy MacLean, *Behind the Mask of Chivalry: The Making of the Second Ku Klux Klan* (New York, 1994), 127 (quotation), chaps. 2–3, 5; Kathleen M. Blee, *Women of the Klan: Racism and Gender in the 1920s* (New York, 1991), chap. 3; Shawn Lay, *Hooded Knights of the Niagara: The Ku Klux Klan in Buffalo, New York* (New York, 1995), 86–101; William D. Jenkins, *Steel Valley Klan: The Ku Klux Klan in Ohio's Mahoning Valley* (Kent, Ohio, 1990), 84, found a wider occupational variation among klansmen, but skilled workers were still overrepresented.

52 On the specific circumstances faced by Germans after World War I, see Richard Bessel, *Germany after the First World War* (New York, 1993).

differences were at least as important as in Germany, but the regions were spread out over a vastly larger area. Equally important, the authority not only of particular states but of individual cities and towns was much more significant than in Germany. When the growth of a "bureaucratic mode of thought" in the United States occurred in the early twentieth century, it did so largely within this context.[53] Despite vast concentrations of power in the economic realm, politically the United States remained a radically decentralized society.

The role of ethnic minorities in the two societies reveals both parallels and important differences. Polish immigrants constituted a significant minority group that became a disquieting presence in a united Germany. Germany's rapid industrialization in the late nineteenth century created opportunities for immigrant labor. Germany ranked as a major producer of steel and nonferrous metals, and Polish immigrants were especially important as a source of skilled labor in the mining industry in the Ruhr.[54] Between 1890 and 1910 the number of Poles living in the Rhineland and Westphalia rose dramatically, from about 30,000 to between 300,000 and 350,000.[55] Much like the new immigrants in the United States, Poles in the Ruhr were both needed as workers and resented as an alien cultural presence. Most Germans considered Poles – and Slavs in general – as an inferior people. The prevalence of such views among German workers and their organizations, John Kulczycki has demonstrated, undercut labor solidarity in the mining industry. Prior to World War I, the Reich attempted to repress the use of the Polish language and, wherever possible, require the use of German; it was not always possible to enforce this policy, but it was nevertheless deeply resented by the Poles.[56]

The acquisition of a sizable Polish population as a result of territorial expansion to the east created more serious internal tensions. Not sur-

---

53 The thesis of growing organization and bureaucracy was stressed by Robert Wiebe in his influential synthesis, *The Search for Order, 1877–1920* (New York, 1967), chaps. 5–6. Wiebe focused mostly on elites, however, and largely ignored the working class, women, African Americans, and others whose lives had little to do with bureaucracy on a day-to-day basis.

54 On the rise of the German metal industry, see Alfred Chandler Jr., *Scale and Scope: The Dynamics of Industrial Capitalism* (Cambridge, Mass., 1990), 486–96. By 1914, Germany had surpassed Great Britain as the second largest industrial economy in the world (after the United States). Ibid., 503.

55 Christopher Klessman, *Polnische Bergarbeiter im Ruhrgebiet 1870–1945* (Göttingen, 1978), 22, 261 (table 2). Exact statistics are not available, because of the difficulty of identifying ethnic groups at that time.

56 Ibid., 63–8; John Kulczycki, *The Foreign Worker and the German Labor Movement: Xenophobia and Solidarity in the Coal Fields of the Ruhr* (Oxford, 1994).

prisingly, from the beginning of the Second Reich, German nationalists viewed the Polish population in East Prussia as a problem. Bismarck inaugurated a kulturkampf against the Poles in the 1870s that included suppression of the Polish language in schools and government bureaucracy, and in 1883–5 he took the extraordinary step of expelling 32,000 Austrian and Russian subjects, two-thirds of them Poles (the other one-third were Jews), who had settled in Berlin or East Prussia. Bismarck also initiated a program of buying out Polish nobility and parceling out their estates to German peasant colonists. These policies were applauded by the Eastern Marches Society (Ostmarkenverein or OMV), a nationalist organization founded in 1893 that continually pressured the government to carry out further Germanization (*Germanisierung*) of the eastern provinces. For the most part, however, this did not happen. Despite the migration of some Poles to western Germany and the United States, their higher birthrate assured their continued domination of the population of Poznan, where they made up 63.6 percent of the inhabitants in 1890.[57] The Ostmarkenverein attracted *völkisch* nationalists who not only wanted to expel the Poles from the eastern provinces but also viewed the Junker landowner class as a hindrance to the development of a German national spirit. Prior to World War I, the OMV was unable to make much progress because of its ties to the Conservatives, who opposed the sale of Junker lands. A radical resettlement plan was seriously discussed during World War I, but Germany's defeat in 1918 ended the nationalists' dream of what today would be called "ethnic cleansing" in the East. As William Hagen notes, however, the idea "remained as a legacy to the National Socialists," who did indeed carry out a policy of massive deportation (often to forced labor camps) in western Poland during World War II.[58]

The Polish question was more significant prior to 1918 than is indicated by the relatively small amount of attention it has received from scholars. As Hans-Ulrich Wehler perceptively notes, Wilhelmine official policy toward the Poles (*die Polenpolitik*) "encouraged a situation in which discrimination against minorities came to be accepted."[59] In the

57 William W. Hagen, *Germans, Poles, and Jews: The Nationality Conflict in the Prussian East, 1772–1914* (Chicago, 1980), 127–35; Klaus J. Bade, "Kulturkampf auf dem Arbeitsmarkt: Bismarcks 'Polenpolitik' 1885–1890," in Otto Pflanze, ed., *Innenpolitische Probleme des Bismarck-Reiches* (Munich, 1983), 121–42.
58 Hagen, *Germans, Poles, and Jews*, 284–6; see also Edward L. Homze, *Foreign Labor in Nazi Germany* (Princeton, N.J., 1967), 27–8.
59 Hans-Ulrich Wehler, *The German Empire, 1871–1918*, trans. Kim Traynor (Dover, N.H., 1985), 113.

immediate postwar period, however, the loss of East Prussian territory to
Poland and the drastic decline in the need for foreign workers as a result
of a severely damaged economy made the problem of a Polish minority
in Germany less urgent. Only 70,000 Polish workers remained in the
Ruhr region (Ruhrgebiet) in 1925, and despite continuing discrimination, the second generation was becoming much more integrated into
German society by that time.[60] This trend was reversed after 1935,
however, as first the revived German economy and then the needs of
wartime production led to a huge increase in the number of Polish laborers in Germany. The Nazi regime responded by bringing the Poles under
increasing surveillance. During World War II leaders of Polish organizations were incarcerated and sometimes murdered, and as the war proceeded the Gestapo carried out an increasingly brutal policy of repression
against foreigners. As a group, however, Polish workers were not sent to
concentration camps.[61]

Although more vicious in some respects, the German treatment of the
Poles during the war bears an uncanny similarity to U.S. policy toward
Japanese Americans. With the exception of a small group of suspected
"troublemakers," the mass internment of individuals of Japanese ancestry
from the West Coast was not duplicated for the Japanese in Hawaii, despite
the glaring fact that the bombing of Pearl Harbor had occurred there.
Like the Polish workers in the Ruhr, the Japanese in Hawaii were strictly
controlled (including repression of their native culture and language), but
they were too valuable as a labor source to remove them to internment
camps. Finally, as Gary Okihero has pointed out, both in Hawaii and on
the mainland the subjugation of the Japanese was intensified by the
wartime crisis, but it had its roots in policies and attitudes dating back
several decades.[62] Much the same could be said of the Polish minority in
Germany.

Although concern about the Poles subsided temporarily after World
War I, the French use of African or Asian colonial troops as part of their
forces occupying the Rhineland raised the specter of a new racial threat

---

60 Klessman, *Polnische Bergarbeiter*, 176, 261 (table 2); and Richard Charles Murphy, *Guestworkers in
    the German Reich: A Polish Community in Wilhelmian Germany* (Boulder, Colo., 1983), which despite
    its title deals with the period up to 1933.
61 Homze, *Foreign Labor*, 23–5; Klessman, *Polnische Bergarbeiter*, 183–6; and Robert Gellately, *The
    Gestapo and German Society: Enforcing Racial Policy, 1933–1945* (Oxford, 1990), chap. 8. See also
    Robert Gellately, "Situating the 'SS-State' in a Social Historical Context: Recent Histories of the
    SS, the Police, and the Courts in the Third Reich," *Journal of Modern History* 64 (1992): 358–9.
62 Gary Okihero, *Cane Fires: The Anti-Japanese Movement in Hawaii, 1865–1945* (Philadelphia, 1991),
    211–24, 272.

in the mind of German nationalists. In the decades prior to World War I, Germans had interacted with dark-skinned people more frequently through travel in the United States and in the newly acquired African colonies. Many of the same stereotypes about blacks common in the United States developed in Germany at this time, communicated through popular travel literature as well as "scientific" studies of race characteristics that became a staple of fascist propaganda in the 1920s and 1930s. Hitler, in *Mein Kampf*, referred to Africans as "half-apes" and argued against missionary work in Africa because in his opinion, the "primitive and inferior" race that lived there was not reclaimable.[63] The intrusion of foreign black troops provoked both racist and xenophobic responses. "Abroad Germany is already humiliated," said Hitler in a speech in 1922, and "the state trembles before every French Negro captain." Revulsion toward the "yellow and black hordes of France . . . raging through our Palatinate" played an important role in attracting early adherents to the Nazi Party.[64]

Apprehension about blacks as an occupying force ended with the withdrawal of French troops from the Rhineland, although the Nazis in their propaganda would repeatedly remind Germans of what they called the *schwarze Schande* (black disgrace).[65] However, the fear of blacks as carriers of alien cultural forms would continue throughout the Weimar era. The sudden appearance of African-American entertainers in Berlin and other large cities elicited a hostile response from cultural conservatives. As in the case of the foreign troops, their response often combined racism with xenophobia, although the latter was aimed primarily at the United States, not France. To many Germans, cabaret entertainment represented all the bad features of American-influenced modernism. As Michael H. Kater has shown, conservative critics particularly singled out jazz – described as

---

63 Adolf Hitler, *Mein Kampf* (Boston, 1943), 403, 430. See also ibid., 395; Adolf Hitler, *The Speeches of Adolf Hitler*, ed. Norman H. Baynes, 2 vols. (New York, 1969), 1:83 (speech at 1924 trial); 2:783–4 (speech of Jan. 27, 1932); 2:1568 (speech of Jan. 30, 1939). For further evidence of black stereotypes in Germany, see Michael Kater, *Different Drummers: Jazz in the Culture of Nazi Germany* (New York, 1992), 19.

64 *Speeches of Adolf Hitler*, 1:37 (speech of July 28, 1922); Peter H. Merkl, *Political Violence Under the Swastika: 581 Early Nazis* (Princeton, N.J., 1975), 193. See also *Speeches of Adolf Hitler*, 1:629, and Gerhard L. Weinberg, *Germany, Hitler, and World War II: Essays on Modern German History* (Cambridge, 1995), 33–4. For examples of racist portrayals of African Americans in travel literature, see Emil Deckert, *Die Neue Welt: Reiseskizzen aus dem Norden und Süden der Vereinigten Staaten sowie Kanada und Mexico* (Berlin, 1892), 271–5, and Hugo Münsterberg, *Die Amerikaner* (Berlin, 1904), 265–73.

65 See, e.g., the memoir of Daniel Guérin's trip through Germany in 1932–33, *The Brown Plague: Travels in Late Weimar and Early Nazi Germany*, trans. Robert Schwartzwald (Durham, N.C., 1994), 100.

"nigger noise" by one commentator – for its detrimental effects on German culture. Hitler called modern artistic trends "trash," something "which a nation of Negroes might just as well have produced." When the National Socialists briefly took over the Thuringian state government in 1930, they quickly prohibited "jazz bands and drum music, Negro dances, Negro songs, [and] Negro plays," along with the paintings of Paul Klee and Wassily Kandinsky.[66]

Only fragments of their story have been told, but it is clear that after 1930 foreigners generally, and African Americans especially, found circumstances in Germany increasingly difficult. Subjected to increasing harassment, by 1931 many American jazz musicians began to leave the country. The African-American biologist Ernest Everett Just, who had intermittently found a relatively accepted place in the cosmopolitan intellectual atmosphere of Berlin during the late Weimar period, decided to leave Germany in the spring of 1933 when he witnessed the rampant racism being fomented by National Socialists. In 1935 the German government barred black jazz artists such as Duke Ellington, as well as the famous African-American singer, Marian Anderson, from performing in Germany.[67] Sexual unions of blacks and Germans were prohibited in the Nuremberg Laws of 1935, and two years later, fearful that a "mixed race" group of "coloreds" similar to that which existed in the United States or South Africa might emerge in Germany, the Nazi regime carried out a program of forced sterilization of all German children with any African ancestry.[68]

German concerns about Poles and blacks fluctuated greatly over time. By contrast, Jews were the one minority group whose place in the social and political order was, for most Germans, the subject of continual, often intense discussion and debate throughout the entire industrialization period.[69] Many of the stereotypes of anti-Semitism had much in common with those applied to the Chinese in the United States – materialism, las-

---

66 Kater, *Different Drummers*, 19, 24–5; Hitler, *Mein Kampf*, 70. See also Mike Zwerin, *La Tristesse de Saint Louis: Swing Under the Nazis* (London, 1985), and Peter Jelavich, *Berlin Cabaret* (Cambridge, Mass., 1993).

67 Kater, *Different Drummers*, 27–8, 30; Kenneth R. Manning, *Black Apollo of Science: The Life of Ernest Everett Just* (New York, 1983), 246.

68 Benno Müller-Hill, *Murderous Science: Elimination by Scientific Selection of Jews, Gypsies, and Others: Germany, 1933–1945* (Oxford, 1988), 11.

69 Gypsies were also perceived as a racially inferior group, and like the Jews would be subject to attack and mass extermination during the Nazi era. Perhaps because they lived outside the main contours of German life, however, their role in German society was never the subject of debate as was that of the Jewish minority. See Angus Fraser, *The Gypsies*, 2d ed. (Oxford, 1995), 249–69.

civiousness, conspiratorial designs. In addition, of course, both groups were non-Christian (a problem that did not apply to Poles in either society). In the United States, however, the Chinese and the Russian Jews each constituted only one racial "problem" among many. German Jews were not perceived in the same manner because they had been a part of German life for centuries. Unlike the Poles and Gypsies, many of them had successfully risen to important positions in trade and the professions by the early twentieth century. Poles were perceived as temporary migratory laborers or as outsiders acquired as part of territorial expansion. Especially after World War I, they were not seen as an intractable problem.

The sudden intrusion of blacks into German society presented quite a different kind of threat. Africans and African Americans were dangerous not because of their numbers but because of their symbolic association with foreign domination or with new, ominous cultural trends. To a much greater degree than in the United States, however, antagonism toward blacks in Germany was more likely to be directly connected to hostility toward Jews. In a flight of ideological fancy and anti-Semitism, Hitler blamed Jews for "bring[ing] the Negroes into the Rhineland," and racist writers readily linked the growth of jazz and cabaret entertainment in Germany with Jews, who were not only musicians but sometimes managers and promoters at jazz clubs.[70] In a remarkable passage in *Mein Kampf*, Hitler expressed his fear that Jews might use black achievements to advance their own cause:

From time to time illustrated papers bring it to the attention of the German petty-bourgeois that some place or other a Negro has for the first time become a lawyer, teacher, even a pastor, in fact a heroic tenor, or something of the sort. While the idiotic bourgeoisie looks with amazement at such miracles of education . . . the Jew shrewdly draws from it a new proof for the soundness of his theory about the *equality of man* that he is trying to funnel into the minds of the nations.[71]

Successful black professionals, like African soldiers, promoted an insidious racial egalitarianism that could all too easily be applied to Jews.[72] To the Nazis, the unwanted intrusion of blacks into German society, horrendous in its own right, was also proof of the pernicious influence of Jews on German life.

In Germany as in the United States, anti-Semitism grew in a broader

70 Hitler, *Mein Kampf*, 325; Kater, *Different Drummers*, 20–3.
71 Hitler, *Mein Kampf*, 430 (original emphasis).
72 The denial of human equality was a central tenet of all fascist doctrines.

atmosphere of intensified racism and xenophobia. In the United States, however, matters of racial and ethnic intolerance were worked out in an incredibly complex demographic and political context, with myriad ethno-racial groups jockeying for position within a system that was not – as the saying goes – a level playing field but one where certain groups were assumed to be inherently inferior and were treated as such, while others were viewed as more or less capable of entering into the social order and the body politic as equals. Germany was a far more homogeneous society, and only one group – the Jews – was perceived (rightly or wrongly) as being in competition with Germans during the formative period of industrialization (1870–1914). Prior to World War I, racialist intellectuals as well as patriotic organizations like the Pan-German League, although they certainly shared the antagonism of the Ostmarkenverein to the Poles, focused primarily on the "Jewish problem" as the key feature of the emergent system of nationalist *völkisch* thought.[73]

Although both animosities played a role in attracting early adherents to the Nazi Party, anti-Semitism was clearly more important than xenophobia in the emerging National Socialist weltanschauung.[74] In Germany (and Austria), xenophobic reaction to the influx of eastern European Jews after World War I simply reinforced an already well established hostility toward Jews as a despised group.[75] In the United States even a rabid racist like Madison Grant, whose antidemocratic elitism and belief in racial purity had much in common with European fascist intellectuals, leveled his broadsides against a wide spectrum of non-Nordic groups. And although people of African or Asian ancestry suffered the most violence and sharpest prejudice, Mexicans and southern and eastern European immigrants were also stereotyped as racially inferior and experienced significant levels of discrimination. The passage of legislation restricting immigration to the United States adversely affected a variety of European and Asian groups.

Prior to World War I nativist and racist organizations were more

73 Fritz Stern, *The Politics of Cultural Despair: The Rise of Germanic Ideology* (Berkeley, Calif., 1961); George L. Mosse, *The Crisis of German Ideology: Intellectual Origins of the Third Reich* (New York, 1964); Roger Chickering, *We Men Who Are Most German: A Cultural History of the Pan-German League, 1886–1914* (Boston, 1984), 1, 230–45.

74 See the data compiled from the statements of 531 early Nazis, who in 1934 described why they became National Socialists. Sixty-six percent showed some evidence of anti-Semitism, whereas only 43 percent demonstrated ethnocentricity other than anti-Semitism. Merkel, *Political Violence*, 499, 517.

75 George L. Mosse, *Germans and Jews: The Right, the Left, and the Search for a "Third Force" in Pre-Nazi Germany* (New York, 1970), 44–7; Evan Burr Bukey, *Hitler's Hometown: Linz, Austria, 1908–1986* (Bloomington, Ind., 1986), 54.

numerous and broad-based in the United States than were anti-Semitic organizations in Germany, where associations such as the Pan-German League were limited mostly to an upper-middle-class membership.[76] Anti-Semitism in the United States was to some extent subsumed under a more general hostility to the "new immigrants" from southern and eastern Europe, but it also operated independently, leading to exclusion of Jews from elite social organizations and middle-class resorts, quotas in admission to Ivy League colleges, and severe discrimination in the legal and, to a lesser extent, medical professions. There can be little doubt that German Jews were far more successful in entering the mainstream of the legal and medical professions than were Jews in the United States. This is especially true of the law. In Prussia in 1880 Jews made up 7.3 percent of all attorneys; by 1904 they comprised an astonishing 27.4 percent. Nor were Jewish lawyers marginalized within the profession. By the end of the Weimar era they were among the most successful members of the bar.

In the United States, however, an old guard of self-consciously elitist Anglo-Saxon lawyers continued to exercise disproportionate influence; they sought to exclude not only Jews but other "new immigrants" and blacks as well from the profession. It was primarily this group that led the unsuccessful effort to prevent Louis D. Brandeis from taking a seat on the Supreme Court in 1916. In the 1920s they loudly supported immigration restriction and fought against the proliferation of "night schools" for legal training, which they feared allowed too many immigrants, Jews, and blacks access to the profession. By 1930 German Jews were totally integrated into the legal profession (indeed they dominated it in Berlin and Frankfurt), while in the United States the bar that emerged following several decades of professionalization was stratified along lines of race and ethnicity, as well as class. Restricted law school admissions and certification procedures channeled most Jewish, immigrant, and black lawyers into smaller law firms or "solo" practice, whereas large law firms dealing with lucrative corporate business continued to be dominated by old-stock Americans.[77] In contrast to law and medicine, Jewish participation in

---

76 On the social basis of the Pan-German League and similar nationalist groups, see Chickering, *We Men*, 107–8; and Geoff Eley, *Reshaping the German Right: Radical Nationalism and Political Change after Bismarck* (New Haven, Conn., 1980), 122.

77 Konrad H. Jarausch, "Jewish Lawyers in Germany, 1848–1938: The Disintegration of a Profession," *Leo Baeck Institute Year Book* 36 (1991): 171–90; Geoffrey Cocks, "Partners and Pariahs: Jews and Medicine in Modern German Society," *Leo Baeck Institute Year Book* 36 (1991): 194–5; Jerold Auerbach, *Unequal Justice: Lawyers and Social Change in Modern America* (New York, 1976), 66–73, 99–100, 106–29.

German academic fields apparently peaked around 1880 and declined steadily thereafter. Although Jews continued to be overrepresented in university positions, by the Weimar era Jewish academics were much less significant, in numbers and influence, than in the medical and legal professions.[78] In business, however, there was only a mild decline in the late 1920s in the significant role that German Jews had played in banking and as managers of industrial concerns since the late nineteenth century.

Jewish success in trade and certain professions in Germany in the decades following emancipation paralleled the rise of a widespread ideological anti-Semitism. Recent investigations of prewar German anti-Semitism have found its main thrust to be either assimilationist or separatist in nature. The former emphasized the conversion of Jews to Christianity and their adoption of German culture; the latter argued for the need to repeal emancipation and resegregate Jews, both socially and economically. Those anti-Semites favoring separatism, however, did not demand the expulsion of Jews from Germany; nor, except in very rare instances, did even extreme anti-Semites urge the destruction (*Vernichtung*) of Jews, as would later be urged – and all too literally carried out – by the Nazis.[79] Furthermore, unlike the anti-Polish Ostmarkenverein, German anti-Semites were largely unsuccessful in translating their ideas into practical political programs, either by influencing the Conservatives or through the short-lived anti-Semitic political parties.[80]

What prewar anti-Semites did accomplish – with profound implications for the Weimar and Nazi eras – was the establishment of anti-Semitism as a respectable part of German culture and politics. Not all elements of German society were equally attracted to anti-Semitism, of course, and most liberals as well as the left-wing parties found it reprehensible.[81] Nevertheless, as Shulamit Volkov has argued, anti-Semitism gained broad acceptance within political/social discourse as a "cultural code" symbolizing many emerging (and, to some extent, threatening) aspects of the new Germany at the turn of the century: democratic pol-

---

78 See Fritz K. Ringer, "Academics in Germany: German and Jew, Some Preliminary Remarks," *Leo Baeck Institute Year Book* 36 (1991): 211, citing unpublished data on Göttingen by David Vampola; W. E. Mosse, *Jews in the German Econoomy: The German-Jewish Economic Elite, 1820–1935* (Oxford, 1987).

79 Donald L. Niewyk, "Solving the 'Jewish Problem': Continuity and Change in German Anti-Semitism," *Leo Baeck Institute Year Book* 35 (1990): 335–70.

80 Richard S. Levy, *The Downfall of the Anti-Semitic Political Parties in Imperial Germany* (New Haven, Conn., 1975).

81 Werner Jochman, "Struktur und Funktion des deutschen Antisemitismus, 1878–1914," in Herbert A. Strauss and Norbert Kampe, eds., *Antisemitismus: Von der Judenfeindschaft zum Holocaust,* Schriftenreihe der Bundeszentrale für Politische Bildung, vol. 213 (Bonn, 1985), 131–4; and Sarah Gordon, *Hitler, Germans, and the "Jewish Question"* (Princeton, N.J., 1984), 24–41.

itics, the expansion of the market economy, and feminism, to name only a few.[82] The growth of anti-Semitism as a "normal" part of German society was also assisted, as Hartmut Lehmann notes, by the development of religious nationalism among German Protestants; during the Weimar era, Protestants fearful of the trend toward secularism and the declining authority of the Lutheran church would find some aspects of the Nazi ideology particularly attractive.[83] The stereotypes that surfaced in the rhetoric of those who urged Jews either to assimilate into German society or separate themselves from it were pervasive and repeatedly connected the image of the Jew to other troubling aspects of German industrial society. What one might call the normalization of anti-Semitic rhetoric in Wilhelmine Germany laid the groundwork that made the more vicious assault (both symbolic and physical) of the Nazis on Jews more generally acceptable, even to those who were attracted to the National Socialists for other reasons.[84] At least as late as the mid-1920s German Jews suffered less discrimination in many professions than their American co-religionists; they were much more prominent than American Jews in the business realm. There is no evidence that German Jews were subject to physical attacks. (It was in the United States, one should remember, not Germany, where Leo Frank was lynched.) Nevertheless, in Germany anti-Semitism was far more pervasive and more focused. In the words of Werner Jochmann, anti-Semitism "became 'socially acceptable' but at the same time more enigmatic and dangerous."[85]

In the *Sonderweg* debate in recent German historiography, one group of scholars has argued that the weakness of liberal democracy and the growth of fascism derived from the persistence of "premodern" mentalities and structures during an era of rapid industrialization, especially among the traditional middle class. Another has argued that the German middle class exhibited a growing complexity at the turn of the century and in social and economic matters was not necessarily "pre-industrial";

82 Shulamit Volkov, "Antisemitism as a Cultural Code: Reflections on the History and Historiography of Antisemitism in Imperial Germany," *Leo Baeck Institute Year Book* 23 (1978): 25–46.

83 Hartmut Lehmann, "The Germans as a Chosen People: Old Testament Themes in German Nationalism," *German Studies Review* 14, no. 2 (1991): 261–73; Uriel Tal, *Christians and Jews in Germany: Religion, Politics and Ideology in the Second Reich, 1870–1914* (Ithaca, N.Y., 1975); Jochmann, "Struktur und Funktion," 134–5; Kurt Nowak, "Protestantismus und Weimarer Republik: Politische Wegmarken in der evangelischen Kirche 1918–1932," in Karl Dietrich Bracher, Manfred Funke, and Hans-Adolf Jacobsen, eds., *Die Weimarer Republik 1918–1933: Politik, Wirtschaft, Gesellschaft*, Bonner Schriften zur Politik und Zeitgeschichte, vol. 22 (Düsseldorf, 1987), 218–37.

84 Shulamit Volkov, "Kontinuität und Diskontinuität im deutschen Antisemitismus 1878–1945," *Vierteljahrshefte für Zeitgeschichte* 33 (1985): 221–43; Niewyk, "Solving the 'Jewish Problem,'" 368–70; Robert Griffith, *The Nature of Fascism* (New York, 1991), 86–7.

85 Jochman, "Struktur und Funktion," 135.

they find the political appeal to corporatist, premodern themes directed at this group to be largely propaganda not related to the actual social or economic behavior of the middle class.[86] As far as the appeal to racism as an important aspect of preindustrial mentalities is concerned, however, much depends on how one defines the troublesome term *modern*. Neither in the United States nor in Germany did those who attacked, excluded, or later sought to exterminate groups deemed deviant or unacceptable necessarily reject modernity in a larger sense. Jackson Lears has shown how antimodern cultural manifestations at the turn of the century iron-ically helped pave the way for modernization in the twentieth century.[87] In some ways racism may have performed a similar function. Far from being "a thoroughly modern weapon used in the conduct of premodern, or at least not exclusively modern, struggles,"[88] as one scholar has said of racism in German history, it appears that racism was an ancient weapon that, in some ways, indirectly promoted modernization. Fear of both the Poles and the Jews in Germany may have helped to overcome class and regional divisions in industrializing Germany, thus smoothing the path to a more modern social order.[89] Fascism, notes Robert Griffith, was inher-ently racist but not necessarily antimodern; to call it such "betrays a set of value judgments about what constitutes the ideal path of moderniza-tion for societies to follow."[90] The racially "pure" community that the Nazis desired was built on age-old myths, but to create it required modern tools of technology, bureaucracy, and, ultimately, a system of impersonal mass murder.

III

In the United States, as in Germany, the era of rapid modernization pro-duced conflict and cultural backlash. Concerns about the "disorderly"

---

86 See Roger Fletcher, "Recent Developments in West German Historiography: The Bielefeld School and Its Critics," *German Studies Review* 7 (1984): 45–80; Helga Grebing, *Der "Deutsche Sonderweg" in Europa, 1806–1945: Eine Kritik* (Stuttgart, 1986).

87 T. J. Jackson Lears, *No Place of Grace: Antimodernism and the Transformation of American Culture, 1880–1920* (New York, 1981).

88 Zygmunt Bauman, *Modernity and the Holocaust* (Ithaca, N.Y., 1989), 62.

89 Hans-Ulrich Wehler, "Polenpolitik im Deutschen Kaiserreich 1871–1918," in Ernst-Wolfgang Böckenförde, ed., *Moderne deutsche Verfassungsgeschichte (1815–1918)* (Cologne, 1972); Jost Hermand, *Old Dreams and a New Reich: Volkish Utopias and National Socialism*, trans. Paul Levesque and Stefan Soldovieri (Bloomington, Ind., 1992).

90 Griffith, *Nature of Fascism*, 47–8. For the argument that National Socialism represented not an antimodern thrust so much as a "dark" version of modernization, see Rainer Zitelmann, *Hitler: Selbstverständnis eines Revolutionärs*, 3d ed. (Frankfurt am Main, 1990).

character of a multi-ethnic society made Benito Mussolini a sympathetic figure in 1920s America.[91] Many of the nativist ideologies and violent actions directed against minority groups in America could be called "fascistic." The growth of the Ku Klux Klan to between two and four million members in the early 1920s, with its desire to impose a conservative morality as well as religious and racial purity on local communities of the South and Midwest, also had many overtones of fascism, whatever normal community activities that "citizen Klansmen" may also have engaged in.[92] "The path to National Socialism," says historian Fritz Stern, "led through a wasteland of personal fears, collective anxiety, and resentments." Much the same could be said of the second Klan, as well as many other racist and nativist groups that preceded it.[93] Both sets of organizations promoted a conservative view of women's place in the social order, and both partly justified their position by positing a sexual threat from a minority group. (The Jewish employer as sexual predator was a staple of Nazi propaganda in the party newspaper *Der Stürmer*.[94]) Once in power, Nazi policies encouraged German women to leave the work force and return to their traditional role as mothers. These views even influenced religious institutions. Some pro-Nazi Protestants wanted to limit women's role in church affairs and create a church where the "manly" (*männlich*) qualities of discipline and soldierly comradeship would be emphasized.[95]

The membership base of the Nazi Party also had much in common with the Klan. Both organizations drew heavily from a predominantly Protestant lower-middle-class group of small businessmen, farmers, white-collar workers, and skilled artisans; neither attracted very many industrial workers.[96] Why then – to turn Werner Sombart's famous question around

---

91 See John P. Diggins, *Mussolini and Fascism: The View from America* (Princeton, N.J., 1972).

92 Leonard J. Moore, *Citizen Klansman: The Ku Klux Klan in Indiana, 1921–28* (Chapel Hill, N.C., 1991), emphasizes the "normality" of Klan activities and downplays their nativism and racism. The two types of behavior are not mutually exclusive, however. Right-wing organizations (even the Nazi Party) in Germany engaged in many activities that were not specifically anti-Semitic, but a virulent anti-Semitism nonetheless remained a key aspect of their weltanschauung.

93 Fritz Stern, *Dreams and Delusions: The Drama of German History* (New York, 1987), 149.

94 Dennis E. Showalter, *Little Man, What Now? Der Stürmer in the Weimar Republic* (Hamden, Conn., 1982), chap. 4.

95 See Claudia Koonz, *Mothers in the Fatherland: Women, the Family, and Nazi Politics* (New York, 1987); and Doris L. Bergen, *Twisted Cross: The German Christian Movement in the Third Reich* (Chapel Hill, N.C., 1996), chap. 4.

96 On the social base of the Nazi Party, see Stern, *Dreams and Delusions*, chap. 3; Johnpeter Horst Grill, *The Nazi Movement in Baden, 1920–1945* (Chapel Hill, N.C., 1983), 82–5; Michael Kater, *The Nazi Party: A Social Profile of Members and Leaders, 1919–1945* (Cambridge, Mass., 1983), 20–31, 242–50 (tables 2–6); Thomas Childers, *The Nazi Voter: The Social Foundations of Fascism in*

to the right – was there no fascism in the United States?[97] By any objective criteria, in the mid-1920s the United States seemed much more likely than Germany to fall under the sway of a right-wing movement. At a time when the Nazi Party in Germany was a small band of fanatics able to capture only a tiny fraction of the vote in 1925, the Ku Klux Klan was a mass movement that had made significant inroads into the Democratic Party, especially in the Midwest and South. In the late 1920s, however, the collapse of the Klan occurred at almost the same time that the National Socialists in Germany rose to influence. In seeking to explain the rapid decline of the Klan, historians have put forward many explanations, including the failure of a corrupt leadership in the Klan itself. MacLean, in drawing a comparison with European fascism, argues that improving economic conditions after 1922 in the United States, plus a perceived decline in black and labor militancy, were the prime reasons for the collapse of the Klan as a major political force.[98] The German economy, however, although far weaker, also improved after 1924; yet this did not prevent organizations such as the Stahlhelm from attracting a disaffected element of the middle class and providing important organizational training for the later development of National Socialism.[99] Nor, if economic causes were pre-eminent, is the argument compelling, because the United States also suffered severely during the Great Depression, yet this did not lead to a significant revival of the Klan.

Surprisingly, historians of the Klan tend to ignore a very specific reason why the organization declined: its success, in 1924, in attaining one of its central goals, the passage of racially discriminatory immigration restriction legislation. Beyond this fact, however, we must look not to economics but more broadly to differences in the social and political systems of the two nations to explain the failure of the xenophobic right in the United States. The continuing diversity of targets among minority groups is one

---

Germany, 1919–1933 (Chapel Hill, N.C., 1983); Peter D. Stachura, "National Socialism and the German Proletariat, 1925–1935: Old Myths and New Perspectives," *Historical Journal* 36 (1993): 701–18. Whereas recent research indicates that Nazism was more broad-based than previously assumed, its core support continued to come from "small shopkeepers, independent artisans, and farmers" (see Thomas Childers, "Who, Indeed, Did Vote for Hitler," *Central European History* 17 [1984]: 51).

97 Werner Sombart, *Warum gibt es in den Vereinigten Staaten keinen Sozialismus?* (Tübingen, 1906). Recently, there has been an upsurge of interest in the second Ku Klux Klan, as well as a new recognition of the significance of conservative movements generally in American history. But scholars have yet to address the failure of fascism in the United States in the same manner in which they have struggled to explain why there was no successful American socialist movement.

98 MacLean, *Behind the Mask of Chivalry*, 179–88.

99 Peter Fritzsche, *Rehearsals for Fascism: Populism and Political Mobilization in Weimar Germany* (New York, 1990).

such cause, but equally important was the nascent political power of some of the minority groups in question. In contrast to Germany, where migrant Polish workers had little political influence, by World War I naturalized European immigrants in America made up a sizeable bloc of voters. As early as 1912 Woodrow Wilson, locked in a close, three-way race for president, was forced to recant prior racist statements about Italians and Hungarians in seeking the support of these ethnic groups.[100] At the local level, however, the influence of (northern) black and immigrant voters was much greater. In some eastern and midwestern cities, African Americans, together with "new immigrants" and their children, made up a clear majority of the population by 1920 and wielded substantial power. In the 1930s, of course, these groups would become essential components of the New Deal coalition.

In contrast to Germany, where the Nazi Party found an important primary core of recruits among elements of the urban lower-middle class, in most major American cities the Ku Klux Klan found only modest support and, indeed, much antagonism to their activities.[101] A factor that inhibited the growth of the Klan in Buffalo, notes one historian, was the existence of "large and politically empowered ethnic populations that were intensely anti-Klan." Even at the height of the Klan's influence, Irish and Italian Catholics, Jews, and African Americans banded together in large urban centers to fight the Klan and its propaganda, sometimes even resorting to violence against local Klan members.[102] In Germany, however, Jews made up less than one percent of the population, and even in Berlin (where one-third of all German Jews lived) they had little political influence. German Jews were an ideal scapegoat group: successful enough in selected, high-profile occupations to attract attention and spur envy, yet excluded from governmental power and not great enough in numbers to sway politicians through the electoral process.

Another distinctive aspect of the United States was the failure of fascism to take root among academic intellectuals or college students.

---

100 Gossett, *Race: The History of an Idea*, 442.
101 Grill, *Nazi Movement in Baden*, 83–4; William Sheridan Allen, *The Nazi Seizure of Power: The Experience of a Single German Town* (Chicago, 1967), 274–6. Kenneth T. Jackson, in *The Ku Klux Klan in the City, 1915–1930* (New York, 1967), overstates the importance of the Klan in the urban (at least big city) context. As his own data indicate, most Klansmen lived outside major urban areas, and given the relative size of cities, heavily white Protestant centers like Indianapolis had a disproportionately large number of Klan members compared to polyglot metropolises like New York and Chicago.
102 Lay, *Hooded Knights of the Niagara*, 145; Jenkins, *Steel Valley Klan*, 117–39; David J. Goldberg, "Unmasking the Ku Klux Klan: The Northern Movement against the KKK, 1920–1925," *Journal of Urban History* 15 (1996): 32–48.

There was widespread discrimination against blacks and Jews in many elite eastern colleges from the late nineteenth century to the 1940s, with blacks virtually (or in some cases, entirely) excluded and the number of Jewish students limited to 10 or 15 percent of those admitted each year. However, these patterns were less true of public universities, especially in the Midwest and West, where admissions policies were more open and discriminatory attitudes less pervasive.[103] In addition, during the 1920s the racist theories purveyed by popular and academic writers were beginning to be contested by sociologist Robert E. Park, cultural anthropologist Franz Boas, and their students. (Not surprisingly, Boas – a Jewish immigrant himself – found a congenial intellectual home at Columbia, the most ethnically diverse of the Ivy League universities.) As a result, among American psychologists and geneticists "the alarm over the effect of intermixture between 'inferior' and 'superior' races had largely subsided by the end of the 1920s."[104]

In contrast, racist theories remained intellectually respectable in Germany throughout the Weimar era. Several prominent German anthropologists produced studies that influenced the racial theories of National Socialism, and during the Third Reich they helped to justify and plan programs of sterilization or extermination of Jews, Gypsies, Poles, and others.[105] Such individuals thrived partly because they operated within an academic milieu that had long encouraged – or at the very least tolerated – racism. As early as the 1880s, a new romantic nationalism had begun to captivate German university students, embodied in organizations like the Association of German Students (Verein Deutscher Studenten or VDSt). Reversing the earlier liberal practices of student groups, the VDSt excluded Jews beginning in 1881. Anti-Semitism was only part of a general illiberalism that came to dominate student life prior to World War I. And as Konrad H. Jarausch has pointed out, it was in the universities that most of the ministers and officials who would lead Germany down the path to fascism in the post-World War I era had their initial training and

---

103 See Laurence R. Veysey, *The Emergence of the American University* (Chicago, 1967), 271, 287–8, and the superb survey by Marcia Graham Synnott, "Anti-Semitism and American Universities: Did Quotas Follow the Jews?" in Gerber, ed., *Anti-Semitism in American History*, 233–71. Some Midwestern private institutions, like the University of Chicago, also early developed a reputation for admitting Jews and blacks.

104 Gossett, *Race: The History of an Idea*, 426 (quotation); Fred Mathews, *Quest for an American Sociology: Robert E. Park and the Chicago School* (Montreal, 1977), 87, 170; Phillip R. Reilly, *The Surgical Solution: A History of Involuntary Sterilization in the United States* (Baltimore, 1991), 115–17.

105 For basic information on Ernst Fischer, Fritz Lenz, and other anthropologists and psychiatrists of the 1920s and 1930s, see the remarkable compendium by Muller-Hill, *Murderous Science*, 66–8.

socialization. German university students formed a key element in the early Nazi Party that helped legitimize it, because to a much greater degree than in American society institutions of higher education in Germany were reserved for the middle class and elite. German professors, while often sympathetic to the Nazis before 1933, seldom became party members, but their acceptance of anti-Semitism, notes Donald Niewyk, made them "more tolerant of their *völkisch* students than they might otherwise have been." German historians, in particular, had little trouble in adapting to National Socialism after Hitler came to power.[106] Nor was the participation of academics in the National Socialist movement limited to propagandizing. In Nuremberg in the late 1920s, 4.3 percent of Nazi stormtroopers (members of the Sturmabteilung or SA) held a Ph.D. degree, and in Munich in 1932, 12 percent of them were university students.[107]

The Ku Klux Klan, in marked contrast, could not look to institutions of higher education for support, and even on southern campuses there does not seem to have been much interest in the secret organization. Available occupational data on Klansmen reveals that very few teachers at any level became members. Nor is there any evidence of close collaboration between Nazi race theorists and American eugenicists, as one scholar has recently contended. In fact, the racial theories of American eugenicists such as Harry Hamilton Laughlin came under increasing attack in the 1930s, and German scientists hardly needed intellectual or moral support from scientific racists in the United States.[108]

The role of the universities in laying the groundwork for fascism in Germany was symptomatic of a general exclusion of Jews from positions of power in German social and political life both before and after World War I. The great prestige of Jews in the legal profession masked their

---

106 Konrad H. Jarausch, *Students, Society, and Politics in Imperial Germany* (Princeton, N.J., 1982), 266–7, 355; Donald Niewyk, *The Jews of Weimar Germany* (Baton Rouge, La., 1980), 69; Karen Schonwalder, *Historiker und Politik: Geschichtswissenschaft im Nationalsozialismus* (Frankfurt am Main, 1992); Stern, *Dreams and Delusions*, 159–61; Ulrich Herbert, *Best: Biographische Studien über Radikalismus, Weltanschauung und Vernunft 1903–1989* (Bonn, 1996), 42–86; and Michael Grüttner, *Studenten im Dritten Reich* (Paderborn, 1995), 19–100. For similar trends in Austria, see Bruce F. Pauley, *From Prejudice to Persecution: A History of Austrian Anti-Semitism* (Chapel Hill, N.C., 1992), 89, 121–30.

107 Conan Fischer, *Stormtroopers: A Social, Economic, and Ideological Analysis, 1929–1935* (London, 1983), 26 (table 3.1); Eric G. Reiche, *The Development of the SA in Nürnberg, 1922–34* (Cambridge, 1986), 69 (table 3.4).

108 Reilly, *Surgical Solution*, 68–70. The slender evidence provided by Stefan Kühl fails to prove his argument for close "collaboration" between Nazi racial scientists and eugenicists in the United States and elsewhere. See Stefan Kühl, *The Nazi Connection: Eugenics, American Racism, and German National Socialism* (New York, 1994).

relative lack of influence in the judiciary, politics, and the higher civil service. Non-baptized Jews were virtually excluded from the latter until the end of World War I. The number of Jews in judicial posts increased during the late imperial era (disproportionately favoring baptized Jews), then declined during the Weimar period. The number of Jews in political offices, elected or appointed, was insignificant after 1922. In this respect, says Peter Pulzer, "the Nazi seizure of power did not initiate the departure of Jews from the center stage of German public life, but gave it a radical acceleration."[109]

In the case of another important elite group, the German officer corps, little change in direction was necessary. Except during the crisis of World War I, since the 1870s Jews had been totally excluded from the Prussian officer corps. Nor were they able to obtain commissions in the reserve officer corps. Membership in the reserves entailed few duties but was socially prestigious and often served as an important stepping stone to a substantial career in the civil service. Despite a concerted effort, no Jews were able to gain commissions in the reserves between 1885 and 1914. As Fritz Stern succinctly notes, in Germany "there was no Dreyfus Affair because there was no Dreyfus."[110] Because of its high prestige and connections, through the reserve corps, to the universities (and, hence, to the positions of influence that would be held by university graduates), the officer corps exercised a disproportionately negative influence on the status of Jews in German society. "In an inward-looking, self-perpetuating hierarchy such as the German officer corps," says one historian, "anti-Semitism was a universally accepted creed." Long before Hitler came to power the officer corps symbolized the racially pure social order that would be glorified by the Nazis.[111]

Equally important for understanding differences between the two societies' response to racial minorities was the ambiguity of party politics and the weakness of the state in America compared to Germany (or, for that matter, most European nations). Thomas Childers, in addressing the *Sonderweg* debate, has persuasively argued that we can learn much about the motivation of voters from an analysis of the social language of poli-

109 John C. G. Röhl, "Higher Civil Servants in Germany, 1890–1910," in James J. Sheehan, ed., *Imperial Germany* (New York, 1976), 138–9; and Peter Pulzer, *Jews and the German State: The Political History of a Minority, 1848–1933* (London, 1992), 44–64, 272–6 (quotation, 276).

110 Stern, *Dreams and Delusions*, 107–8; Werner T. Angress, "Prussia's Army and the Jewish Reserve Officer Controversy Before World War I," in Sheehan, ed., *Imperial Germany*, 95, 101–3.

111 Wehler, *German Empire*, 125–7; Stern, *Dreams and Delusions*, 108; Martin Kitchen, *The German Officer Corps, 1890–1914* (Oxford, 1968), 37 (quotation).

tics in Germany during the 1920s.[112] It is unlikely, however, that his discovery of ideological appeals to specific occupational groups would be
duplicated by a comparative study of American political imagery of that
decade or any other period. Except for the obligatory nod to farmers,
American political rhetoric has seldom been aimed at particular occupational groups. Traditionally, such language has been vague and pitched to
a broad middle class – as it almost must be in a two-party system. Nor,
in American politics, has the corporatist mentality ever been popular (at
least since the death of the Whig Party). This remained true to a considerable degree even in the 1930s. Despite the expansion of state power
under the New Deal, studies of the ways in which the New Deal
policies were carried out have revealed substantial limitations on that
power at the local level.

In assessing the politics of the Depression decade, one is struck by
the fact that the enormous popularity of the anti-Semitic radio commentator, Father Charles Coughlin, yielded such a tiny political harvest.
Explicitly fascist political groups in America during the 1930s had very
little support compared to such movements in other Western nations,
partly because of the American right's traditional anti-statism.[113] Ironically,
Coughlin's own attempt to move from his role as the "radio priest" to
being the head of an organization (the National Union for Social Justice)
that would influence political decisions foundered on resistance to his plan
to control the organization from the top down. In promulgating his
philosophy over the airwaves, Coughlin himself had stressed the virtues
of small, locally controlled organizations as an alternative to big government and bureaucracy.[114]

Except for the World War I and II eras (and even then only to a
relatively limited degree, compared to European nations), in racial matters
the federal government often played a role only in a negative sense – as
in 1877, when it withdrew from the South, allowing white supremacy to

---

112 Thomas Childers, "The Social Language of Politics in Germany: The Sociology of Political Dis-
     course in the Weimar Republic," *American Historical Review* 95 (1990): 331–58.
113 On American right-wing radicalism, see Jürgen Kocka, *Angestellte zwischen Faschismus und
     Demokratie: Zur politischen Sozialgeschichte der Angestellten USA 1890–1940 im internationalen Ver-
     gleich* (Göttingen, 1977), 285–6. Coughlin did inspire the establishment of some fascist groups
     at the local level, e.g., the heavily Irish "Christian Front" in New York. See Ronald Baylor,
     Neighbors in Conflict: The Irish, Germans, Jews, and Italians of New York City, 1929–1941 (Baltimore,
     1978), 97–100, 139–41, 165–6. On the weakness of the American state in the 1930s, see the
     perceptive comments of Alan Dawley in *Struggles for Justice: Social Responsibility and the Liberal
     State* (Cambridge, Mass., 1991), 406–7.
114 See Alan Brinkley, *Voices of Protest: Huey Long, Father Coughlin, and the Great Depression* (New
     York, 1982), 186–92.

begin its resurgence, or in 1882 and 1924, when it excluded certain immigrant groups from entrance into the United States. In Germany, the Nazis were able to gain control and carry out their program rapidly because the machinery of centralization was already partly in place. The merging of the police and the SS (Schutzstaffel) in 1936 created the basis for a police state, but for decades the police had been far more intrusive in the lives of civilians in Germany than in America and were not accountable to local control. Most members of the Gestapo, Robert Gellately notes, had been "trained policemen, and many were carry-overs from the Weimar days."[115] The federal government in the United States, by contrast, usually allowed local communities to handle criminal justice matters, especially when they involved race. For decades the National Association for the Advancement of Colored People (NAACP) struggled in vain to get a federal anti-lynching bill through Congress.[116] Local control, as Richard Hofstadter emphasized in his last book documenting the history of violence in America, has certainly not always meant democratic control – especially for America's embattled racial minorities.[117] One might argue, however, that whatever limitations a weak central state has imposed on the struggle for progressive social change in the United States, it has at least prevented the development of organized terror from above.

"The story of racism is not pleasant to tell, and perhaps that is why it has been told so rarely in the fullness it deserves: not as the history of an aberration of European thought or as scattered moments of madness, but as an integral part of the European experience."[118] This statement, by the late George Mosse, is equally valid when applied to the United States. In both the United States and Germany, the period of rapid industrialization and urbanization coincided with the upsurge of racism and xenophobia, which in important ways controlled and channeled the social and political response to the new society that was coming into being.

115 See Elaine Glovka Spencer, *Police and the Social Order in German Cities: The Düsseldorf District, 1848–1914* (Dekalb, Ill., 1992), and George C. Browder, *Foundations of the Nazi Police State: The Formation of Sipo and the SD* (Lexington, Ky., 1990); and Gellately, *Gestapo and German Society*, 75.

116 Robert Zangrando, *The NAACP's Crusade Against Lynching, 1909–50* (Philadelphia, 1980). A parallel between the inability (or lack of will) in dealing with violence against racial minorities in the American South and West in the late nineteenth century may be found in Russia, where pogroms against Jews became commonplace after 1881. See I. Michael Aronson, *Troubled Waters: The Origins of the 1881 Anti-Jewish Pogroms in Russia* (Pittsburgh, 1991).

117 Richard Hofstadter, "Introduction," in Richard Hofstadter and Michael Wallace, eds., *Violence in America: A Documentary History* (New York, 1970), 28.

118 George L. Mosse, *Toward the Final Solution: A History of European Racism* (New York, 1985), xiv–xv.

Clearly, racism infected some social classes and (in the United States) ethnic groups more than others, with skilled workers, lower middle-class white-collar workers, and small businessmen most likely to adopt hostile or prejudiced attitudes toward minorities. Unskilled and semiskilled workers had little interest in the Ku Klux Klan, and in Germany the industrial working class strongly resisted Nazi propaganda aimed at them prior to 1930. Few industrial workers joined the Nazi Party, and even fewer became stormtroopers.[119] During the crisis-filled years 1930–3, blue-collar voters' support for National Socialism increased significantly in some localities but overall remained "underrepresented in relation to their size in the German population."[120]

The same cannot be said for elites. In fact, racism and xenophobia among the upper-middle class of substantial businessmen and professionals, although it affected fewer individuals in absolute terms than was true of other classes, was proportionately much higher in both Germany and the United States than is usually acknowledged. In Germany this was especially true of the salaried white-collar workers (*Angestellte*), a group particularly known for its virulent anti-Semitism. During 1930–2, as Eric Reiche has shown, almost 10 percent of Nazi stormtroopers in Nuremberg were professionals, managers, merchants, or leading civil servants.[121] During the Third Reich it was middle-level bureaucrats and planners who worked tirelessly and imaginatively to carry out the systematic destruction of Jews and other "inferior" groups throughout the Nazi-controlled

119 For a recent case study that re-emphasizes the appeal of Nazism to the middle class, see Benjamin Lapp, *Revolution from the Right: Politics, Class, and the Rise of Nazism in Saxony, 1919–1933* (Atlantic Highlands, N.J., 1997). Only 2 percent of Königsberg's industrial workers joined the SA at a time when this occupational group made up a quarter of the male workforce. In Nuremberg, unskilled workers made up only 3 percent of the SA prior to 1929 and only 5.3 percent during 1930–32. Richard Bessel, *Political Violence and the Rise of Nazism: The Storm Troopers of Eastern Germany, 1925–1934* (New Haven, Conn., 1984), 37; Reiche, *Development of the SA*, 68 (table 3.3), 108 (table 4.5). Conan Fischer's *Stormtroopers: A Social, Economic, and Ideological Analysis, 1929–1935* (London, 1983) is somewhat confusing because it fails to distinguish skilled workers from semi-skilled and unskilled workers. Skilled workers were much more likely to become party or SA members than were less skilled workers. On the function of anti-Semitism in the weltanschauung of skilled workers, see Shulamit Volkov, *The Rise of Popular Anti-Modernism in Germany: The Urban Master Artisans, 1873–1896* (Princeton, N.J., 1987), chaps. 8, 10.

120 Reiche, *Development of the SA*, 98–100; Stachura, "National Socialism and the German Proletariat," 707–8 (quotation), summarizes recent literature on this subject. As he points out (717), whereas blue-collar support for the Nazis has received attention from scholars, "working-class racism and anti-semitism is to date a virtually unploughed field."

121 Kater, *Nazi Party*, 62–70; and Reiche, *Development of the SA*, 108 (table 4.5). Almost 8 percent of early SA members (1922–3) were professionals and equally significant, 10 percent were the sons of managers or leading civil servants. Ibid., 30 (table 2.4). Because of downward occupational mobility in Germany during the Weimar era, the proportion of Nazis coming from the upper middle class or middle class may be understated.

empire.[122] Available evidence on Klan membership also points to active participation and leadership on the part of the upper-middle class.[123] Members of the elite were also participants in some race riots, and they instigated or took part in numerous lynchings in the South.

The blame for the vicious racism of the industrial era cannot, however, be laid exclusively at the door of the middle and upper classes. All social classes participated to some degree in racist behavior. Although perceived threats to economic or social status or to changing gender relations help explain hostile or violent actions against specific groups, an underlying pattern of racist thought was an essential foundation of all racist activity. In the case of African Americans, racist images whose origins lay in the colonial era were readily adapted to new circumstances in the nineteenth and early twentieth centuries. In industrializing Germany, age-old stereotypes of Jews were reforged and put to novel uses. In both nations, a growing racist climate of opinion throughout the period legitimized racist behavior and made the struggle against the racist worldview more difficult.

"Racism substituted myth for reality," says Mosse, "and the world that it created, with its stereotypes, virtues, and vices, was a fairy-tale world."[124] Blacks, Asians, and some European immigrants in the United States; Poles, blacks, Gypsies, and especially Jews in Germany became imagined enemies in the minds of racists and xenophobes, often for reasons having little or nothing to do with these groups' actual place in the social-economic order. In neither country were extensive contacts with the despised minority necessary to produce a hostile response from the majority. As early as the 1850s, the first nativist movement in the United States found its firmest adherents in rural areas of the Midwest where few immigrants had settled, and in Germany anti-Semitic or pro-Nazi attitudes were sometimes strongest in regions or communities with few Jews or even none at all.[125] Nothing better demonstrated the irrationality of the racism

---

122 Michael Prinz, *Vom neuen Mittelstand zum Volkgenossen: Die Entwicklung des sozialen Status der Angestellten von der Weimarer Republik bis zum Ende der NS-Zeit* (Munich, 1986); Götz Aly and Susanne Heim, *Vordenker der Vernichtung: Auschwitz und die deutschen Pläne für eine neue europäische Ordnung* (Frankfurt am Main, 1993). In *Who Voted for Hitler?* (Princeton, N.J., 1982), Richard Hamilton does not disprove the strong support of the lower middle class for National Socialism, but he does provide important evidence of support by higher income groups.

123 See Jenkins, *Steel Valley Klan*, 84; Lay, *Hooded Knights*, 86–101; and MacLean, *Beyond the Mask of Chivalry*, 55–6, which I think (contrary to her interpretation) demonstrates that upper-middle-class participation was proportionate to the size of this group in the total population.

124 Mosse, *Toward the Final Solution*, xiii.

125 See Tyler Anbinder, *Nativism and Slavery: The Northern Know-Nothings and the Politics of the 1850s* (New York, 1992); James H. Harris, *The People Speak! Anti-Semitism and Emancipation in Nineteenth-Century Bavaria* (Ann Arbor, Mich., 1994), 145–7; Walter Rinderle and Bernard Novling, *The Nazi Impact on a German Village* (Lexington, Ky., 1993).

and xenophobia that pervaded the two societies throughout the industrial era. A "fairy-tale world"? Perhaps. But one with very real consequences for the minority groups in the societies that embraced it – and, in the case of Germany, devastating consequences for the society as a whole.

8

Movie Stereotypes, 1890–1918

Some German and American National Perceptions

DANIEL J. LEAB

Elitists in Wilhelmine Germany and Progressive-era America condemned the movies. Films were classified as low culture, inferior to classical music, serious drama, and the fine arts. Movies lacked the mark of bourgeois respectability and were snubbed by the upper classes. A Düsseldorf banker discussing a movie theater remarked: "I am not embarrassed to enter it, but I am embarrassed to emerge from it after the show." A similar point of view held sway among many in the United States: They thought of movies as entertainment for the lower classes, "helping civilization to permeate downwards."[1]

Perceptions of the cinema, especially in recent years, have changed drastically. Film studies has become a major field of intellectual endeavor, with an intellectual jargon all its own. Movies have become a respectable art form. For the past few decades film has been the subject of vigorous, sometimes foolish debate as the moving image has been scrutinized almost microscopically – sometimes this study has unfortunately centered on marginalia at the edge of important substantive areas. But, as film scholar Miriam Hansen asserts, cinema "intersects and interacts with . . . public life."[2]

Already in the early days of what critic Walter Benjamin called "the age of mechanical reproduction" (that is, the film epoch), movies had a significant impact on public perceptions. Whatever private restrictions or official censorship may have existed in the United States and Germany,

---

1 Quoted in Ursula Hardt, *From Caligari to California: Eric Pommer's Life in the International Film Wars* (Providence, R.I., 1996), 14; John W. Dodds, *Everyday Life in Twentieth-Century America* (New York, 1965), 74.
2 Miriam Hansen, *Babel and Babylon: Spectatorship in American Silent Film* (Cambridge, Mass., 1991), 7.

the bulk of the movies produced in both countries never lost their ability to set forth images, no matter what their character, to capture viewers. Film may be art, but even more so it is commerce – and movies, with rare exceptions, were produced to capture an audience, to provide a return on investment. Whatever ambivalent images such movies may now project, at the time of their release the producers in both countries did not intend to alienate viewers.[3]

The treatment of such films has varied considerably during the past few years. There are constant shifts in interpretation with regard, for example, to technique, content, and attitudes. Certainly, academic discourse has not remained constant. But as various scholars have pointed out, the resultant images, although periodically inconsistent and occasionally contradictory, ultimately form a "national cinema" that grapples with the present, the past, and sometimes even the future. Pierre Sorlin has astutely declared that film is a "framework, serving as a basis or counterpoint," with each particular national cinema differing dramatically.[4]

The movies produced before the end of World War I in both the United States and Germany frequently plagiarized each other in terms of genre, but they did highlight various separate concepts of nationhood as well as individual destiny for men and women. Both German and American cinemas articulate specific and general viewpoints. As Eric Rentschler perceptively argues (albeit for a different time frame), the process is really one "bound in the quest of a national cinema for a sense of cultural identity." The movies served to establish views of "others" and of an ideal that was an idiomatic shorthand for "us."[5]

In the two decades before 1918 in both Germany and the United States, the movies went from being "flickers" to being big business, from a mere curiosity to a ubiquitous, dominant form of popular entertainment. Despite the hostility of the elites in both countries, movies became a mass medium between the mid-1890s, when public film presentations first took place, and the end of World War I, during which film served all sides as an important propaganda vehicle. The Germans had a fascinating love-hate relationship with the United States during those years. A survey of the various images of the United States presented in various media found, among other things, that "the extreme romantic and ideal-

3 Walter Benjamin, "The Work of Art in the Age of Mechanical Reproduction," in Walter Benjamin, *Illuminations*, trans. Harry Zohn (New York, 1969), 217.
4 Pierre Sorlin, *The Film as History* (Totowa, N.J., 1980), 208.
5 Eric Rentschler, "How American Is It: The U.S. as Image and Imaginary in German Film," *German Quarterly* 54 (1984): 614, 618.

istic traits . . . had almost disappeared" and that "American utilitarianism, lack of culture, profit orientation, superficiality, and coldness had . . . greatly gained in weight and credibility." The American image of Germany had also fluctuated wildly during that same time: What has been described as "the ambivalent American attitude toward German culture and institutions" (such as education and public administration) during the course of World War I gave way to extremely negative perceptions. Already before the end of the first decade of the twentieth century in the movies, as in much else in German and American cultures, as a recent study puts it, "each country is overburdened with prejudices against each other."[6]

The American film image of Germany during the latter years of this time remains important because of the global cultural hegemony that came to be exercised by movies produced in the United States. By 1919 the movies, to use critic Gilbert Seldes's phrase, "came from America." World War I made that hegemony possible. European film activity declined precipitously after war's outbreak in 1914. Prior to that moment French films, production companies, and capital controlled the screens of most European nations, including Germany. According to one account, "fully 80 percent of the films shown in Germany were foreign-made, mainly by French companies."[7]

However, as a recent history points out, after 1914 the continental film-makers "increasingly felt the effect of lost personnel, lost resources, lost markets." Britain and France quickly lost access to Germany's screens, as did Italy once it entered the war on the Allied side in 1915. In continental Europe, as has been recently pointed out, "only the film industries of neutral Scandinavia continued to prosper." German producers also took up the slack, obviously benefiting enormously from wartime restrictions.[8]

The American film industry benefited most of all. It took great advantage of the stall in European film production, for as one history succinctly points out, "the American companies found themselves with a unique opportunity." The statistics speak for themselves: Film exports from the

6 Wolfgang Helbich, "Different, But Not Out of This World: German Images of the United States Between Two Wars, 1871–1914," and Jörg Nagler, "From Culture to *Kultur*: Changing American Perceptions of Imperial Germany," both in David E. Barclay and Elizabeth Glaser-Schmidt, eds., *Transatlantic Images and Perceptions: Germany and America Since 1776* (New York, 1997), 129 and 154, respectively; John Graham Brooks, *As Others See Us* (New York, 1908), 253.
7 Gilbert Seldes, *The Movies Come from America* (New York, 1937); Hardt, *From Caligari to California*, 15.
8 David Parkinson, *History of Film* (New York, 1995), 54; Robert Sklar, *Film: An Illustrated History of the Medium* (New York, 1994), 47.

United States (which did not enter the war until 1917) rose from 36,000,000 feet in 1915 to over 158,000,000 in 1916. By war's end in 1918 the United States was said to produce "some 85 percent of the films shown throughout the world."[9]

Germans (whether portrayed in their homeland or in the United States, in the past or in the present) did not fare well in most American films in which they appeared during these years. Despite the fact – as many a history has pointed out – that Germans "had been probably the most esteemed immigrant group in America," and notwithstanding that Wilhelmine Germany was regarded highly by many Americans, generally negative images prevailed. One account argues that "no portrayal . . . was complete without recourse to a series of stereotypes and damning stereotypes at that." Why did American film, even before the outbreak of World War I, in the main eschew a positive view of Germans? How does one explain these particular images of Germans? What, if any, is the correlation between such images and the social, cultural, and political issues of the day?[10]

Germans never did suffer the overall demeaning, hostile treatment meted out to other ethnic groups, such as the Italians. No easy answer exists that explains the negative stereotyping, but American popular culture did not cotton to the Germans. A too-glib explanation would point to the Anglophilia of the movers and shakers of American society: A thick 1901 memoir, for example, by an effective participant in the "Lyceum business," discusses famous men and women "of the platform and stage" but "includes no German names." Nor can one simply argue that various classes in the United States resented the ordered society that Wilhelmine Germany represented. Yet, such feelings cannot be overlooked. Typically, the educator John Dewey apotheosized the German "systematic attention to education" but expressed grave concern about its "realization of the ideal of the national state . . . substituted for humanity."[11]

In the decades before World War I, German men and women (and German–Americans, who could be viewed as their surrogates) elicited

---

9 Ruth Vasey, *The World According to Hollywood, 1918–1939* (Exeter, U.K., 1997), 14; Robert Sklar, *Movie-Made America*, rev. ed. (New York, 1994), 47.

10 David M. Kennedy, *Over Here: The First World War and American Society* (New York, 1980), 67–8; Beverly Crawford and James Martel, "Representations of Germans and What Germans Represent: American Film Images and Public Perceptions in the Postwar Era," in Barclay and Glaser-Schmidt, eds., *Transatlantic Images and Perceptions*, 285.

11 J. B. Pond, *Eccentricities of Genius* (New York, 1901), xvii; John Dewey, *Democracy and Education* (1916; reprint, New York, 1966), 93.

much admiration for qualities of thrift, honesty, industriousness, and perseverance. In 1908, as John Higham reports, "a group of professional people in rating the traits of various immigrant nationalities ranked the Germans above the English and in some respects superior to native whites." Wilhelmine Germany received high marks from many Americans for its scientific, industrial, and cultural achievements, for its university system (as Frederick Leubke notes, "at the time American leaders in higher education . . . repeatedly expressed their indebtedness to the German example"), and for its value system." (Theodore Roosevelt, among others, extolled its "genius for order and efficiency.") Indeed, in his best-selling autobiography from 1913 Roosevelt declared it "impossible" to feel that "Germans were really foreigners."[12]

During World War I, Roosevelt would change his mind dramatically. Others had never been so friendly as he had been and just did not cotton to Germany or the Germans, even before the wartime mobilization of American public opinion resulted in a virulent discoloring of the German in the average citizen's consciousness. Some of the very characteristics that had resulted in a positive view of the Germans now underlay a negative reaction that found its most forceful response in 1917–18. The commitment of many Germans to socialism produced friction; as Richard Krickus indicates, they became "the first serious exponents of Marxism in America." In the United States, German was the language of Marxist radicalism, which came into conflict – sometimes violently – with perceived American values.[13]

Many in Germany, and not just the elite classes, denigrated American values, manners, and standards as raw, barbaric, and insignificant; in championing a German culture that Carl Wittke years ago argued convincingly "perpetuated a culturally static *Deutschtum*," critics of America aroused suspicions and anger. Already by the first years of the twentieth century the over-hyped enthusiasm for the empire established in 1871 had annoyed many Americans, who for all Germany's virtues perceived the new Germany as undemocratic, arrogant, reactionary, and class-ridden.[14]

Scholars have pointed out that Americans often found ominous a "mil-

---

12 John Higham, *Strangers in the Land: Patterns of American Nativism* (New York, 1963), 196; Frederick C. Luebke, *Bonds of Loyalty: German Americans and World War I* (DeKalb, Ill., 1974), 58; William Henry Harbaugh, *Power and Responsibility: The Life and Times of Theodore Roosevelt* (New York, 1961), 288; Theodore Roosevelt, *An Autobiography* (New York, 1913), 26.
13 Richard Krickus, *Pursuing the American Dream: White Ethnics and the New Populism* (New York, 1976), 47.
14 Carl Wittke, "American Germans in Two World Wars," *Annals of the American Academy of Political and Social Science* 223 (Sept. 1942): 86.

itaristic . . . Imperial Germany that followed Bismarck's 'blood and iron' policy," which was seen as the "subordination of civilians to military considerations in the conduct of government." Because of the Kaiser's capricious foreign policy, maintains Detlef Junker, "the generally benign image of the German Empire" in the 1870s underwent "a great transformation" in the next decades and by 1917 "had become an integral part of the American image of the enemy." This transformation resulted from "the changing positions of both countries as they sought to become world powers" and "found themselves confronting each other as rivals in the Pacific, the Far East, and Latin America."[15]

Nor should the influence of Great Britain on the Anglophilic attitude of America's "Establishment" be overlooked. Hans-Jürgen Schröder, a German scholar much concerned with his country's relations with the United States, finds that their deterioration before World War I stemmed in considerable part from Great Britain's willingness to appease and woo the United States in order to achieve (as it did) a "rapprochement" with an obvious rival who until recently had been hostile. That wooing was made easier by the Anglophilia of "the directors of American industry, government, and culture, many of whom also were concerned about international issues," to use Mel Small's words.[16]

In the years before World War I the American image of the German (both in the homeland and in the United States) left something to be desired. Americans may have respected, admired, at times emulated, and more than just occasionally feared Germany and the Germans, but in the context of American popular culture, notwithstanding such positive aspects, Germany and its *Volk* were not well liked. And for many, Wilhelmine Germany evoked what has been characterized as "increasing uneasiness."[17]

15 Allen L. Woll and Randall M. Miller, *Ethnic and Racial Images in American Film and Television* (New York, 1987), 33, 221; Geoff Eley, *From Unification to Nazism* (New York, 1990), 390; Detlef Junker, *The Manichean Trap: American Perceptions of the German Empire*, German Historical Institute, Washington, D.C., Occasional Paper series, no. 12 (Washington, D.C., 1995), 15–16.
16 Hans-Jürgen Schröder, *Deutschland und Amerika in der Epoche des Ersten Weltkriegs 1900–1924* (Stuttgart, 1993), 15. A great deal has been written about German-American relations before World War I. Among the most important efforts are those by Ragnhild Fiebig-von Hase, *Lateinamerika als Konfliktherd der deutsch-amerikanischen Beziehungen 1890–1903*, 2 vols. (Göttingen, 1986), and "The United States and Germany in the World Arena, 1900–1917," in Hans-Jürgen Schröder, ed., *Confrontation and Cooperation: Germany and the United States in the Era of World War I, 1900–1924* (Oxford, 1993), 33–68; Melvin Small, "Misunderstanding or Realpolitik? America and Germany in the Progressive Era," paper presented at Recurrent Patterns of Mutual Misunderstanding in German-American Relations, a symposium at the University of North Carolina, Chapel Hill, Sept. 1986, 18.
17 Richard A. Oehling, "The German Americans, Germany, and the American Media," in Randall M. Miller, ed., *Ethnic Images in American Film and Television* (Philadelphia, 1978), 52.

That uneasiness, that lack of affection, manifested itself in the image of the German (and the German–American) prevalent in American popular culture for a generation before World War I. In an era when social libels abounded (for example, a song such as "You May Be a Hawaiian on Old Broadway but You're Just Another Nigger to Me," or movies such as *The Greaser and His Gun* or *The Wop by the Door*) the German stereotype did not deteriorate into nastiness but was unkind, condescending, disparaging, ridiculous, all too often mean-spirited, and sometimes arrogantly ruthless. The stereotype had, as I have pointed out elsewhere, generally "few positive qualities" and all too often took on what Mark Sullivan has described as "a mocking note . . . a little touched by jeering."[18]

One of the many popular pre-World War I songs dealing with Germans (in this instance German Americans), "Dot Leedle German Band," typifies this attitude:

> Dot leedle German band, dot leedle German band;
> De beoble cry and say "oh my!" as we march drough de land
> Ve go around de screeds almost every day
> Und sit de beoble vild mit dc music dot ve blay;
> "Goodbye Sourheart," und "Heime Sweet Heime," we blay so fine,
> But ve always do our best ven ve blay "De Wacht am Rhein."[19]

Such fracturing of the language also occurred in the newly developing newspaper comic strips, especially *The Katzenjammer Kids*, which almost immediately after its debut in 1897 attained enormous popularity. Openly based on the German cartoonist Wilhelm Busch's *Max und Moritz*, the illustrated adventures of the two quite mischievous young boys, *The Katzenjammer Kids* depicts "the guerilla war conducted against society itself." Rudolph Dirks, the strip's creator, made very effective use of Anglo-German pidgin. Thus, for the boys, "society ist nix," and their chief targets include "die Mama" (their mother, a rotund, middle-aged, stereotypical hausfrau), "der Captain" (their adoptive father, a shipwrecked sailor rescued by die Mama), and "der Inspector" (a long-white-bearded truant officer resembling the stereotypical rigid German civil servant of the time, who apparently came for the boys and stayed).[20]

Popular verses and songs mocked Germans' overly serious "traits." And the stage, burlesque, and vaudeville abounded with stereotypical Germans. The typical hausfrau was shown as dowdy and too willingly subject to

---

18 Daniel J. Leab, "Goethe or Attila? The Celluloid German," in Miller, *Ethnic Images*, 64; Mark Sullivan, *Pre-War America* (New York, 1930), 390.
19 Quoted in Maldwyn Jones, *Destination America* (New York, 1976), 139.
20 Maurice Horn, ed., *The World Encyclopedia of Comics* (New York, 1976), 421.

her comically bellicose husband. More often than not, according to one show-business history, he had "padded stomachs, . . . chin whiskers, wore small brown derbys, checkered trousers, fancy vests with big watch chains, and murdered the English language."[21]

The movies quickly adopted these stereotypes, in due course refining and transforming them as well as adding others – perhaps most notably what has been dubbed "the monstrous image of the Teutonic Prussian . . . a barbaric bayoneter of babies." That image developed some time after commercial production and exhibition of motion pictures (in one form or another) began in the United States during the mid-1890s. Into the first years of the twentieth century the movie industry produced only short films, most of them running only a few minutes. Exhibitors strung them together to make up a program. However, by the end of 1904 over half the films produced by American companies were story films. And between 1907 and 1908 the number of such films increased to over 95 percent of the total output.[22]

The already prevalent stereotypes of the German easily found their way into all types of films. Even blacks, usually objects of derision, could be found holding their own against the German stereotype. In *A Bucket of Cream Ale*, a 1904 Biograph film that ran less than 360 seconds and was meant to be funny, a black serving woman, after considerable provocation, is shown "dumping a bucket of beer on the head of a stereotypical German burgher."[23]

Utilizing such stereotypes, American filmmakers presented various representations of German men and women. Because the movies drew heavily on the contemporary popular culture, the images presented in the main retained somewhat negative connotations in the early films. As I have indicated elsewhere, if "not cruelly labeled in the manner of . . . other ethnic groups . . . [the Germans] were ridiculed and made the butt of nasty humor." As World War I progressed the humor rapidly gave way, and with American entry into World War I, nastiness prevailed as movie imagery, in the words of one historian, shifted in response to "events on the national and international . . . fronts."[24]

As the saying goes, "the devil lies in the details." In dealing with the

21 Abel Green and Joe Laurie Jr., *Show Biz: Variety from Vaude to Video* (New York, 1951), 7.
22 Crawford and Martel, "Representations of Germans," 287.
23 Daniel J. Leab, "The Gamut From A to B; the Image of the Black in Pre-1915 Movies," *Political Science Quarterly* 88 (1973): 61.
24 Leab, "Goethe or Atilla?" 64; Leslie M. De Bauche, *Reel Patriotism: The Movies and World War I* (Madison, Wis., 1997), 18.

following films my purpose is to use the texts, the contents if you wish, to highlight various aspects of the changing American film image of the German. To repeat, these themes varied somewhat, albeit reinforcing the already prevalent stereotypes until, after the outbreak of the war, anti-German bias became ever more intense – even before the United States became a belligerent in 1917. Garth Jowett correctly assesses the situation with his belief that "the cinemas were mobilized against Germany well before [President Woodrow] Wilson led the nation into war."[25]

More than just occasionally a positive note does creep in. The 1909 Biograph drama *The Voice of the Violin* represents this aspect, but it had relatively few imitators. In this short film Herr von Schmitt, an immigrant who makes his living as a violin teacher, falls in love with the daughter of what the Biograph plot synopsis describes as "a wealthy capitalist." The violinist saves the lives of father and daughter in a stirring climax: A bomb has been planted in the basement of the family mansion; "bound hand and foot von Schmitt crawls towards the bomb," and as the company publicity blurb declares, "with his teeth bites the fuse in two as it is within a few inches of igniting the terror bomb."[26]

Such unambiguously positive representation found little duplication in the longer feature films that became the bulk of the American industry's output in the years immediately preceding and following the outbreak of World War I. The traditional stereotypes of the German found their way into these features. To cite just a few examples: Cecil B. DeMille's 1915 drama *The Kindling* (based on a 1911 Broadway play) centered on "Honest" Heinie Schultz and his family, who escaped from the snares of New York City slum life; the actor Lew Fields transferred from the stage to the movies his characterization of "an old-fashioned . . . German" who finds his way in America; in November 1915 Triangle films, then an important studio, successfully released *Old Heidelberg* with the rising star Wallace Reid as the lead, which dealt with the heir to a Central European throne who temporarily finds happiness while enrolled at a German university (any similarity to *The Student Prince* is not coincidental).[27]

These representations of the German gave way to other, much more antagonistic images as the war strongly and adversely affected American popular culture even before America entered the fray in April 1917. In 1914 when the war began, President Wilson urged citizens of the neutral

25 Garth Jowett, *Film: The Democratic Art* (Boston, 1976), 66.
26 *Biograph Bulletins, 1908–1912* (New York, 1973), 73.
27 *Motion Picture News*, Nov. 4, 1916, 2863.

United States to be "impartial in thought as well as action," neutral "in fact as well as name." He even urged that movie audiences "refrain from demonstrating in any way in favor of either side." Wilson successfully ran for re-election in 1916 as a "peace candidate."[28]

Americans may have voted for peace, but at the movies they opted for war. One of the greatest box-office triumphs of 1916 was Thomas Ince's *Civilization*, a mammoth spectacle that ended with Christ successfully preaching his gospel of peace to a mythical, aggressive war-making king; but as *Variety* pointed out at the time, "while the 'foreword' . . . announces the spectacle as pure allegory, the mythical kingdom, the king . . . and the soldiers . . . were unmistakably Teutonic types."[29]

Such anti-German sentiment pervaded more propagandistic films. Thus, *The Battle Cry of Peace* (1915), another box-office hit in which New York City is shelled into submission by an invading fleet, made a shrill cry for "preparedness." Captured American civilians are machine-gunned, and a mother kills her two daughters to spare them "a fate worse than death." The film avoided identifying the enemy, but as the American Film Institute catalog points out, "the beer drinking parties and the Kaiser Wilhelm moustaches of the invading soldiers typified prevailing German stereotypes."[30]

This kind of "political fiction" found its counterpart in other sorts of films that also presented a negative view of the German. In *Arms and the Woman* (1916), an overwrought drama centered on a Hungarian immigrant who becomes a successful opera singer in America, German spies blow up a munitions factory. Toward the end of *The Ivory Snuff Box*, an indifferent 1915 mystery, the German head of a Brussels sanitarium tortures an American detective in front of his new wife. *The Ordeal*, a 1914 film set in part during the Franco-Prussian War, includes a scene in which a German general strongly resembling Kaiser Wilhelm fails to extract information from a French officer and so shoots the officer's mother, sister, and sweetheart before his eyes. (This film was so biased that during the height of the anti-German hate campaign of 1918 it was re-released as *The Mother of Liberty*.)[31]

Social scientists and others concerned with the impact of movies on

---

28 Wilson quoted in Richard Morris, ed., *Encyclopedia of American History* (New York, 1976), 358; Arthur S. Link, *Woodrow Wilson and the Progressive Era* (New York, 1954), 148n.
29 *Variety*, June 9, 1916, 23.
30 Patricia King Hanson et al., eds., *The American Film Institute Catalog of Motion Pictures Produced in the United States: Feature Films, 1911–1920* (Berkeley, Calif., 1988), 48.
31 Leif Fruhammar and Folke Isaksson, *Politics and Film* (New York, 1971), 9; *Variety*, Oct. 23, 1914, 22.

public opinion have long been sharply divided as to whether films influence an audience or mirror its ideas and feelings. However one views that influence, it is clear that during the three war years when the United States was officially neutral, Germans on screen (as in many other areas of American popular culture) fared badly, and any positive aspects of the German image dribbled away.

Whatever chance there might have been of improving the image of the German collapsed upon American entry into the war in 1917. The administration's frenzied rousing of support for the war resulted in an anti-German hysteria that swept over the United States. For the next years every possible manifestation of German influence came under attack. Operas, symphonic music, even hymns of German origin were boycotted. The syndicators of *The Katzenjammer Kids* found it expedient to rename the comic strip *The Shenanigan Kids*. Renaming became a popular pastime: Sauerkraut became "liberty cabbage," hamburgers became "liberty sandwiches," and dachshunds became "liberty pups"; the well-known actor Gustav von Seyfferitz changed his name to C. Butler Clonburgh, explaining that he had "a perfect right" to this new name as it "belonged to his mother"; after the war he reverted to the original. Anything of German origin became suspect.[32]

Significantly contributing to this chorus of hate was a propaganda-oriented American film industry that participated with a vengeance, so much so that, as Kevin Brownlow quite rightly points out, the industry "must take a large part of the responsibility for the campaign launched . . . in the United States during World War I." That campaign, although directed at German–Americans, contributed significantly to the extremely negative view of the citizens of "the fatherland." Many an American movie in 1917 and 1918 expressed concern about the loyalty of German–Americans and stigmatized Germans ad infinitum, ad nauseam. *Draft 258* laid bare, according to the *Motion Picture News*, "the workings of German intrigue . . . to enlist the . . . pacifist as a tool . . . against the United States." In a 1918 William S. Hart vehicle, *The Border Wireless*, a German-American mine owner supervises a gang of spies transmitting intelligence that they had gathered to Berlin. *On the Jump*, a 1918 action film, has a dashing reporter expose his newspaper's owner as "custodian of a German fund to establish anti-Allied newspapers in the United States."[33]

32 Lewis Jacobs, *The Rise of American Film* (New York, 1939), 259.
33 Kevin Brownlow, *The War, the West, and the Wilderness* (New York, 1979), 134; *Motion Picture News*, Dec. 1, 1917, 3857, Oct. 19, 1918, 2594.

In 1900 Kaiser Wilhelm II, while inspecting German troops being sent to participate in the international response to the Boxer Rebellion in China, with his usual exuberant thoughtlessness exhorted the troops to "Give no quarter! Take no prisoners! Kill the foe. . . . Even as a thousand years ago, the Huns under . . . Attila." His speech received a great deal of publicity both inside and outside Germany. When World War I broke out, a highly effective British propaganda campaign made "Hun" a common derogatory synonym for German, and on American entry into the war the American movie industry became a very active part of the "Hate-the-Hun" campaign.[34]

The Hun behaved with vile brutality on screen. In the 1917 melodrama *For France* the Huns humble a French mother. The 1918 Cecil B. DeMille production *Till I Come Back to You* included scenes of Belgian children working in German war industries as whipped and starved slave labor. Master filmmaker D. W. Griffith's *Hearts of the World* (1918), much of which is set in a French village, depicted what a *New York Times* critic described as "the horrors of German occupation." The Hun did not even scruple to unleash the "yellow peril"; one of the advertising tag lines of Samuel Goldwyn's *For the Freedom of the East* (1918) was "Berlin's sinister sneering agent advanced to raise the floodgate and drown the world under the flood of China's 400 million people."[35]

Two of the most sensational and commercially successful of the atrocity films were *The Little American*, a 1917 feature starring "America's Sweetheart," Mary Pickford, and *My Four Years in Germany*, a 1918 effort loosely based on the memoirs of James Gerard, a wealthy Democratic politician who served as the American ambassador in Berlin from 1913 to 1917.

In Pickford's film, as the result of what can be described as an extraordinary series of circumstances, the eponymous heroine witnesses the drowning of women and children in the aftermath of a U-boat attack, the burning of priceless antiques from a French chateau by indifferent German soldiers in need of firewood, the execution of innocent civilian hostages by heartless Hun officers; and she barely escapes being raped by one of them.

My Four Years in Germany, an ambitious film dealing with Gerard's tenure, included scenes set in German prisoner-of-war camps. People are

---

34 Quoted in Virginia Cowles, *The Kaiser* (New York, 1963), 177.
35 Quoted in Jack Spears, *Hollywood: The Golden Era* (New York, 1971), 33; *Moving Picture World*, Oct. 19, 1918, 448.

shown being beaten, set on by vicious guard dogs, scrambling for scraps
of bread. British soldiers are thrown in with Russians suffering from
typhus; a German officer who is asked why the Russians are not quar-
antined responds that "they're Allies. Let them get acquainted." A trade
journal summed up this film when it admiringly declared that "there is
no stone left unturned to arouse the audience to a sense that the German
manner of conducting war is synonymous with barbarism." Brownlow has
found "the simplemindedness of the film . . . beyond belief," but points
out that audience reaction "everywhere was ecstatic . . . enthusiastic."[36]

In many a film the Kaiser became the focal point for anti-German
propaganda. He served the same purpose as Goldstein (Big Brother's
archrival) in Orwell's *1984*; the Kaiser was an object of "HATE." He fit
perfectly the stereotype of the "hated Hun," with his arrogant stare,
upturned mustache, and arched eyebrows. Winsor McCay's animated one-
reeler, *The Sinking of the Lusitania* (1918), ends with the title "The man
who fired the shot was decorated for it by the Kaiser! – AND YET THEY
TELL US NOT TO HATE THE HUN." And in movie after movie the
Hun in the form of the Kaiser was vilified and so were the actions of
his people. The most notorious of these films, *The Kaiser – The Beast of
Berlin* (1918), was advertised as "giving insight into the man guiding the
most horrible outrages."[37]

A common thread ran through all these films, whatever their subject
matter or length, and that was a generally less-than-positive representation of things and people German, a representation that turned highly
negative as a result of the war. Interestingly, until the outbreak of World
War I, the movies, like other parts of American popular culture, had never
been as outspokenly hostile to Wilhelmine Germany as occasionally had
been the case with Great Britain. "Tweaking the lion's tail" had always
been a part of the political culture of the United States, sometimes good-
naturedly and sometimes not. From time to time there were intense outbursts of Anglophobia that rivaled any World War I indictment of
Germany. The Populists, for instance, in the 1890s issued "bitter philip-
pics" against England. One of their most influential tracts argued forcefully that "a war with England would be . . . most popular." But for all
the attacks on "perfidious Albion" and the supposed effete, ignorant snob-
bishness of the English upper classes, there was a constantly reiterated
belief among U.S. elites (with which many other citizens concurred)

36 *Motion Picture News*, Mar. 23, 1918, 1768; Brownlow, *War, the West, and the Wilderness*, 136–7.
37 Quoted in Jacobs, *Rise of American Film*, 257.

about the "oneness of British and U.S. interests." Germany never evoked such a response.[38]

The generally favorable stereotyping of the British, as with the less favorable depiction of African Americans, lasted for generations. Unfortunately, because of subsequent circumstances (for example, the Nazis, World War II, the Holocaust) Germans who were not unique in being perceived negatively on screen or off never really managed to achieve a movie depiction that did not in the main judge them harshly. This view of the Germans arrived at during World War I, although ultimately modified (especially in the immediate past decades by the exigencies of international politics) remained, in one critic's words, "like a bad stain in a washed garment."[39]

There is no dichotomy between what might be considered American official policy in terms of international politics and the stereotypes set forth in American popular culture. Any admiration for things German was skin-deep, not widespread, and easily dispensed with. As the movies of the era demonstrate, individuals were not segregated from the overall less than positive stereotypes. After American entry into the war, President Wilson may have declared that the United States did not make war on the German people, only on their government and ruling class, but the movies made no such distinction. On screen there were few if any "good" Germans. In the absence of reliable polls the American response to Germany and the Germans must be read through the stereotypical response to them. It never improved, and serious tensions set in as a result of the war. Praise for German *Kultur* (culture) easily gave way to references to the German *Schweinehund* (bastard) in that public opinion available for measurement.

In Wilhelmine Germany the image of the United States never suffered such a serious recession, never received such on-screen treatment, not even after American entry into World War I in 1917. The Germans had never been of one mind about the United States between the mid-1890s and the end of World War I. During these years the emphasis on what a German critic has termed "cliché ideas" about the United States and its inhabitants obviously were influenced not only by events on the world stage but also by class attitudes. These ideas, as Hans J. Gatzke has remarked, "tended towards extremes of admiration or condescension."[40]

38 Coin's Financial School, quoted in Richard Hofstadter, *The Age of Reform* (New York, 1955), 88; Howard K. Beale, *Theodore Roosevelt and the Rise of America to World Power* (New York, 1956), 92.
39 Oehling, "German Americans," 51.
40 "Introduction," in Alfred Gong, ed., *Interview mit Amerika* (Munich, 1962), 11; Hans W. Gatzke, *Germany and the United States* (Cambridge, Mass., 1980), 48.

The latter included a view of Americans as unceasingly violent and crassly materialistic. In 1908 a writer found that Germans thought of the American man as "a haggard creature, with vulgar tastes and brutal manners, who drinks whiskey and chews tobacco, spits, fights, puts his feet on the table, and habitually rushes along in wild haste, absorbed by a greedy desire for the dollars of his neighbors." German elites especially considered the United States "a land without culture," given to excesses of democracy. Intellectuals may have admired American democracy, but they dreaded the materialism of American culture. One described it as "the pairing of originality and triviality"; another (Felix Salten, the creator of Bambi) argued in 1913 that America, "in all aspects the finer culture . . . so completely without style, so childish, noisy and brutal, behaves in a way that one gets nervous complaints." One German professor at the time maintained that "as a result of . . . the immodest striving after success . . . Americans have had their nerves overstrained and . . . become an unhealthy nation."[41]

Germany's social elite in the main shared the disdain for American culture and generally denigrated America's democratic political traditions. For many in the middle class, what Erich Angermann has described as "a fear that the German soul" might be lost in a "materialistic, democratized, and egalitarian . . . world" was an "old theme that reached back to . . . those who had criticized America" before the 1848 Revolution. Others had a different view of the "social totality" of America: It was "a good idea." And aspects of the United States such as the romance of "the Wild West," the abundant opportunities available in the burgeoning cities, the innovative technology, and the egalitarianism of society tilted the overall view in a more positive direction.[42]

Andrew Dickson White, American ambassador to Germany between 1897 and 1902, was "especially concerned" about the "strong anti-American disposition among the highly educated." And it existed on both sides of the political fence. After his 1910 tour of the United States, the radical Social Democrat Karl Liebknecht expressed deep concern at "the

---

41 Brooks, *As Others See Us*, 255; Franz Pfemfert and Felix Salten, quoted in Joerge Schweinitz, ed., *Prolog vor dem Film: Nachdenken über ein neues Medium 1909–1914* (Leipzig, 1992), 49; Eduard Mayer, quoted in W. W. Coole and M. F. Potter, eds., *Thus Spake Germany* (London, 1941), 192.

42 Hans A. Joachim quoted in Anton Kaes, "Mass Culture and Modernity: Notes Towards a Social History of Early American and German Cinema," in Frank Trommler and Joseph McVeigh, eds., *America and the Germans: An Assessment of a Three Hundred Year History*, 2 vols. (Philadelphia, 1985), 2:323; Erich Angermann, "Coming to Grips with Modern Society: Germany and the United States in the 'Golden Twenties,'" in Erich Angermann, ed., *Deutschland und die USA / Germany and the USA 1918–1933* (Braunschweig, 1968), 73.

effort to secure the almighty dollar" and the "worship of the god Mammon." His equally radical father, a few years earlier, had concluded that "we were going to bow-wows, but were having a great deal of fun getting there." But that was an unusual opinion. In looking back on this era, Fritz Stern reports that "conservative writers in Imperial Germany" feared that its "soul would be destroyed by 'Americanization,' that is by mammonism, materialism, mechanization, and the mass society."[43]

Many other Germans, however, saw America in a very different, more positive light. They drew their inspiration from the judgment expressed decades earlier by Goethe: "Amerika, du hast es besser / Als unser Kontinent, das alte." They believed that the United States was "ein goldenes Land," a country ripe with opportunity, the prototypical democratic society where everybody had a chance to make good. What one historian has characterized as "open-minded Germans trying to modernize their country" looked to the United States like a model for political and economic systems. For them, Americanization was not a blight but a guidepost to a better future.[44]

That belief in America had led tens of thousands of Germans to emigrate to the United States in "the great Atlantic migration" that took place during the half-century before World War I. Kathleen N. Conzen estimates that "between 1850 and 1900 Germans were never less than a quarter of all the foreign-born" in the United States and that between 1880 and 1920 they were the "largest single element among first-generation immigrants." Many of these emigrants wrote home about the wondrous opportunities available in America or in due course returned home for a visit (such visits by a "rich uncle from America" became a recurrent motif in Wilhelmine Germany's popular culture, including the movies).[45]

An admiration for America and things American manifested itself in a

---

43 Reinhard Doerries, "Empire and Republic: German-American Relations Before 1917," in Trommler and McVeigh, eds., *America and the Germans*, 2:15n14; Philip S. Foner, *Karl Liebknecht and the United States* (Chicago, 1978), 18; Wilhelm Liebknecht, quoted in Brooks, *As Others See Us*, 274; Fritz Stern, *The Politics of Cultural Despair* (Berkeley, Calif., 1961), 131n.

44 Goethe quoted in J. W. Schulte Nordholt, "Anti-Americanism in European Culture: Its Early Manifestations," in Rob Kroes and Maarten Van Rossem, eds., *Anti-Americanism in Europe* (Amsterdam, 1986), 12; Peter Krüger, "Traditional Patterns of Ambiguous Misunderstanding in a Period of Transition," paper presented at Recurrent Patterns of Mutual Understanding in German-American Relations, a symposium at the University of North Carolina, Chapel Hill, Sept. 1986, 12.

45 Walter Nugent, *Crossings: The Great Atlantic Migrations, 1870–1914* (Bloomington, Ind., 1992), 69; Kathleen Neils Conzen, "Germans," in Stephan Thernstrom et al., eds., *Harvard Encyclopedia of American Ethnic Groups* (Cambridge, Mass., 1980), 406; Deniz Göktürk, *Künstler, Cowboys, Ingenieure: Kultur- und mediengeschichtliche Studien zu deutschen Amerika-Texten 1912–1920* (Munich, 1998), 8.

variety of ways. Interest in America remained strong. Between 1903 and 1906 at least seventeen German travel books on America were published, and by 1913 over 250 translations of Mark Twain and Brett Harte had appeared. Germany's capital, Berlin, was characterized by an English observer as among "the most American of European cities." Situated along the Spree River, this bustling, dynamic city was often referred to by many Germans as "Spreechicago" in those years. A logo of crossed German and American flags was on top of the proscenium framing the screen in that city's first large movie theater (opened in 1909). Two years earlier the company opening a movie theater in Frankfurt am Main utilized a vigorous, attractive full-length figure of "Uncle Sam" on its first posters – then already an American icon. For contemporary writers and critics such as Walter Hasenclever, Eric Schlaikjer, and Alfred Kerr, film was a very important "bridge" between nineteenth-century *Amerika Bilder* (images of America) and the Americanization they supported for Wilhelmine Germany: For them, the movies were among "the most important means of Americanization."[46]

Until recently the early years of German cinema have been a neglected field of study, in large measure because of the late Siegfried Kracauer's 1947 book *From Caligari to Hitler*, a seminal work on "Weimar cinema" that maintained that "it was only after the first World War that the German cinema really came into being. Its history up to that time . . . was insignificant." A dynamic new generation of scholars (mostly but not exclusively German, many of them women) have provided new insights and have revised older arguments.[47]

As in the United States the film industry in Germany began in the mid-1890s but developed more slowly. Production, distribution, and exhibition evolved at a less frenetic pace – in part because of a culture committed to "Denker und Dichter" – philosophers and poets. But it did nevertheless develop, as evidenced, for example, by the remarkable increase

---

46 W. T. Stead, *The Americanization of the World or the Trend of the Twentieth Century* (1902; reprint, London, 1972), 67. In 1899 the noted German businessman/statesman Walter Rathenau observed that "the Athens on the Spree is dead and the Chicago on the Spree grows apace" (quoted in Peter Jelavich, *Berlin Cabaret* [Cambridge, Mass., 1993], 110). Wolfgang Jacobsen et al., *Geschichte des Deutschen Films* (Stuttgart, 1993), 13; advertisement in Michael Hanisch, *Auf den Spuren der Filmgeschichte: Berliner Schauplatz* (Berlin, 1991), 209; poster reproduced in *Lebende Bilder: Kino und Film in Frankfurt am Main* (Frankfurt am Main, 1995), 37; Paolo Cherchi Usai et al., eds., *Before Caligari: German Cinema, 1895–1920* (n. p., 1990), 16.

47 Siegfried Kracauer, *From Caligari to Hitler* (Princeton, N.J., 1947), 15. A good cross section of the new scholars and their attitudes may be found in Corinna Müller and Harro Segenberg, eds., *Die Modellierung des Kinofilms: Zur Geschichte des Kinoprogramms zwischen Kurzfilm und Langfilm (1905/6–1918)* (Munich, 1998).

in the number of movie theaters and their size. In 1910, just a few years after public exhibition of films had begun, there were approximately 1,000 theaters in Wilhelmine Germany; in 1912 there were 1,500; in 1914 over 2,400; and in 1918 over 2,800. More important, in 1910 the 1,000 or so theaters could accommodate about 200,000 viewers; by 1918 the number of theaters had more than doubled, but the number of seats available had more than quadrupled. Yet, only because of the war was the German screen able to break free from foreign domination and establish what Corinna Müller, one of the best practitioners of the new film history, has termed an "indigenous *Kinokultur*." At war's outbreak, although the German cinema was, as a recent survey demonstrates, "very rich and complex, with unique and specific characteristics," it produced only about 15 percent of the films playing on the nation's screens. War meant an end to British, French, and Italian imports, but until 1917 American films continued to be shown in somewhat increased numbers in Germany.[48]

The cutoff from the international film market stimulated the German film industry in various ways. In 1913 there were eleven production companies, in 1918 over 130; in 1913 there were nineteen distributors, by 1918 over fifty. Initially, after war started, the industry produced what one history aptly described as "feldgrau Filmkitsch" (uniformed kitsch), such as *Wie Max das Eiserne Kreuz erwarb* (How Max earned his iron cross). But moviegoers wanted escapism, not celluloid excesses of patriotism.[49]

Germany's ruling classes recognized the importance of the movies as a force to raise morale at home and counter Allied propaganda abroad, especially among European neutrals. In early 1917 at the initiative of General Erich Ludendorff, by then the all-powerful virtual dictator of wartime Wilhelmine Germany, the army set up the Picture and Film Office (Bild und Film Amt or BUFA) to create and distribute cultural propaganda. Anxious to enhance BUFA's mission, Ludendorff, who believed that "the war has demonstrated the superiority of . . . film as a means of informa-

---

48 *Handbuch der Filmwirtschaft* (Berlin, 1930–), 1:61. Corinna Müller, "Emergence of the Feature Film in Germany between 1910 and 1911," in Bruce A. Murray and Christopher J. Wickham, eds., *Framing the Past: The Historiography of German Cinema and Television* (Carbondale, Ill., 1992), 94. It has been argued that German productions accounted for the majority of dramatic films seen by Germans but that there were a limited number of such films shown. Herbert Birett, *Das Filmangebot in Deutschland* (Munich, 1991), xvi, a systematic study of the films released, confirms Müller's projections.

49 Friedrich von Zglinicki, *Der Weg des Films: Die Geschichte der Kinematographie und ihrer Vorläufer* (Berlin, 1956), 389; Deutsche Kinemathek, ed., *Rot für Gefahr, Feuer und Liebe: Frühe deutsche Stummfilme* (Berlin, 1995), 9.

tion and persuasion," helped in the formation in December 1917 of the Universium Film AG (UFA), which incorporated most of Germany's leading film companies.[50]

Neither BUFA nor UFA lived up to Ludendorff's expectations. The exigencies of the war kept UFA, which later became a giant, in *Windeln* (diapers), to use Angermann's term. Moreover, UFA's leadership, in decisions that reportedly "enraged" Ludendorff, emphasized entertainment at the expense of propaganda. A trade journal in 1917 found the industry's propaganda efforts to be "pathetically laughable" as well as primitive "kitsch."[51]

The general presided over a country increasingly weary of war. Real life was very different from the censored war on the nation's movie screens. The troops had marched off in 1914 certain of victory and a quick return home. Instead, they stumbled into a deadly war of attrition in the trenches on the western front. Meanwhile, on the home front, for many Germans the standard of living steadily deteriorated because there were shortages of almost everything. Given the ongoing massive casualties, few families escaped unscathed. Yet, the country escaped the ecstasy of hate that had spread so rapidly across America in 1917.

The German patriotic zeal of 1914 did have an effect on the country's public life: For instance, UFA established its offices on Berlin's Potsdamer Platz in an establishment called Haus Vaterland (called Picadilly until the war); a song favorite in revue shows was the "Song of Hate Against England" (Hassgesang gegen England) – "Wir lieben vereint, wir hassen vereint / Wir haben alle nur einen Feind" (United in love, united in hate / We have only one enemy); Max Winterfeld, a composer who before 1914 had adopted the French pseudonym Jean Gilbert, found it expedient to drop the first name and pronunciation "a la français" for the duration of the war; and the Chat Noir cabaret became the Schwarzer Kater; German newsreels mocked French use of black colonial troops, implying that "the French were importing barbarians onto European soil."[52]

Even after its entry into the war, America remained less of a propaganda target than Britain or France. The United States was, as Frank

---

50 Quoted in Leif Furhammar and Folke Isaksson, *Politics and Film*, trans. Kersti French (New York, 1971), 12.
51 Erich Angermann, "1917: Jahr der Entscheidungen," in Schröder, ed., *Deutschland und Amerika*, 64; Thomas J. Saunders, "History in the Making: Weimar Cinema and National Identity," in Murray and Wickham, eds., *Framing the Past*, 46; *Illustrierte Filmwoche*, quoted in Hans Borgelt, *Die UFA: Ein Traum – 100 Jahre deutscher Film* (Berlin, 1993), 22.
52 Hanisch, *Spuren der Filmgeschichte*, 292–3; Jelavich, *Berlin Cabaret*, 119, 174.

Trommler has argued, "only a thin silhouette on the western horizon behind" them. Consider Fern Andra, a specialist in what have been called "demimondaine" roles who had been born in Illinois in the early 1890s. As Fern Andrews, she had worked her way to Europe as a dancer. She made her first German film in 1913 and quickly became a leading player, Germany's first "vamp." Sexy, charming, talented, she reportedly wore only enough clothes on-screen to make clear what she would have looked like naked. Expert at public relations, she was described by a German journalist as a "Genie der Reklame" (genius of marketing) and in 1917 overcame hostile feelings toward her as an American; the Fern Andra Film Co. and its principal carried on successfully throughout the war. Harry Piel, one of Germany's outstanding action filmmakers, in August 1917 did make a film about a German and an American who apparently are deadly enemies. But at the end of *Sein Todfeind* it turns out that the "bad" American is actually a "good" German who has been playing a role.[53]

In the main, World War I had little impact on how the German cinema portrayed America and Americans. Although American entry into the war ultimately ended the exhibition of American movies, the image of America they had created still remained. That image drew on others prevalent in the popular culture of prewar Wilhelmine Germany. Thus, the "Westerns" built on images created by the fanciful writings of Karl May, novels that Kracauer, among many others, described as "set in an imaginary American West and full of fabulous events involving Indian tribes, covered wagons, traders, hunters, tramps, and adventurers." A German trade paper enthused about "die famosen" (splendid) American cowboy and Indian films. During the 1912–13 movie season alone, seventeen Westerns starring the American cowboy star "Bronco Billy" achieved wide distribution. And the American out-of-doors attracted German audiences. A 1908 article emphasized the efforts of a German exhibitor to obtain American films for showing with "scenes from the Rocky Mountains, forest views, and flowing cascades."[54]

53 Frank Trommler, "The Rise and Fall of Americanism in Germany," in Trommler and McVeigh, eds., *America and the Germans*, 2:334; Klaus Kreimeier, *Die UFA-Story* (Munich, 1992), 181 (according to Oskar Kalbus, *Vom Werden deutscher Filmkunst: Der Stumm Film* [Hamburg, 1935], 26, she began her German film career as Fern Andra); Ute Schneider, "Fern Andra," in Hans-Michael Bock, ed., *Cinegraph* (Stuttgart, 1984–), E2. A less than kind contemporary of Andra later argued that she should have kept her clothes on, "denn für so etwas, hatte sie einfach nicht die geeignete Figur" (Heinrich Fraenkel, *Unsterblicher Film* [Munich, 1956], 80).

54 Matias Bleckman, *Harry Piel: Ein Kino-Mythos und seine Zeit* (Düsseldorf, 1994), 68; Kracauer, *From Caligari to Hitler*, 20; very early on, German moviegoers could see "Indianer und Cowboys" as part of a group of short films (advertisement dated 1905 for a Berlin theater in Zglinicki, *Weg*

What was described as "amerikanische Knock-about-Farce," with comedians such as John Bunny and Fatty Arbuckle, achieved great acceptance. The artist George Grosz remembered with pleasure laughing at Bunny and his jokes. But with their emphasis on slapstick and action, American movies were judged to have a touch of "brutality." Thus, even many of the popular Bronco Billy Westerns were "verboten" by the censor for children or would have scenes such as a lynching cut from the released prints. In 1912 the Prussian police authorities banned the showing of the 1909 American film *A Corner in Wheat*, the director D. W. Griffith's powerful tract attacking speculation in a staple food – censorship in Germany as elsewhere was based not just on the film's "social argument" but also on "its depiction of suicide, dumbing, and riotous living" (especially among the well-to-do speculators).[55]

The very qualities that made American films popular were part of what the "better elements" (who emphasized the quality of German *Kultur*) denigrated and denounced as trash (*Schundfilme*). Indeed, if there was any agreement between "German attitudes toward cinema and [toward] the United States it lay in the assumption that neither had a serious contribution to make to culture." Yet, interestingly, the Kaiser, contemporaries agreed, "had a personal interest in movies." He was a fan; he had a secret private screening room, and he gave filmmakers what now would be called photo opportunities for all kinds of functions, such as state visits or military maneuvers. The industry characterized him as a "Freund des Kinos" (pro-cinema). Generally speaking, criticism of what was shown in cinemas did not come from him.[56]

In order to meet such criticisms, the nascent German film industry just as it was turning to feature production in 1912–13 began producing films

des Films, 695); *Erste Internationale Film Zeitung*, Mar. 18, 1911, quoted in Herbert Birett, *Licht-spiele: Kino in Deutschland bis 1914* (Munich, 1994), cxiv; Schweinitz, *Prolog vor dem Film*, 343; Hansen, *Babel and Babylon*, 110.

55 Urban Gad, "Der Film (1918)," in Uta Berg-Ganschow, ed., *Berlin: Aussen und Innen – 53 Filme aus 90 Jahren* (Berlin, 1984), 104; Grosz quoted in Fritz Göttinger, *Der Stummfilm im Zitat der Zeit* (Frankfurt am Main, 1984), 62; Sabine Hake, *The Cinema's 3rd Machine: Writing on Film in Germany, 1907–1933* (Lincoln, Neb., 1993), 17; Russell Merritt, "D. W. Griffith's *A Corner in Wheat*," *Grif-fithiana*, nos. 61–2 (1997): 5.

56 Thomas J. Saunders, *Hollywood in Berlin: American Cinema and Weimar Germany* (Berkeley, Calif., 1994), 3; Hanisch, *Babel und Babylon*, 226. *Hätte ich das Kino: Die Schriftsteller und der Stummfilm* (Munich, 1976), 25; on the occasion of the twenty-fifth anniversary of the Kaiser's ascension to the throne, *Der Deutsche Kaiser im Film* (Berlin, 1912) was published; among other things, it was generously illustrated with photos taken from "actualities" of numerous film companies including Path, Union, Decla-Bishop, and Vitascope. An excellent overview of the "Kaiserzeit" is Martin Loiperdinger, "Das frühe Kino der Kaiserzeit," in Uli Jung, ed., *Der deutsche Film* (Trier, 1993), 21–50.

based on plays and novels of recognized value or on scripts by established literary figures. One result was movies that did not move. An irritated German writer of the time who did not think much of American movies (which he judged as "ein ganz kleines Kaliber" [of a very small caliber]) ultimately declared in exasperation at the unattractiveness of much of the domestic film product that it should be possible to go to the movies without running into "Hamlet, Dostoyevsky, Ibsen, Maeterlinck, Stefan George, Nietzsche, Freud, and Schopenhauer" or adaptations of sonnets, psychological novels, and "theories of relativity." Anton Kaes has usefully summed up this situation: "The literarization of the German cinema between 1910 and 1920 did not win many friends either among the working class public who went to the movies for . . . entertainment . . . or among intellectuals who . . . deplored the debasement of 'high art' . . . into the unrefined language of film."[57]

Certain themes mark the appearance of America and Americans in German films between the 1890s and 1918. Americans generally are seen as easygoing, happy-go-lucky, not difficult. In 1912 the American film company Universal Studios sent a director (Herbert Brenon) and a small team of actors to London, Paris, and Berlin as part of a "carefully planned assault on Europe – they made eight films in a few months. The films shot in London and Paris included *Ivanhoe* and *The Child Stealers of Paris*; those shot in Berlin were lighter in tone and included a farcical comedy of "two hard-up Americans in Berlin, each thinking the other rich." The treatment of these two was generally in keeping with the pleasant treatment on screen of Americans in German films.[58]

The German films of this era favorably depict cities such as New York and Chicago as bustling, attractive metropolises, and fascinating if perhaps occasionally dangerous urban centers. There are many examples of how the American city is treated. In the 1915 movie of Bernhard Kellerman's futuristic novel *Der Tunnel*, New York is the port city chosen as the North American terminus for a transatlantic tunnel, and it remained a desirable goal despite the nefarious machinations of the financiers who opposed the project. New York's Flatiron Building, then among the best known of the city's skyscrapers, shown flying the American flag, figured prominently in the film's advertisements.

The city also remains a place to go to in the Danish filming of a novel

---

57 Hans Siemsen, "Deutsch-amerikanischer Filmkrieg," in Fritz Göttinger, ed., *Kein Tag ohne Kino* (Frankfurt am Main, 1984), 435; Anton Kaes, "Mass Culture and Modernity," in Trommler and McVeigh, 320–1.
58 Jack Lodge, "The Career of Herbert Brenon," *Griffithiana*, no. 60 (Oct. 1996): 15.

by the well-known German author Gerhart Hauptmann. The production company found his script for *Atlantis* "vollkommen unbrauchbar" (completely unusable), but the subsequent writers on the project hewed closely to the novel because it had been released shortly before the *Titanic* disaster in 1912, and Hauptmann's effort had included such a disaster. The proponents of "high culture" used the failure of the film to attack American cultural influences, arguing that "die Vernichtung" (destruction) of a respectable novel by the film industry was "amerikanisch" – as "unhappily the whole film industry has something American to it."[59]

New York, Chicago, and other American cities also were featured prominently, if briefly, in the various popular adventure films produced in the 1910s, which sent their protagonists hither and yon. A typical example is the 1913 adventure film *Die Jagd nach der Hundertpfundnote* (The hunt for the hundred-pound bill) or *Die Reise um die Welt* (The trip around the world). This film also included scenes placing its protagonists in "the Wild West."

Westerns flourished in Wilhelmine Germany. The Kaiser enjoyed them; his interest went back to his childhood days when he had happily played "cowboys and Indians" with the son of an American diplomat. Cinema scholar Deniz Göktürk, in reviewing the Western's impact on Wilhelmine Germany, maintains that the genre held an "ungeheure Faszinationskraft" (an immense power to fascinate). American cowboy stars had quickly captured the affection of German audiences. They projected a strong, brave image, the "good bad man" with a tough exterior and a sentimental core.[60]

The Germans also tried their hand at Westerns, which projected an American image like that found in the homegrown product. They did so in films such as *Der Pferdedieb* (The horse thief) and *Wild-West-Romantik* (The romantic Wild West). The German film industry also produced a significant number of films that included Western sequences with the usual stalwart characters; these projected a positive image of the American. Typical were three adventure films from 1913. Gold mines and the prairie are part of *Evinrude: Die Geschichte eines Abenteuers* (Evinrude: The history of an adventure). Part two of *Menschen und Maske* (People and masks) continued the adventures of detective Kelly Brown, whose efforts also took him out West. The family melodrama *Heimat und Fremde* (At home and abroad) began in a European metropolis but included,

---

59 The Danish newspaper *Politiken*, quoted in Zglinicki, *Weg des Films*, 375.
60 Edward Taylor, *The Fate of the Dynasties* (Garden City, N.Y., 1963), 157; Deniz Göktürk, "Neckar Western, statt Donau Walzer," *KINtopp* 2 (1993): 118.

as advertised, scenes "im wilden Westen" that one critic found *hübsch* (pretty).[61]

That same year Harry Piel directed *Erblich Belastet* (Burdened by heredity), which dealt with an innocent man who, suspected of murder, is forced to flee: his name, Ferry Hudson; the locale supposedly was the Wild West, but the film's suggestions of America foundered on views of what was obviously "the heath of the Mark Brandenburg, the Havel lakes, and the Potsdamer Platz in Berlin."Yet, Piel's effort, even if lambasted critically in the trade journals, succeeded at the box office, for such was the pull of the genre.[62]

Notwithstanding the war, censorship, and the patriotic mien of the industry, Western films that set forth a positive view of Americans continued to be made and shown. Two soon-to-be-major industry figures were involved in cowboy films. In the early stages of his career the estimable director and producer Richard Oswald wrote the screenplay for the 1915 *Die Goldfelder von Jacksonville* (The gold mines of Jacksonville), described as a "Drama aus dem amerikanischen West." Just before the end of the war Erich Pommer, subsequently a major force in the pre-Hitler German film industry, produced *Der Cowboy*, whose hero traveled to a castle "irgendwo in Europa" in the last reel.[63]

Westerns were not the only German films during the war in which Americans featured prominently and not unfavorably. Another example is the Anglo-American detective film, which became even more popular. The *übermensch* of detectives (according to a German trade journal in December 1917) was Tom Shark, advertised as "the best snooper in America." The talented Alwin Neuss directed and starred in a number of Shark films during World War I. In these films Shark seems to have been positive and typical of the "can-do" spirit that typified the American in other genres. The production of such movies, despite what has been described as "the militarization of cinema," is what led to General Ludendorff's rage about UFA's failure as a propaganda vehicle.[64]

Still another approach to the representation of the American was reflected in the depiction of "the rich uncle" who returns to Germany from the United States after many years. In 1913 the 29-year-old Max

---

61 Quoted in Hanisch, *Babel and Babylon*, 147.
62 Bleckman, *Harry Piel*, 40, originally cited as "die märkische Heide, die Havelseen, und in Berlin der Potsdamer Platz."
63 Helga Belach and Wolfgang Jacobsen, eds., *Richard Oswald: Regisseur und Produzent* (Munich, 1990), 140; "Alwin Neuss," in Hans-Michael Bock, ed., *Cinegraph*, D11.
64 *Der Kinematograph*, Dec. 12, 1917, quoted in "Alwin Neuss," Hans-Michael Bock, ed., *Cinegraph*, D1; Kreimeier, *UFA-Story*, 31.

Brod contributed a plot outline centering on the character of "Der Dol-
laronkel" (Rich American uncle) to a collection edited by Kurt Pinthus
on the movies. In *Das Kinobuch* Pinthus, a 27-year-old Leipzig journalist
– and a not unimportant theater and film critic whose 1920 anthology
of expressionistic poetry remains useful – brought together seventeen
writers (mostly young Expressionists) whose suggested film scenarios
underscored Pinthus's sharp rejection of the "elitist attitudes of German
intellectuals." In Brod's effort a young student's uncle returns for a visit.
This uncle, although extremely well off and generous in the student's
daydreams, in which he appears wearing a high hat with the stars of the
union on it and with money flowing endlessly out of his pants' pockets,
on first appearance seems old and shabby. After a series of fantastic events
that mix daydreams and reality, he turns out to be a generous
millionaire.[65]

Variations on this theme were to be found in a significant number of
films made before 1918. Even Germany's first great silent movie star, the
Dane Asta Nielsen, the "[Eleonora] Duse of film" (as she was called), made
a movie centering on a rich uncle. Nielsen, who after her 1911 breakthrough in Denmark made films in Germany for the next two decades,
in 1913 starred in *Engelein* (Little angel). The 32-year-old Nielsen convincingly played a 17-year-old who impersonated a 12-year-old in order
to stop a rich uncle from America from letting his fortune leave the
family. As exemplified by the returning uncle, the American in these films
was presented as energetic, determined, and hard-working, even if (as in
the Nielsen film) a bit comic.[66]

In German films "the American" was composed of a series of often
contradictory images. Cowboys did not seek wealth; the primitivism of
the "Wild West" was a far cry from urban technological progress; energy
and determination failed to compensate for the much-heralded lack of
culture; money-grubbing overshadowed sentiment and emotion. Moreover, most of the images were male. The madcap American heiress, "die
Dollarprinzessin" (also found elsewhere in Wilhelmine culture) only occasionally made her way on-screen before and during World War I. For all
the drawbacks found in the presentation of the American by German
filmmakers, they never demonized this image, as was the case with the
American wartime Hate-the-Hun campaign.

65 Max Brod, "Ein Tag aus dem Leben Kühnbecks, des jungen Idealisten," in Kurt Pinthus, ed., *Das
   Kinobuch* (1913; reprint, Zurich, 1963), 71–6; Hake, *Cinema's 3rd Machine*, 71.
66 "Asta Nielsen," in Bock, ed., *Cinegraph*, B2.

Indeed, over the next half-century during which movies dominated the mass media, the only truly venomous German depictions of Americans on a broad scale came after World War II in East German films. Such movies carefully and convincingly present what has been called a *Feindbild* (image of the enemy). No Hitler-period film attacked the American self as venomously, as diligently, as concretely as did some GDR films. During the Nazi era hate films were made excoriating Jews, communists, the Soviets, and the British. Americans, as in the business epic *Diesel* (1942), did come under attack, but only rarely.[67]

Conversely, during World War II American moviemakers did not produce en masse German-bashing movies World War I–style. After 1918 the German, with a few notable exceptions, disappeared from American films. Even as American antipathy to the Nazis became ever stronger after 1933, the American film industry – hesitant about losing the German market (which grew with the 1938 annexation of Austria, the 1939 occupation of Czechoslovakia and Poland, and the 1940 conquest of much of western Europe) – overall avoided explicit anti-German or anti-Nazi films until 1941. And during World War II, although Hollywood turned out its fair share of "nasty Nazi" propaganda, it avoided the excesses of the earlier Hate-the-Hun films.

The industry followed the guidelines of the Office of War Information (coordinating American propaganda), which urged "don't make blanket condemnations of all Germans . . . as this country does not regard the German people as our enemies, only their leaders." Not all filmmakers followed this advice, and Germans often were presented virulently, but even the staunchest anti-Nazi films could contain what later came to be called "Good Germans." Over a generation after the war's end a West German critic noted with some awe and astonishment that "even at the height of the war, American films were released that showed good Germans in a sentimental and respectful way, as though Hitler and the war had never existed."[68]

After 1945 communism replaced Nazism as the chief threat to the American way of life; the "nasty Nazi" gave way to the "rotten Red." The exculpation of Germany (or at least anticommunist West Germany) meant

---

67 Wolfgang Gersh, "Film in der DDR: Die verlorene Alternative," in Jacobsen et al., eds., *Geschichte des deutschen Films* (Stuttgart, 1993), 340.

68 Bureau of Motion Pictures, Office of War Information, quoted in Richard Lingeman, *Don't You Know There's a War On: The American Home Front, 1941–1945* (New York, 1970), 186; Hans C. Blumenberg, "Hollywood und Hakenkreuz," in Alice Goetz, ed., *Hollywood und die Nazis: Eine Dokumentation*, 2d enlarged and rev. ed. (Hamburg, 1977), 9.

that American movies increasingly drew a very clear distinction between "the good German who fought for his country and the Nazi fanatical beasts." As the movies (and other media) refurbished German society, it became a victim of rather than an accessory to the Nazis. Although Nazis did not disappear from American film, they became distinct from Germans.[69]

But the years since 1918 are another story, which must be dealt with in more detail. As it is for the years prior to 1918, a comprehensive analysis of the image in films remains difficult. The interpretation of the intertext in these films poses various questions. In an attempt to catch up with the scholarship available and continuing about early American film, those on both sides of the Atlantic interested in German cinema prior to 1918 have undertaken yeoman, broadbased, and in the main successful efforts. Typical is Heide Schlüpmann's work in which, through a close reading of selected films, she has set forth intelligent ideas about the relationship between cinematography and women's emancipation in Wilhelmine society. She surveys broadly but must do so on the basis of reading relatively few films, because not many of the movies produced during those early years have survived. The very well-versed scholar Thomas Elsaesser, in one of his recent challenges to Kracauer, has succinctly summed up the situation: "We know too few films, and we possess too little information about the ones we do have."[70]

Yet, even the limited number of films available are valuable because of how a movie is created. Filmmaking is a team effort, the auteur theory notwithstanding. Even a short film of the early 1900s can be assumed to have been the product of collaboration. Such joint effort explains in part why movies have a closer relationship to the group processes in society than individual efforts like a painting or a short story. It may well be that early movies were what Kracauer in 1930 called *Wirklichkeitsflucht* (escape from reality) or these films may have been what in 1933 was described as *Wunschbilder* (desired images). However these early movies are categorized, placing them in historical context makes it possible to avoid just a nostalgic recycling of images.[71]

---

69 Oehling, "German Americans," 60; for an overview of American treatment of Germans since 1941, see Daniel J. Leab, "Good Germans/Bad Nazis: Amerikanische Bilder aus dem Kalten Krieg und ihre Ursprünge," *Deutsches Historisches Museum Magazin* 5 (1992): 25–39.

70 Heide Schlüpmann, *Unheimlichkeit des Blicks: Das Drama des frühen deutschen Kinos* (Basel, 1990), 8; Thomas Elsaesser, "National Subjects, International Style," in Usai et al., eds., *Before Caligari*, 342.

71 Kracauer, quoted in Thomas G. Plummer, "Introduction," in Thomas G. Plummer et al., eds., *Film and Politics in the Weimar Republic* (Minneapolis, 1982), 7; Hans Traub, *Der Film als politisches Machtmittel* (Munich, 1933), 6.

To come to definite conclusions may be premature, but certain implications are clear. Film (like any other discourse) is never really neutral.
Movies, even at their most primitive in the latter 1890s and early 1900s,
were connected to and influenced by the larger culture in complex, not
always comprehensible or rational ways. Factors involved (and often overlooked until relatively recently) included class, gender, race, ethnicity, and
sexual preference, as well as audience response, production history, and the
impact of technique in conjunction with technological developments.
Film developed its own language with explicit and implicit prejudices.

In both Germany and the United States, the movies, even during these
nascent years, contributed mightily toward the rapid transformation of the
public sphere. As the late Jay Leyda – still among the most prescient of
commentators on early film – asserted years ago, "each film historian . . .
is struck by the speed with which the peculiar expressiveness of the
medium was developed." We know more about national images in older
German and American films than we did a generation ago, even more
than we did just five years ago. As scholarship progresses on both sides of
the Atlantic, as more resources are discovered, we shall be able increasingly to move from tentative theorizing to assertive conclusions.[72]

72 Jay Leyda, "A Note on Progress," *Film Quarterly* 21 (summer 1968): 28.

PART FOUR

Transatlantic Politics and Economics

9

Franklin Delano Roosevelt and Adolf Hitler

A Contemporary Comparison Revisited

GERHARD L. WEINBERG

Roosevelt and Hitler came to power in the same year; the former died shortly before the latter committed suicide. This contemporaneity was one of the very few things they had in common, but it did lead to one other very important shared experience, or perhaps one should say nonexperience: neither was able to write his memoirs. This has meant that neither had the opportunity to present his own version of events the way so many of their other contemporaries did; in fact, it almost invited others to present their versions in a manner that might well have been impossible had these others been obliged to consider the possibility of a rebuttal. This was to be particularly true in the case of Hitler. Dozens if not hundreds of those who had happily collected promotions, bribes, estates, and medals from him would discover after his death that they had not only been vastly more intelligent and far-sighted than the leader they had once praised so loudly and served with such devotion, but they had both despised him the whole time and had invariably given him the good advice whose disregard had led Germany to disaster.[1]

Now that more time has passed, most of the memoir writers have departed from the scene, and much more of the record has become available, it might be of interest to look at these two leaders in terms of their own perceptions of themselves as well as their places in the great drama of the twelve years during which they led their respective countries. There is an enormous difference that immediately strikes the observer. Whereas both men had a great deal of self-confidence, there was a self-assurance about Roosevelt that Hitler entirely lacked. This cannot simply be attrib-

---

1 An example would be the distortions and fakeries in the memoirs of Field Marshall Erich von Manstein; a selection is exposed and corrected in Manfred Kehrig, *Stalingrad: Analyse und Dokumentation einer Schlacht* (Stuttgart, 1974), 224, 390–1, 395–6.

uted to their different socioeconomic backgrounds. Roosevelt could easily have become self-conscious about his polio-induced handicap, and Hitler could as easily have developed his father's assurance about his status. The fact is that Roosevelt was comfortable with all sorts of people from all walks of life and from a great variety of backgrounds – even when his mother did not approve of them. Hitler, in contrast, was extraordinarily diffident about dealing with men and women from social backgrounds different from his own.

There is an interesting comparison that illustrates this point. During World War II Roosevelt went over all proposed promotions to star and flag rank in the army and navy, and occasionally he would turn down specific individuals proposed for higher rank by General George Marshall or Admiral Ernest King, striking them from the lists to be sent to Congress for action.[2] When one looks at his objections, one factor *never* appears: that of background or nationality. A German-born Walter Krueger could rise to three-star rank as commander of the Sixth Army fighting in the Pacific; such individuals of German-American background as Albert Wedemeyer and Robert Eichelberger, Dwight Eisenhower and Chester Nimitz, Clarence Huebner and others could advance in rank without Roosevelt ever raising an eyebrow. At the same time, the German military was directed to discharge all officers suspected by Hitler of having too much blue blood in their veins. He considered it dangerous for members of Germany's old princely families to have a chance to earn decorations, promotions, or a hero's death at the front.

In some ways this diffidence on the one hand and self-assurance on the other may be related to the two leaders' respective outlooks on the future. Roosevelt was confident not only about himself but about the future of his country. Rightly or wrongly, he not only put on an air of confidence, he really shared it. Few things seemed impossible to him; the country was not only headed for victory but for a better future; the colonial empires he detested seemed to him certain to disintegrate; and the challenges of the future would be met successfully. Hitler, though, was always in a desperate hurry lest things go wrong; no other German leader was likely to do as well and take the risks he was prepared to take; Germany's future was a grim one if he did not rush forward to seize the chances that he imagined lay before him.

As is well known, the two men never met; but it is too often forgotten that Roosevelt did invite Hitler to Washington in 1933. Hitler sent

2 The promotion correspondence is in the Franklin D. Roosevelt Library at Hyde Park, N.Y.

Hjalmar Schacht instead. The latter made a fool of himself in Washington by announcing a German transfer payment moratorium while in the American capital – right after publicly promising not to do so – as a means of cheating Germany's American creditors by devaluing the securities they held so that these could be repurchased by Germany at bargain-basement prices with the allegedly nonexistent foreign exchange. Roosevelt was furious, to put it mildly, refused to see Schacht once more, and instead arranged for Secretary of State Cordell Hull to tell him off in no uncertain terms. This had to be done in so "undiplomatic" a manner that the American record of the conversation was not sent to the State Department's main file for years and hence escaped the editors of the *Foreign Relations of the United States* series.[3] Although the twentieth century was one of almost endless personal diplomacy, the first contact between the two governments at the ministerial level was also to be the last in the twelve years under review.

If Roosevelt and Hitler never met in person, they did have one very public exchange of messages. After Germany tore up the Munich agreement and it looked increasingly as if a war was likely to break out soon, Roosevelt sent a public message to Hitler on April 15, 1939, asking him (as well as Mussolini) to promise not to attack a lengthy list of countries for a period of ten years.[4] Hitler, who had by this time already decided to attack one country on the list later that year and three others in the course of his planned war with France and Britain, decided that the way to deal with the president's request was by a speech to the Reichstag on April 28 ridiculing Roosevelt. The Reichstag members all laughed and applauded at the appropriate points in the speech; one cannot help wondering whether any of them recalled the occasion in subsequent years when Germany invaded countries on the list one by one.

By the time of this exchange, the two leaders were no longer in contact through ambassadors, Roosevelt having recalled the United States ambassador to Germany after the November 1938 pogrom and the Germans then following suit.[5] Occasional subsequent consideration of a return of ambassadors never led to such a step in the interval before the German declaration of war on the United States ended the possibility. That formal

---

3 Gerhard L. Weinberg, "Schachts Besuch in den USA im Jahre 1933," *Vierteljahrshefte für Zeitgeschichte* 11 (1963): 166–80; the critical document is cited in note 56.

4 Günter Moltmann, "Franklin D. Roosevelts Friedensappell vom 14. April 1939: Ein fehlgeschlagener Versuch zur Friedenssicherung," *Jahrbuch für Amerikastudien* 9 (1964): 91–101.

5 See Roosevelt's handwritten emendations on the draft announcement of November 15, 1938, about the recall of Ambassador Hugh Wilson, in Franklin D. Roosevelt Library, Hyde Park, N.Y., PSF Germany.

declaration came several days *after* Hitler ordered hostilities against the United States to begin; he was as so often in a great hurry, and after receiving the news of the Japanese attack on Pearl Harbor in his East Prussian headquarters did not want to wait until he could get to Berlin. Because of his personal role in this step, Hitler's view of war with the United States deserves further examination, as does Roosevelt's view of possible war with Germany.

Already when dictating his second book in the summer of 1928 Hitler was certain that preparing for war with the United States would be one of the main responsibilities of a National Socialist government.[6] He followed up on this concept as chancellor in 1937 by ordering the building of airplanes and super battleships for the coming war against the United States.[7] Here was clearly a high priority for him: Both in the summer of 1940 and in the summer of 1941, just as soon as he believed victory had been attained – in the West in 1940 and in the East in 1941 – his first *formal* step was to order resumption of construction on the huge navy Germany in his opinion needed to fight the United States. I have covered the details elsewhere,[8] but the point that seems to me to be important for an understanding of the way Hitler saw things and the priorities that affected his planning for the future is the way in which on every occasion when he thought he had some choices, this one appears to have come to his mind first. And in 1940 he was willing to sacrifice the possibility of having Spain come into the war on Germany's side rather than give up on his insistence on the German-owned bases on and off the coast of Northwest Africa, which he believed Germany needed for war with the United States.[9]

Until Germany had a navy that Hitler believed adequate for coping with the Americans, he would restrain the German navy, which itself had been calling for war with the United States since October 1939; but he was always looking for the obvious short-cut: an ally who already had a big navy. The repeated promises to the Japanese that Germany would join

6 Gerhard L. Weinberg, ed., *Hitler's zweites Buch: Ein Dokument aus dem Jahr 1928* (Stuttgart, 1961), 130. A new edition of this book has been published as vol. IIA: *Aussenpolitische Standortbestimmung nach der Reichstagswahl Juni – Juli 1928* (Munich, 1995) in the series *Hitler: Reden Schriften Anordnungen Februar 1925 bis Januar 1933.* The reference is on 90.

7 See Jost Dülffer, *Weimar, Hitler und die Marine: Reichspolitik und Flottenbau 1920–1939* (Düsseldorf, 1973), 546; Jochen Thies, *Architekt der Weltherrschaft: Die "Endziele" Hitlers* (Düsseldorf, 1976), 128–46.

8 These issues are covered with detailed references in Gerhard L. Weinberg, *A World at Arms: A Global History of World War II* (New York, 1994), chaps. 3–5.

9 See Norman J. W. Goda, *Tomorrow the World: Hitler, Northwest Africa, and the Path Toward America* (College Station, Tex., 1998).

them as soon as they went to war with the United States have to be understood in this context; and because the Japanese picked their own time to act, all Hitler could do was start hostilities as soon as Tokyo moved. He would have preferred for them to strike earlier, but the moment they did so, he wanted to move against the United States.

There was no specific plan for how Germany was to fight the United States when Hitler brought the good news of war with America to a cheering Reichstag; only at sea was there an immediate opportunity to strike at the United States, as the German navy had long urged. What evidence we have suggests that Hitler believed that the Japanese would keep the bulk of American military power tied up in the Pacific for a long time so that Germany could complete its conquest of the Soviet Union and defeat of England while making its plans and completing its preparations for other aspects of the clash with the power across the Atlantic. It is too often forgotten, however, that massive allocations of German resources to the construction of U-boats and to the development and production of new weapons for use against England characterized the German war effort for the balance of the war and must be seen as indicators of Hitler's priorities. His designation of Admiral Karl Dönitz as his successor surely shows the direction of his final thoughts.

At the time that Hitler was dictating his views on the need for war with the United States in the summer of 1928, Roosevelt had not yet agreed to run for the office of governor of New York as he was being urged to do in the context of an election in which it was the hope of many Democrats that his running would assist presidential candidate Al Smith, whom Roosevelt had nominated at the Democratic National Convention in Houston on June 17. Whatever was on Roosevelt's mind that difficult summer, as he was trying out the braces on his legs and as he had to decide whether to become a candidate for the first time since his defeat in the run for the vice presidency in 1920 – he only agreed to run at the beginning of October – another war with Germany was surely not one of the issues he was considering. He had been something of a "hawk" in 1914–17, if that expression had existed then, and there are indications that he favored the demand for unconditional surrender rather than the official policy of granting an armistice to Germany adopted by the Wilson administration of which he was a part.[10] Insofar as he was concerned with foreign affairs after the 1918 armistice, however, it had

10 Raymond G. O'Connor, *Diplomacy for Victory: FDR and Unconditional Surrender* (New York, 1971), 3–5.

been the issues of the peace treaty and the League of Nations that drew his attention; and thereafter, of course, he had his bout with polio. Nothing suggests that the possibility of another war with Germany entered his thoughts while his political comeback took place even as Al Smith was defeated.

As already mentioned, Roosevelt invited Hitler to Washington in 1933, but his immediate concerns as president were focused on the depression that had hit the United States much harder than Germany. As I have explained elsewhere, Roosevelt did follow events in Nazi Germany quite carefully, with a combination of apprehension and disgust.[11] The material available in the National Archives and at Hyde Park clearly shows that Roosevelt took the danger that Hitler's Germany posed to the peace of the world very seriously; the question that has been a subject of some dispute is, what did he want to do about it? Slowly he began to push for some rearmament, first with the navy in 1936–37, then with the air force in 1938, and finally with the army in 1939 and 1940. The fact that the army came *last* in the chronological sequence of rearmament as Roosevelt saw it seems to me to reinforce the view that he was thinking of what today would be called deterrence rather than any armed confrontation with Germany in Europe. It should be noted that the naval rearmament program originally aimed more at Japan than Germany because that country had denounced the naval limitation treaties that hobbled American rather than Japanese naval construction as the Japanese were to learn to their great regret later. But here too deterrence rather than provocation was Roosevelt's aim; the subsequent movement of large naval forces from the West Coast to Pearl Harbor as well as the early allocation of a substantial number of new four-engine bombers to the Pacific must be seen as parts of a policy of deterrence that failed in its purpose.

Roosevelt was hardly an eager confrontationist; one of the major studies of American policy in the 1930s, that of Arnold Offner, is titled *American Appeasement: United States Foreign Policy and Germany, 1933–1938*.[12] Roosevelt undoubtedly played a central role in the American effort to assist the rebuilding of the French air force,[13] but nothing he

---

11 Detailed accounts in Gerhard L. Weinberg, *The Foreign Policy of Hitler's Germany: Diplomatic Revolution in Europe, 1933–1936* (Atlantic Highlands, N.J., 1994), chap. 6; and Gerhard L. Weinberg, *The Foreign Policy of Hitler's Germany: Starting World War II, 1937–1939* (Atlantic Highlands, N.J., 1994), chap. 8.

12 Arnold Offner, *American Appeasement: United States Foreign Policy and Germany, 1933–1938* (Cambridge, Mass., 1969).

13 John McVickar Haight Jr., *American Aid to France, 1938–1940* (New York, 1970).

heard from his ambassadors to France, Jesse Strauss and William Bullitt, can possibly have suggested to him anything other than a defensive posture and policy on the part of that country. Anyone is entitled to the opinion that Roosevelt's policy in the face of what was increasingly looking like another war started by Germany was not especially clear or imaginative, but it is difficult to see his actions as anything other than defensive.

In the months immediately preceding Germany's invasion of Poland, Roosevelt's policy seemed calculated once again more to deter than to confront Germany. The special peace appeal of April 15, 1939, has already been mentioned. The president tried two other approaches, both of which also failed, but both also were designed to give Germany pause if successful. On the domestic front, Roosevelt tried to get Congress to repeal the prohibition on the sale of war materiel and equipment in this country to belligerents, a move designed to make clear that Britain and France could purchase arms in the United States in case of war. As is well known, Congress refused to act on this proposal before Germany began the war.[14] On the international front, Roosevelt urged the Soviet government through both the Soviet ambassador in Washington and his newly appointed ambassador to Moscow to join with the Western Powers lest a Germany triumphant in the West thereafter menace both the Soviet Union and the United States.[15] We shall never know whether such a step by the Soviet Union would have deterred Hitler from war – I am inclined to doubt it – but Roosevelt was not alone in thinking of that possibility. Joseph Stalin, of course, was certain that he knew better and aligned himself with Hitler. It deserves to be recalled that when Roosevelt's prediction proved entirely correct, and the Germans, victorious in the West, decided to attack the Soviet Union, a summary of the German plan that the United States had obtained from an internal opponent of Hitler was, on Roosevelt's instruction, handed to the Soviet ambassador in February 1941. As before, Stalin was certain that he knew better.[16]

By this time, the war in Europe was under way, and the Japanese were in the process of deciding to join their war against China with the conflict that Germany appeared to be winning in Europe. It remained Roosevelt's hope that the United States could keep out of hostilities by

14 The account of this in Cordell Hull, *The Memoirs of Cordell Hull*, 2 vols. (New York, 1948), 1:chap. 45: "Neutrality Disaster," is still worth reading.
15 See Weinberg, *Foreign Policy, 1937–1939*, 578n178.
16 The evidence is cited in Gerhard L. Weinberg, *Germany, Hitler, and World War II* (New York, 1995), 185–8.

assisting those fighting Germany and Japan. As we know today, the ability of the British to read German naval signals in 1941 and to share the information gleaned with the Americans was utilized to do everything possible to *avoid* incidents in the Atlantic.[17] The widely held view that Roosevelt was looking for incidents and opportunities to confront Germany and draw the United States into the war is directly contradicted by the evidence on this point that has been available in the National Archives for twenty-five years, but few scholars have allowed the facts to interfere with their preconceived notions.

The same thing has been true for discussion of Roosevelt's policy toward Japan. Here, too, there were in 1941 extraordinary opportunities for confronting Japan that the president deliberately refused to take in the hope of avoiding hostilities. He spent endless hours in conversations with the Japanese ambassador at a time when the American ambassador in Tokyo was complaining about his inability to see anyone of importance there. Perhaps even more significant for the insight it gives us into the president's general orientation was the handling he and Secretary Hull accorded to what was certainly their most dramatic opportunity to arouse the population of the country against Japan.

In the summer of 1941 the Office of Naval Intelligence and the Federal Bureau of Investigation uncovered a major Japanese spy ring in southern California; several high-ranking Japanese naval officers were caught with evidence. A number of Americans whom they had bribed or tried to bribe also were caught. It was undoubtedly the largest Japanese espionage network discovered in the United States in the twentieth century, and the authorities involved wanted to put the Japanese officers on trial. Such a trial would, of course, have attracted enormous interest and it would have provided an ideal opportunity to whip up public opinion. However, in the hope of protecting whatever chances of success the negotiations with Japan might have, Roosevelt and Hull instead, at the special request of Japan's ambassador Nomura Kichisaburo, arranged for the release and expulsion of the Japanese officers and aborted a sensational trial.[18]

All hopes for continued peace with Japan were dashed by the Japanese attack on Pearl Harbor and the immediate German and Italian declarations of war on the United States that followed. The very insistence

---

17 See Jürgen Rohwer, "Die USA und die Schlacht im Atlantik 1941," in Jürgen Rohwer and Eberhard Jäckel, eds., *Kriegswende Dezember 1941* (Koblenz, 1984), 81–103.

18 A recent summary in Pedro R. Loureiro, "Japanese Espionage and American Countermeasures in Pre–Pearl Harbor California," *Journal of American–East Asian Relations* 3 (1994): 205–8.

of the Tripartite Pact powers on waging war on the United States, an insistence shared by Hungary, Romania, and Bulgaria in the face of American efforts to have them withdraw their declarations of war, must be seen as part of the background for Roosevelt's insistence on unconditional surrender. As previously mentioned, there are indications that he had favored such a demand in 1918, rather than the Wilson administration's agreement to an armistice for Germany; everything we now know shows that he favored such a course in World War II from the day the United States was forced into it. The public announcement of that policy did not come until the Casablanca Conference, but it is clear from Roosevelt's comments before then that he agreed with the conclusion of the State Department's Advisory Committee on Post-War Foreign Policy reported to him on May 20, 1942, that unconditional surrender should be demanded. As Assistant Secretary of State Breckinridge Long had stated in the committee, "We are fighting this war because we did not have an unconditional surrender at the end of the last one."[19] Looking to the future beyond hostilities, Roosevelt was absolutely determined that American soldiers would not have to fight Germany a third time or Japan a second time.

As for how to fight Germany, Roosevelt and his military and civilian advisers never had any serious doubts: The Third Reich would have to be defeated by striking at its heart, not by stepping on its toes. It would take years to get to that stage, but it was probably just as well that this approach carried the day. The alternative strategy, climbing every mountain in the Balkans, would have produced an iron curtain running East–West rather than North–South, with all of Germany under Soviet control.

For the future of Germany, Roosevelt was extremely reluctant to make detailed plans during hostilities. This was not simply a matter of postponing decisions, as is often suggested; already in 1942 he expressed a preference for American soldiers getting to Berlin first. What Roosevelt was reluctant about was the making of agreements about the future of a country the Allies had not reached and in particular doing so at a time when American military power and the ability to project it into Europe were unfolding and likely to get stronger. Here was the basis of his difference with Winston Churchill over concessions to the Soviet Union. The British leader, from the standpoint of a power that was steadily getting weaker, preferred to make the best deal possible and to offer what-

19 O'Connor, *Diplomacy for Victory*, 36–8.

ever concessions seemed to him to be necessary as early as possible lest
he have to make a poorer deal later. This is most obvious in regard to
the occupation zones: Roosevelt drew maps showing the eastern and
western zones meeting in Berlin, whereas the British drafted and proposed in the European Advisory Committee the line that was quickly
agreed to by the Soviets and then pushed onto the reluctant Americans.[20]
The events of 1945 would show that Roosevelt's inclination had been
correct; Churchill then changed his mind, but it was far too late.

Roosevelt would have to give way on one other aspect of the future
of Germany, this time not to the British but to the Soviets. He had agreed
to Henry Morgenthau's idea of reorienting Germany into a country with
a high standard of living but little or no heavy industry on the model of
Holland and Denmark. But as Morgenthau's map showed, this meant
leaving Germany a majority of the land between the Oder-Neisse Line
and the 1937 border – a point subsequent observers have ignored but
which was immediately recognized as critical by the Soviets, who turned
the plan down forthwith.[21] One could either try to transform Germany
into a predominantly agricultural country or take away much of its agricultural land and expel the millions of Germans living on it, but one
could not do both. So the plan was dropped; it was too soft, not too hard,
on the Germans.

As is well known, Roosevelt died before the end of the war in Europe
and at a time when it was assumed that the war in the Pacific would last
another year and a half. Roosevelt's prediction that the Allies would be
well advised to see what the situation in Germany was like before they
made detailed arrangements for it ironically presaged the development of
American policy after his death.[22]

There is a final personal aspect in the comparison between Hitler and
Roosevelt that deserves our attention. Roosevelt had been stricken with
polio and had, in a special way, triumphed over it. In the 1950s the
medical discoveries of Drs. Albert Sabin and Jonas Salk in turn triumphed
over polio. Hitler had nothing but contempt for Roosevelt and no doubt
thought that the election of such an individual to the highest office in

20 On Roosevelt's proposed zonal boundaries and the British-Soviet proposal, see Earl F. Ziemke,
   The U.S. Army in the Occupation of Germany, 1944–1946 (Washington, D.C., 1975), 115–26.
21 The map that accompanied Morgenthau's proposal and has been overlooked by 99 percent of
   those writing on the subject was published in Henry Morgenthau Jr., *Germany Is Our Problem*
   (New York, 1945), facing 160. An early draft was published in David Rees, *Harry Dexter White*
   (New York, 1973), 444.
22 See Roosevelt's "Memorandum for the Secretary of State," Oct. 20, 1944, in *Foreign Relations of
   the United States: The Conferences at Malta and Yalta 1945* (Washignton, D.C., 1955), 158–9.

the land demonstrated just what dolts the Americans must be. In a country run as well as his Germany, such individuals would be put to death as living lives unworthy of life in the so-called euthanasia program.[23] But that was not all. As he explained in considerable detail to the Grand Mufti of Jerusalem, not only were all Jews in Europe to be killed but, in addition, all those living on the globe elsewhere – the interpreter records him as referring to those living among "aussereuropäische Völker" (non-European peoples) – also were to be killed.[24] As Jews, both Sabin and Salk were destined to be killed if Germany won the war, and presumably people inside and outside Germany would have continued to suffer the ravages of polio – to be followed by euthanasia if they survived – under those circumstances. This is by no means the only reason why it is fortunate for the world that Roosevelt, not Hitler, triumphed in the contest between the two, but it is a facet of the comparison that deserves to be mentioned that a recent Miss America, handicapped by deafness, belonged to the category of those Hitler considered unworthy of living.

The memory of the 1930s and 1940s is dimming, and with time it will recede further as those decades become a portion of the distant past the way prior centuries appear to us now. But it seems very likely that even then the two men under discussion will continue to be analyzed both as extremely interesting individuals in and of themselves and, in a certain way, as symbols of an era in history that is both terrible and hopeful at the same time.

23 Ernst Klee, *"Euthanasie" im NS-Staat: Die "Vernichtung lebensunwerten Lebens"* (Frankfurt am Main, 1983), 80, 118–19. I am not aware of any separate study of the fate of survivors of polio in the Third Reich. The whole subject has now been covered in greater detail in Henry Friedlander, *The Origins of Nazi Genocide: From Euthanasia to the Final Solution* (Chapel Hill, N.C., 1995).
24 *Akten zur deutschen auswärtigen Politik 1918–1945*, ser. D: 1937–1945, vol. 13.2: *Die Kriegsjahre*, vol. 6/2: *15. September bis 11. Dezember 1941* (Göttingen, 1970), 720.

10

The Role of the Banker in Transatlantic History

J. P. Morgan & Co. and Aid for the Allies, 1914–1916

ELISABETH GLASER

The outcome of World War I hinged largely on the economic and financial resources that each side commanded. To a considerable extent it depended just on bankers and financiers in Great Britain and the United States. Georges Clemenceau illustrated this by his remark, "War is too serious a matter to entrust to military men."[1] The United States played an increasing role in supplying the Allies from 1915 until the end of the war and thereby contributed considerably to Germany's defeat in 1918. In the first eighteen months of the war the American banking firm J. P. Morgan & Co. took the lead in shaping America's material and financial aid to the Allies. J. P. Morgan assumed the risk and the responsibility of exploring the hitherto uncharted field of large-scale private financing of European needs at a critical juncture. This venture proved successful in facilitating the unprecedented flow of American resources in support of Allied warfare in Europe. Yet the initiative came back to haunt the banking concern in 1936, when those who had marshaled aid for the Allies in World War I had to face hostile interrogation from the Senate Special Committee Investigating the Munitions Industry, chaired by Senator Gerald P. Nye (R-North Dakota).

The Anglo-French loan of 1915 constituted the first large American loan for the Allies. It attracted the attention of the Nye Committee in 1936 because it served as the cornerstone in the evolution of American financial aid in World War I. The 1915 loan likewise occasioned a review of official American policy with regard to private advances to the Allies that brought about a more conciliatory attitude in the administration of Woodrow Wilson. A closer examination of J. P. Morgan & Co.'s stake in

---

1 Hampdon Jackson, *Clemenceau and the Third Republic* (New York, 1946), 228.

the Anglo-French loan of 1915 reveals the extent to which the main players in the British and American banking community shaped a major episode in transatlantic history. The bankers, however, did not exert the pernicious pressure that muscled an unwitting American government into World War I, as later foes of another American intervention would suggest. Rather, they did what they did best by making a rational contribution to a worthy and only mildly profitable cause, based on a sober assessment of the available options.

In 1914 J. P. Morgan & Co. ranked as one of the largest American banks and certainly as the most influential one.[2] Reorganized in 1894, the banking concern consisted of the American partnership with its headquarters at 23 Wall Street; Morgan, Harjes & Co., the Paris house partly controlled by New York; and the independent London partnership, soon to be called Morgan, Grenfell & Co.[3] Morgan's rise to pre-eminence on Wall Street resulted from the bank's controlling position as the banking institution for European investments in American railroads during the nineteenth century, its successful refunding of the Civil War debt, and its financing of large-scale industrial mergers. The bank was responsible for the financial reorganization of Andrew Carnegie's steel companies into U.S. Steel in 1901. In such consolidations, it drew on the managerial expertise that it had acquired through its pivotal role in railroad financing at the turn of the century. During the panic of 1907 John Pierpoint Morgan organized the New York banking community's rescue operations, which headed off a more fundamental crash.

Conspiracy theories and the re-emergence of traditional antimonopoly sentiments led to a hostile interrogation of Morgan by the Pujo Committee in 1913 and generated more heat than light. After Morgan's death in 1913, soon after the Pujo Committee hearings, his son, John "Jack" Pierpoint Morgan Jr., became the chief partner of the firm. Two other close associates and partners, Thomas W. Lamont and Henry P. Davison, joined him on the steering committee that managed Morgan's financial participation in World War I.[4]

For America, a sharp drop in stock prices and the resulting panic

---

2 Standard histories of the bank include Vincent P. Carosso, *The Morgans: Private International Bankers* (Cambridge, Mass., 1987); and the more popular account by Ron Chernow, *The House of Morgan: An American Banking Dynasty and the Rise of Modern Finance* (New York, 1990).

3 Carosso, *Morgans*, 302–7.

4 Carosso, *Morgans*, 303–7; 433–54, 466–74, 536–49, 624–41; John Douglas Forbes, *J. P. Morgan, Jr., 1867–1943* (Charlottesville, Va., 1981); Edward M. Lamont, *The Ambassador from Wall Street: The Story of Thomas W. Lamont, J. P. Morgan's Chief Executive* (Lanham, Md., 1994); Thomas W. Lamont, *Henry P. Davison: The Record of A Useful Life* (1933; reprint, New York, 1975).

figured as the first sizeable consequences of the outbreak of war in Europe. The German invasion of Belgium and the English declaration of war on August 4 caught New York's financial community by surprise. Many bankers and financiers on Wall Street, among them Davison, had hoped until the last minute that a large-scale European conflict could be averted. Commencement of hostilities in Europe ended a century-long regime of free gold exchange. The value of the pound in New York rose sharply. Turmoil on the financial markets almost led to a default by the City of New York. Owing to the sudden rise of sterling, by early August the city found itself unable to pay September loan reinstallments in London and Paris, amounting respectively to £2.1 million and 7 million francs. Led by Morgan and Davison, the city's banks pledged their gold for repayment. Morgan and Davison organized a syndicate of participating banks, and the rescue scheme that they successfully engineered saved New York City from an almost certain default.[5] Following a decision by the governors of the New York Stock Exchange, the exchange closed its doors on July 31 and reopened for unrestricted trading only in April 1915.[6]

American neutrality in the European war was dictated from the outset by the nation's diplomatic tradition as well as a lack of other choices.[7] The operation of American neutrality remained to be spelled out by an administration that seemed inexperienced in foreign policy matters and hostile to business interests. That much, at least, could be inferred from Wilson's decision in March 1913 to withdraw official support from the American bank consortium's participation in the Six-Power Chinese loan. J. P. Morgan & Co. had participated in the consortium, and its directors expressed shock at the president's censorious attitude. Wilson had indeed faulted the loan scheme for touching "very nearly the administrative independence of China."[8] The incident constitutes more than an isolated episode in Wilson's early foreign policy; it reflects the president's fundamental dislike of big business, monopoly, and East Coast banking. Wilson shared those opinions with Secretary of State William Jennings Bryan, who in 1896 had rallied his Democratic campaign against the "Cross of Gold." Wilson's position on the China consortium also foreshadowed his later foreign policy course, in which he visualized the United States as

5 Lamont, *Henry P. Davison*, 172–85.
6 Alexander Noyes, *The War Period of American Finance, 1908–1925* (New York, 1926), 56–8; Forbes, *J. P. Morgan*, 87–8.
7 Ernest R. May, *The World War and American Isolation, 1914–1917* (1959; reprint, Chicago, 1966), 1–5; Arthur S. Link, *Wilson: The Struggle for Neutrality, 1914–1915* (Princeton, N.J., 1960), 1–6.
8 Carosso, *Morgans*, 573–8.

educator of the world. His country would become nothing less than "the light which shall shine unto all generations and guide the feet of mankind to the goal of justice and liberty and peace."[9]

On domestic matters as well, there was not much love lost between Washington and Wall Street. The partners at J. P. Morgan & Co. were staunch Republicans who were in favor of a Federal Reserve System controlled by private banks. Wilson, by contrast, sought to reserve political directorship of the new system for his own appointees.[10] The Federal Reserve System developed into a dual agency, directed by private bankers and nominated in part by the government, who acted in an official position. Still, the governor of the leading Federal Reserve Bank of New York, Benjamin Strong, cooperated with the Morgans in many ways.[11] J. P. Morgan & Co. held no special political enmity against the Wilson administration but rather sought above all to preserve its pre-eminent position in American banking.

American neutrality, as Wilson and Bryan spelled out in the first three weeks of August 1914, precluded further activities by the Morgans in support of the Allies. In the early days of August, Herman Harjes, Morgan's senior partner in Paris, had asked the New York house for funds in order to support Americans in Paris as well as to underwrite a large French government loan. Short of that he proposed that New York banks should discount French treasury bills, in order to steal a march on houses such as Kuhn Loeb & Co., which might seek to conduct analogous transactions for Germany.[12] In light of the Morgans' previous sale of British bonds during the Boer War (1899–1902), these operations represented business as usual in New York, just as Wilson's assertion on July 28, 1914, that the United States declined to take part in political affairs outside the hemisphere figured as routine boilerplate in Washington.[13]

Bryan however, faced with Morgan's request for authorization to float a $100,000 loan for the French government, saw the matter differently. A religious pacifist, Bryan proclaimed that American loans to belligerent nations were inconsistent with the true spirit of neutrality. Before

9 Thomas J. Knock, *To End All Wars: Woodrow Wilson and the Quest for a New World Order* (New York, 1992), 20.
10 Chernow, *House of Morgan*, 181.
11 Lester V. Chandler, *Benjamin Strong, Central Banker* (Washington, D.C., 1958), 88, passim.
12 Herman Harjes to J. P. Morgan & Co., Aug. 8, 1914, *Hearings Before the Special Committee Investigating the Munitions Industry: United States Senate, 74th Congress, Second Session, Parts 26, 28: World War Financing and United States Industrial Expansion: J. P. Morgan & Company* (Washington, D.C., 1937), 7490–1 (hereafter *HSCIMI*).
13 Link, *Wilson*, 3; Carosso, *Morgans*, 510–13.

announcing his decision, the secretary of state had obtained Wilson's consent. This was very shortly after the death of Wilson's first wife Ellen, and the grief-stricken and preoccupied president was in no mood for a searching review of a policy that invoked the true spirit of neutrality and that drew no objection from the State Department's counselor and senior professional, Robert Lansing. Whereas Wilson, and even Bryan, emotionally abhorred the German invasion of Belgium and most of Washington officialdom sympathized to a greater or lesser extent with Britain and France, the administration embarked on a foreign policy course that was truly impartial.[14]

At 23 Wall Street, Jack Morgan took the opposite view. Morgan was clear in his mind from the outset, as he would later recall, that he could not heed Wilson's call for impartiality "even in thought." He and his associates "found it quite impossible to be impartial as between right and wrong." From the moment that the battle became ineluctable, "We, in common with many others, realized that if the Germans should obtain a quick and easy victory the freedom of the rest of the world would be lost."[15] Lamont, Morgan's partner and soon to become the Morgans' image-maker as well as its leading policy executor in the foreign sphere, felt strongly about the irrationality of German behavior: "Yet, even as general war became a certainty, thoughtful men were still asking themselves what in the world there was to fight about. Germany's domestic economy was prospering. Her foreign trade was constantly making new records in volume and profit."[16] Although the Morgan partners did not agree with Wilson's and Bryan's neutrality policy, they unhappily abided by it. Not only were they preoccupied by business difficulties at home, but there seemed no occasion for activity abroad because sterling rose well above par during the first four months of the war (Figure 10.1).

The growing strength of sterling propelled Treasury Secretary William Gibbs McAdoo into action.[17] Combined with the shipping crisis that paralyzed trade during the first weeks of the war, the disorderly exchange hampered cotton exports, a politically sensitive problem for a Democratic administration beholden to the South. At the outbreak of the war the United States had just emerged from an economic downturn, and

14 Link, *Wilson*, 62–4; Bryan to J. P. Morgan & Co., *Foreign Relations of the United States 1915, Supplement*, 580.
15 Jack Morgan's statement, Jan. 7, 1936, *HSCIMI*, 7483.
16 Quoted in Lamont, *Ambassador*, 67.
17 On McAdoo, see John Broesamle, *William Gibbs McAdoo: A Passion for Change, 1863–1917* (Port Washington, N.Y., 1973); McAdoo's economic policy is examined by Dale N. Shook, *William G. McAdoo and the Development of National Economic Policy, 1913–1918* (New York, 1987).

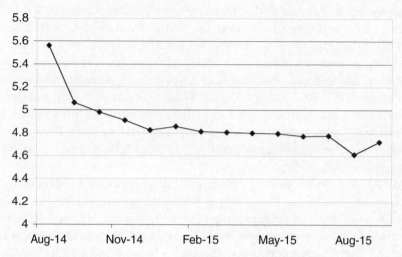

Figure 10.1 New York dollar rate on Sterling, London, 1914–1915. *Source: Federal Reserve Bulletin,* Nov. 1, 1918, 837.

McAdoo, not to be outdone by William Howard Taft's record in this matter, sought to promote American foreign trade. The war offered the prospect of large-scale sales both of commodities and manufactures, once initial hindrances could be overcome. Exports of American goods, even those declared contraband by the belligerents, stood fully in line with traditional U.S. neutrality policy. Bryan favored continued exports from early August and underscored his support with a public statement in October when trade began to decline.[18] McAdoo sought consultations, and in October the British Treasury dispatched a mission to the United States. George Paish and Basil Blackett arrived in Washington on October 16 with two principal items on their agenda: exchange stabilization and the facilitating of cotton purchases for Great Britain. Initially, McAdoo seriously desired an agreement on both matters, but the negotiations produced an agreement only to strike cotton from the British contraband list. The resurgence of the dollar in October and November removed all urgency from deliberations about the exchange rate, and the Paish mission returned to London in December without having accomplished much in the course of their communications with the American government.[19]

18 Bryan to McAdoo, Aug. 7, 1914, *Foreign Relations 1915, Supplement,* 571; public circular by the secretary of state, Oct. 15, 1914, ibid., 573–4.
19 The standard account on this mission and the subsequent financial and economic wartime relationship between Great Britain and the United States is Kathleen Burk, *Britain, America, and the Sinews of War, 1914–1918* (Boston, 1985), 54–61. My sketch differs from Burk's mainly by empha-

The economic and financial impasse between the Paish mission and their interlocutors at the Treasury Department and the Federal Reserve thus had created more anxiety than confidence. The fact that Paul Warburg, newly appointed to the Federal Reserve Board, took part in the negotiations on the side of the U.S. Treasury led the British ambassador in Washington, Sir Cecil Spring Rice, to warn of growing German-Jewish influence in America:

The Jews show a strong preference for the Emperor, and there must be some bargain. Since [the elder] Morgan's death the Jewish banks are supreme and they have captured the Treasury Department by the simple expedient of financing the bills of the Secretary of the Treasury and forcing on him the appointment of the German Warburg on the Federal Reserve Board which he dominates. . . . The President quoted to me the text "he that keepeth Israel shall neither slumber nor sleep." One by one the Jews are capturing the principal newspapers and are bringing them over as much as they dare to the German side.[20]

Anti-Semitism, conflated with anti-German sentiment, helped to shape Jack Morgan's attitudes and strengthened his fervent wish to assist Great Britain, where he maintained a part-time residence, by marshaling the resources of the New York banking community.[21]

During the confused period in the first months of the war, the National City Bank slipped through a French loan amounting to $10 million by taking up one-year French treasury bonds payable in New York. The Morgans quietly took half of that loan, which was finalized in November.[22] Until that point, in order not to antagonize the Wilson administration, the Morgans kept watching and waiting while seeking common ground with Washington in vain.[23] The National City Bank loan, inconspicuous as it was, induced the Wilson administration to quietly re-evaluate its foreign-loan rules. Bryan did not object to the loan, partly motivated by his friendship with a National City Bank official and partly by what Wilson's biographer has described as his curious mental

---

sizing the American and Morgan's perspective. For McAdoo's initial optimism about negotiations with Paish's mission, see McAdoo to Wilson, Oct. 29, 1914, Arthur S. Link et al., eds., *The Papers of Woodrow Wilson* (Princeton, N.J., 1979), 31:249–52 (hereafter *PWW*).

20 Spring Rice to Sir Edward Grey, Nov. 13, 1914, *PWW*, 31:315–16.

21 On Jack Morgan's Anglophilia, see Forbes, *J. P. Morgan*, 31–45, passim; Chernow, *House of Morgan*, 196–7, passim, describes Morgan's growing anti-Semitism; for an assessment of German propaganda among American Jews, see Reinhard R. Doerries, *Imperial Challenge: Ambassador Count Bernstorff, and German-American Relations, 1908–1917* (Chapel Hill, N.C., 1989), 57–67.

22 National City Bank to George M. Reynolds et al., Nov. 4, 1914, *HSCIMI*, 7665.

23 J. P. Morgan & Co., New York to Morgan, Harjes, Aug. 12, *HSCIMI*, 7494; Jack Morgan's sparing efforts to consult with Wilson are documented in his letter to Wilson, Sept. 24, 1914, *PWW*, 31:82–3; Wilson to J. P. Morgan Jr., ibid., 39–40.

processes.[24] Whatever may have motivated Bryan's volte-face, in reality approval of the National City Bank loan marked the crossing of the Rubicon in foreign-loan policy. Yet, the administration did not acknowledge the extent of the reversal. Wilson made no public statement. He privately explained his attitude to Lansing, who defined the new policy in an ambiguous memorandum that demonstrates the administration's unease with the whole matter:

As trade with belligerents is legitimate and proper it is desirable that obstacles, such as interference with arrangement of credits or easy methods of exchange, should be removed. The question of an arrangement of this sort should not be submitted to this Government for its opinion, since it has given its views on loans in general, although an arrangement as to credits has to do with a commercial debt rather than with a loan of money.

The decision was communicated to officials at the National City Bank and at J. P. Morgan & Co. The latter had recently approached the administration with a request for a Russian trade loan.[25]

Wilson's turnabout in the loan question was paralleled in Britain by a growing realization that the war would certainly not be over by Christmas. One of the major requirements for a more successful strategy in the field, as Sir Maurice Hankey of the British Cabinet Secretariat emphasized, was to increase the production of rifles and munitions.[26] Here America could become the main supplier. While the Paish mission still remained in the United States, a meeting of minds took place. Morgan partner Harry Davison met Paish in mid-November and discussed prospects for expanding munitions production in the United States. Davison addressed both ends of the problem, namely, expanding exports of American products to Britain and having those exports financed by the Morgans.[27] Paish realized that while the British government was not yet ready to discuss a major loan with the Americans, it would prove helpful to line up the main players. He intimated to Davison that if the American partners were to take up a large international loan for Britain, they would probably find themselves in a position "to render services in connection with British purchases."[28] Paish knew the world of American

24 Link, *Wilson*, 131–6.
25 Memorandum by Robert Lansing, Oct. 23, 1914, *PWW*, 31:219–20.
26 Winston Churchill to Lord Kitchener, Sept. 3, 1914, Martin Gilbert, *Winston S. Churchill: Companion Volume III*, pt. 1 (Boston, 1973), 81; Lloyd George, *War Memoirs, 1914–1915* (Boston, 1933), 167–70.
27 Lamont, *Ambassador*, 186, passim, if not always wholly reliable, presents indisputable evidence for this point.
28 Davison to E. C. Grenfell, *HSCIMI*, 8098–9.

finance well and seems to have concluded that, while several firms could serve as central purchasing agencies, only the Morgans had the international standing and the partners of good reputation necessary to become Britain's American financing agency. The first sizeable result of these deliberations came with the establishment of "Demand Loan no. 1" in February 1915, a credit line for British purchases established by a bank triumvirate consisting of First National Bank of New York, National City Bank, and J. P. Morgan & Co. Through the cooperation of the trio the demand loan helped to stabilize sterling until the following summer. Unofficial promises by the Bank of England to maintain a sufficient amount of gold in Ottawa to cover payments due formed the financial basis for Demand Loan no. 1.[29]

Davison subsequently accompanied the Paish mission back to London. There he negotiated a purchasing agreement between the bank and the British government. This arrangement made the bank the procuring agency for all orders by the War Office and the Admiralty in the United States. Previous contacts between Lloyd George and Edward C. Grenfell as well as persistent lobbying on the part of Spring Rice had helped to pave the way for this accord. The Foreign Office took the precaution of directing Spring Rice to remind Morgan not to exert any political influence on the Wilson administration before signing the agreement on January 15, 1915.[30] Subsequently, French Finance Minister Alexandre Ribot visited London and met Thomas Lamont. They agreed that France should join with Britain and designate the Morgans as the French purchasing agency. On May 15, France concluded its own purchasing agreement with the Morgans. Both agreements were nonexclusive, allowing Britain and France to buy from whomever they wanted.[31]

The Morgans' new role as Allied purchasing agency – it also came to arrange a large part of Britain's orders for Russia – transformed the bank and its business. While Davison was negotiating in London, Lamont persuaded Edward Reilly Stettinius to direct Morgan's Allied purchasing agency.[32] At that time Stettinius served as an executive of the Babcock and Wilcox Company, a major water-tube boiler producer, as well as for Diamond Match. The bank's new Allied purchasing manager, who became

---

29 *HSCIMI*, 7226–7; Richard S. Sayers, *The Bank of England, 1891–1944*, 3 vols. (Cambridge, 1976), 1:85–9.

30 *HSCIMI*, 7795–802; Edward Grey to Spring Rice, Dec. 28, 1914; Spring Rice to Grey, Dec. 29, 1914, ibid., 7802–3; Burk, *Britain, America*, 13–18, gives a detailed account of the negotiations leading to the purchasing agreement that however ignores Paish's early interest in a major loan.

31 See Lamont's testimony, *HSCIMI*, 7484, 7808–10.

32 John D. Forbes, *Stettinius, Sr. Portrait of a Morgan Partner* (Charlottesville, Va., 1974), 29–64.

Table 10.1. *J. P. Morgan & Company contract payments 1915–1917 in million of current dollars (A) and exports as percentage share of total United States exports, 1915–1917 (B).*

Country	A	B
France	997	49
Russia	412	44
United Kingdom	1447	32

HSCIMI, 7934.

a full partner in 1916, immediately began to set up the Export Department. Until 1916 the department was connected with the bank merely by means of a brokerage agreement. This arrangement nominally freed the Morgans from actual purchasing responsibilities while allowing the bank to devote most of its resources to the endeavor.[33] Stettinius had to develop large-scale industrial production according to very specific British requirements. Starting from scratch, he devoted all his energies to this aim. He drove his growing number of subordinates – his staff comprised 175 members by spring 1917 – relentlessly. Stettinius later stated that 90 percent of munitions deliveries to Britain were made by companies that had to be trained in this business by British war orders. This illustrates the scope of Stettinius's work.[34] In the next three years Stettinius would almost single-handedly develop American mass production capacity for the manufacture of rifles, cartridges, shells, fuses, and other military matériel.[35] Owing to Stettinius's efforts, by April 1917 J. P. Morgan & Co. emerged as the chief supplier of the Allied war effort (Table 10.1).

In accordance with its agreements with Britain and France, the bank received a 1 percent commission on orders, after having obtained 2 percent on the initial $47 million of orders. Lamont later totaled Allied purchases at roughly 3 billion dollars and estimated commissions received by the Morgans at 30 million dollars.[36]

Arms and ammunition, as well as iron, steel, and their manufactures,

33 Burk, *Britain, America*, 22–4.
34 Stettinius to Thomas Lamont, Apr. 22, 1918, in Thomas W. Lamont papers, 131–2, Baker Library, Harvard University.
35 Forbes, *Stettinius*, 62–3.
36 Lamont, *Ambassador*, 69; *HSCIMI*, 7484. A more detailed estimate arrived at British and French commission payments of $30.5 million, *HSCIMI*, 8098.

Table 10.2. *Arms, ammunition, iron, steel, and manufactures exports, millions of current dollars: 1911–1913 (A), 1915–1917 (B), percentage of J. P. Morgan & Co. exports 1915–1917 (C).*

A	B	C
125	2187	84

HSCIMI, 7935.

formed the largest part of the Morgans' wartime exports. The bank's connections with U.S. Steel as well as its multifold ties with Pennsylvania's manufacturing sector helped to facilitate business contracts and production. The Morgans, however, largely downsized their own investments in contract companies in which they held an equity stake. Stettinius's orders, out of necessity, were placed with companies in the northeastern United States, although the export department bought from whatever firm could make delivery the earliest because rapid shipments of supplies proved crucial for battlefield performance. Bethlehem Steel ($201 million), E. I. Du Pont de Nemours ($329 million), and U.S. Steel ($123 million) figured as the largest suppliers among hundreds of large and mid-size companies. The Morgans owned shares or had a controlling interest in fifteen among those hundreds of supplying firms and, in order to avoid the appearance of impropriety, sought to reduce the bank's stake in those companies in the course of 1915 and 1916. Cambria Steel Company represented the sole exception. The bank owned 42,000 Cambria shares, which it sold to Midvale in 1915. In a subsequent stock swap, the Morgans obtained 7,500 shares of Midvale.[37] The purchasing contracts meant a profitable business for the bank because prices and, therefore, commissions tended to be high, for reasons that the Morgans could not influence. The bank, however, did not show any favoritism in contract negotiations and refrained from acquiring stock of Bethlehem Steel and other contract companies that were in financial trouble (Table 10.2).[38]

Although Morgan's assumption of responsibility as the central Allied purchasing agency gratified Spring Rice and others who had pushed for

37 *HSCIMI*, Summary total British contract payments, 7694–712, 7941–8090.
38 Lamont to H. P. Davison, Jan. 31, 1917, Lamont papers, 91–2; Lamont to C. F. Wigham, Mar. 16, 1915, Lamont papers, 136–8.

the arrangement, formidable technical difficulties remained to be over-come in early 1915. The shell scandal in Britain and battlefield setbacks on the western front as well as in Russia led authorities in Britain suddenly to realize that purchases from America were of utmost importance. The steep increase in orders during the spring of 1915 created numerous bottlenecks in American production. Stettinius's team had to deal with chaotic condi-tions. While gross production figures in the United States increased rapidly, prospects for the fulfillment of specific contracts remained uncertain, owing to scrambles for raw materials and parts among major suppliers. France joined the scheme only in May 1915, and Russia continued to order independently until the summer of that year.[39] Competing orders from different British governmental purchasing institutions created bureau-cratic havoc, and ongoing changes in technical specifications compounded the difficulties. A major crisis occurred in 1916 when the Remington Company delayed deliveries. Subsequently, the British demanded several design changes and threatened to cancel orders. It took explicit warnings from the Morgans about the detrimental effects of cancellation on further purchasing and financing arrangements to bring the British Ministry of Munitions back to the negotiating table in the fall of 1916.[40]

The British-American trading network could function smoothly only if sufficient dollar supplies were available to meet British payments due in New York. Financing became more difficult because sterling began to fall, starting in December 1914. From a high of 4.86 (average in Decem-ber 1914: 4.82), sterling plummeted to 4.795 by mid-February 1915.[41] By July 1915 the rising purchases of the British government had exhausted the trio's initial demand loan. The Morgans immediately recognized that a serious financial crisis was imminent. Davison started negotiations with Chancellor of the Exchequer Reginald McKenna seeking to overcome the threatening dollar shortage. Davison proposed several mechanisms, including acceptances, loans on British-owned American securities, and, for the first time, a large government loan.[42] The critical state of Britain's finances by the summer made this step unavoidable. On June 21 the British government issued the Second War Loan, seeking to tap public money at home, but by July it had become obvious that the loan had failed. McKenna had to admit that the government lacked the dollars to

39 For the background in 1915, see David French, *British Strategy and War Aims, 1914–1916* (London, 1986), 116–35.
40 Lamont to Davison, Sept. 27, 1916, Lamont papers, 81–15; Lamont, *Ambassador*, 82–3.
41 Burk, *Britain, America*, 62.
42 Davison to J. P. Morgan & Co., Export Department, July 8, 1915, *HSCIMI*, 8106–7.

pay for Russian purchases in the United States. John Maynard Keynes, a member of the Treasury's division concerned with finance since May, expressed such pessimism about the financial prospects that he took the necessity of a large American loan – something unprecedented in British financial history – for granted. Meanwhile, the Bank of England weakened prospects for future constructive interallied financial cooperation by demanding gold shipments for its increased credits to the Allies, creating serious frictions in Anglo-French financial negotiations.[43]

The Morgans saw themselves faced with British resistance to shipping gold across the Atlantic. Neither side contemplated gold shipments except as a last resort.[44] By June 1915, the Bank of England had started to buy American securities from British owners instead and transported them to New York for sale. Until the end of that year, $233 million worth of British-owned American securities were sold in New York.[45] Once hopes faded that the British War Loan would procure further British-owned American securities and thus produce the necessary dollar exchange, it became obvious that a large British government loan made in the United States remained the sole possibility to alleviate the situation. The necessity of a government loan in America was underlined by the continuing slide of sterling. Davison discussed a possible loan with the governor of the Bank of England, Walter Cunliffe, in late June.[46]

Yet, several obstacles militated against a quick issuance of British war bonds in America. The main problem, which all British financial experts, including Keynes, curiously overlooked, was that a large public foreign loan had never been issued in the United States. The American public had grown accustomed to railroad bonds only after the late 1890s. Those obligations were secured by solid collateral and paid interest rates much above the prevailing European level. Accordingly, there existed little incentive for small investors in America to buy risky foreign bonds. Only the sale of Liberty bonds from 1917 onward accustomed the American investing public to large public-bond issues. Thus, although the social classes in America that made up the bond-buying public largely sympathized with the Allies, even more so after the sinking of the *Lusitania*, chances seemed

43 French, *Strategy and War Aims*, 123; Keynes's memorandum of Aug. 23, 1915, cited in John Maynard Keynes, *The Collected Writings of John Maynard Keynes*, ed. Elizabeth Johnson, 30 vols. (Cambridge, 1971–89), 16:110–15; Robert Skidelsky, *John Maynard Keynes: Hopes Betrayed 1883–1920* (London, 1983), 307–9.

44 Davison to J. P. Morgan & Co., Export Department, June 25, 1915, *HSCIMI*, 8109–10.

45 E. Victor Morgan, *Studies in British Financial Policy, 1914–1925* (London, 1952), 327.

46 For exchange rate movements, see Figure 10.1. Davison to J. P. Morgan & Co., Export Department, June 23, 1915, *HSCIMI*, 8108.

considerable that a large British loan in the United States would fail. Such an outcome would impede American-British trade relations by hastening the decline of sterling. Even in the strongly pro-British Northeast, the bond market seemed uninterested in purchasing British bonds. Articles and rumors regarding increased German military strength, possibly planted by German agents, had created uneasiness on financial markets. An attempt on Jack Morgan's life in July reinforced presentiments of an omnipresent German menace. Prevailing doubts about the outcome of the war further undermined investors' willingness to wager money on the Allies. The situation was not rendered easier by the $1 million worth of French treasury notes that overhung the New York financial markets at that time. The Morgans found themselves the buyer of last resort.[47]

Edward C. Grenfell, the senior partner of the London house, again jumped into the breach and did his utmost to convince the British government that it had to take sensible measures to prevent a collapse of the pound.[48] Yet, as Keynes's reflections demonstrated, the British Treasury and the American banks that wanted to support it had reached no meeting of the minds. The Treasury clung with unwarranted optimism to the notion that a British loan amounting to £240 million or more could be placed in the United States in order to supply Britain with liquid funds over the next months. Yet, McKenna remained unaccountably lethargic.[49] Morgan, eager to give his partners at Morgan Grenfell a clear picture of the true situation in the United States, wrote in the last weeks of June:

Whether caused by German propaganda or simply by the usual idiocy of newspaper men, [there] has been considerable discussion in the last few weeks in newspapers of how impossible it is for belligerent countries in Europe to pay for the amounts they are taking from the United States. Amounts are exaggerated and resources for payment minimized, and there has been a feeling of considerable apprehension during the past few weeks.

Nevertheless, Morgan believed a loan could be placed if the right precautions were taken.[50] But the British refused to take the hint and remained passive.

By midsummer financial conditions in New York had worsened con-

---

47 Lamont, *Ambassador*, 72; J. P. Morgan & Co., Export Department to Morgan, London, for H. P. Davison, July 7 and 9, 1915, *HSCIMI*, 8112–14.
48 On Grenfell, see Kathleen Burk, *Morgan Grenfell, 1838–1988: The Biography of a Merchant Bank* (Oxford, 1989), 64–134.
49 Keynes, "The Financial Prospects of This Financial Year," in Keynes, *Collected Writings*, 16:117–25; Lamont testimony, *HSCIMI*, 7854.
50 Jack Morgan to Morgan, London, June 26, 1915, *HSCIMI*, 8110–11.

siderably. Davison reported his own impressions of the American bond market to Grenfell:

Am surprised to find a markedly unfavorable change toward the placing of any important amount of a loan, even of Great Britain. Bear in mind that our investors, unlike yours, have never been taught to absorb foreign loans on a large scale, even in peace times, and to introduce such loans in war period meets much resistance. Since the *Lusitania* incident, the bond market, even for well-seasoned securities, has very materially lessened. This, coupled with the continued flow of securities from London, has practically brought general investment market to a standstill, so that all our associates here feel that it is quite out of the question to handle a British loan on comprehensive basis.[51]

Faced with this impasse, Cunliffe sent a message to the Morgans on July 22 signifying that he stood ready, as a last resort, to ship gold – "naturally most unwilling[ly]."[52] Once one key institution in Britain seemed to offer cooperation, the New York partners evinced greater optimism about an Allied loan. They now proposed that $500 million could be raised if several parties, that is, Britain and France, joined in the undertaking.[53]

Despite these intimations of American receptivity, the next weeks passed without advancing the matter further, mainly owing to the continued lethargy of the British Treasury. Grenfell felt so exasperated that on August 10 he openly denounced McKenna in a confidential cable to New York – a not-too-risky undertaking because the Morgans used their private code: "I cannot move Chancellor of the Exchequer. As H. P. Davison will explain to you, Chancellor is not efficient and is inclined to pay attention to second class advisers who really cannot do anything for him."[54] Two days later the Morgans, given the lack of funds, felt compelled to cease supporting the British exchange in order to forestall a more violent drop later on. Sterling slid further over the next two weeks. By August 13, however, Grenfell had finally made definite progress in lining up Cunliffe's and McKenna's support for placing a public loan in the United States: "At least I think I have got ministers and all concerned thoroughly aware of situation. From your personal knowledge of the Chancellor of the Exchequer you may perhaps understand how difficult task has been."[55]

51 Davison to Morgan, London, July 20, 1915, *HSCIMI*, 8114–15.
52 E. C. Grenfell to J. P. Morgan & Co., July 22, 1915, *HSCIMI*, 7845–6.
53 J. P. Morgan & Co. to Morgan, Grenfell, July 23, 1915, *HSCIMI*, 8116.
54 Grenfell to Morgan, New York, Aug. 10, 1915, *HSCIMI*, 7850.
55 Grenfell to Davison, Aug. 13, 1915, *HSCIMI*, 7851.

During the following two weeks a major change in official American loan policy took place. Under three mutually reinforcing impulses, Wilson agreed to acquiesce to a major Anglo-French loan in the United States and quietly waived his prerogative to make Wall Street's financial help for the Allies subject to his continuing review.[56] First, the sinking of the *U.S.S. Arabic* by a German submarine on August 19 brought the administration close to a rupture with Germany.[57] Simultaneously, McAdoo grew more exasperated with Warburg's open attempts on the Federal Reserve Board to block the rediscounting of acceptances for munitions exports to the Allies. Warburg had marshaled his efforts chiefly against the pro-Allied policy line of Benjamin Strong.[58] McAdoo forced the issue and denounced Warburg's pro-German position to Wilson. Simultaneously, the treasury secretary openly embraced the prospect of a large British loan in the United States.[59] Robert Lansing, now secretary of state, supported the proposal, which reflected his growing belief that peace with Germany would not last. Given Lansing's ties to the New York banking community, he found it natural to endorse private American support for the Allies once Wilson had ceased to object. Likewise, Colonel Edward M. House also backed this new policy line and helped to bring Wilson around.[60] When Spring Rice exasperatedly told House in early September that the United States had to save England in spite of itself, House replied that he had been working assiduously to solve the international financial problems.[61] With official tolerance of an Allied loan assured, the British government sent an Anglo-French loan commission, led by Lord Reading, to the United States on September 1.[62] Announcement of the mission almost immediately buoyed sterling.

The British government had accepted Morgan's reasoning that only a joint Allied loan in the United States would prove successful. The British commissioners nevertheless still clung to the notion that a loan of £250 million at the European interest rate of 3 percent would be feasible. It took considerable effort and patience on the Morgans' part to educate Reading and his associates about the constraints of the American bond market. By September 23, after protracted negotiations, the British

---

56 Wilson to Lansing, Aug. 26, 1915, *PWW*, 34:329.
57 Doerries, *Imperial Challenge*, 112–15, McAdoo to Wilson, Aug. 23, 1915, *PWW*, 34:294.
58 Shook, *William G. McAdoo*, 208–16.
59 McAdoo to Wilson, Aug. 21, 1915, *PWW*, 34:275–80.
60 Daniel M. Smith, *Robert Lansing and American Neutrality, 1914–1917* (New York, 1972), 93–5.
61 Extract from House's diary, Sept. 8, 1915, *HSCIMI*, 7862.
62 Burk, *Britain, America*, 67; H. Montgomery Hyde, *Lord Reading: The Life of Rufus Isaacs, First Marquess of Reading* (London, 1967), 187–93.

and French parties in the mission had accepted the Morgans' offer of a £100 million loan at 5 percent. The dollar proceeds had to be spent in the United States. The British Cabinet endorsed the proposal on September 28. It was, as Prime Minister Herbert Henry Asquith wrote, the best available plan in the circumstances.[63]

Now the scheme had to be sold to the American investing public. The failure of such an offering might very well doom further foreign loans; hence, education of the public formed the most critical issue ahead. Lamont personally took the British and French commissioners on an advertising campaign trip to Chicago, starting on September 27, even before the Cabinet in London had formally approved the loan. Chicago represented the most important roadblock in Lamont's proselytizing effort because, owing to the large number of German depositors, the support of midwestern banks could not be taken for granted. As early as the beginning of July, Lamont had conferred with the president of Chicago's First National Bank, James Forgan. Forgan informed Lamont that prospects for an unsecured British loan in Chicago were practically nil.[64] Not surprisingly, the commissioners met with a chilly reception in Chicago. When Lamont appealed to members of the banking community on September 27 to subscribe to the loan, he encountered only silence. A quiet but massive withdrawal of funds from the Illinois Trust and Savings Bank by foreign depositors strengthened the resolve of Chicago's bankers, few of whom needed persuasion, to give the allied loan a wide berth.[65]

It took all of Lamont's political and social skills to move Charles G. Dawes, the outspoken president of the Central Trust Company of Illinois, to break the consensus of his brethren and support the loan publicly. In order to alleviate Dawes's fears of a run on his bank, Lamont gave his word that the Morgans would back him up. With that, a lasting friendship began. Both men participated in key positions in the solution of the German reparations problem in 1924. When Dawes made his public announcement supporting the Anglo-French loan, the anticipated run did not materialize. Four hundred small depositors withdrew a total of $99,000. Central Trust's banking department registered withdrawals of $131,000. And over the next ten weeks, bolstered by public appreciation of his courage, Dawes seems to have gained around $5 million in

63 Burk, *Britain, America*, 69–72; Lamont, *Ambassador*, 74.
64 J. P. Morgan & Co. to Morgan, Grenfell, July 8, 1915, *HSCIMI*, 8113.
65 Thomas W. Lamont, memorandum about the trip to Chicago, Sept. 27–9, 1915, Lamont papers, 81–15.

deposits.[66] The commission's visit to Chicago thus turned out to be a political, if not a financial, success. Only Dawes joined the underwriting syndicate, yet Forgan and George M. Reynolds, another prominent Chicago banker, as well as other Chicagoans, quietly bought the bonds.[67] Similar meetings followed in New York, Philadelphia, Boston, and Pittsburgh in order to organize distribution of the largest public loan ever offered in the United States.

A banking syndicate led by the Morgans distributed the loan. The managing underwriters, sixty-one New York banks, renounced the usual management fee for distributing the loan.[68] Owing to the Morgans' public relations effort, banks throughout the Midwest cautiously joined the underwriting syndicate. Participation in Ohio was prominent, and bankers from Michigan, Missouri, and even Nebraska followed suit, although Bryan, a private citizen since his resignation over Wilson's *Lusitania* note of June 9, had threatened to propagandize against the loan.[69] Subscriptions to the bond issue started slowly, mainly owing to the sluggish sale of the French tranche. The Morgans then organized the intervention of its major contract companies. E. I. Du Pont de Nemours and Bethlehem Steel took $55 million worth of bonds together, and the total taken up by the contracting companies amounted to $90 million. By October 15 the whole issue had been oversubscribed by the banks, although the resale of the bonds by the public proceeded slowly.[70] However, public perception of the loan depended mainly on the proceeds of institutional subscriptions. Judged from that perspective the loan was, in the words of one Wall Street observer outside the Morgan circle, "quite a success."[71] Even more important, the Morgans prepared the American bond market for future Allied loans. By April 1917, Britain and France had secured loans of $450 million in the United States by means of public bond sales.[72]

66 Lamont to E. C. Grenfell, Dec. 7, 1915, Lamont papers, 81–20; Dawes to Lamont, Sept. 29, 1915, Lamont papers, 81–15; Stephen A. Schuker, "Charles Gates Dawes," in Larry Schweikart, ed., *Encyclopedia of American Business History and Biography: Banking and Finance, 1913–1989* (New York, 1990), 482–92.

67 F. Cyril James, *The Growth of Chicago Banks: The Modern Age* (New York, 1938), 888–91.

68 Lamont, *Ambassador*, 74.

69 J. P. Morgan & Co. to Messrs. White, Weld & Co., Sept. 29, 1915, *HSCIMI*, 8139–42; Franklin Knight Lane to Wilson, Sept. 16, 1915, *PWW*, 34:477–8.

70 By May 31, 1916, 296.3 million dollars had been sold, Arthur Young & Co. to J. P. Morgan & Co., May 31, 1915, *HSCIMI*, 8144–5.

71 George Blumenthal to Lazard Brothers, London, Oct. 8, 1915, *HSCIMI*, 7916.

72 Purchases of Anglo-French bonds by companies having British and French contracts through J. P. Morgan & Co., Oct. 15, 1915, *HSCIMI*, 8138. The fact that most of the bonds were subscribed by institutional investors and not by the public has induced some writers, like Burk, to call the loan a failure. See Burk, *Britain, America*, 73–4; Link, *Wilson*, 628. Burk and Link discount the fact

The Morgans' help for the Allies in World War I made a lasting impression on the memory of those who received it. At home the bank experienced a period of prosperity and good business, after the postwar depression had ended. Their participation in war finance and the peace process made Lamont and Morrow, and their partners, the most renowned international financial experts of their day. Yet, the Morgans' voluntary and generous help for the Allied and then American-Allied war cause did not save them from two hostile and distorting hearings during the 1930s. The Pecora hearings of 1933 constituted a restaging of the 1913 Pujo interrogations.[73] In 1936 the circus-like Senate Munitions Committee Hearings followed. Sponsored by the head of the Women's International League for Peace, Dorothy Detzer, the hearings aimed to produce evidence in support of more stringent neutrality legislation rather than to document with any objectivity America's involvement in the munitions trade during World War I.[74]

The attempt to distort the Morgans' role produced disillusionment and dismay among those who had led the successful private American drive to support the Allies. The wartime assistant secretary of the treasury, Russell Leffingwell, who became a Morgan partner in 1923, summarized his partners' reaction to Senator Nye's fishing expedition when writing to his old chief, Carter Glass:

Of course, Morgans have nothing to conceal, nothing to hide and nothing that they are not proud of. The propriety of investigating the business of great and friendly nations by indirection in this manner, the question whether that is the best way to promote peace and good will among nations, I have nothing to do with. The suggestion that President Wilson or you or McAdoo or the American people went to war for the Morgans and the munitions makers is so grotesque that it must defeat itself. Surely, there must be enough men living to remember the violation of Belgian neutrality, the sinking of the *Lusitania*, and finally the unrestricted U-boat campaign, on the one hand, and the antagonism and even hostility between Wall Street and Wilson, Bryan, and McAdoo, on the other, to make such a canard fall flat.[75]

---

that the issue established the indispensable institutional and organizational requirements for further war bond issues in the United States. The first Anglo-French bond issue thus overcame the political and institutional obstacles that had occasioned such anxiety on the part of those most familiar with the American scene, like British ambassador Spring Rice; see David Henry Burton, *Cecil Spring Rice* (Cranbury, N.J., 1990), 178.

73 Lamont, *Ambassador*, 336–40.

74 Wayne S. Cole, *Senator Gerald P. Nye and American Foreign Relations* (Minneapolis, 1962), 60–96; John E. Wiltz, *In Search of Peace: The Senate Munitions Inquiry, 1934–1936* (Baton Rouge, La., 1963), 3–47, 191–220, passim.

75 Russell Leffingwell to Carter Glass, May 3, 1935, Carter Glass papers, box 4, University of Virginia Library, Charlottesville.

Conflicts between banks and American political leaders form a continuing pattern in American history. Yet American bankers in this case not only pursued the enlightened self-interest of U.S. business and commerce as a whole but also furthered the Allied cause and the hopes that democratic forces on both sides of the ocean increasingly placed in an Allied victory. They thus served as important transatlantic communicators at a crucial juncture in the history of Western civilization. Good deeds, however, rarely go unpunished, and magnanimity is seldom the truest wisdom of domestic politics.[76]

76 In variation of Burke's remark in *On Conciliation with America* (1775), 62: "Magnanimity in politics is not seldom the truest wisdom; and a great empire and little minds go ill together."

PART FIVE

Transatlantic History and American Exceptionalism

11

Transatlantic History as National History?
Thoughts on German Post–World War II Historiography

PETER KRÜGER

When I considered the problems of writing about the subject of this chapter, I hesitated because they turned out to be comprehensive enough for more than one essay. It fascinated and puzzled me, and provoked, at first, a kind of forestalling reaction: Is there a question? Is there an answer? Subsequently, I decided to put this challenging subject to the test – at the risk of finding a host of answers that would leave me in a still worse predicament. Nevertheless, at least some of the questions seem worth discussing here, all of them considering the tension between "transatlantic" and "national."

First, "transatlantic" is usually limited to the North Atlantic and signifies a particular relationship, a dynamic interrelation of Europe and North America kept apart by an ocean that became a challenge to all those who were determined to make it a link and a symbol of a common space and history in spite of a sometimes strong propensity to make it a huge natural boundary allowing a retreat into oneself on both sides. The linkage function has proven particularly important to West Germany since 1945, thus providing an extraordinary test case for the compatibility of transatlantic and national history and historiography.

Second, transatlantic history might be an effort to trace back into the past a real or imagined European-American intertwining, a transatlantic world of shared values and continuous contacts in different ways and on different levels irrespective of national contrasts, rivalries, and conflicts.

Third, it is possible to understand "transatlantic history as national history," connoting a connection that resulted in mutual influences on the national history of both sides. For example, we cannot avoid taking into account the transatlantic origins of and persistent transatlantic influences

245

on that apparently most national of topics, namely, the "frontier" of the American West.

Fourth, another important interaction between transatlantic and national history might manifest itself in the way that at least part of German historiography after 1945 strove to catch up with American historiography as one way toward modernization and a rebirth of national history after the Third Reich.

Fifth, a fundamental message is revealed in the prefix "trans" taken from the title of this chapter. Again, different meanings and lines of argument may be pursued by stressing that syllable: (1) One essential connotation of transatlantic history is that transcending one's own national history has become the only feasible response in writing national history, given the modern overlapping, intertwining, and growing interdependence of structures, processes, and decisions. Because it is doubtful, however, that national history may be transcended at random, a cautious scrutiny of relevant areas with important transnational linkages, thus concentrating on the transatlantic realm, may prove useful. (2) To go one step further in this direction is to substitute "transnational" for "transatlantic," whereby "transatlantic" may be seen only as a specification, although arguably one of prime priority, of "transnational." This could lead us to an exciting and salutary paradox: transnational history as national history.

Sixth and finally, it seems necessary to take into account two concrete problems of the transatlantic connection: the European dimension and the size of the transatlantic world.

Regarding the European dimension, it is obvious that Germany cannot escape the implications of the more comprehensive relationship between America and Europe. This is an important point because of tendencies toward mutual self-segregation. About seventy years ago, during a long and intensive debate in Germany on the advantages of a European customs union, the well-known economist Ludwig Mises already stated that merely substituting European chauvinism for small-scale national chauvinism was unacceptable and the worst solution of the problems of the international economy.[1] This is but one enduring example of a difficult and complex transatlantic relationship that concerns Europe as a whole and not just its component states.

Regarding the size of the transatlantic world, the difficult question of

---

1 H. A. Wirsching, "Der Kampf um die handelspolitische Einigung Europas," Ph.D. diss., University of Würzburg, 1928, 66. In general, see Erhard Forndran, *Die Vereinigten Staaten von Amerika und Europa: Erfahrungen und Perspektiven transatlantischer Beziehungen seit dem Ersten Weltkrieg* (Baden-Baden, 1991).

inclusion and borders has always depended on the changing situation in Europe. For a couple of years after June 1940 it appeared, on the European side, restricted to Great Britain. Between 1945 and 1989, especially during the Cold War era, numerous more-or-less obvious forces deepened the rift between eastern and western Europe, entrenched the dividing line, and limited the Atlantic community to NATO and some neutral states. A major issue that will have to be taken up by future research, therefore, is the situation of East-Central Europe both before and after 1989. The countries in this region resolutely wish to belong to the transatlantic world, to its community of shared values, interests, opportunities, and institutions; this was a driving force in their resistance to Soviet rule. Now, transatlantic research approaches and strategies are acquiring a new dimension and should henceforth see East Central Europe as part of the transatlantic world. This will mean studying the changes in that particular region within a transatlantic framework and incorporating both the work of leading scholars of Eastern European history and contemporary issues.

In practical terms, these considerations would appear to require three or four different essays. Nevertheless, I shall try to keep these approaches in mind and make use of them by concentrating on certain integrative points, such as the importance of transatlantic history for writing German and American national histories; the place of transatlantic history in German historiography after 1945; the role of a modern political and national history; and, finally, an assessment of some approaches to transatlantic history. Within this framework, some reflections on West German historiography after 1945 will follow, combined with a short section on the status and substance of transatlantic history in Germany. Suggestions on the writing of and possible topics for transatlantic history will conclude the chapter.

I

Many historians have dealt with German historiography after World War II, and I shall therefore limit my contribution to a few summary remarks and critical questions.[2] The catastrophe Germany brought down

2 Ernst Schulin, "Zur Entwicklung der deutschen Geschichtswissenschaft nach dem Zweiten Weltkrieg. Versuch eines Überblicks," in Jürgen Kocka, Hans-Jürgen Puhle, and Klaus Tenfelde, eds., *Von der Arbeiterbewegung zum modernen Sozialstaat: Festschrift für Gerhard A. Ritter zum 65. Geburtstag* (Munich, 1994), 831–46; Hartmut Lehmann and James Van Horn Melton, eds., *Paths of Continuity: Central European Historiography from the 1930s to the 1950s* (New York, 1994); Georg G. Iggers, *Geschichtswissenschaft im 20. Jahrhundert* (Göttingen, 1993); Winfried Schulze, *Deutsche Geschichtswissenschaft nach 1945*, Beiheft Nr. 10 *Historische Zeitschrift* (Munich, 1989).

on Europe and the world with the increasing dynamics of destruction, persecution, murder, and genocide during the Third Reich clearly marked an epoch in German historiography.[3] Whether it was a turning point still remains a matter for debate, although the signs of a reorientation, even in the so-called restoration period until the end of the 1950s, are obvious ("restoration" is a misnomer in most historical cases or at least a misleading overall label). What was indeed restored after 1945, as a last resort and virtually as a means of intellectual survival, was the critical method, which was seen as a pledge of objectivity and the only reliable instrument for purifying German historiography of all the political and ideological constraints of the past. The destruction of the old national conception of history was inevitable and irrevocable but was a shock whose reverberations hit hard, even to the point of fundamental disorientation.[4] During the postwar years Friedrich Meinecke's *Die deutsche Katastrophe* (The German catastrophe, 1946) remained, despite its methodological limitations, the most penetrating analysis of the origins and causes of that catastrophe.

To many historians the cathartic effect of the critical method in the field of historical processes and events as well as the clarification of traditional patterns and aberrations in the history of politics and ideas seemed to offer the only solid basis for dealing with an incriminating past, insufficient as this may appear today to analyze the rise to power of National Socialism, its historical roots, and its incorporation into modern German history. Such an analysis was a far cry from what the majority of German historians – with Gerhard Ritter as their leading figure – strove for. Their attitude was by no means exceptional but rather typical of times of cataclysmic crises: the desire to preserve not only the objectivity and independence of historical science but a familiar or even existential set of principles and beliefs by specifying the distortion, violation, and injury inflicted on them. This conviction that the principles are right and have merely been mismanaged, perverted, or abused by criminal rulers

---

3 As Friedrich Meinecke explained in his influential and still impressive analysis, *Die deutsche Katastrophe: Betrachtungen und Erinnerungen* (Wiesbaden, 1946), this catastrophe was preceded by and a result of a catastrophe of German moral and intellectual development, the tragic futility of the German struggle for liberty since 1848 and the supremacy of the Prussian authoritarian and military state and its power politics in spite of its "other soul," the Prussia of reform, modernization, arts and sciences. See also Friedrich Meinecke, *1848: Eine Säkularbetrachtung* (Berlin, 1948). In a "transatlantic" effort already to attribute the outbreak of World War I to a catastrophe of German thinking, in particular of the German school of philosophical idealism, John Dewey published a book on *German Philosophy and Politics* (New York, 1915).
4 Schulze, *Geschichtswissenschaft*, 89, 114.

reappeared, albeit under quite different circumstances, after 1989. This attitude, combined with some sort of political vacuum, was likely to promote adaptation to new principles, especially to that of a western European and occidental community in sharp contrast to Bolshevism and communism. It also favored the Federal Republic's redirection toward and integration into the Western community.

Changes in West German historiography were slow in coming, and to a certain extent the process was a return to a past normalcy. Again, history became a moral institution with yet little innovation. Where it did appear, as in the new strands of structural folk history (*Volksgeschichte*) encompassing economic, social, cultural – including everyday life – and regional history, it was discredited because of its links with Nazism. Innovation also could be found in the work of outsiders such as Hans Freyer, who came from historical sociology and developed a model of the history of industrial society; yet he also was not beyond all suspicion.[5] Such innovations had better chances to make an impact later on.

To state this, however, is not enough. As Ernst Schulin has concluded, German historiography after 1945 could not have influenced public life in Germany in a constructive way without being methodologically conservative because "only on the traditional level of political and intellectual history was it possible to overcome the history of National Socialism. To argue in terms of social and structural history would have meant to evade responsibility."[6] Some historians did avoid these thorny political topics by means of a lofty cultural history. However, the biting criticism of Hermann Heimpel and others exposed them.[7]

Dealing with National Socialism – as far as it was done – was again a stimulus to concentrate on national history; transatlantic history and new methods and fields of historical analysis remained a subject for few historians. Nevertheless, the first signs of new approaches and unconventional views, questions, and methods cannot be denied: here it was a question of certain trends and institutions as well as leading figures. Such trends, strengthened or even caused by major international developments during the Cold War, are well documented in general accounts of German historiography. The impulse came from the desire to reintegrate Germany into Europe, often hailed as a major achievement, as the discovery of a

5 Willi Oberkrome, *Volksgeschichte: Methodische Innovation und völkische Ideologisierung in der deutschen Geschichtswissenschaft 1918–1945* (Göttingen, 1993); Jerry Z. Muller, *The Other God That Failed: Hans Freyer and the Deradicalization of German Conservatism* (Princeton, N.J., 1987).
6 Schulin, *Entwicklung*, 837.
7 Schulze, *Geschichtswissenschaft*, 22, 89.

new basis and identity. As Peter Rassow put it in November 1946: "Out of German history and right into European history!"[8]

Less well documented and still limited to special studies or casual remarks were – admittedly rather infrequent – initiatives to go beyond the European sphere into the transatlantic dimension of the history of the Western world. Particularly stimulating and attractive to this kind of transatlanticism was a fresh study of Western civilization, its foundations, and its values as a response to the dangers and threats to it culminating in World War II. This new start was promoted by new approaches in American political science, mainly on the basis of modern institutionalism, which included the study of norms, rules of behavior, and so forth. It was supported by German emigrants in the United States, historians, social scientists, and jurists, who were interested in a more thorough, generalized explanation of contemporary history. This explanation was based on typologies and theories applicable to the very conditions of democracy and constitutionalism in modern societies as well as to the origins and different forms of authoritarian and totalitarian, rightist and leftist movements. In particular, the theories of totalitarianism developed by Hannah Arendt and Carl J. Friedrich gained influence in West Germany in the field of contemporary history, for example, in the works of Karl Dietrich Bracher on the dissolution of the Weimar Republic and on the rise of National Socialism.[9] Scholars turned to the study of forces that threatened liberal democracy, human rights, and the independence of the individual, values that were to form the very basis of the Federal Republic's political identity. Some influential historians, often with a new comparative approach that transcended the traditional history of politics, were emigrants who returned to Germany, at least for a time, as guest professors or wanderers between two worlds.[10] One example is Dietrich Gerhard, one of Erich Angermann's predecessors, who was appointed to a chair of American history at the University of Cologne in 1955 and yet retained his position at the University of St. Louis.[11] This position at

---

8 Schulze, *Geschichtswissenschaft* 89, 160.

9 Hannah Arendt, *The Origins of Totalitarianism* (New York, 1951); Carl J. Friedrich, *Totalitäre Diktatur* (Stuttgart, 1957); Konrad Löw, ed., *Totalitarismus* (Berlin, 1988).

10 Hartmut Lehmann and James J. Sheehan, eds., *An Interrupted Past: German-Speaking Refugee Historians in the United States After 1933* (New York, 1991).

11 Dietrich Gerhard's career as an example: privatdozent (Berlin, 1931); visiting professor (Cambridge, Mass., 1935); assistant professor (1936) and full professor (1944), Washington University, St. Louis; chair, department of history, University of Cologne, 1955; emeritus, 1961; director, Max-Planck-Institut für Geschichte, Göttingen, 1961–7.

Cologne became the institutional foundation for the virtually transatlantic Institute of Anglo-American History, which flourished under Angermann's direction for nearly three decades and continues to prosper.

Franz Schnabel, Angermann's mentor, also was important in this process. He would influence two generations of historians. In his works he developed a much broader concept of national history, embedded in the currents of modern history and including such hitherto neglected historical forces as education and sciences, religion, political mentality, technology, engineering, and industry. Even more interesting in the transatlantic context were his lectures in the late 1940s, especially on "Revolutions and Wars of Liberation" from the American War of Independence to the era of decolonization. By themselves, these topics yielded a new approach and a deeper analysis of the transformations of state and society that led to far-reaching convulsions as well as to dangerous uncertainty or disorientation in the nineteenth century and the catastrophes of the twentieth. Another historian who must be mentioned here is Hans Herzfeld, who published a two-volume history of the modern world in 1950–2.[12]

As to new institutional impulses toward transatlantic history, the prospects were fascinating in the late 1940s but soon proved disappointing. This outcome is important and surprising, and requires explanation, yet the leading professional accounts of German history generally show little interest in the problem. Cultural politics in connection with re-education by the occupational powers seemed to lay the foundation for a conception of history oriented toward the West, under the influence in particular of the Western integration of the early Federal Republic. A unique opportunity was embodied in the founding of the Free University of Berlin, which was supported by strong American financial and academic involvement.[13] The numerous guest professors, the first exchange programs and institutionalized connections to leading American universities, an institute of interdisciplinary North American studies (the John F. Kennedy Institute, established in 1963) – all this later bore fruit, but for various reasons did not become the center or starting point of an innovative renewal of German history based on the broader aspects of transatlantic history. Transatlantic history depended, despite a general, if

12 On Schnabel, see Erich Angermann, " 'Sapientia et eloquentia': Überlegungen zur Geschichts-darstellung Franz Schnabels," in *Franz Schnabel: Zu Leben und Werk (1887–1966): Vorträge zur Feier seines 100. Geburtstages* (Munich, 1988); Hans Herzfeld, *Die moderne Welt*, 2 vols. (Braunschweig, 1950–2).

13 James F. Tent, *Freie Universität Berlin 1948–1988* (Berlin, 1988).

superficial, interest in the history of the United States, on the personal involvement and initiative of a handful of scholars. It should be noted, however, that innovation in subjects and methods as well as the setting of new research agendas required time. Historians' belated interest in the social sciences, their particular questions, statements of the problem, methods, and conclusions all took their toll. Interdisciplinary approaches were first tried only in the late 1950s through the initiatives of historians such as Werner Conze and, in part, by building on the influential work of Hermann Aubin, Otto Brunner, and Hans Freyer, among others, and – a factor that is often neglected – on the study of comparative regional history.[14]

Criticism of the majority of German historians for their conservative stance in the reorientation of the profession between 1945 and the end of the 1950s is certainly justified. But to understand the reasons for this situation it would be more useful to begin with an analysis of their reactions to the catastrophe of World War I and their entrenched conservative nationalism, accompanied by more-or-less outspoken anti-Western and anti-American sentiments.[15] Moreover, because of the persecution and expulsion of Jewish but also of liberal and leftist historians during Nazi rule there was no incentive for and, even worse, no interest in discussing transatlantic connections. This may partly explain the limited success of returning emigrants and of transatlantic history in the decade after World War II, as well as the success of these fields in a few cases owing to the desire of students in many universities to learn more about the transatlantic world. Because there was no established tradition of transatlantic history in 1945, a new exploration of unknown areas was necessary – the new, almost preordained pro-American and pro-Western attitude notwithstanding. It was an unfamiliar world still to be explored, and it was by no means grotesque when a G.I. college lecturer wanted to talk with Freyer about Oswald Spengler upon their first meeting in the spring of 1945. The lecturer justifiably expected the subject to be of some importance in this period of re-evaluation, but his interest was not shared by the distressed German mandarin.[16] Even for Freyer, the catastrophic change had

---

14 For the progress of regional history since the 1880s, see Alois Gerlach, *Geschichtliche Landeskunde des Mittelalters: Genese und Probleme* (Darmstadt, 1986).

15 See, among others, Frank Trommler, "Inventing the Enemy: German-American Cultural Relations, 1900–1917," and Peter Krüger, "German Disappointment and Anti-Western Resentment, 1918–19," both in Hans-Jürgen Schröder, ed., *Confrontation and Cooperation: Germany and the United States in the Era of World War I, 1900–1924* (Providence, R.I., 1993), 99–125 and 323–35, respectively. On the history of World War I generally, see Michael Epkenhans, "Neuere Forschungen zur Geschichte des Ersten Weltkriegs," *Archiv für Sozialgeschichte* 38 (1998): 458–87.

16 Schulze, *Geschichtswissenschaft*, 27.

come all too suddenly, despite the fact that he was one of the very few to view Germany's and Europe's situation within a global context.

For most historians the process of coming to terms with the past resulted in a retreat to the best traditions of their profession. In general they did not conceive of the theme of transatlantic history, now pressing in with all its dimensions, as leading the way toward new perspectives. This is a fascinating subject in itself and has to be related to West German history after 1945 (a somewhat more promising approach to the elucidation of the course of German historiography than following only its methods and institutions) and to the unwavering and determined policy of German integration into the West, which was not matched by a similar promotion of transatlantic history.

With the exception of individual and small group efforts, a longer transition period was needed for German historians to discover the value of a European or Western identity as a substitute for a now discredited traditional nationalism. From the late 1960s onward the history of a larger identity was overshadowed, although sometimes supported by the powerful rise of the new social history. But the really striking neglect, both in German historiography after 1945 and in its later critical study and reappraisal, lay elsewhere. Today, it is generally acknowledged that for almost fifteen years there was a serious lag in the introduction of new methods and subjects. What was needed, however, was not only an *alternative to the history of politics but an alternative history of politics*, especially as an integrated approach. With the triumphant march of social history, the history of politics was considered old fashioned, and the history of foreign relations and international politics was contemptuously labeled "diplomatic history." To the detriment of a new transatlantic history, these fields were replaced, not reformed. Transatlantic historians viewed their subject not only as a set of structures, social and economic forces, and different levels of interdependence, which were to be compared, but also as a complicated processes of political decision making.

It is possible to trace the effects of an innovative political history. One outstanding early example is Bracher's book on the collapse of the Weimar Republic, a brilliant work on the edge between contemporary history and political science.[17] Bracher combined an analysis of the disintegration of power and the decay of an unstable democracy with structural and functional approaches to clarify the concurrence of institutional disarray,

---

17 Karl-Dietrich Bracher, *Die Auflösung der Weimarer Republik: Eine Studie zum Problem des Machtverfalls in der Demokratie* (Stuttgart, 1955).

a fragmented society, antiliberalism, and the arrival of new ideologies and political movements that demonstrated an increasing tendency toward violence. And all of these were found in a state overstrained by political and economic pressures. Hans Mommsen's recent vigorous inquiry has again demonstrated how the end of the Weimar Republic challenged modern political history based on an analysis of political and socioeconomic structures but with an emphasis on the priority of a fateful struggle for power between republican and antirepublican forces.[18]

It should be noted that it was a similar integrated approach, in view of the relative importance of political dynamics, that has guided new concepts of transatlantic history since the 1960s. However, only a small number of historians – Angermann, Günter Moltmann, and a few others – supported by a limited if well-organized and effective institutional basis, especially Angermann's Institute of Anglo-American History at the University of Cologne, brought lofty ideas of a Western world and a fated occidental community back to earth.

In the 1960s the famous Fischer controversy over German war aims and Germany's responsibility for the outbreak of World War I dominated mainstream historiography in the Federal Republic. This debate soon extended to the structural weaknesses of the German Empire and unleashed a wave of innovative, albeit sometimes one-sided studies that concentrated on the socioeconomic preconditions and organized interests, on the dynamics of change, technical development, and economic growth, on uneven processes of rapid modernization and the deficits of the political system. Furthermore, this discussion was energized in the 1970s by scholarly efforts to uncover the roots of National Socialism and the German *Sonderweg* (special path) that produced the Third Reich. These strands were connected to the international debate on imperialism and then dominated by the new patterns of social history that revealed the determining factors of political processes. This work was based in particular on concepts of a historical social science and a history of society developed at the University of Bielefeld. The Bielefeld school of historical studies was able to produce impressive achievements as a result of academic reform and a farsighted concentration of resources in a new university. Whereas the focus on German problems received fresh impetus, the transnational character and comparative potential of social history was not completely dismissed, although a transatlantic perspective was rare. In

18 Hans Mommsen, *Die verspielte Freiheit: Der Weg der Weimarer Republik in den Untergang 1918 bis 1933*, Propyläen Geschichte Deutschlands, vol. 8 (Berlin, 1989).

any case, the leading figures in the Bielefeld school exemplified the possibilities of comparative history: Hans-Ulrich Wehler, who studied with Theodor Schieder and Angermann, focused on American and German social imperialism, and Jürgen Kocka investigated white-collar workers.[19] Methods and results of social history were applied, from the beginning, to historical interpretation by the still quite small number of historians specializing in American history. Even among these scholars, only a few concentrated on transatlantic history instead of the history of the United States.

The evolution of postwar German historiography need not be repeated here: The Fischer controversy; social history as historical social science; the new history of basic concepts as an expression of their changing social and political environment; the anthropological enrichment of social history, sometimes coupled with new methods of individual or collective biography; gender history; the history of mentalities; the history of everyday life; and of course the linguistic turn – these impressive developments in modern historiography also have left their marks in the sphere of American studies. The same applies to the much-debated recent development of cultural history. Its new methodological framework, although by no means homogeneous, is quite different from the old-fashioned portrayal of the customs and manners of an epoch. Cultural history now includes a consideration of spheres, conditions, and traditions of living, the ways in which they are digested and reflected in human experience, consciousness, and behavior, as well as in belief systems, competence in interpreting culture, and the construction of meaning.[20] Political history, especially the history of foreign policy and international politics, however, although important and well done, did not attract much attention among those analyzing German historical writing.

For any transnational concept, including transatlantic history, there are rivals. In the postwar years there was a penchant for global history, the great turning points, and other general subjects that attracted a certain

19 Hans-Ulrich Wehler, *Der Aufstieg des amerikanischen Imperialismus: Studien zur Entwicklung des Imperium Americanum 1865–1900* (Göttingen, 1974); Jürgen Kocka, *Angestellte zwischen Faschismus und Demokratie: Zur politischen Sozialgeschichte der Angestellten: USA 1890–1940 im internationalen Vergleich* (Göttingen, 1977). For a brief overview, see Gerhard A. Ritter, *The New Social History in the Federal Republic of Germany* (London, 1991).

20 Wolfgang Hardtwig and Hans-Ulrich Wehler, eds., *Kulturgeschichte heute* (Göttingen, 1996); Otto Gerhard Oexle and Jörn Rüsen, eds., *Historismus in den Kulturwissenschaften: Geschichtskonzepte, historische Einschätzungen, Grundlagenprobleme* (Cologne, 1996); on religious aspects, see Hartmut Lehmann, *Säkularisierung, Dechristianisierung, Rechristianisierung im neuzeitlichen Europa: Bilanz und Perspektiven der Forschung* (Göttingen, 1997). See also the ongoing debate in *Geschichte und Gesellschaft*.

amount of attention. Later on, European integration became the dominant theme together with the history of Germany's integration into the West, which included transatlantic history only inasmuch as it was necessary to explain the steps of this process from the Marshall Plan and NATO to the German question and its place in East–West relations. Transatlantic history always had a hard time.

II

What was transatlantic history in actual practice? My answer goes back to Angermann, not only because this book is dedicated to his memory but also because he had a genuine and clear concept of transatlantic history and of the institution through which to realize it, namely, his institute at the University of Cologne. His concept was based on the perception of a longstanding and specific cultural network of connections and relations across the Atlantic between Europe and the British colonies and later the United States. This network existed despite sometimes far-reaching controversies, conflicts, and critical attitudes on both sides. I would even suggest that they belong to this special relationship, and to use a well-known metaphor: If Europe was the mother of North America, the child did not seem to have loved her very much most of the time. This critical view, however, stemming from familiarity and differences, as well as common assumptions and the endeavor to stand out against each other, is a promising yet complicated prerequisite for a lasting special relationship. This state of affairs enables European historians "to take a different view" of American history and transatlantic relations from that of American historians. However, one must always remain aware of the transatlantic network, that is, the "Atlantic culture" that is interested not only in special problems of the history of the United States.[21]

This briefly sketched concept of transatlantic history explains, in part, the apparent paradox of its coincidence with national history. Transatlantic history as national history thus means elucidating national history within

---

21 Erich Angermann, "Ständische Rechtstraditionen in der amerikanischen Unabhängigkeitserklärung," *Historische Zeitschrift* 200 (1965): 91; in addition, see Erich Angermann, "Was heisst und zu welchem Ende studiert man anglo-amerikanische Geschichte?" *Historische Zeitschrift* 256 (1993): 637–59, and Jürgen Heideking and Vera Nünning, *Einführung in die amerikanische Geschichte* (Munich, 1998). Michael Geyer and Konrad H. Jarausch, "The Future of the German Past: Transatlantic Reflections for the 1990s," *Central European History* 22 (1989): 228–59, provides a good example of how to consider the essence and influence of transatlantic connections as well as of how to make use of them for an agenda of transatlantic history as a method and a way of thinking, even if there is no special transatlantic subject.

the framework of the close intertwining of nations in a common Atlantic culture. This can be done successfully and with a good chance of stimulating an ongoing and thought-provoking discussion from the outside when German historians analyze American history within its broader context. Of course, this context can be enlarged by the new perspectives, ranging from gender to cultural history, and vice versa. But there is more to it than that. Germans and Americans can make a fresh start in studying their own national history in terms of transatlantic history. Yet, four points, I think, should be taken into consideration:

First, the concept of transatlantic history is based on actual but changing circumstances, on existing states as well as other forms of political and social organization, on the real linkages – the network, as I have called it – among them, and on transnational relations. Therefore, it does not consist in such generalities as basic values, the capitalist world, industrial or postindustrial society, class structures, minorities, and so forth. Each of these subjects may be integral to concrete transatlantic research projects, but none of them, in their vague abstractness, is the essence of transatlantic history.

Second, such concreteness also should be used to avoid a particular danger: Transatlantic history must by no means become a myth with some kind of transatlanticism as its core. We know how strong the temptation is in our complicated world to strive for any available reduction of complexity; the unholy trinity of catchword, ideology, and myth is often the only explanation available. Transatlantic history changes constantly, and historians are obliged to observe these changes carefully; the Atlantic system, or even its culture, can fall apart. Other systems, connections, or spaces may become more important. In any case, transatlantic history, or the special network of an Atlantic system, is by no means insulated and exclusive. Modern interlocking systems never are, and arguing that the concept of an Atlantic system and transatlantic history neglects other connections, spaces, or systems to which the United States belongs misses the point.[22] Modern states and societies are by definition interwoven – perhaps entangled – in a multitude of systems, and it is therefore one of the most challenging and fascinating tasks of transatlantic history to inquire into the relationships and tensions among those different orientations – not only in the United States but also in Europe.

Third, from what has been said already, it would seem conclusive that

---

22 Ian Tyrrell, "American Exceptionalism in an Age of International History," *American Historical Review* 96 (1991): 1040–1.

transatlantic history is no substitute for national history, rather an advanced stage of it that has to change according to the profound changes in the nation-state in an age of increasing transnational linkages and even of supranational integration. The nation-state, in its so-called Western type, based on human and civil rights, individual liberty, political participation, and constitutional guarantees, has proven capable and flexible enough to cope with these new developments. The European Union is an achievement of nation-states that has organized a limited group of them along admittedly contested lines of political agreement on functional and institutionalized forms of integration. Even today the nation-state remains by far the biggest and most effective constitutional and political unit in modern history.[23] It is undergoing fundamental changes and may one day disappear. But the historian must carefully study these changes as well as the new actors competing successfully with national governments to prepare or anticipate political decisions in domestic or foreign affairs. Yet, however weak the government and however strong the interest groups, legitimate and binding decisions can be made only on the national level (or by those subnational or supranational institutions to which certain competencies are delegated). Therefore, the demand to renounce the concept of national history would appear unworkable, provided the changed functions and position of the nation-state find due consideration.

As Ian Tyrrell has recently suggested, Germans may share responsibility for even another *Sonderweg*: American exceptionalism.[24] The influence of the nineteenth-century German pattern of national history may have been great, but now the debate has traveled far beyond this point. Carl N. Degler has made a well-considered comment "in pursuit of an American history" in speaking of "national character not exceptionalism," because "to ask what differentiates one people from another does not mean one has to insist on deviation from a norm . . . in various ways, the history of each nation is unique."[25] John Higham has summarized the recent debate with the "conviction that the nation-state will remain for a long time the strongest political structure in the world."[26] Advancing a

23 Peter Krüger, ed., *Deutschland, deutscher Staat, deutsche Nation: Historische Erkundungen eines Span-nungsverhältnisses* (Marburg an der Lahn, 1993); Peter Krüger, ed., *Ethnicity and Nationalism: Case Studies in Their Intrinsic Tension and Political Dynamics* (Marburg an der Lahn, 1993); Peter Krüger, *Wege und Widersprüche der europäischen Integration im 20. Jahrhundert,* Schriften des Historischen Kollegs, no. 45 (Munich, 1995).
24 Tyrrell, "American Exceptionalism," 1031.
25 Carl N. Degler, "In Pursuit of American History," *American Historical Review* 92 (1987): 4.
26 John Higham, "The Future of American History," *Journal of American History* 80 (1993): 1289.

modern concept of American history, Higham stresses three points that are of special interest. He warns against a shapeless pluralism between the extremes of macro- and microhistory that neglect the nation-state (I would even dispute that such an idea of pluralism is theoretically possible), demands a contextualized concept of transnational history (he emphasizes its complimentarity with national history) as well as transatlantic history, and substantiates the mediating character of the nation-state in its ability to connect "subnational particulars with supranational patterns."[27] This confirms my own attempts to locate the western European nation-state in a balance between the regional level and the European Union.[28]

Fourth, to draw a conclusion from the points made I would like to plead for a modern political history as integrated history. It has its virtues if an integrated approach is needed; it is quite different from any kind of "total" history but capable of concentrating on political decisions as a result of various strands of modern history, thus bringing together events and structures. The sphere of political decisions, from the local to the supranational level, is needed by all those who represent certain interests and attempt to reach certain solutions to pressing needs or to plan for the future. The political system provides the legal framework and the rules for individual life and the functioning and development of society. The influence of social forces, economic pressures, international politics, mentalities, traditions, and so forth, may be paramount yet does not alone determine political decisions and systems. Politics, domestic as well as international, is a system and a force in its own right, interdependent with other systems and forces but with a relative autonomy and with systemic interactions and mutual influences among political decisions not directly dependent on other factors. Every social activity takes place and has its limits in a political and legal order. Therefore, it is obviously impossible to analyze even local or family affairs adequately without this framework.

There is another, more fundamental reason for the importance of political history. For some time there has been much talk about a history oriented toward "man," a *science de l'homme*. But again it is discussed only in terms of additional structures, social anthropology, habits and customs, mentalities, everyday life, and so forth – man as a collective phenomenon. Despite all structures, however, prefiguring human behavior, there remains the very essence of man, his free will, his thinking, his creativity, his consciousness, and his character: All this makes him capable of per-

27 Ibid., 1290.   28 Krüger, *Ethnicity and Nationalism*, 97–108.

sonal decisions in order to form his life and his environment. It makes him capable of reaching political decisions and of establishing a political system. Although it is self-evident that, in history, individuality as such cannot be explained, analyzing human decisions comes as close as possible to it, especially as a sequence of decisions. Therefore, the political decision – and that means political history – should be central to historical analysis, integrating the invaluable and indispensable results of structural history to explain the preconditions of political decisions and processes. Political history is integrative to an extent that the history of society will never be able to achieve.[29]

III

My concluding remarks attempt to touch on some promising fields of transatlantic history, which should, wherever practicable, allow for interdisciplinary cooperation.[30] To begin with, it would seem obvious that the development of political history in general and transatlantic history in particular is a rewarding, far-too-neglected subject in the history of history. There is a remarkably conventional aspect even to the most modern and sophisticated accounts of German historiography. They are mainly interested in the innovative mainstream and the spectacular novelties, and much less in the so-called traditional fields or even in the consequences of modern approaches, not to mention transatlantic history. This is more than an incomplete treatment of the currents of modern historiography; it is an incomplete perception and analysis of what modern history is and what its tasks should be. Transatlantic history includes a variety of factors that may be investigated: the degree of interconnectedness, shared values, constitutional principles, patterns of organization, common and conflicting interests, as well as the procedures to reconcile them, especially in the realm of security, strategy, economic prosperity, social welfare, and in response to global challenges.

The history of the creation of a new Atlantic community after 1945 is relatively well known; close examination of fundamental decisions, their background, and their accepted implications (for instance, the partition of Europe and Germany) remains to be done. A considerable number of studies have been published in the last few years. Besides a detailed history

---

29 Manfred Hettling et al., eds., *Was ist Gesellschaftsgeschichte? Themen und Analysen: Festschrift für Hans Ulrich Wehler* (Munich, 1991).

30 To some extent, this means to continue Angermann's considerations and suggestions stated in his "Was heisst und zu welchem Ende studiert man anglo-amerikanische Geschichte?"

of NATO, a historical analysis of the handling of nuclear issues – strategy, proliferation, military and nonmilitary use of atomic energy, acceptance and protest – should be a priority.[31] These developments deepened the division between East and West and limited the Atlantic community to NATO and some neutral states. As already mentioned, a major problem of future research is the situation of East-Central Europe before and after 1989. The countries in this region want to belong to the transatlantic world; and the role of mediator between East and West that the Germans cast for themselves, sometimes in a dubious way, will become more confined yet more precise and significant, namely, to help to bring these countries into the Atlantic community. Here, transatlantic history means studying these changes and including the work of the experts on the history of eastern Europe. This is only one example of a necessary transgression of the borders of transatlantic history.

Comparative studies of nationalism and the nation-state, as suggested by Erich Angermann, are also of basic and present importance.[32] In a comparative study of nationalism it may not be advisable to concentrate on nationalism alone, but it could become a nucleus or indeed a leitmotif in transnational analysis by pursuing, on a comparative basis among various nations, the influence of nationalism and the way it affects or even shapes constitutional principles; law; governmental, economic, and social systems; mentalities; cultural preferences, and so forth; or to put it more generally: What is the significance of the nation-state for the existence and development of those vital forces of modern society and what does nationalism make of them?

Considering the rapid change taking place in Western societies, comparative studies in constitutional history assume high priority because constitutional law and practice, judicial review, and the rules for the functioning and the adaptability of institutions to new situations are paramount for the functioning and the survival of an open, pluralistic society in a state of flux. Insights into the different constitutional traditions and potentials, as revealed through the study of history, may become vital for coping with ensuing problems in times of increasing numbers of actors (domestic as well as transnational), be they new social groups, organiza-

---

31 See, most recently, Beatrice Heuser, *Transatlantic Relations: Sharing Ideals and Costs* (London, 1996); Beatrice Heuser, *NATO, Britain, France, and the FRG Nuclear Strategies and Forces for Europe, 1949–2000* (London, 1997); and Beatrice Heuser, *Nuclear Mentalities? Strategies and Beliefs in Britain, France, and the FRG* (London, 1998).

32 Erich Angermann, *Challenges of Ambiguity: Doing Comparative History*, German Historical Institute, Washington, D.C., Annual Lecture series, no. 4 (New York, 1991), 13.

tions, minorities, municipalities or regions, which question the legitimacy of the state and lay claim to their own.[33]

To some extent, linked to the importance of constitutional history in broad terms is another fascinating and promising field of research: comparative regional history, including center-periphery interdependence. An outstanding case is the new history of the frontier and the American West,[34] the different European influences in different parts of the old colonial West, the persistent influence of Europe through its emigrants on the westward expansion of the United States, its coincidence with the settlement expansion in the British Empire and in Russia, and last but not least, the comparison of methods and of regions over time on both sides of the Atlantic. Regional history, an old domain of German historiography and now an impressive achievement of American history, too, offers a comprehensive view within a small area, from the large historical processes down to everyday life and environmental history.[35] Frontier history is an extraordinary example and can be compared to Germany's eastward expansion from the twelfth to the fourteenth centuries as part of an enormous European settlement of cultivated areas. Such a comparison reveals parallels and differences in the development from frontier to region, from periphery to partly powerful regional centers, from the overcoming of backwardness to modernization and state-building.[36] This is only one impressive example; similar comparisons of modern regions in the United States and the European Union are rewarding.

A somewhat neglected field is the historical development of transatlantic traffic and communication, and their tremendous effects on other structures, causing, for example, massive changes in entire regions. There are close connections to migration. Here not only the mass movements and the classic migration process of the nineteenth century are important, but also the migration of special groups and needed experts, the

33 Yale H. Ferguson and Richard W. Mansbach, *The State, Conceptual Chaos and the Future of International Relations Theory* (Denver, 1989); Yale H. Ferguson and Richard W. Mansbach, "Between Celebration and Despair. Constructive Suggestions for Future International Relations Theory," *International Studies Quarterly* 35 (1991): 363–86.

34 Patricia Nelson Limerick, Clyde A. Milner II, and Carles E. Rankin, *Trails: Toward a New Western History* (Lawrence, Kans., 1991); William Cronon, George Miles, and Jay Gitlin, eds., *Under an Open Sky: Rethinking American's Western Past* (New York, 1992); John Mack Faragher, "The Frontier Trail: Rethinking Turner and Reimagining the American West," *American Historical Review* 98 (1993): 106–17.

35 Donald Worster, *Under Western Skies: Nature and History in the American West* (New York, 1992).

36 For greater detail on this comparison, see Peter Krüger, "Der Wandel der Funktion von Grenzen im internationalen System Ostmitteleuropas im 20. Jahrhundert," in Hans Lemberg, ed., *Grenzen in Ostmitteleuropa im 19. und 20. Jahrhundert: Aktuelle Forschungsprobleme* (forthcoming).

mobility of the labor force, the influence of multinational corporations and the traffic and communication networks, and the effects of temporary migration.

Finally, I would like to emphasize that the complicated relationship between North America and European integration remains one of the classic and most important themes of transatlantic history. This agenda includes the concrete forms of interconnectedness; the "special relationship" between several European countries and the United States; the sometimes delicate or even crucial triangular relations between Germany, the United States, and the rest of Europe, particularly France; the complicated mixture of common goals, cooperation, tension and rivalry between the United States and Europe; and their relationships with the outside world, to list only a few important topics. Transatlantic history or transatlanticism should become neither a doctrine nor a myth, but it should be taken seriously.

12

American Exceptionalism as National History?

HANS R. GUGGISBERG

I would like to start out from two seemingly contradictory premises. The first is that every national history, American or non-American, is based on a more or less dominating and comprehensive notion of exceptionalism. In other words, exceptionalism is one of the fundamental driving forces impelling the writing of national history. However – and this is my second premise – no serious work on national history can ever rest on exceptionalism alone. In order to satisfy the critical reader it also has to take into consideration supranational structures and contexts. In surveying the history of American national historiography we observe that much of it has been dominated by exceptionalism, that is, by the emphasis on what is usually called "the uniqueness of the American historical experience." This observation does not, however, do justice to American national historiography in its entirety. Since the time when the study of history became professionalized in the United States, many American historians have also emphasized the transatlantic contexts of the history of the United States, the different aspects of ethnic and national Old World heritage, as well as the combined impacts of European ideas, institutions, inventions, and ways of thinking, that is, all those elements that came to America with the immigrants and helped shape the unique and in many ways exceptional history of American society. It also must be noted that since the colonial period of American history a very great number of European visitors were deeply impressed with the otherness and uniqueness of mentalities, social structures, and political institutions they had encountered in the New World. In describing what they had seen, many of them became defenders of American exceptionalism. Most prominent among them was Alexis de Tocqueville, who coined the phrase by observing that "The position of the Americans is therefore quite exceptional, and it may be believed that no democratic people will ever be placed in a similar one."

This statement is quite well known, but when quoting it we should not forget that it stands in a somewhat contradictory context. Immediately preceding it we find the following passage:

In spite of the ocean that intervenes, I cannot consent to separate America from Europe. I consider the people of the United States as that portion of the English people who are commissioned to explore the forests of the New World, while the rest of the nation, enjoying more leisure and less harassed by the drudgery of life, may devote their energies to thought and enlarge in all directions the empire of mind.[1]

What we have before us here sounds like a rather elaborate, even if not fully comprehensive circumscription of the dichotomy of the theme of this book, "Transatlantic History and American Exceptionalism." Tocqueville seems to have felt that the two notions cannot be separated from each other.

As Seymour Martin Lipset has pointed out, an emphasis on American uniqueness always raises the obvious question as to how and in what respects Americans were and are different from the rest of the world, particularly from Europeans.[2] There is a large literature on this subject dating back to the eighteenth century and attempting to define the special character of America (that is, the British colonies and the new American republic) in political and social terms. One of the most interesting of these texts is the speech on "Conciliation with America," which Edmund Burke gave before the House of Commons in 1775 and in which he noted that Americans were not simply transplanted Englishmen but a different people culturally.[3] In his *Letters from an American Farmer* (1782), Hector St. John de Crèvecoeur explicitly raised the question "What is an American?" He told his readers that Americans behaved differently in their social relations and were much more egalitarian in their political thinking than other nationalities.[4] Tocqueville agreed with this and also stressed American individualism as distinct from the group ties that, in his opinion, essentially characterized the social structures of European countries.[5]

---

1 Alexis de Tocqueville, *Democracy in America*, ed. Phillips Bradley, 2 vols. (New York, 1948), 2:36–7. See *De la Démocratie en Amérique*. Biographie, préface et bibliographie par François Furet, 2 vols. (Paris, 1981), 2:48–9.

2 Seymour Martin Lipset, "American Exceptionalism Reaffirmed," in Byron E.Shafer, ed., *Is America Different? A New Look at American Exceptionialism* (Oxford, 1991), 4.

3 Edmund Burke, *Speeches and Letters on American Affairs*, Introd. by Peter McKevitt, Everyman's Library (London, 1961), 90ff.

4 Hector St. John de Crèvecoeur, *Letters from an American Farmer*. Introd. by Warren Barton Blake, Everyman's Library (London, 1962), 39ff.

5 Tocqueville, *Democracy in America*, 2:100–1, 103, 121 (*De la Démocratie en Amérique*, 2:129–30, 132, 153ff.)

In the course of the nineteenth and twentieth centuries those commentaries were followed by a very large number of books and articles written by educated and interested Europeans. All these visitors stressed American exceptionalism and looked at it (as Burke, Crèvecoeur, and Tocqueville had done) in a comparative way. Among them were Harriet Martineau, Friedrich Engels, and Max Weber.[6]

In spite of what has already been said about American exceptionalism, let me point to some definitions that will help clarify my argument: "American exceptionalism," to the student of American historiography and of European writing on U.S. history, is – and here I am following Byron E. Shafer – "the notion that the United States was created differently, developed differently, and thus has to be *understood* differently – essentially on its own terms and within its own context."[7] This statement is suggestively supplemented by Lipset, to whom I should like to refer once more:

American exceptionalism could only have arisen in a comparative context. It basically means that America is unique, is different in crucial ways from most other countries. . . . In dealing with national characteristics it is important to recognize that comparative evaluations are never absolutes, that they always are made in terms of more or less. The statement that the United States is an egalitarian society obviously does not imply that all Americans are equal in any way that can be defined. This generalization usually means . . . that the United States is more egalitarian than Europe.[8]

From the earliest beginnings of European colonization the concept of America stood not only for a specific geographical space but also for meanings and characterizations that were attached to that space by its many contemporary observers and interpreters. These meanings reflected not only the aspirations of the immigrants but also their manifold experiences of indigenous resistance against their advance. The same meanings were chiefly responsible for shaping the changing identities of America as well as the images by which America has been known, characterized, and rendered comprehensible to both its inhabitants and the rest of the world. These observations summarize the basic thesis of Jack P. Greene's book, *The Intellectual Construction of America*. Greene very convincingly shows that American exceptionalism is tightly linked to various elements of national identity. The exploration of this amalgamation he calls a "venerable subject of American historiography." I would permit myself to add

6 Lipset, "American Exceptionalism Reaffirmed," 5.
7 Shafer, ed., *Is America Different?*, v.
8 Lipset, "American Exceptionalism Reaffirmed," 1.

that besides being a venerable subject it is also a fruitful and important one because its investigation helps us – and here I explicitly include the European students of the American past – find answers to fundamental questions as to what American civilization and society basically were and are about. Greene is surely right in stating that if a society's sense of its collective self depends to a large extent on conceptions of its past, then historians have played a principal role in the formation of this society.[9] It cannot be doubted that this has happened very often in American historiography, even if some images of history proved to be simplistic or one-sided, and the ensuing articulations of identity remained problematic.

In his *History of the United States* (1843–76), George Bancroft created an image of history guided by divine providence that is, of course, no longer tenable and was criticized very severely well before the end of the nineteenth century. Bancroft taught reverence for the American past, elucidated the "Manifest Destiny," and assured the American nation that it was the instrument of Divine Providence for bringing liberty and democracy to all of humanity.[10] That was true American exceptionalism in its romantic form, preached by an historian whose aim was not only to inform but also to edify his readers. In spite of its defects, however, Bancroft's *History of the United States* still ranks among the classical works of preprofessional American historiography. That it has exerted an enormous influence on a large reading public (also outside the Unites States) cannot be denied.[11] Like many other classical works of historiography it has become an historical monument in itself. No history of American historiography can leave it unmentioned. Besides this, another point should not be overlooked: Even if Bancroft's vision of providential history no longer is accepted today, there is no denying that many Americans believed in it in the past, not only the Puritans themselves but many of their spiritual descendants in later periods as well as perhaps some enlightened deists during the American Revolution and in the decades immediately following it.

Another nineteenth-century example of American exceptionalism functioning as a driving force for the writing of national history is provided by the works of Frederick Jackson Turner. To a much larger extent

9 Jack P. Greene, *The Intellectual Construction of America: Exceptionalism and Identity from 1492 to 1800* (Chapel Hill, N.C., 1993), 3.

10 Ernst A. Breisach, *American Progressive History: An Experiment in Modernization* (Chicago, 1993), 17–18.

11 Ibid., 19. On Bancroft and romantic historiography, see David Levin, *History as Romantic Art: Bancroft, Prescott, Motley, and Parkman* (Stanford, Calif., 1959), 3ff., 49ff.

than in Bancroft's *History of the United States*, exceptionalism here works as the master key to understanding the American past.

Turner's frontier thesis stressed the extent to which the open spaces and extensive resources of the American West and the opportunities they offered to the immigrant proved incompatible with Old World institutions and mentalities. More open, more expansive, more equal, and more democratic than the societies of the Old World, the American frontier society was distinctly American.[12] In the West, American history had found a new beginning. Once the westward movement started, American history no longer could be seen and explained as an offshoot of European history. At the frontier the colonist became a new man, a democrat, a self-made individualist, a true American. Turner's vision had a tremendous impact on his colleagues who heard him deliver his famous address at the annual meeting of the American Historical Association held in Chicago in July 1893.[13] For a while it seemed to dominate all American historical writing.

In a recent essay the Dutch-American historian Jan Willem Schulte Nordholt stated his impression that Turner "was more a poet than a historian, more a man of great visions than of careful analysis of the past," in fact the "true heir" of Rousseau and Jefferson.[14] I think that if we are cautious not to exaggerate the historical similarities, there is something to be said for this judgment. Although he belonged to a generation of historians who considered themselves professionals, Turner was in many ways an exception to the rules of the craft. He worked in archives, to be sure, but he seemed less interested in describing facts and developments than in formulating provocative theses and suggestive phrases. His agrarianist message was simple and sweeping: It certainly contained some romantic elements, but it also remained in conformity with older intellectual traditions. Turner saw America's past as a great covenant, not between the Puritans' God and his chosen people in the "City upon a Hill" but between Nature's God (in the Jeffersonian sense) and the innocent colonists conquering and exploiting the American wilderness. At this point we cannot overlook the fact that when Turner started to propagate his radically exceptionalist message concerning "The Significance of the Frontier in American History," the westward movement had virtually

---

12 Greene, *Intellectual Construction of America*, 3.
13 American Historical Association, *Annual Report for 1893* (Washington, D.C., 1894), 199–227.
14 Jan Willem Schulte Nordholt, "The Turner Thesis Revisited," in David K. Adams and Cornelis A. van Minnen, eds., *Reflections on American Exceptionalism*, European Papers in American History, no. 1 (Staffordshire, U.K., 1994), 10.

come to its end. At the same time, the United States had also completed its transformation into an industrialized nation. In view of these developments it is not surprising that criticism of the Turner thesis spread very quickly.

When formulating his interpretation of American history in the early 1890s Turner himself had done this as a critic of an older historiographical tradition. With his frontier thesis he had attacked the "Teutonic theory" that the so-called scientific historians of the history seminar at Johns Hopkins University had put forth and that claimed that American democracy had its roots in Germanic antiquity. That was, of course, a romantic idea, too, but it was developed with great methodological meticulousness. Striking parallels between the administrative systems of the ancient German villages and the early New England towns were discovered (they mainly concerned the town meeting), and most "scientific historians" believed that the "germs" of American democracy were to be found in the forests of ancient Germany, from whence they had been transferred to Anglo-Saxon England and, much later, to North America. This "germ theory," vehemently rejected by Turner, was obviously nonexceptionalist.[15]

Turner's early critics did not defend the "germ theory" of the "Scientific School," but they, too, were inclined toward nonexceptionalist interpretations of the American past. They criticized what appeared to them as Turner's parochialism and chauvinism as well as the fact that he hardly ever mentioned the fate of the West's original inhabitants. The historians of the so-called Imperial School – among its most prominent representatives were Herbert Levi Osgood, George Louis Beer, and George McLean Andrews – insisted that North America's colonial past should be seen and described in terms of the general context of the British colonial empire. They also emphasized the close connection between the continental colonies in North America and those in the West Indies, and they held that the history of the postrevolutionary relationship between the United States and Britain should always be studied with special care.[16] Whereas the adherents of the Imperial School were mainly interested in political and institutional history, Turner's "progressive" colleagues and contemporaries who became prominent during the first two decades of the twentieth century also occupied themselves with problems of Amer-

---

15 Ibid., 13.

16 Greene, *Intellectual Construction of America*, 4; On the "Imperial School of Colonial History," see Michael Kraus and Davis D. Joyce, *The Writing of American History*, rev. ed. (Norman, Okla., 1985), 210–38.

ican social, cultural, and economic history. They endeavored to demonstrate that the political and economic life of the nation could and had to be interpreted in terms of the same analytical categories that were being used by European historians engaged in describing the development of the Old World. In its criticism of the Turner thesis, the "Progressive School" of American historiography was essentially non- or rather antiexceptionalist. I believe that the same can be said of at least one particularly radical strain of Turner criticism in our own time. Most members of this group, which is generally referred to as the "School of New Western History," seem basically to be influenced by their common predecessor Henry Nash Smith, who, in his famous book *Virgin Land: The American West as Symbol and Myth* (1950), also was a critic of Turner. He held that the development of the West had not been determined by realities but by mythical visions and dreams of innocence and progress. The new critics – Patricia Nelson Limerick, Richard White, and Donald Worster, among others – are considerably more radical. They reject not only Turner's central idea of a moving frontier but also the definition of the frontier as a borderline between civilization and wilderness. To them such a definition presupposes that the Indians always were and still are uncultured savages and that their own history can be ignored altogether. They also criticize Turner for his lack of interest in Hispanic borderline history. Thus, after the criticism of the New Western History School, practically nothing is left of Turner's exeptionalist assessment of the frontier in American history.[17] If his critics in the New Western History School seem to express exceptionalist views here and there, it is a negatively defined exceptionalism resting on concepts such as racism, discrimination, and negligence. But negative exceptionalism, as we shall see, is also an aspect of our topic.

In spite of a long tradition of sharp criticism and rejection, Turner – as Schulte Northolt emphasizes – has not been forgotten.[18] Like Bancroft,

---

17 Schulte Nordholt, "Turner Thesis Revisited," 15. On the progressive historians' criticism of Turner and especially on that of Benjamin F. Wright and George W. Pierson, see Richard Hofstadter, *The Progressive Historians: Turner, Beard, Parrington* (London, 1969), 123–31. For Henry Nash Smith's critical comments on Turner, see *Virgin Land: The American West as Symbol and Myth* (New York, 1950), 291–305. A good introduction to the "New Western History School" is provided by Patricia Nelson Limerick et al., eds., *Trails Toward a New Western History* (Lawrence, Kans., 1991). Among the most informative articles in this collective volume are the following: Donald Worster, "Beyond the Agrarian Myth," 3–25; Richard White, "Trashing the Trails," 26–39; Patricia N. Limerick, "What on Earth Is the New Western History?" 81–8. Of fundamental importance is Limerick's book *The Legacy of Conquest: The Unbroken Past of the American West* (Lawrence, Kans., 1987), 253ff., for Turner. A comprehensive textbook has been written by Richard White, *"It's Your Misfortune and None of My Own": A History of the American West* (Norman, Okla., 1991).

18 Schulte Nordholt, "Turner Thesis Revisited," 9, 16.

he cannot be ignored by students of American historiography and intellectual history. His work has also become something of a historical monument, and his notion of the frontier, although today considered highly problematic, is still used in daily language. It has undoubtedly contributed much to the strengthening of cultural and national identity, mainly among those Americans who can claim descent from westward-moving immigrants. For the American Indians, however, the exceptionalist Turner thesis remains irrelevant and even discriminatory. For Hispanic Americans, particularly for the Chicanos, a national exceptionalism based on the vision of a migratory movement from east to west is equally irrelevant. As I have tried to explain elsewhere, the course of history for them does not move from east to west but from south to north.[19]

Although criticism of Turner's interpretation of American history has mostly been based on non- or antiexceptionalist concepts, exceptionalist tendencies certainly have not vanished from more recent American national historiography. What seems to have disappeared is the exclusive concentration of American historical exceptionalism on the "winning of the West."

Progressive historians, as we have seen, raised serious questions about the exceptionalist idea that the United States had a distinctive history that could be written only in its own terms. They never succeeded, however, in entirely supplanting it. They may not have been energetic enough or perhaps not even willing to really defeat the concept of historical exceptionalism. Whereas Charles Beard diversified his economic interpretation of history, others like James Harvey Robinson and Harry Elmer Barnes urged their fellow historians to cooperate with the social sciences, and the most radical relativist, Carl L. Becker, still contemplated the uniqueness of the American struggle for national independence.[20]

During the 1920s and 1930s exceptionalist concepts also were kept alive by the debates over the question of why both working-class radicalism and socialism had never developed much vigor in the United States. This phenomenon was explained by numerous factors, such as the

---

19 Hans R. Guggisberg, "Traditionen und Ideale nationaler Identität in den USA," in Hans R. Guggisberg, *Zusammenhänge in historischer Vielfalt: Humanismus, Spanien, Nordamerika* (Basel, 1994), 398.
20 Breisach, *American Progressive History*, 123–4, 130ff. On the rise of relativism in American historiography see 159–60, 165ff.: To some extent, historical relativism was a reaction to the still prevailing positivism of the "mainline Scientific History." It was strengthened also by the experience of the Great Depression, which shook the general faith in the intrinsic benevolence of the industrial age more violently than the horrors of World War I had done. See Breisach, *American Progressive History*, 165, and Peter Novick, *That Noble Dream: The "Objectivity Question" and the American Historical Profession* (Cambridge, 1988), 335.

material environment and economic wealth, the electoral systems geared to inhibit third parties, the egalitarian elements in the class structure, the widespread antistatist and populist beliefs that help determine American political culture, and – one might add – the "American dream," with its promise of material success for everyone willing to work for it.[21] It is impossible here to discuss the vast literature on this complex topic, but one should not forget that the absence of socialism had been pointed out as a conspicuous element of American exceptionalism by a considerable number of prominent European observers, politicians, and political theorists already at the turn of the century. Among them were Vladimir Lenin, Leon Trotsky, H. G. Wells, James Bryce, and, of course, Werner Sombart. It has been rightly pointed out that the latter's well-known book *Why Is There No Socialism in the United States?* (1906) should really have been titled *Why Should There Be Socialism in the United States?* and that in his argument the German sociologist who had never visited the United States himself heavily drew on Bryce's earlier book, *The American Commonwealth* (1894).[22]

After World War II, that is, during the period from the late 1940s to the late 1960s, the concept of American exceptionalism enjoyed an astonishing revival, as Jack P. Greene has noted. This revival was essentially supported by both the emerging American studies movement and the so-called consensus historians. These two groups of scholars represented the strengthening of American cultural self-consciousness after the victories over fascism and totalitarianism. They shared the assumption that America had always been fundamentally different from Europe and that any variations among localities, regions, and ethnic groups within the United States were generally less important than the similarities that constituted American culture and made it different from that of Europe. Building on Tocqueville's already quoted observation concerning the "entirely exceptional situation" of Americans in the world, the consensus historians endeavored to identify the distinctive elements of American life and mentalities that seemed to make the United States "different in crucial ways from most other countries." In the exceptionalist statements of some commentators (which were again quite radical) we encounter designa-

---

21 Lipset, "American Exceptionalism Reaffirmed," 6.
22 Sombart's work had been published in German in 1906. The English translation is by P. M. Hocking and C. T. Husbands (London, 1976). For Bryce's remarks on the American working class, see *The American Commonwealth*, new ed., 2 vols. (New York, 1910), 2:300ff. On Sombart and America, see Daniel Bell, "The 'Hegelian Secret': Civil Society and American Exceptionalism," in Shafer, ed., *Is America Different?* 52–4.

tions of the United States as an "exemplary nation," "the first new, self-conscious nation able to control its own fate," and here and there even allusions to "Providence" as the guiding force of American history.[23] One of the most prominent and eloquent advocates of this "consensus history exceptionalism" was Daniel J. Boorstin. In his opinion, the uniqueness of American history basically derived from American pragmatism. This he illustrated clearly in the introduction to *The Genius of American Politics* (1953). In his own words, the thesis of this book is "that nothing could be more un-American than to urge other countries to imitate America," because "America has no philosophy which can be exported." On the basis of this thesis, the argument is disarmingly simple:

American democracy is unique. It possesses a genius all its own. . . . Our unique history has thus offered us those benefits which come (in Edmund Burke's words) "from considering our liberties in the light of an inheritance" and has led us away from "extravagant and presumptuous speculations." . . . To understand the uniqueness of American history is to begin to understand why no adequate theory of our political life can be written.[24]

The New Left historians of the 1970s took up some ideas and interpretations of the Progressives, for example, the skeptical attitude toward traditional and positive exceptionalism. In 1970 Howard Zinn published a collection of essays under the title *The Politics of History*. In the chapter on "Inequality" he attacked the patriotic exceptionalists of his own time with bitter irony. His words were leveled at Jacques Barzun, but they could just as well have been meant as an answer to Boorstin's statement quoted previously: "Somehow," Zinn asserted, "the notion of American uniqueness persists." And then he went on to explain:

There is a common belief that our country has from birth been favored, by Providence or by Circumstance, in being unencumbered with harsh class lines, with solidified privilege, with a stubborn aristocracy, with a mass of illiterate peasantry, with all those things that plagued Europe until the dawn of modern times. A naked continent, rare idealism and courage among settlers weeded out by hardship and three thousand miles of ocean, the egalitarian demands of the frontier – these combined, we are often told, for a physically crude but socially immaculate conception.[25]

While emphasizing the basic dishonesty of this image of history, Zinn urged American historians to stop comparing an idealized America with an oversimplified notion of Europe's rigid class system: "There is some-

23 Greene, *The Intellectual Construction of America*, 4–5.
24 Daniel J. Boorstin, *The Genius of American Politics*, 6th ed. (Chicago, 1964), 1, 2, 5.
25 Howard Zinn, *The Politics of History* (Boston, 1970), 57.

thing wrong," he said, "with the use of other countries as a basis of evaluation." He continued in truly utopian and somewhat romanticizing fashion: "Why not use as our norm the ideal society, that which has never existed on earth, that mythic society which has eliminated (to use Jacques Barzun's phrase) 'irrational privilege.' I would call irrational that privilege which comes from the distorted distribution of abundant resources."[26]

Whenever the New Left historians tended toward exceptionalist interpretations themselves, their exceptionalism was negatively defined and rested on notions like racial discrimination, degradation of minorities, poverty, social inequality, and aggressively imperialist foreign policy. This can be observed in many radical publications of the time, notably in such books as Barton J. Bernstein's *Towards a New Past* (1968), a well-known collection of essays which very clearly elucidated the antiprogressive and anticonsensus revisionism of the New Left historians.[27]

In more recent years negative exceptionalism has also appeared in politically less committed studies on violence, crime, and divorce rates.[28] In addition to this, a definitely antiexceptionalist trend has become notable in the work of some younger specialists of the American colonial period. The emergence of a deepening interest in its social history – in itself not so new any more – has led to many indications that the basic conditions of life in the colonies differed less radically from those of the contemporary rural and small-town society in Britain than had been contended in the past. Thus, in the 1980s and early 1990s historians such as Joyce Appleby and John Murrin could state that at least for the colonial period, American exceptionalism has been practically refuted as a concept of historical interpretation. Greene has protested this assertion quite vehemently and the debate continues.[29]

It is not easy to conclude these reflections with a few summarizing and generalizing remarks. In spite of everything, as a motivation to think about and to write American national history, positive or negative exceptionalism seems to come back again and again. Historians mainly

---

26 Ibid., 58–9.
27 Barton J. Bernstein, ed., *Towards a New Past: Dissenting Essays in American History* (New York, 1968; reprint, London, 1970); see especially Bernstein's introduction and the following two articles: Jesse Lemisch, "The American Revolution Seen from the Bottom Up," 3–45; and Staughton Lynd, "Beyond Beard," 46–64.
28 Lipset, "American Exceptionalism Reaffirmed," 30–1.
29 Greene, *Intellectual Construction of America*, 5–6. See Joyce Appleby, "Value and Society," in Jack P. Greene and J. R. Pole, eds., *Colonial British America: Essays in the New History of the Early Modern Era* (Baltimore, 1984), 304 and John M. Murrin, "The Irrelevance and Relevance of Colonial New England," *Reviews of American History* 18 (1990): 180.

interested in analyzing social developments may be reluctant to adopt exceptionalist concepts and rather stress supranational contexts, whereas specialists of political and intellectual history may be more readily disposed to emphasize the notion of American uniqueness. In my opinion, it would be quite wrong to simplify the situation by asserting that conservative historians are necessarily more exceptionalist than those who consider themselves progressive, liberal, or radically revisionist. It seems to me that without a certain amount of exceptionalism national history is basically inconceivable. And national history, as long as it avoids nationalistic tendencies, is certainly not an obsolete concern in our time. Exceptionalism, again defined positively *and* negatively, is and remains a legitimate motivation for national history, but only as long as it does not minimize or obscure the nonexceptional aspects. Carl Degler's admonition to beware of the dangers brought about by the "specter of exceptionalism" certainly deserves our consideration. The same is true of Ian Tyrrell's skeptical and dispassionate observations on "American Exceptionalism in an Age of International History," which culminate in the assertion that "the growth of the American nation-state can be depicted not as an exception to patterns of national power in a world of nations but as a particular, and constantly changing, expression of complex forces."[30] All this said and done, we should, however, not overlook the fact (already mentioned at the outset) that the topic discussed here is not a distinctively American one. American exceptionalism consists of many elements distinctively American that we do not find in the exceptionalist concepts of other countries. As an agent of national identity and as an incentive to the writing of national history, American exceptionalism is problematic in many ways, but it is in itself not exceptional.

---

30 Carl N. Degler, "In Pursuit of American History," *American Historical Review* 92 (Feb. 1987): 3; Ian Tyrrell, "American Exceptionalism in an Age of International History," *American Historical Review* 96 (Oct. 1991): 1055.

13

The Historical World of Erich Angermann

HERMANN WELLENREUTHER

The pride expressed in John F. Kennedy's confession "Ich bin ein Berliner!" (I am a Berliner!) could have colored Erich Angermann's own admission "Ich bin ein Sachse!" (I am a Saxon!). Yet everyone who knew him would have noted the thick irony, whereas all others would have classified this as a blatant and shameless lie. For who could have been more Bavarian, who was in a greater hurry to get out of Cologne and back to Munich after the end of the term, who had his dentist in Munich, who bought all his clothes and most of his shoes there, and who refused to admit that Kölsch, the local Cologne brew, was drinkable – Erich Angermann. But who was Erich Angermann?

There are various approaches to this question. We could turn to his wife, and she would probably answer, with a pensive smile: "Well, he was many things, but first of all he was a very lovable person." His students would admit to the first part of the sentence but would then add: He was a fine academic teacher, easily accessible, but as a supervisor of doctoral dissertations something of a "precisionist." Had Angermann been listening in, he would have agreed with this description but added that the term *precisionist* in its historical meaning carried connotations – a word he was rather fond of – that probably fit him less well. And soon he would have engaged us in a discussion about the meaning of the term in early modern religious history in England, North America, and Germany.

"Precisionist" stood for the determination to reform the English church according to the biblical description of the first Christian congregations. But, he would have added, it was somewhat less clear how this first congregation was structured. The Bible, which he knew better than most of us, is open to interpretation; this not only explains the fierce polemics in England between radical precisionists but also the attacks of Ann Hutchinson and Henry Vane Jr., on the one hand, and Roger Williams and the

Rhode Island secessionists, on the other, on those who sought to re-create biblical reality in Massachusetts. Historically, the term *precisionist* was intimately linked to illiberal and radical endeavors to cleanse the church of the unbiblical additions of the Middle Ages. In the sense that the term defines a search for a concept of life according to the true dicta of the Bible, Angermann would have carefully pointed out, "precisionist" would ill fit his own attitude toward life. He most likely would have added, as he did in his introduction to the session on "Religion – Politics – Society in the Seventeenth and Eighteenth Centuries" at the annual meeting of German historians in 1970, that it was the "moral rigidity of the lifestyle of its followers out of which arose the inability for tolera-tion" characterizing "precisionists" in the Puritan, Jansenist, and Pietist movements that did not belong to the values he particularly cherished or shared.[1]

In short, Angermann would once more have demonstrated that, in some sense, the adjective "precisionist" fit him after all. The example, which is of course purely fictitious, would have demonstrated one other important facet of Angermann's historical world: his constant effort to set his insights as a historian into a wider Atlantic setting. It is the purpose of this chapter to offer some suggestions on how Angermann arrived at this particular mode of thought and to delineate the contours of his his-torical world.

I

Erich Angermann was born in Chemnitz, and that is about as Saxon as you can get. But early in his childhood the family moved to Bavaria, where his father accepted a position in the adult education system. It was his father, with his liberal and practical attitude and his pointed rejection of anything that smacked of National Socialism and fascism, who shaped his early world view. His father's firm beliefs in the educability of mankind and in the possibility that even the most complex matter could be phrased so that every halfway educated person would understand it, deeply impressed the adolescent. These beliefs were part of Angermann's firm principles as an academic teacher. Later, he would be more interested than most of his fellow historians in ways of translating historical insights into modes and materials suitable for secondary school use.[2] A second insight

1 Erich Angermann, "Religion – Politik – Gesellschaft im 17. und 18. Jahrhundert: Ein Versuch in vergleichender Sozialgeschichte. Einführung," *Historische Zeitschrift* 214 (1972): 27.
2 Erich Angermann, ed., *Der Aufstieg der Vereinigten Staaten von Amerika: Innen- und aussenpolitische*

is an outgrowth of the first: Angermann thought little of theoretical chatter when it became en vogue toward the latter part of the 1960s. He would react to the question about the theoretical underpinnings of his concept of history with the disarming and cheerful admission that he had none. He simply enjoyed doing history.[3]

The second person that shaped Angermann's intellectual world was Franz Schnabel (1887–1966), author of the particularly influential *German History of the Nineteenth Century*.[4] Forced out of Karlsruhe's Technical University by the Nazis, after World War II Schnabel resumed his career at the University of Munich. Angermann was deeply influenced by Schnabel's liberalism as well as his exceptionally broad concept of history. There was a group of Schnabel's students who at the time were friends: Friedrich Hermann Schubert, Eberhard Weis, Karl Otmar Freiherr von Aretin, and Heinrich Lutz are the names that he frequently mentioned. This group, to which Heinz Angermaier and Johanna Autenrieth should be added and who became his friends during his early association with the *Neue Deutsche Biographie* (New German Biography),[5] bespeaks a diversity of intellectual interests that is quite remarkable[6] and parallels the diversity of interests of Angermann's own students.[7]

Entwicklung (Stuttgart, 1959–60); Erich Angermann, "Die Auseinandersetzung mit der Moderne in Deutschland und den USA in den 'Goldenen zwanziger Jahren,'" *Internationales Jahrbuch für Geschichts- und Geographie-Unterricht* 11 (1967): 76–87; Erich Angermann, "Franklin Delano Roosevelt als Politiker: Ein didaktischer Versuch," in Akademie Eichholz, ed., *Möglichkeiten der Behandlung Amerikas im Geschichts- und Gemeinschaftskunde-Unterricht* (Wesseling bei Köln, 1970), 28–36.

3 Erich Angemann repeatedly stressed that being a historian should provide joy. See introduction to Erich Angermann et al., eds., *New Wine in Old Skins: A Comparative View of Socio-Political Structures and Values Affecting the American Revolution* (Stuttgart, 1976), 5; see also Erich Angermann, *Challenges of Ambiguity: Doing Comparative History*, German Historical Institute, Washington, D.C., Annual Lecture series, no. 4 (New York, 1991), 6. It is no coincidence that Erich Angermann was particularly fond of J. H. Hexter, *Doing History* (London, 1971).

4 Franz Schnabel, *Deutsche Geschichte im neunzehnten Jahrhundert*, 4 vols. (Freiburg im Breisgau, 1929–37; reprinted, with a biographical essay by Eberhard Weis, Munich, 1987).

5 Erich Angermann was associated with the *Neue Deutsche Biographie*, first as a student assistant between 1949 and 1952 and then until 1955 as a *wissenschaftlicher Mitarbeiter*.

6 A measure may be the titles of the doctoral dissertations of these historians: Eberhard Weis, "Geschichtsschreibung und Staatsauffassung in der französischen Enzyklopädie," Diss. phil., University of Munich, 1952; Erich Angermann, "Karl Mathy als Sozial- und Wirtschaftspolitiker (1842–1848)," Diss. phil., University of Munich, 1952; Friedrich Hermann Schubert, "Ludwig Camerarius (1573–1654) als Staatsmann im Dreissigjährigen Krieg," Diss. phil., University of Munich, 1953; Heinrich Lutz, "Conrad Peutinger: Beiträge zu einer politischen Biographie," Diss. phil., University of Munich, 1953; Karl Otmar Freiherr von Aretin, "Die deutsche Politik Bayerns in der Zeit der staatlichen Entwicklung des Deutschen Bundes 1814–1820," Diss. phil., University of Munich, 1954.

7 Among the dissertations he supervised are: Hermann Wellenreuther, *Glaube und Politik in Pennsylvania 1681–1776: Die Wandlungen der Obrigkeitsdoktrin und des Peace Testimony der Quäker* (Cologne, 1972), and Norbert Finzsch, *Die Goldgräber Kaliforniens: Arbeitsbedingungen, Lebensstandard und politisches System um die Mitte des 19. Jahrhunderts* (Göttingen, 1982). He supervised the following *Habili-*

Angermann retained a deep, life-long affection for Schnabel. On the hundredth anniversary of Schnabel's birth, Angermann paid moving tribute to his former teacher as a historian. Schnabel's portrait had a prominent place in his office. The picture he cherished of Schnabel offers further clues to his own world. In his tribute he used two key terms: *sapientia* and *eloquentia*, and what he meant with these terms he put into the formula "out of a humanistic spirit, artfully formed presentations of history."[8] In Schnabel he admired "the breadth of his interests and the unusual talent of getting to the essence of historical epochs, developments, and events"[9]; he also considered Schnabel's ability to re-create and view "the interconnectedness of historical developments" as Schnabel's most important achievement.[10]

Schnabel's vision of history was all-inclusive, and that set him apart from many of his contemporary colleagues; indeed, he was something of an outsider. History to Schnabel was not only foreign policy and domestic affairs but also the life of the simple citizen, the culture, the technology, and the environments that shaped life and politics. In a sense this vision forced the historian to mold these endless factors and facets into a coherent whole – that was the "geistige Durchdringung," the analysis as the intellectual duty and achievement of the good historian.

In rereading Angermann's introduction to the sixth edition of his successful history of *Die Vereinigten Staaten von Amerika seit 1917* (The United States of America since 1917) I am struck by the similarity of the two men's approaches. He wanted to set American politics into the context of the "sociocultural and socioeconomic life-background" but stressed the necessity of an "appropriate weighting that is representative." In doing so he discarded the possibility of taking a theoretical interest as his guideline and confessed that he was merely led by a "curiosity that strives toward penetrating the intellectual structure of historical interconnections and their generally understandable representation."[11]

---

tationsschriften: Peter Krüger, *Deutschland und die Reparationen 1918/19: Die Genesis des Reparationsproblems in Deutschland zwischen Waffenstillstand und Versailler Friedensschluss*, Schriftenreihe der *Vierteljahreshefte für Zeitgeschichte*, no. 25 (Stuttgart, 1973); Hermann Wellenreuther, *Repräsentation und Grossgrundbesitz in England 1730–1770* (Stuttgart, 1979); and Norbert Finzsch, *Obrigkeit und Unterschichten: Zur Geschichte der rheinischen Unterschichten gegen Ende des 18. und zu Beginn des 19. Jahrhunderts* (Stuttgart, 1990).

8 Erich Angermann, "'Sapientia et Eloquentia': Überlegungen zur Geschichtsdarstellung Franz Schnabels," in Historische Kommission bei der Bayerischen Akademie der Wissenschaften, ed., *Franz Schnabel: Zu Leben und Werk (1887–1966)* (Munich, 1988), 41–92, 71.

9 Ibid., 70. 10 Ibid.

11 Erich Angermann, *Die Vereinigten Staaten von Amerika seit 1917, mit einem ergänzenden Beitrag von Hermann Wellenreuther: Von Gerald Ford zu Bill Clinton: Die Zeit von 1974 bis 1994*, 9th ed. (Munich,

The purpose and aims of Angermann's book on the history of the United States, which first appeared in 1966, mark the union of two influences: his father's (communicating with the general public) and his academic mentor's (penetrating the intellectual structure of historical interconnections). History to him was not only *événements* (events) and political decisions but also the "background of life," which imbeds everyone's life in historical culture. Thus, his concept of history was not restricted to one particular part of a person's life and activities but consciously sought to take an all-inclusive approach.

This approach could of course easily lead to those wonderful rambling accounts that pile up more and more information without ever arriving at the essence of a person. What Angermann learned from Schnabel was both the broad concept of history and the necessity to structure the various forces shaping a person's life and ideas: Individuality, contexts, and purposeful intellectual analysis prompted his efforts to energetically conceptualize and tell the reader so in his first paragraphs. Thus, his *dispositiones* (dispositions) were double-edged: They presented the reader with the subject matter he was to expect in the article or book and with the concept and contours, the *rote Faden* (red thread) of his general argument.[12]

As my reference to rhetorical terms already indicates, Angermann was intensely aware of the potential of language. First, language and style were to him the means by which the historian communicated with the public. This sounds like a truism, but it bears repetition for two reasons: First, Angermann rejected the tendency to subjugate language and style to the so-called necessities of the historical sciences. To him, this betrayed one of the fundamental trusts placed in historians, for the historian was not only writing for the specialist but had to re-create and explain the past to contemporary readers, scholars and laymen alike. He was acutely aware that this exercise was intimately bound up with the intellectual trends of the times in which the historian lived. Indeed, this view informed a lengthy analysis of American historiography on the American Revolution

---

1995), 9. These general remarks only appeared in his introduction to the revised edition dated "Fall 1977" and not in the first edition (1966), where he restricted his remarks to a brief discussion of the difficulties in writing a history of the United States in the twentieth century. He then offered a brief outline of his overall argument.

12 See his introduction to his doctoral dissertation, "Karl Mathy als Sozial- und Wirtschaftspolitiker"; the introduction to Erich Angermann, "Die Vereinigten Staaten von Amerika vom Frieden von Gent (1814) bis zum Frieden von Versailles (1919)," in Fritz Valjavec, ed., *Historia Mundi: Ein Handbuch der Weltgeschichte in zehn Bänden*, 10 vols. (Bern, 1952–61); and the introduction to the first edition of *Die Vereinigten Staaten von Amerika seit 1917* (1966).

that was published in 1979.[13] Yet, these convictions also prompted him, earlier than most other colleagues, to accept invitations from broadcasting services and television stations to contribute essays and talks on historical subjects – all related to American history.[14]

My second point has a wider bearing: It is a comment on Angermann's own "artistic presentation of history." For to him, language was more than just a means of communicating with the readers. Language was like clay, ready and waiting to be "artfully" molded. For hours he would brood over a sentence until he had cast it into its perfect shape. And "perfect shape" not only meant that it carried his meanings and thoughts with all their ramifications but that it did so in its most elegant form. He read and accepted the thoughts of the American scholars Peter Gay and J. H. Hexter – both for their craftsmanship and elegance of style – and recommended their books to his students.[15] To the best of my knowledge, he never thought about the theoretical implications of his attitude toward language. He was aware of Hayden White's writings but probably shrugged off his theories as reading too much into something that came naturally to him.[16] Yet, the reader of Angermann's works will wonder whether the increasing complexity of his style, his longer and progressively more involved sentence structures, which occasionally drove some of his close friends to mild desperation, may not have reflected his increasingly more complex, detached, and pessimistic perception of where the world was headed. In a world bent on producing and reproducing platitudes and simplifications – and after 1968 he was often furious about

13 Erich Angermann, "Die amerikanische Revolution im Spiegel der Geschichte," in Erich Angermann, ed., *Revolution und Bewahrung: Untersuchungen zum Spannungsgefüge von revolutionärem Selbstverständnis und politischer Praxis in den Vereinigten Staaten von Amerika,* supplement, no. 5, n.s., *Historische Zeitschrift* (Munich, 1979), 13–88.

14 He contributed the following talks to the Hessische Rundfunk: "Vom Blockhaus zum Computer: Vom Sinn der Arbeit in den USA," in the series "Arbeit: Fluch oder Würde des Menschen?" (ca. 1980); "Das Mandat auf Zeit: Spielregeln der Demokratie in den USA," in the series "Der König ist tot, es lebe der König! Zur politischen Kultur des Machtwechsels" (Jan. 2, 1983); "'. . . dass diese Nation eine Wiedergeburt der Freiheit erlebe': Rechtfertigungsethik im Amerikanischen Bürgerkrieg," in the series "Der gerechte Krieg" (Nov. 13, 1983); "'Sic Temper Tyrannis!' Die Absurdität der Ermordung von Abraham Lincoln" (Mar. 31, 1985); "'Das war kein Krieg – das war Mord!' Der Amerikanische Bürgerkrieg, 1861–1865," in the series "Kriegsende: Kleine Bilanz der grossen Kriege" (May 8, 1988); on Nov. 7, 1976, the Zweites Deutsches Fernsehen (ZDF) broadcast an extensive interview with Erich Angermann on the question "Wie mächtig ist der amerikanische Präsident?" I am grateful to Manuela Friedrich, Documentation Office, Hessischer Rundfunk, for helping me to locate the dates of these programs.

15 Hexter, *Doing History;* Peter Gay, *Style in History* (New York, 1974).

16 I am referring here to Hayden White, *Metahistory: The Historical Imagination in Nineteenth-Century Europe* (Baltimore, 1975), which he bought immediately after the German edition was published in 1991 but with which he was not overly impressed.

these tendencies – the duty to counteract these trends by being ever more precise, by demonstrating that things were not simple, easy, and uncomplicated fell more heavily on the historian.

Let me demonstrate this development toward increasing complexity in style and thought by comparing the first with the sixth edition of Angermann's *Die Vereinigten Staaten von Amerika seit 1917*. In 1966 he ended his brief introduction into the origins of the Cold War with the reminder: "Indeed, in this case it also would be good to remember that it usually takes two to have a quarrel." Ten years later he recast this sentence: "The truism that it takes two to quarrel, of course, makes it less easy to demonize one side or the other and less likely to lead to an amorphous relativism."[17] The sentence carries the same message but qualifies it with reminders that stating that it takes two to pick a fight does not imply judgment on one party nor avoids judging at all.

II

In reconstructing the basic features of Angermann's early ideas about history I have somewhat freely drawn on some of his later writings. Yet, how many of these features *inform* his early writings? Angermann received his Ph.D. in 1952 for his thesis on "Karl Mathy: Social and Economic Policy Maker (1842–8)."[18] This work marked the beginning of his lifelong interest in nineteenth-century liberalism. His second book or qualifying second doctorate (*Habilitationsschrift*) on Robert von Mohl, some smaller later studies like that on Ludolf Camphausen, and finally in the 1980s his last big, albeit unfinished, comparative study of the unification processes in mid-nineteenth-century Germany, Italy, and the United States are the results of this abiding fascination with this period.[19] A large part

---

17 Angermann, *Die Vereinigten Staaten von Amerika seit 1917*, 234; Erich Angermann, *Die Vereinigten Staaten von Amerika*, 6th ed. (Munich, 1978), 268–9.
18 Published under this title in *Zeitschrift für die Geschichte des Oberrheins* 103, n.s. 64 (1955): 499–622.
19 Erich Angermann, *Robert von Mohl 1799–1875: Leben und Werk eines altliberalen Staatsgelehrten* (Neuwied, 1962); Erich Angermann, "Zwei Typen des Ausgleichs gesellschaftlicher Interessen durch die Staatsgewalt: Ein Vergleich der Lehren Lorenz Steins und Robert Mohls," in Werner Conze, ed., *Staat und Gesellschaft im deutschen Vormärz 1815–1848* (Stuttgart, 1962), 173–205; Erich Angermann, "Ludolf Camphausen (1803–1890)," in Bernhard Poll, ed., *Rheinische Lebensbilder*, 17 vols. (Düsseldorf, 1966–97), 2:195–219; Erich Angermann, "Die deutsche Frage 1806–1866," in Theodor Schieder and Ernst Deuerlein, eds., *Reichsgründung 1870/71: Tatsachen, Kontroversen, Interpretationen* (Stuttgart, 1970), 9–32; Erich Angermann, "Germany's 'Peculiar Institution': The Beamtentum," in Erich Angermann and Marie-Luise Frings, eds., *Oceans Apart? Comparing Germany and the United States: Studies in Commemoration of the 150th Anniversary of the Birth of Carl Schurz* (Stuttgart, 1981), 77–101.

of his historical world centered on this period, whose liberal values shaped his own world views to a considerable extent. But this progression from Mathy to the Atlantic world demonstrates, too, the gradual enlargement of his historical world from German history to that of the western hemisphere.

Karl Mathy was one of the leading liberals of Baden. In his dissertation, Angermann does, as the title indicates, not study the whole man but focuses on Mathy's economic and social ideas, as he carefully points out in his circumspect introduction. Yet, these are indeed not narrowly conceived. He initially defines the term *social and economic policy* rather loosely so that it encompasses all of Mathy's thoughts. These extended well beyond the narrow confines of social and economic concepts to "the social question, the creation of a liberal state, social, and economic order as well as the realization of German unity"; extended in other words, to the practical political implications of Mathy's concepts on economy and society.[20]

By and large he stuck fairly closely to his stated purposes. He carefully delineates Mathy's ideas, reconstructs their contemporary national and international contexts, and never forgets to argue their practicability. Mathy was, we learn, a pragmatic politician, well informed for his times but no doctrinaire. Basically discursive in its narrative style, the work demonstrates Angermann's keen interest in social forces and formations as fundamental factors shaping political attitudes as well as movements. His crisp analysis of the emergence of the "social question" (*soziale Frage*), for example, foreshadowed some of the key points that in 1954 informed Werner Conze's seminal article on the emergence of the "proletariat" in the *Vormärz* (pre-March 1848 Germany).[21]

Yet, a feature that loomed large in my preliminary definition of Angermann's concept of history is somewhat underdeveloped, namely, the *Lebenshintergrund* or personal background. We learn next to nothing about Mathy's biography, his own economic activities, his lifestyle, his family, his friends. True, Angermann had not set out to write a biography. But there is a lingering suspicion that more information would have been helpful. Only occasionally does he break through this self-imposed silence and draw Mathy's own social position into the argument. When Mathy has

---

20 Angermann, "Mathy," 500, 508.
21 Ibid., 501–4; Werner Conze, "Vom 'Pöbel' zum 'Proletariat': Sozialgeschichtliche Voraussetzungen für den Sozialismus in Deutschland," *Vierteljahrsschrift für Sozial- und Wirtschaftsgeschichte* 41 (1954): 333–64, reprinted in Werner Conze, *Gesellschaft – Staat – Nation: Gesammelte Aufsätze*, ed. Ulrich Engelhardt et al. (Stuttgart, 1992), 220–46.

one of the leading revolutionaries arrested, Angermann carefully points out that this act should not be interpreted as a betrayal of the just cause but rather be seen as the result of Mathy being a "typical representative of the rising middle classes" bent on reform rather than on revolution.[22] Nevertheless: Mathy remains a public figure – his private life and his personal feelings are left out of the argument. And this shyness that so starkly contrasts with today's historians' preoccupation with the private self was to remain one of the important features of Angermann's historical writing. Thus, although his next major publication promised an analysis of the "life and work" of Robert von Mohl, his private life was condensed onto a dozen pages. The bulk of this book deals with the extensive writings, teachings, and ideas of Mohl as one of the finest *Staatswissenschaftler* (political scientists) and legal minds of his time. Again, the historical role and historical developments are presented in the shape of Mohl's intellectual discussions with his contemporaries and about the problems of his times.

By the early 1960s Angermann had developed a concept of history that was essentially discursive. To him, history was not a sequence of events or decisions; his books are not fast-moving action thrillers. To him history was argument. True, it was argument set in historical context – but argument it was nevertheless. His wars were not battles but debates about strategies; he viewed the rivalry between Alexander Hamilton and Thomas Jefferson as a clash of two diametrically opposed yet well-reasoned world views, in which Hamilton seemed to have the more convincing arguments. He viewed history as a process of reasoning, and this concept stayed with him throughout his life.

But lest I be misunderstood: Angermann never lost sight of the context. I have already cited his deft and concise description of the social dilemma liberals in Baden faced in the 1840s; many other examples could be added. But these were contexts. The dynamics and drama of history were the debates, the arguments, the rhetoric of history. And that, of course, also meant that he was interested neither in pure politics nor in social or family history. Gender history he considered ideological presentism. He was, however, very knowledgeable about these new developments in the profession – to be so he considered simply part of his craftsmanship – and encouraged his students to try all these new methodologies and approaches. But he himself stuck to his idea of history as an argument.

---

22 Angermann, "Mathy," 506; see also ibid., 511.

III

Between his doctoral dissertation and his *Habilitationsschrift*, Angermann discovered the New World.[23] This discovery was the somewhat fortuitous result of happy circumstances: Shortly after the completion of his doctorate Franz Schnabel suggested to Angermann that Robert von Mohl would be a suitable subject for his next book.[24] By then, Angermann knew that Mohl – like Mathy a member of the southern German group of liberals – was not only an important legal mind but also the author of a very good analysis of the American constitutional system. Of equal importance was the philosopher Helmut Kuhn. Angermann became Kuhn's assistant (*wissenschaftlicher Assistent*) in 1955. After his return from his enforced exile in the United States, Kuhn had first held a chair at the University of Erlangen and then in 1952 had taken over the directorship of the America Institute at the University of Munich. Kuhn immediately suggested that Angermann travel to the United States. During the winter of 1956–7 a Fulbright fellowship allowed Angermann to spend time at Columbia University's library.[25] The fruits were soon published. In 1958 he discussed at some length new publications on Pearl Harbor and the significance of the Venezuela Crisis as a turning point for the Monroe Doctrine and for German–American relations.[26] Within the next three years, four more contributions to the literature dealt with aspects of American history, among them a popular collection of sources on American history for use in secondary schools and a survey of American history from 1812 to 1919 in one of the leading handbooks of the time.[27]

---

23 Eberhard Weis informs me that, in a sense, this is an oversimplification (personal communication, Mar. 15, 1995). Angermann and his friends were first introduced to the New World by Graf Stolberg von Wernigerode, who at that time held a chair for American history at the University of Munich.

24 Angermann, *Robert von Mohl*, "Vorbemerkung"; personal communication from Eberhard Weis, Mar. 12, 1995.

25 On the important role of American-funded programs to bring young German scholars and intellectuals to the United States, see Hermann-Josef Rupieper, *Die Wurzeln der Westdeutschen Nachkriegsdemokratie: Der amerikanische Beitrag 1945–1952* (Opladen 1993), 390–420.

26 Erich Angermann, "Pearl Harbor und kein Ende. Zur Problematik der Zeitgeschichte," *Neue Politische Literatur* 3 (1958): 961–76; Erich Angermann, "Ein Wendepunkt in der Geschichte der Monroe-Doktrin und der deutsch-amerikanischen Beziehungen: Die Venezuelakrise von 1902/03 im Spiegel der amerikanischen Tagespresse," *Jahrbuch für Amerikastudien* 3 (1958): 22–58. In the 1970s, he supervised the definitive study on the Venezuela crisis: Ragnhild Fiebig von Hase, *Lateinamerika als Konfliktherd der deutsch-amerikanischen Beziehungen 1890–1903: Vom Beginn der Panamerikapolitik bis zur Venezuelakrise 1902/03*, 2 vols. (Göttingen, 1986).

27 Erich Angermann, "Amerika im Wandel," *Neue Politische Literatur* 4 (1959): 513–38; Angermann, ed., *Aufstieg der Vereinigten Staaten von Amerika*; Angermann, "Republikanismus, amerikanisches Vorbild und soziale Frage 1848: Eine unveröffentlichte Flugschrift Robert Mohls," *Die Welt als*

The last publication offers some important clues to Angermann's approach to American history. The first paragraph sets the tone: Comparing American to European history reveals, so we are informed, a different chronology, for despite all cultural and political interconnectedness both followed separate paths. The American path can only be understood by studying the "inner developments" within the United States. Yet, he hastened to add that studying these alone would not do. He insisted that the course of American history "has been determined more from within than from without, even if many internal ideas were borrowed from abroad."[28]

It is not necessary to follow his argument any further. His insistence that American history was shaped by the dynamic relationship between collectivism and individualism, by a tendency to look inward with occasional outbursts of chauvinism, was always quickly balanced by an awareness of America's obligations to and interests in the wider world – "the tug of war between inner developments and dependence on outward influences and forces on the one hand and between individualism and subordination to the will of the majority on the other."[29] This point encapsulated the contours of his argument.

What then do we have here? First, American developments are firmly set in an Atlantic context. But this is more declarative than part of his narrative. European influences are but rarely mentioned and nowhere pursued and described. Yet, in a different sense, the Atlantic context acquires a new importance, for to him America represents in *pure culture*, his term,[30] the tendency toward a majoritarian democracy that took so long to develop in the Old World; the concept as such was, as Angermann carefully points out, "originally no American particularity." Yet, owing to especially favorable circumstances, it developed faster and in a purer form in the United States than in Europe.[31] Studying the factors

Geschichte 21 (1961): 185–93; Angermann, "Die Vereinigten Staaten von Amerika," in Valjavec, ed., *Historia Mundi*, 10:253–331.

28 Angermann, "Die Vereinigten Staaten von Amerika," in Valjavec, ed., *Historia Mundi*, 10:253.

29 "Freilich muss man sich immer vor Augen halten, dass in den USA Individualismus und Unterordnung unter die Gesellschaft sich stärker die Waage gehalten haben als gemeinhin auf dem Alten Kontinent, und dass jede Störung dieses Gleichgewichts alsbald zu einer Gegenbewegung geführt hat: Dies ist das Hauptthema der neueren amerikanischen Geschichte" (ibid., 254).

30 Ibid., 254.

31 The notion that republican and democratic ideas would work in America because that continent was not burdened by European historical traditions was often voiced between 1790 and 1850 by German liberals and conservatives alike; see Hermann Wellenreuther, "Die USA: Ein politisches Vorbild der bürgerlich-liberalen Kräfte des Vormärz?" in Jürgen Elvert and Michael Salewski, eds., *Deutschland und der Westen im 19. und 20. Jahrhundert*, pt. 1: *Transatlantische Beziehungen*, special issue no. 7 of *Historische Mitteilungen* (Stuttgart, 1993), 30.

and forces that enabled this achievement requires the historian to become deeply involved with the inner development of America. On the one hand, America thus becomes something of a laboratory of European ideas; in this laboratory European ideas developed under conditions purer and more favorable than in the Old World. On the other hand, American conditions shaped these Old World concepts and gave them their peculiar twist and character out of which North America's "separate" history sui generis emerged.

Thus, he faced the old dilemma of the historian: to strike a balance between the particular and the general, between the _Sonderweg_ (special path) and the course of the _abendländische Geschichte_ (history of the West), between "American exceptionalism" and Atlantic history. At this stage, Angermann perhaps did not yet recognize this fundamental historiographical problem – although in retrospect he himself dated his thinking about Atlantic history to the beginning of his career in Cologne.[32]

Aside from a continuing flow of articles, first on Angermann's "own period," the _Vormärz_, and then more generally on nineteenth-century German history,[33] after 1965 Angermann published an increasing number of studies on American history proper. The thematic range was broad indeed. After the survey texts of the early 1960s he began with the publication of his Cologne inaugural address on "Corporative Legal Traditions in the American Declaration of Independence," which in many ways continued an argument set out in his inaugural address in Munich in 1961. The latter focused on the gradual separation of the concepts of government and society in eighteenth-century German thought, and the former looked at the reverse process in North America: how concepts of government and society were rejoined under the idea of the common good and functionalized with the help of European concepts as a means to legitimize the abjuration from the British king.[34]

---

32 Erich Angermann, "Was heisst und zu welchem Ende studiert man anglo-amerikanische Geschichte? Eine akademische Abschiedsrede," _Historische Zeitschrift_ 256 (1993): 658.
33 Erich Angermann, "Eine Rede Robert Mohls über den Saint-Simonismus aus dem Jahr 1832," _Vierteljahrsschrift für Sozial- und Wirtschaftsgeschichte_ 49 (1962): 195–214; Angermann, "Typen des Ausgleichs," 173–205; Angermann, "Camphausen," 195–219; Angermann, "Die deutsche Frage 1806–1866," 9–32; Angermann, "Germany's 'Peculiar Institution,'" 77–101; Angermann, "Überlegungen zum Demokratieverständnis Alexis de Tocquevilles und Max Webers: Ein historischer Vergleich," in Ralph Melville, ed., _Deutschland und Europa in der Neuzeit: Festschrift für Karl Otmar Freiherr von Aretin zum 65. Geburtstag_ (Wiesbaden, 1988), 49–59.
34 Erich Angermann, "Das Auseinandertreten von 'Staat' und 'Gesellschaft' im Denken des 18. Jahrhunderts," _Zeitschrift für Politik_, n.s. 10 (1963): 89–101; Erich Angermann, "Ständische Rechtstradition in der amerikanischen Unabhängigkeitserklärung," _Historische Zeitschrift_ 200 (1965): 61–91.

Angermann concluded his analysis of the indebtedness and connections of the Declaration of Independence to European legal traditions with some general remarks about the possible contributions European historians could make to American history and offered reasons why they should bother at all with the history of that far distant world. As to the latter, he pointed out that European historians viewed sources on American history differently than American historians did – a general observation regarding how outsiders look at the history of a particular nation. How valid such an argument was he had, of course, just demonstrated. As to the former he suggested a principal reason: He argued that his analysis had shown, "particularly from the perspective of recent German historical scholarship, where one can make a contribution to American history and to its proper placement in what might be broadly called 'Atlantic culture.'"[35]

As far as I know this was the first time that Angermann used the term *Atlantic culture*. In this context Atlantic culture meant more specifically "European legal traditions." But these implied more than that Jefferson drew on European legal traditions; for as a result the Declaration of Independence could be understood by European courts and politicians as the "high- and endpoint of the British-American constitutional conflict," which declared the former colonies not only independent but rightful partners in a legitimate war and potential partners for international treaties. Thus, for Angermann Atlantic culture meant not only that Americans profitably used older European concepts but that in doing so they accepted European rules that guided relations between nations and that at the same time explained their actions to Europeans.

As previously mentioned, Angermann published his history of the United States in the twentieth century in 1966. The following year he published two articles that focused on the late nineteenth century, particularly on the problem of imperialism as a continuation of expansionism and on the conflict over modernity in Germany and America in the 1920s. This, incidentally, was Angermann's first explicit comparative venture.[36] Two years later two articles on Franklin Delano Roosevelt

---

35 Angermann, "Rechtstradition," 91.
36 Erich Angermann, "Der Imperialismus als Formwandel des amerikanischen Expansionismus: Eine Studie über den Gedanken einer zivilisatorischen Sendung der Vereinigten Staaten," *Jahrbuch für Geschichte von Staat, Wirtschaft und Gesellschaft Lateinamerikas* 4 (1967): 694–724; Erich Angermann, "Die Auseinandersetzung mit der Moderne in Deutschland und den USA in den 'Goldenen zwanziger Jahren,'" *Internationales Jahrbuch für Geschichts- und Geographie-Unterricht* 11 (1967): 76–87.

marked a temporary end to Angermann's concentration on the twentieth century.[37]

The pendulum now swung back to the eighteenth and nineteenth centuries.[38] In a sense he returned not only to his Cologne inaugural address but also to his earlier work on the *Vormärz*, and he combined the two in what obviously was conceived as a monographic study of, to quote the title of the unpublished manuscript, "Some British and American Influences on German Social and Political Thought Between the American and German Revolutions."[39] In a sense, but on a larger scale, this inquiry represents the counterpiece to Angermann's analysis of the indebtedness of the Declaration of Independence to European legal traditions. Now the focus is reversed, for his inquiry describes and analyzes English and American influences on German economic, social, legal, administrative, and political thought. The last chapter discusses "National Unification: Federalism from *Staatenbund* to *Bundesstaat*." As usual, Angermann began with clearly stating his purpose and aims:

I do intend to discuss mainly the British, or rather Anglo-Saxon, impact on German social and political thought. . . . I say Anglo-Saxon, for American political experience . . . was in many respects really an offspring of British constitutional life. And in Europe, and especially among German liberals, the United States was widely looked on as the shining example (or the reverse) of the creation of a new body politic on truly constitutional and federalist principles, somehow lacking certain debasing experiences of Old World politics and therefore . . . in a state of moral virginity. I think it thus both relevant and legitimate to include American influences in our discussion. Yet they are not simply to be treated as part and parcel of an essentially British tradition. They will rather have to be considered as a branch of a peculiar Anglo-Saxon body of ideas derived in part from a common tradition and in part from widely different political experiences, as distinguished from French political thought following rather the line of what Hippolyte Taine called the *esprit classique*.[40]

In other words, what Angermann set out to do in this manuscript was to describe more fully "aspects" of what he in 1965 had called "Atlantic

---

37 Angermann, "Franklin Delano Roosevelt als Politiker," 28–36; Erich Angermann, "Franklin Roosevelt (1882–1945)," in Rolf K. Hocevar, Hans Maier, and Paul-Ludwig Weinacht, eds., *Politiker des 20. Jahrhunderts*, vol. 1: *Die Epoche der Weltkriege* (Munich, 1970), 239–60.

38 Except for the publication of another synthesis, entitled "Die weltpolitische Lage 1933–1935: Die Vereinigten Staaten von America," in Oswald Hauser, ed., *Weltpolitik 1933–1935: 13 Vorträge* (Göttingen, 1973), 110–45.

39 Unpublished manuscript in author's possession. It was probably written during Angermann's sabbatical at St. Anthony's College, Oxford, in 1970. Without the numerous extensions and the copious annotations the manuscript numbers 140 typed pages. It is organized in seven chapters. Originally, the manuscript was obviously used as a series of lectures for an English-speaking as well as for a German-speaking audience.

40 Angermann, "Some British and American Influences," fol. 2.

culture." Did he succeed? Certainly he was not satisfied with the results of his inquiry, and that was the reason why sometime between 1973 and 1975 he broke off his efforts at revision. A careful study of the manuscript reveals some reasons. The difficulties stemmed from his general approach: He attempted to study British and American influences on Germany first through a description of the experiences of German travelers to England and North America, then by way of an analysis of the reception of English and American writings in Germany, and finally through a discussion of German writings that mirrored experiences and reflections in England and North America. Thus, we learn a lot about Friedrich Christoph Dahlmann, Rudolf Gneist, Franz Lieber, Friedrich List, Robert von Mohl, Friedrich Julius Stahl, and Albrecht Thaer; but what comes through clearly was the by-and-large dominant influence of England on the German economy, technology, and agriculture, and on constitutional thought. Only in two areas did Angermann find American influences that attracted German liberal attention: In the arena of economic thought, where Franz Lieber provided a most important connection through his revision of Adam Smith's insights in light of the emergence of the nation-state, and in the reception and discussion of American federalism in the context of the 1848 debates in the Frankfurt Parliament on the formation of a German *Bund* (federation). True, Angermann notes other areas, such as transatlantic efforts at prison reform. But there is simply no escaping the conclusion that the description of the Atlantic culture he had set out to provide had really largely turned into a description of England's role in German liberal thought.

Some fruits of his inquiries appeared in the following years. In 1974, 1975, and 1976 he published reflections on the influence of the American Revolution on German liberals in the 1830s and 1840s as well as his first essay on Abraham Lincoln.[41] In 1976 he chaired a symposium that commemorated the bicentennial of the American Revolution.[42] His work on the Revolution produced more articles, a shorter reflection on Washington's advice "to Steer Clear of Permanent Alliances," a long and well informed discussion of American historiography of the American Revolution, and a history of the American Revolution itself.[43]

41 Erich Angermann, "Der deutsche Frühkonstitutionalismus und das amerikanische Vorbild," *Historische Zeitschrift* 219 (1974): 1–32; Erich Angermann, "The Impact of the American Revolution on Germany: A Comment," in Library of Congress Symposia on the American Revolution, ed., *The Impact of the American Revolution Abroad: Papers Presented at the Fourth Symposium May 8 and 9, 1975* (Washington, D.C., 1976), 160–3.
42 The proceedings were published as Angermann et al., eds., *New Wine in Old Skins.*
43 Erich Angermann, "'To Steer Clear of Permanent Alliances': Neutralität, Parteipolitik und nationale Konsolidation in der Frühgeschichte der Vereinigten Staaten von Amerika," in Helmut

On a more general level I would argue that the 1970s marked the shift from what I would call his study of "influence" and "relations," which had informed his work until he stopped revising his "Some British and American Influences," to comparative history proper. By 1976 he was firmly sold on the latter approach, as his introduction to the published proceedings of the bicentennial symposium makes very clear.[44] When talks began the following year about the needs to reinvigorate American-German intellectual relations in general and those between historians in particular he agreed especially with Carl N. Degler that one of the major aims of such an effort should result in fostering truly comparative studies of both countries ranging from early modern to contemporary times.

Angermann's most energetic involvement with the problems of comparative history occurred in the 1980s.[45] In 1982–3 as a fellow of the Historisches Kolleg in Munich he began work on a comparison of movements toward national unity in Italy, Germany, and the United States during the mid-nineteenth century – a project that for health reasons he never finished. At the end of this period he summed up his thoughts and experiences on this methodology in his Annual Lecture at the German Historical Institute (GHI) in Washington, D.C., titled: "Challenges of Ambiguity: Doing Comparative History."[46] The formula seemed deceptively simple: If you want to do comparative history, first "ask whether the people we wish to study are fairly alike in terms of ethnocultural homogeneity, including racial prejudices, religion, language, moral values, etc., or whether there are differences possibly relevant to the dominant theme."[47] After you have overcome this sky-high mountain, you will then have to "devise a set of what might be called *core questions*,"[48] and having mastered that test, you then just do the comparing preferably in what, to

---

Berding et al., eds., *Vom Staat des Ancien Régime zum modernen Parteienstaat: Festschrift für Theodor Schieder zu seinem 70. Geburtstag* (Munich, 1978), 133–44; a similar version appeared as Erich Angermann, "'Entangling Alliances with None': Neutralität und Bündnispolitik in den Anfängen der amerikanischen Aussenpolitik," in Heinz Dollinger et al., eds., *Weltpolitik, Europagedanke, Regionalismus: Festschrift für Heinz Gollwitzer zum 65. Geburtstag am 30. Januar 1982* (Münster 1982), 93–107; Erich Angermann, "Die amerikanische Revolution im Spiegel der Geschichte," 13–88. He gave his manuscript on the American Revolution the significant title "Grundlegung einer neuen Grossmacht: Geschichte der Vereinigten Staaten von Amerika 1776–1815."

44 Angermann et al., eds., *New Wine in Old Skins*, 8–9.
45 Erich Angermann, "Abraham Lincoln und die Erneuerung der nationalen Identität der Vereinigten Staaten von Amerika," *Historische Zeitschrift* 239 (1984): 77–109; as fellow of the Historisches Kolleg, 1982–3, Angermann began work on the comparative project tentatively entitled, "Einigkeit und Recht und Freiheit: Eine Untersuchung des amerikanischen Bürgerkriegs im Vergleich mit den mitteleuropäischen Einigungskämpfen im dritten Viertel des 19. Jahrhunderts."
46 Angermann, *Challenges of Ambiguity.*
47 Ibid., 9–10.   48 Ibid., 11.

quote Angermann again, "my much admired academic mentor Franz Schnabel referred to as *Geschichtsschreibung grossen Stils*" (history writing in grand style).[49]

Despite his disclaimers of not being interested in "theoretical history, cognitive patterns, social scientist generalizations, and God knows what," Angermann displayed an awe-inspiring awareness of the difficulties of doing comparative history that resulted in two very straightforward conclusions: Whatever the historian compares, he must be sensitive to all aspects of both indigenous cultures in their broadest sense; second, he simply had to be an expert in the history and domestic affairs of *both* nations. It could be done, he insisted, and added that he looked forward to his retirement and the leisure requisite for completing the research for his "Einigkeit und Recht und Freiheit" (unity, law, and freedom) project. But to the listeners a somewhat different message came through. Degler expressed it in his cautious remarks that "the difficulties, obstacles, and ambiguities" in doing comparative history should not turn us into "cowards and [lead us to] shirk our obligations."[50]

In a sense, then, Angermann's lecture at the GHI summed up his experience that things were very complex and required careful consideration and stupendous knowledge. He also stressed that he was speaking from experience, which he scrupulously described in his introduction. He had learned the hard way that the history of connections and reception (*Beziehungs- und Rezeptionsgeschichte*) would not do if one truly believed in the existence of an Atlantic culture. But more particularly, both were not enough if one wanted to re-create an improved understanding between Americans and Europeans. The increasing trend toward specialization even in the historical profession, he felt, was rather counterproductive to the needs of Europe and North America. What was needed was deep immersion in the history and culture of other nations in order to overcome the provincialism inherent in the increasing specialization of the profession.

Angermann's argument was simple: Intellectual provincialism sooner or later bred political provincialism, and that would harm both countries, Germany and America. What was needed – and the honor of first suggesting this argument and drawing this conclusion albeit with suggestive

49 Ibid., 18–19.
50 Carl N. Degler, "In Making Historical Comparisons Focus on Common National Issues," in ibid., 21.

political overtones belongs to Michael Stürmer – was some kind of institutionalization of relations between German and American historians. The vision was clear: An institute modeled to some extent on the historical institutes in London, Paris, and Rome should provide the setting for German historians to totally immerse themselves into all aspects of American history, thus broadening their intellectual horizons and paving the way for truly comparative history; it should at the same time serve as a meeting place for American, German, and European historians who would learn from each other and, by doing so, broaden their own vision. Angermann was adamant that the subjects of such meetings should not be restricted to contemporary history but rather that they include the whole of history – after all, Atlantic history had been a reality since the sixteenth century. In the margin of one position paper that suggested a particular emphasis on contemporary history (*Zeitgeschichte*), he penned the angry remark: "Why 'contemporary history' when it already is sufficiently supported!"[51]

With his memorandum written at the suggestion of the German general consul in Boston, Stürmer started a movement in which Angermann very soon played a key role. At a meeting in Munich it was decided that he would coordinate and organize five symposia designed to explore German and American needs and opinions about strengthening relations between the two historical professions. It was hoped that the Volkswagen Foundation would provide the necessary funds. Early on in this process Angermann was convinced that only a historical institute would do. It should be an institute free from political influence dedicated to furthering historical understanding and creating an Atlantic historical consciousness. It is therefore appropriate that – whatever course the German Historical Institute in Washington takes in the future – the symposium honoring Erich Angermann took place at that institution and that his ideas and thoughts concerning the role of the institute should be recalled and discussed in Washington, particularly in the light of events since his death. For after all, the German Historical Institute would most likely not exist had he not devoted his energies to this goal since 1978.

IV

Angermann's lecture at the GHI in 1990 formed part of a triptych of lectures he had carefully planned. The first was his public lecture at

---

51 Memorandum of the president of the Alexander von Humboldt Foundation.

Krefeld on the significance of the year 1917; the second, his lecture in Washington; and the third, his academic farewell address (*akademische Abschiedsrede*) when he retired from his Cologne position. Time does not permit me to discuss his critical, stirring, and counterfactual thoughts on the importance of the year 1917 – thoughts that I began to appreciate only when I thought closely about them in preparation for a translation of the German text into English.[52] But I must discuss Angermann's *akademische Abschiedsrede*, for it truly offers in many ways a summation of his academic career and thus provides us with final and vitally important clues to his "historical world."

The address is divided into three parts: The first reflects on the European perspective of the New World and the American relationship with Europe; the second is a breathtaking and brilliant outline of the history of the United States; and the final part combines a summary with some tantalizing short remarks on Atlantic history (*atlantische Geschichte*).

Angermann's argument was essentially based on three convictions: First and foremost, American history has to be studied, interpreted, and taught "in relation to the rest of history," or, as he repeated in his closing remarks, the historian specializing in American history had to abide by the rule "that one must relate everything to everything else."[53] Second, American history should properly be viewed as Anglo-American history characterized by a progression from close dependence on European mother countries to gradual emancipation, evolution of self-government, independence, territorial expansion, and finally, in the twentieth century, the rise to hemispheric and global domination. True, influences from other continents gradually made themselves felt. But Angermann insisted that it was the European influences and connections that shaped the fundamental political, social, cultural, religious, and demographic structures of North America and that this fundamental truism provided the rational justification for a "Eurocentric approach" to North American history. Third, Angermann demanded that historians approach and study Anglo-American history "in the spirit of European independence."[54] Based on these convictions, he offered the following definition of the field: "The specialty of Anglo-American history encompasses the motherland and its Atlantic colonies since the late Middle Ages, and indeed beginning

---

52 Erich Angermann, "1917 Reconsidered," in Hans-Jürgen Schröder, ed., *Confrontation and Cooperation: Germany and the United States in the Era of World War I, 1900–1924* (Providence, R.I., 1993), 423–35.

53 Angermann, "Anglo-Amerikanische Geschichte," 638, 659.

54 Ibid., 642.

with a Eurocentric perspective in the context of general modern history."[55]

These thoughts imply a challenge and a critique of how American history is practiced in Europe and Germany, a challenge never to lose sight of the interconnectedness of American and European history, the whole – of which the two were the dominant parts – he again called Atlantic history,[56] a challenge, too, to keep the whole course of Atlantic history from the sixteenth to the twentieth century in view and not to focus arbitrarily on one or the other century and elevate it to the status of a paradigm of American national development. His definition is a challenge to those who want to limit German work on American history to German–American relations. His concept, as it had evolved in discussions with colleagues like Theodor Schieder and Richard Konetzke, "banned . . . narrow reflection on specific aspects, even bilateral wherever possible, of just a peculiar German-American relationship."[57] These challenges contain the core of his critique. They are the logical result of his insistence on bearing constantly in mind the "total connectedness" (*Gesamtzusammenhang*) and on always rooting his analysis of a particular historical phenomenon firmly in the wider field of Atlantic history.

Finally, his view and definition of Anglo-American history had clear and obvious political implications: To approach Anglo-American history in the "spirit of European independence" liberated the European historian from the need to identify with his subject in order to be able to cope with it – an often unspoken assumption guiding contacts between historians of different nationalities; at the same time this conviction implies a criticism of European scholarly tendencies to accept American paradigms as a precondition for finding acceptance from North American colleagues. Angermann was a proud and self-conscious European liberal deeply concerned about the state of European-American relations. He was convinced that improving these relations could only be based on mutual recognition, respect, and acceptance of the other, "warts and all," from a position of independent, honest, and craftsmanlike scholarship. Only on such a basis could scholars and citizens meet and learn from each other. Learn, he insisted, and do not attempt to influence or dictate to the other. In the past scholarship may have been considered a means to influence and dominate other nations. Yet, these were bygone days and,

---

55 Ibid., 643.   56 Ibid., 658.
57 Ibid., 638.

as Germany had painfully learned, subjecting scholarship to the vainglo-
rious nationalistic aims of politicians eventually ended in disaster. Instead,
he insisted that getting involved in Anglo-American history in the spirit
of European independence put scholarship on the unencumbered footing
necessary for providing the basis for a better understanding of the history
and culture of the other, the American nation.

V

Angermann's historical world stretched from the eighteenth to the twentieth century.[58] Each of the ages received book-length treatments. But
more than that, it was Germany and Europe on the one hand and North
America on the other. From the beginning he never thought of both as
separate entities, although he did not deny either its own very specific
identity. If one looks closer at those areas on which he focused, one is
struck by one important similarity: They represent fundamental turning
points in the modern history of the Western world. That is true of the
Vormärz, of his writings on the early twentieth century of American
history, as well as his preoccupation with the American Revolution, the
period of the American Civil War, and the European movements toward
national unity. And finally, Angermann conceived of all these turning
points primarily as intellectual reflections and processes of social
formation.

To Angermann history was a rational argument. This idea highlights
a number of qualities as well as limitations: An argument superimposes a
structure on a text and on the historical subject. Thus, it is no coincidence that Angermann's writings begin with a disposition that represents
his argument. Yet, here "argument" has a larger and deeper meaning, for
argument to him represented thinking about a decision, an act, an event;
in a sense the argument was more important than the decision, the act,
and the event itself. The decisions, acts, and events, by arguing their rationality, their legitimacy, and their origins, tended to dissolve into rational
constructs. In doing so they were re-created as a set of ideas and concepts. And as ideas and concepts they were part of an endless process that
ached for finality yet never achieved it.

This essential open-endedness of his concept of history represents the

---

58 Indeed, in his lectures on American history at the University of Cologne, Erich Angermann began
   correctly with the sixteenth century.

key to his historical world; yet, in another sense, it supplies the key to his increasing awareness of the problems and difficulties of comparative history. For it is next to impossible to compare essentially open-ended phenomena with each other because comparison requires definite entities. In Angermann's historical world, however, there were no definite entities but only arguments about the possibilities of definite entities, which were embedded in countless phenomenological and semantic ramifications. His sense of the difficulties and complexities of comparative history thus could be read on a deeper level as an expression of his awareness that his concept of history-as-argument was in a fundamental sense incompatible with the idea of comparing definite and clear-cut entities – be they ideas, institutions, lifestyles, or cultural and political concepts. Comparative history requires a price, the price is substitution of the infinity of things with the definite entity of things, requires the substitution of the endless argument about an act, event, or decision with the act, event, or decision. Angermann was not willing or prepared to pay this intellectual price because it ran counter to his fundamental notions of history as an open-ended argument. Nothing was simple, final, and clear. History was a process full of dynamics and changing meanings. No one was more aware of this than Angermann. In a world that believes in simplicity, in simple arguments, and in calculating with finite entities he staunchly held out for the opposite, the endless complexity, the challenge of the ever-questioning mind that refused to accept that there was an end to arguments. We admire his inquisitive mind; he believed in the endless rationality of essentially limitless phenomena that shape the historical world; yet at the same time this kind of historical world, this approach to history in the final sense, effectively precluded any meaningful approach to and methodology of comparative history.

Erich Angermann was a scholar and a citizen, for he never believed in keeping the two separate. As a scholar and citizen he believed in educating his students and the public; and as a citizen and scholar he acted on principles and values he had found and cherished in nineteenth-century liberalism: emancipation from the shackles of authority, freedom of opinion, rejection of political censorship, responsibility of the citizenry for the commonwealth and for the world. He rejected revolution and licentiousness, believed in freedom *and* order, hated intolerance, strove for *sapientia* and *eloquentia*, respected the ordinary citizen, hated deceit, and thought corruption is a viable and necessary means to keep a social system functioning; he was curious and a ferocious worker, and he enjoyed his work too; he was a wonderful friend and an excellent teacher. But, above all, he was a model scholar because he believed in the improvement of mankind. His methods and his weapons were those of intellectual discourse and argument. He believed in rationality. His historical world was the rational argument stretching from Christopher Columbus to Richard M. Nixon. For contributors to this book and for the German Historical Institute in Washington, this remains an enduring challenge.

Index